Elementary Reading Instruction

Elementary Reading Instruction

EDWARD B. FRY

Graduate School of Education
Rutgers University

McGraw-Hill Book Company

New York   St. Louis   San Francisco   Auckland   Bogotá   Düsseldorf
Johannesburg   London   Madrid   Mexico   Montreal   New Delhi
Panama   Paris   São Paulo   Singapore   Sydney   Tokyo   Toronto

ELEMENTARY READING INSTRUCTION

1234567890 DODO 783210987

This book was set in Times Roman by Allen Wayne Technical Corp.
The editors were Stephen D. Dragin, Alison Meersschaert, and Barry Benjamin;
the cover was designed by Al Cetta;
the production supervisor was Charles Hess.
R. R. Donnelley & Sons Company was printer and binder.

Library of Congress Cataloging in Publication Data

Fry, Edward Bernard, date
    Elementary reading instruction.

    Includes index
    1. Reading (Elementary) I. Title.
LB1573.F72   372.4'1   76-45796
ISBN 0-07-022585-0

Contents

Part 3   Evaluation, Grouping, and Individual Differences

Preface

The dear people do not know how long it takes to learn to read. I have been at it all my life, and I cannot yet say I have reached the goal.

Goethe, at age eighty

The purpose of this text is to help present teachers and future teachers improve reading instruction in the elementary schools. It is written for students in a first course in reading, and for experienced teachers who wish an overview or refresher course.

Teachers of reading, like all classroom instructors, must bring a wide range of expertise and knowledge to their teaching. They need to know how to divide their classes into reading groups and how to plan for individual instruction. They need to know what materials are available and, if there is a choice, how to judge which ones are best. If the materials are not comprehensive enough for students' needs, they must be able to identify and supply what is missing. Hopefully, before they even begin teaching, instructors will find out whether or not each student already knows what they plan to teach.

Elementary teachers who do not teach beginning reading need to know how to teach the more advanced reading skills of comprehension, vocabulary improvement, study skills, and rate flexibility. If they are in schools that regularly give tests, as many do, they need to know how to interpret those tests so that test scores will be most useful.

Both the tests and daily experiences in the classroom will show up wide individual differences, so that few elementary teachers can afford to be unaware of beginning reading methods for the slowest children or of the higher reading skills and book selection for the most advanced children. The causes of these wide differences in individuals cannot always be known, but there are a number of things which correlate with reading success and failure.

Students who progress at slower rates provide a special challenge. Few schools have an adequate number of remedial reading instructors, leaving the responsibility for special needs with the regular classroom teacher. This is one reason why it is necessary for all teachers to know basic phonics principles and have some notion of their progression. That is why it is important to know about basic vocabularies and lists of comprehension skills. And that is also why you need to know many methods of teaching these skills.

While there are individual variations among students, the reading skills do not differ that greatly. However, it is important to know alternate methods; if one method has proved unsuccessful with a student, another can be tried. This text is about reading instruction for all children—from bright to slow learners, from poverty-stricken, culturally different children to children of wealthy, highly educated parents. It is a book that will give you basic principles and many of the standard methods. You will have to use your creativity in applying them to your particular students.

Truly professional teachers who understand the principles of reading instruction have little difficulty in understanding new methods as they come along. Changing the labels on the back of basal readers from Grades 1, 2, 3 to Levels A, B, C did not disturb the good teacher who was already providing for individual differences in the classroom, but it might have caused some anxiety for less flexible teachers who have always believed that in third grade you use only third-grade books. Some of the newer methods, like programmed instruction and computer-assisted instruction, did not provide any new or startling changes in the content of phonic skills or comprehension skills.

THE CONTENTS OF THIS TEXT

Determining the extent of coverage in a text such as this involves many decisions on exactly what to include and what to exclude. There are a multitude of volumes on the subject of reading, as well as books devoted to such areas as experimental psychology and linguistics, which have a bearing on the reading process. The contents of this text are based on two national research surveys in which professors of reading and classroom teachers were asked to indicate their opinions on just what should be included in an elementary reading text.* We have included nearly every topic requested.

As for sequence of topics, the survey results showed that individual college professors have a wide divergence of opinion about what should come first in a reading course. Some teachers begin with principles; some want to cover methods first; others

---

*One survey of 500 professors and 500 classroom teachers was conducted by Professor Florence Mooney, now at Monmouth College in New Jersey. The other survey, of over 1,100 college reading instructors, was conducted by Stephen Dragin of the McGraw-Hill Book Company.

prefer a combination of the two. Topics cited by various respondents as most appropriate for beginning the course ranged from readiness to tests to the language experience approach. As a result, the chapters in this text have been developed to allow maximum flexibility in the sequencing of topics. Instructors may assign chapters in any order to suit their course outline.

The text is organized in three major sections, beginning with Part 1, The Basis of Reading. Chapter 1 includes a definition of reading, an overview of the basic steps which comprise most of this part, and some commentary on theoretical models of the reading process. Chapter 2 covers phonics, one of the most highly placed topics in the research surveys. Phonics instruction is an important part of a majority of reading courses; some studies, however, have shown that it is not one of the best known areas among teachers. Following a rough "unit size" progression, Chapter 3 covers word analysis: phonograms and other units. (Terminology differences are prevalent in the reading field, and some authors might organize the material in Chapters 2 and 3 under the heading "Word-Attack Skills." Hopefully, minor differences in preferred terminology will not mar the validity of the content or its usefulness.) Chapter 4 covers sight words and vocabulary building. Comprehension is the subject of Chapter 5, and in many ways it is the most important chapter in the book, for comprehension is the purpose of reading. This chapter covers reading larger units—like sentences and paragraphs—and gets into teaching methods.

Part 2 of the book begins with a chapter on readiness, and then gets right into methodology. In short, this part attempts to "put it all together." The skills and principles discussed in the earlier part now come back again in the form of basal readers, directed reading activities, and a host of methods from programmed instruction to television. The higher skills covered in Chapter 9 might be thought of as an extension of comprehension, but they also include some newer skills, such as rate improvement and study skills. The language experience approach is discussed in Chapter 10 on writing, but writing is also looked at from the viewpoint of readability and what makes writing easy to read.

Part 3 begins with evaluation, covering the process in some depth, including some of the concepts (often covered in a tests and measurements course) which have direct application to reading tests. Modern teachers will be working with evaluation in many ways—from interpreting computerized test printouts to teaching by test management systems—which are part of the diagnostic-prescriptive approach. Part 3 also includes chapters on alternate ways of grouping students for reading and on individual differences that affect reading achievement.

There are different ways of learning and, if this is true for children, it is equally true for us. Readers of this text are encouraged to use it to meet their individual needs and preferences. If you want practical information on teaching in a specific classroom situation, Chapter 7 on basal readers, Chapter 8 on methods, and Chapter 10 on the language experience approach will be useful. For material on teaching older or advanced students, read Chapter 9 on higher skills. In addition, there are teaching suggestions and implications in the word attack, vocabulary, and comprehension chapters (2, 3, 4, and 5). To facilitate appropriate application of methods, and to ensure that your expectations of students are soundly based, read the chapters on readiness, evaluation, and individual differences (6, 11, and 13).

Some additional tools to aid learning and to enhance teaching effectiveness are provided at the ends of chapters. The suggested learning activities are designed to provide the reader with opportunities to apply some of the principles and ideas discussed in each chapter. There are specific types of observations to be made of children in classrooms and the use of reading materials. College instructors may wish to select among them or add to them, but they are kernels of meaningful activities to enhance learning about the teaching of reading.

Other types of learning aid are the Vocabulary and Study Terms listed at the end of each chapter, including terms that will be useful to readers in their professional careers. The list also serves as a chapter outline which can be used in study and review. College instructors may wish to use the list of Vocabulary and Study Terms as a partial basis for lecture outlines, class discussions, or examination questions. The references at the end of each chapter include suggested readings for further exploring topics discussed in the chapter.

The Postscript on continued professional growth should be useful in acquainting students with the resources of information available to reading teachers. Hopefully, this text will prove to be of lasting value to its readers, whether they are preparing for a career in elementary education or are already involved in the challenging role of teaching young people how to read.

I would like to acknowledge the following valuable assistance in preparing this text: Mrs. Gloria Luckas for secretarial assistance, Professor Josephine Goldsmith for proofreading and content suggestions, Professor Florence Mooney for help with the outline, and to the many other colleagues in the National Reading Conference and the International Reading Association for their contributions to my education. Last but not least, I, like all of you, stand on the shoulders of my previous teachers, both live and in print, to see what lies ahead and, hopefully, to achieve the goal of improving reading instruction.

Edward B. Fry

Elementary Reading Instruction

Part One

The Basis of Reading

Chapter 1

Introduction:
Definition, Basic Steps,
The Reading Process

It is both interesting and rewarding to teach reading. It is interesting because there are so many different ways to teach reading, and there are so many different kinds of students that need to learn to read better.

It is rewarding because often you can see students improve their reading skills over the course of a few weeks or months. It is also rewarding because you know that you are helping students acquire a priceless skill that will have lifelong usefulness.

Reading is also a source of great pleasure. It can change a lonely hour into an exciting hour. It can provide experiences which are all but unobtainable by other means. Through reading you can experience sitting in at a president's cabinet meeting or fleeing through a rain forest. Reading can stretch your emotions from laughter to tears, or cause you to reflect the warm glow of love.

Reading is a prime source of education. You can learn how to repair your car or save your life by seeing a doctor if you have a certain kind of pain. You can learn how your ancestors lived one century or twenty centuries ago, or even how your great-grandchildren may live a century in the future. You can learn how to make more money—or how to save what money you already have. You can learn, sometimes first-hand, the teachings of the great philosophers and religious leaders. Best of all, you can learn these things when you are ready, any time of the morning, noon, or night . . . *if* you can read.

Most people can learn how to read. And most of the people who do learn how to read do so by taking lessons from a teacher. The purpose of this book is to help teachers do a better job teaching reading.

Society places in the hands of the teaching profession the serious responsibility of teaching children, and sometimes adults, how to read. This responsibility falls directly on the shoulders of the classroom teacher. But the classroom teacher is not left alone with this important task; help is available from books like this, from college courses, and from inservice training.

DEFINITION OF READING

It is important to have a definition of reading because it will help to keep your thinking on track and give your lessons the proper emphasis: *Reading is the process of getting meaning from written language.*

Reading can also be defined as "the receptive half of the written communication system"—the other half is writing. In order to read anything, somebody must have written it. Hence reading is only part of the process of transferring ideas from one mind to another. Sometimes ideas do not transfer well because they are not well formed in the author's mind, or the author did not write them well. At other times, the ideas do not transfer well because the reader has trouble interpreting the symbols or because the reader does not "think like"—share a common body of experience and language use with—the author.

The reading teacher concentrates chiefly on one part of the visual communication process, that part which has to do with the efficient interpretation of the written symbols. Some aspects of reading instruction are more clearly the responsibility of the reading teacher. For example, phonics (the relationship between symbols and speech sounds) and basic word recognition are clearly in the reading teacher's province. Perhaps some aspects of reading comprehension—the somewhat general skills, such as "getting the main idea" or "getting the proper time sequence"—are partly his or her province, but partly also the province of the subject-matter teacher. The subject-matter teacher might be the same person, particularly in a traditional classroom organization where one teacher does everything, but the lessons involved may be in some subject other than reading. To get the main idea of a paragraph in a biology book, it often takes some background knowledge in biology and the words and phrases used in biology. This is how teachers in other subjects are also partly reading teachers.

By defining reading as "the process of getting meaning," it helps to keep the teacher from undue emphasis on oral reading (reading aloud), phonics, recognizing words in isolation, or reading rate (speed). Each of these skills is important and needs development, but none of them should distract from the central purpose of reading—that of getting the meaning.

Another interesting aspect of reading as part of the communication process is that it transcends the time-space barrier (see Figure 1-1). Writing is the process of encoding ideas in symbolic form in some medium, such as ink on paper (or electronic

Figure 1-1   Reading is the receptive part of the visual communication process. Because the idea can be stored in symbols on paper (or other means), it can transcend the time-space barrier. The author can communicate with the reader minutes or hundreds of years later at any place near or far away.

charges on magnetic tape). These symbols then can be stored indefinitely or transmitted in some fashion (such as in the postal system). Thus, symbols can be sent to any part of the world or, in this space age, even out of the world. Reading is that process which the receiver performs in order to get these symbols into his or her mind. To transmit an idea from one person to another does not mean that they have to be face to face; they can be thousands of miles apart or thousands of years apart.

BASIC STEPS IN TEACHING READING

While it is important to have a good definition of reading and to understand the value of being able to read, if you are really going to teach reading, you must consider these questions: "What do you do first?" "What are some basic principles or steps that you should keep in mind?"

A partial answer to these questions will be answered in the five steps that follow. They are not a complete reading program, but they will help you to get started. They will help you to see how many of the chapters which follow are related to the basic process of teaching reading and to specific lesson plans. If you have a little bit of each of these five steps in every lesson you teach, you will have a fairly solid reading program. There is much more to the teaching of reading—as you will see as you progress through the chapters of this book—but these basic steps are a good foundation (see Figure 1-2).

Basic Step 1: Matching

Before you can begin teaching reading to a child, or a whole class for that matter, you must assess reading abilities in order to provide reading material at the proper level of difficulty. This is important, for a mismatch in reading material can result in disinterested readers. Material that is too difficult is frustrating and breeds failure, which in turn often causes a dislike of reading. Similarly, asking a child to read material that is not challenging may not be advisable.

You can find out a child's reading ability by looking at recent reading tests, or by using informal reading tests, or—in a pinch—by using the one-out-of-twenty rule.

No. 1   **Match reading ability with difficult material.**

No. 2   **Phonics and word attack skills**

No. 3   **Words**

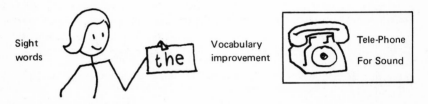

No. 4   **Comprehension**

No. 5   **Motivation and practice**

Figure 1-2 The five basic steps.

("When the student makes more than one mistake out of twenty words while reading aloud, the material is probably too difficult and you should select something easier.") Chapter 11 on evaluation, particularly the section on oral tests, will be helpful. Chapter 8 will discuss teaching methods, such as Directed Reading Activity.

Determining the difficulty of the reading material is an area called "readability." You can get some help in determining the difficulty of written material by using readability formulas, but your own judgment is also valuable. Information on readability and book selection is provided in Chapter 10.

Basic Step 2: Phonics

Phonics instruction involves breaking words into phonetic elements (speech sounds) rather than into individual letters. Part of many reading lessons, and sometimes a whole lesson, is devoted to phonics or word analysis. Informally, you can get an idea of what phonic or word-attack skills the student knows by listening carefully to oral reading errors, or by asking him or her to sound out unknown words. For a more formal assessment, phonics criterion referenced tests can be used. Informally, you can even ask the child to try to sound out some nonsense syllables that you make up. Chapter 2 on Phonics and Chapter 3 on Word Analysis will give you some knowledge of needed word analysis skills. Those chapters also contain some more formal tests and some specific teaching methods. More phonic teaching methods are discussed in Chapter 8. There are many ways to teach word-attack skills, varying from workbook pages to audiovisual devices. The teacher can explain phonics principles to the student from charts or play card games with them.

Basic Step 3: Words

Many teachers see words as the building blocks of the reading process. Certainly they are important. As you will see in Chapter 4, a very few high-frequency words make up a high percentage of all reading material. Instant recognition of these words is important. If a child has to sound out words like "of" and "this," comprehension will be lost in slowing down to try to sound them out. Hence, sight recognition of basic vocabulary is important for beginning readers, and vocabulary improvement (learning the meaning of more difficult words) is important for more advanced readers. Both sight vocabulary and vocabulary improvement are basic reading skills that can be taught. Vocabulary knowledge can also be assessed. There are many types of vocabulary tests, and almost all of the major formal reading tests include a vocabulary section. You will find suggestions for both teaching and testing vocabulary in Chapter 4, and additional teaching methods in Chapter 8. Since many basal reading systems do a good job of teaching sight vocabulary, you can look at them for further suggestions and actual materials.

In an individual or small group situation you can help a child build his or her vocabulary by simply writing down a list of words that the child doesn't know during oral or silent reading. Use the child's individual list to explain meaning, regular and irregular uses, and even phonic or syllabification elements.

Basic Step 4: Comprehension

As I stated before and will state again, the major purpose of reading is comprehension, so the teacher must regularly attempt to assess comprehension, call attention to its importance, and teach it in a wide variety of reading situations. Chapter 5 will give you lists of comprehensive skills, but don't overlook the study skills discussed in Chapter 9, as they, too, are closely related to both the concept and the teaching methods of comprehension.

One of the simplest ways to test and teach comprehension is simply to ask the child to tell you about what he or she has read. If the child hesitates or does a weak job, your questions can help elicit whether he or she is getting all the facts, and assess higher comprehension skills. Particularly for bright children, you can have an enjoyable and intellectually challenging experience by trying to apply some of the principles of critical reading from Chapter 5, or propaganda analysis from Chapter 9. There is a multitude of commercially prepared comprehension materials available at all levels, and you will find some of the more common ones mentioned in Chapters 5, 8, and 9.

Basic Step 5: Motivation and Practice

Last but not least, one of the reading teacher's most important functions is to help provide motivation and practice. Motivation to learn to read starts in the home. In some homes, there is excellent motivation by parents' examples and exhortations, but in others, the atmosphere is indifferent. Schools can help to overcome some home deficiencies with individual attention and interesting experiences. They can also foster a good group attitude, as children take many of their values from their peers.

Few children learn to read well without much practice in both structured reading lessons and informal or leisure reading experiences. The teacher needs to provide structured lessons and create opportunities for reading under less formal conditions. There is a clear and definite relationship between time spent in school and skill in reading. There are exceptions, but on the average, the more time spent in school, the better the reader. United States Census Bureau estimates of literacy levels are based on years of schooling. Historically, one of the reasons for the founding of the public school system was to increase the percentage of the population that could read. It has been known for a long time that the best way, and certainly the most common way, for a child or an adult to learn to read is to be under the instruction of a professional teacher. While a small number of children are first taught to read by parents or friends, most children learn to read in school. Teachers need to take their responsibility seriously, and providing interesting, motivating reading lessons on a regular basis is the way that this charge is carried out.

One of the most important ways of maintaining or increasing motivation is to *provide lessons and situations in which the student can usually be successful.* If a child "fails" a lesson, it is frequently the method or content that has "failed." Good teachers build success on success.

To fulfill their responsibilities, teachers should provide interesting, motivating lessons to get students involved and actively learning. *(De Wys Inc.)*

Success should not be limited to reading skills lessons. While they are often important, it is reading itself that is *most* important. It is the teacher's job to see that reading is meaningfully used in learning other subjects and in expanding the whole child through pleasurable and informative reading of books, articles, poetry, and creative hobby directions. All of these are reading *practice* and, if done correctly, are *motivating*.

THEORETICAL MODELS OF THE READING PROCESS

It is very difficult to describe exactly what happens when we read. Perhaps if we understood it better, we could have more effective reading lessons, but there is little agreement among authorities on what happens when we read. It is not that there hasn't been much research, and even some brilliant theorizing, but we still don't *know* how a child learns to read or what happens when a mature reader reads a book. Fortunately, we do know enough to be able to teach reading to most people, but this has evolved more through teaching experience than from experimental psychological research or from definitive theories.

Nonetheless, it might help you to at least hear about some of the definitions or descriptions of process. I will not attempt to systematically cover the field of reading theories and models, but rather present a sufficient variety of opinions to give you a bit of insight into this sometimes fascinating, sometimes boring, field. It is too important to ignore, but not developed well enough to be of definite help for the classroom teacher.

Let's look again at the definition given earlier and see its implications. *"Reading is getting meaning from written language."* This is probably close to what most people mean by "reading." You could "read" a person's face for signs of sadness, or clouds for signs of rain, but this is not the kind of reading we will be dealing with in this book. Reading various symbols, such as nonverbal traffic signs, might be a type of reading, but that, too, is not the kind of reading that is our main concern.

Note that our definition stressed "meaning." Thus, merely saying words out loud, while a type of reading, is not really central or the most important type of reading. It might be well to point out that, in most universities, programs for training people to read aloud are found in the drama or radio broadcasting department. The implication for teachers is that while oral reading might be important as a diagnostic tool or as a type of lesson, the goal of reading instruction is to teach the student to efficiently extract the meaning. Incidentally, up until this century, oral reading had much more central importance as an end product because reading aloud after dinner was family entertainment.

Finally, our definition implies that a person is involved, and states that language is involved; thus, the two large realms of psychology and language study or linguistics are really very much a part of understanding the reading process.

Our alternate definition of reading as "the written half of the communication system" might be considered as a simplified "communications model," which sees reading as only part of the larger area of human communication and is similar to "an information model" which emphasizes a "sender" (the author) and a "receiver" (the reader).

Now, let us look at some other opinions, definitions, and process descriptions. In reading them you might become aware of the many sides and angles from which the subject of reading can be approached.

In his classical textbook, Edmond Burke Huey wrote that

Reading, for our Anglo-Saxon forefathers, meant counseling or advising oneself or others (A.S., *radan*, to advise). To read was to get or to give counsel from a book, originally from a piece of bark on which characters were inscribed, at least if the reputed connection of *book* and *beech* can be sustained. The accessory notion of talking aloud seems to have been implied in the word, as it was also in the Roman word for reading. To the Roman, on the other hand, reading meant gathering or choosing (*lection*, reading, from *lego*, to gather) from what was written, suggesting that constant feeling of values which goes on in all effective reading. (*The Psychology of Reading*, 1908.)

While Huey was strong in a historical approach to both reading instruction and the development of languages, he was also quite fond of the relatively new "scientific" movement starting with Professor Javel's discovery of eye movements in 1879 and, later, studies in visual perception.

Another early prominent psychologist, Edward L. Thorndike, wrote that *reading was reasoning,* or more specifically,

> Reading is a very elaborate procedure, involving a weighing of each of many elements in a sentence, their organization in proper relations to one another, the selection of certain of their connotations and the rejection of others, and the cooperation of many forces to determine final response. . . . Understanding a paragraph is like solving a problem in mathematics. It consists in selecting the right elements of the situation and putting them together in the right relations, and also with the right amount of weight or influence or force for each. (Reading as Reasoning: A Study of Mistakes in Paragraph Reading," *Journal of Educational Psychology,* June 1917.)

Here we see that "thinking" is very much involved in the reading process. Thorndike sees reading as a problem to be solved: Given the symbols—what is the meaning?

Thorndike's ideas are the predecessors of more modern theoretical models which might be called "information searching." Typical of these would be Kenneth Goodman's (1970) "Reading: A Psycholinguistic Guessing Game."

The idea of infusing reading with the thinking process is also found in a later model which Theodore Clymer calls the Gray-Robinson Comprehensive Skills Model. William S. Gray was one of the fathers of modern reading instruction, from both his post as professor at the University of Chicago and his position as senior author of the old Scott, Foresman basal readers. He influenced the reading instruction of millions of children in America and throughout the world. Helen Robinson was one of his pupils and his successor to both positions. Their reading process model would include:

1 Word perception, including pronunciation and meaning;
2 Comprehension, which includes a clear grasp of what is read;
3 Reaction to, and evaluation of, ideas the author presents;
4 Assimilation of what is read, through fusion of old ideas and information obtained through reading.

More specific ideas of what Gray would include as skills will be found in Chapter 5 on Comprehension.

The above-described models are based largely on what we might call learned speculation (based, no doubt, on wide reading and personal experiences), but not on research data. A major attempt to build a model on research data was made by Jack Holmes and Harry Singer when using a statistical procedure they called the "substrata analysis." They attempted to see which tests of many factors, such as vision, word knowledge, IQ, hearing, etc., "accounted for the variance" in scores of reading comprehension and reading speed tests. This analysis caused Holmes to publish the following definition of reading in 1960:

> Reading is an audio-visual verbal processing skill of symbolic reasoning, sustained by the interfacilitation of an intricate hierarchy of substrata factors that have been mobilized as psychological working system and pressed into service in accordance with the purposes of the reader.

While this is a little difficult to interpret without reading the contents of their studies, you can get the idea that the reading process is complex. As a practical outcome, Singer felt that there was a definite rise in the importance of knowledge of word meanings between grades three and six. In other words, one important thing that teachers in the upper elementary school can do is teach vocabulary improvement.

Attempts to understand some of the components of the reading process have also had other practical outputs. For example, Frederick Davis used factor analysis of many test items to try to find the elements involved in comprehension. He isolated nine factors, such as word knowledge, ability to select the main idea, ability to determine the writer's purpose, etc. These factors were used in constructing his reading comprehension test, published by Educational Testing Service, and probably have influenced numerous curriculum materials. A list of the nine factors can be found in Chapter 5.

Another type of reading model is patterned after the computer. For example, Jane Mackworth's reading model is based partly on visual processing time and neurological knowledge. It contains boxes with such labels as "short-term memory," "long-term memory," etc.

Yet other models of reading have a heavy linguistic emphasis. A simple one would see *reading as a decoding process:*—If you can sound out the symbols you can get it into auditory language, and this is the prime function of the reading process. This heavy emphasis on the decoding process is advocated by such linguists as Charles Fries and Leonard Bloomfield. If you accept this model, obviously all you have to do is to teach phonics and everything else will take care of itself.

Linguists (like reading people) disagree on nearly everything, and quite a different "linguistic theory of reading" is held by Noam Chomsky, who feels that the actual words or sound symbol correspondence (sight words and phonics) represent only *surface structure,* while the important "meaning" would be found in *deep structure.* Deep structure is the basic underlying idea of the sentence. In part, he would be interested in the relationship between grammar and comprehension. One of the implications of this type of theory is that teachers can improve the teaching of reading comprehension by either teaching about or utilizing syntax. This would mean using units of language somewhat larger than single words for meaning or comprehension lessons. It might also include lessons teaching the underlying grammatical or syntactical rules, and showing that the same thought (deep structure) can be written a number of different ways (surface structure).

SCIENTIFIC OBSERVATIONS OF THE READING PROCESS

Any theory must of course be based upon some kind of fact or direct observation. Psychologists use many types of laboratory observations to aid theorists, but classroom teachers can observe many of the same inputs informally. Here are a few reading process observations you can make:

1 *Oral reading* gives a strong indication of ability. This was the basis of one of the first standardized published tests in the reading field, *Gray's Oral Reading Paragraphs.* Besides simply observing the total number of errors, thus getting a general indication of level, errors can be analyzed and classified. Does the student typically leave off endings, or is he unable to use any phonic cues? Do errors indicate that she seems to understand the passage, or not? Reading specialists from William Gray to Kenneth Goodman, who developed Reading Miscue Analysis, have been interested in oral reading errors.

2 *Silent reading* output can be observed in the form of various types of test questions or performance requirements. The type of questions that can be answered show us something of mental process.

3 *Eye movements* can be observed during reading. You can see the difference in eye movements between beginning readers and more mature readers (movements can be seen, photographed, and timed).

4 *Eye-Voice Span* can be observed. When a child is reading aloud, simply take a sheet of paper and quickly cover the page. The number of words he can continue to say is one measure of eye-voice span. Repeat this experiment with an older student reading easier material, and you will see a greater eye-voice span. The fact that there is any eye-voice span at all indicates that a certain amount of "processing time" is going on inside the head.

5 *Latency or response time* is another observable part of the reading process. If you flash a difficult word (flip a card over) for a fraction of a second, the amount of time it takes the reader to respond might vary with the student's familiarity with the word. Why do less familiar words take a longer response time? Some theorists would say that different areas of the brain, or a different type of "processing," is being used with the less familiar word. *Reading speed* or total time to complete a passage is another time measurement.

6 What *parts of the word* are attended to? If you type a passage omitting the vowels, and another passage omitting the consonants, which is easier to read? If the first or last part of a word is omitted, which is easier to read? See Figure 1-3.

7 Which *parts of a passage* are easier? If you omit verbs, or nouns, or prepositions, how does it affect recall or comprehension?

8 *Correlation studies,* or studies which use part of a population, attempt to answer such questions as "Do boys read better than girls?" or "Do children from wealthy homes read better than children from poor homes?"

9 *Varying teaching condition studies* investigate all manner of learning conditions. Typical questions would be "Is the phonics method better than the whole word method?" or "Do children learn to read better if taught in their own speech dialect?"

No. 1   **Listen to oral reading.**

1. Are more errors made if a harder book is given?
2. What kinds of errors are made? Endings left off, meaningful substitutions made, omissions?
3. How successful are attempts to sound out difficult words?

No. 2   **After silent reading, ask various kinds of questions.**

1. What were the facts?
2. Which event occurred first, next?
3. What was the author trying to do?
4. Also analyze printed comprehension questions in a reading drill book.

No. 3   **Observe eye movements while reading silently.**

1. See eyes stop about every word and swing back at end of line.
2. Regressions and hesitations occur on difficult words.
3. Are there more regressions on difficult material?

No. 4   **Observe eye-voice span while reading orally.**

1. With a sheet of paper, quickly cover page while student reads aloud.
2. Note the number of words student continues to read after page is covered (this is the eye-voice span).
3. Is the span greater for easier books?

No. 5   **Observe latency (time it takes to say word) after word has been flashed.**

1. Prepare word cards with easy, medium, and difficult words.
2. Flash words very fast (flip over and instantly flip back).
3. Note how long it takes a child to respond to words of varying difficulty.
4. Time the reading of a passage.

Figure 1-3 Reading process observations.

No. 6   **Observe which parts of the word are most useful for reading.**

XXGER   or   TIGXX
ıııʋʋıı   or   mɔɔn
XEXXEX   or   LXTTXR

1. Using flash cards or a paragraph, try omitting various parts of words such as first half or second half, top half or bottom half, vowels or consonants, and see which are easier to read.

2. Try making the words easy or hard.

No. 7   **Observe which parts of a passage are most necessary for comprehension.**

the old boy
was   the
floor next to
the   He
was going

1. Omit (by retyping or blacking out) different kinds of words in a passage: (a) nouns and verbs versus articles and conjunctions or (b) every 10th word versus every 5th word.

2. See if student can tell you omitted words.

3. How do omissions affect comprehension?

No. 8   **Correlation studies (and parts of population). Who reads better?**

Girls

Boys

No. 9   **Vary teaching conditions.**

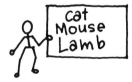

Figure 1-3 Reading process observations (continued).

These are some of the types of observations that reading specialists, psychologists, and linguists make to attempt to understand the reading process, and there are many more areas of investigation.

Thus we can see that there are many ways of looking at the reading process. It is not the intent of this book to delve extensively into research studies or theoretical models, but they sometimes are interesting and, on a practical level, teachers will often see curriculum materials and suggested teaching methods which are closely related to one kind of model or another. Should you be interested in more depth about this topic, the references at the end of the chapter will help you get started.

SUMMARY AND CONCLUSIONS

This chapter serves as an orientation to the rest of the book. By giving you our definition—"reading is the process of getting meaning from written language"—you can see how phonics, vocabulary, and the various comprehension skills all contribute toward that goal.

The five basic steps will also orient you to the subject in general, and this book in particular. There are so many aspects to the topic of teaching reading that, without some orientation, it is easy to get lost in the details or, even worse, to confuse minor details with major goals.

The reading process is complex, and I apologize for not doing it full justice, but it is not the intent of this book to emphasize theoretical models or the many controversies and conflicting research studies which surround them. They should be discussed in more advanced books and more advanced courses. There are some excellent references at the end of this chapter which will allow you to go more thoroughly into the theoretical aspects of reading.

Likewise, in mentioning some of the scientific observations of reading, I have shown only some of the major types of observations. This is not a book on how to do reading research, but it is interesting to know a bit about how the reading process can be observed, and you will undoubtedly come across many of these observational techniques in your later professional reading.

What this book will help you with is the teaching of reading in the classroom. The five basic steps suggest actual lesson plans. The later chapters will not only give you much more information on the underlying principles, but will provide you with some definite teaching techniques and lists of some commercially available materials that can be of further specific help.

For your own learning, at the end of each chapter I have placed a list of vocabulary and study terms. This list is a bit like an outline of the chapter and a bit like a vocabulary drill. After reading the chapter you should be able to associate something meaningful, or a brief definition, with each of the terms; if you can't, then reread that part of the chapter. When you are teaching reading, particularly in the subject matter areas (like science and social studies), one of the things you will be teaching is the vocabulary of the subject. I am suggesting that you learn the vocabulary of the reading field. The vocabulary of this chapter is not very technical, but in the next chapter, on phonics, there may be many new terms for you to learn (for example, what is the difference between a "digraph" and a "diphthong?"). It is a good idea to learn all of these terms chapter by chapter rather than waiting until midterm or the end of the course. Facility with the vocabulary will help you greatly in later professional reading, and in using the teachers' manuals of basal series and other commercially prepared reading teaching material.

The "Suggested Learning Activities," at the ends of all the chapters, are another learning aid for you. Most of them have been tried out in classes at Rutgers University, and they have the very valuable feature of helping you to see that things talked about in this book really do exist in the outside world. Many of them ask you to observe in classrooms, so it is advisable to have some time set up for at least several classroom observations. But some of them merely require that you have some reading material or work with a child. Most colleges and most public schools have some kind of curriculum library, so it will behoove you to start getting familiar with the tools of teaching reading. Doctors would have a difficult time learning to cure people if they never observed patients or handled a stethoscope during training; likewise reading teachers should have some children to observe and some materials to examine and use. You may not be able to do all of the suggested learning activities at the end of each chapter, though it wouldn't hurt you. If you are using this book as part of a reading course or inservice training procedure, your instructor may suggest those activities which are more important or more feasible. But if you are really eager, try to do as many as you can—it will make the discussions in this book more meaningful and more insightful. We want the best-trained teachers possible.

SUGGESTED LEARNING ACTIVITIES

1 Go into an elementary classroom at reading lesson time and observe what is going on. Have a list of the five basic steps handy, and see how many of them are being covered in a particular reading lesson and follow-up activities.

2 Conduct some of your own scientific observations of the reading process, using some of the seven methods listed in this chapter: observe oral reading errors, types of comprehension questions, eye movements, eye-voice span, latency, and reading with parts of words or parts of the passage removed. You can use either a child or an adult for these observations or, better yet, contrast the difference between a younger reader and a more mature reader.

3 Apply models. See if you can take one or two of the theoretical models discussed in this chapter and show how they apply to a reading lesson of some commercial set of reading materials. Perhaps you can write a brief description showing how two or more models are followed in the same lesson.

4 Start building your own reading glossary, notebook, or card file. If you are new to the reading field, one of the goals of reading this book should be to build your vocabulary of reading terms. Start with some of the terms used in this chapter and keep your own list of new, unique, or particularly important terms, along with a brief definition.

VOCABULARY AND STUDY TERMS

Definition of reading
  Meaning
  Part of communication
  Time-space barrier
Basic steps
  1 Match reading ability and readability
  2 Phonics and word attack
  3 Words: sight words and vocabulary
  4 Comprehension
  5 Motivation and practice (success)
The reading process
  Meaning definition
  Communication muddle
  Hughey, Javel, Thorndike, Goodman, Gray-Robinson,
  Holmes-Singer, Davis, Mackworth, Fries, Chomsky (surface structure–deep structure)
Scientific observations
  Oral reading
  Silent reading
  Eye movements
  Eye-voice span
  Latency (reading speed)
  Word parts
  Passage parts
  Correlation (part of population)
  Vary teaching conditions

REFERENCES

Bloomfield, Leonard, and Clarence L. Barnhart. *Let's Read: A Linguistic Approach.* Detroit: Wayne State University Press, 1961.

Carroll, J. B. "The Analysis of Reading Instruction: Perspectives from Psychology and Linguistics." In E. R. Hilgard (Ed.), *Theories of Learning and Instruction.* Chicago: National Society for the Study of Education, 1964.

Carroll, John B., and Jeanne S. Chall. *Toward a Literate Society.* New York: McGraw-Hill, 1975.

Chomsky, Noam. "Phonology and Reading." In H. Levin and J. P. Williams (Eds.), *Basic Studies on Reading.* New York: Basic Books, 1970.

Clymer, Theodore. "What is 'Reading'?: Some Current Concepts." In Helen M. Robinson (Ed.), *Innovation and Change in Reading Instruction*, '67 Yearbook of the National Society for the Study of Education. Chicago: University of Chicago Press, 1968.

Corder, Reginald, *The Information Base for Reading.* Berkeley, Calif.: Educational Testing Service (ERIC), 1971.

Courtney, Brother Leonard (Ed.). *Reading Interaction, The Teacher, The Pupil, The Materials*. Newark, Del.: International Reading Association, 1976.

Davis, Frederick B. "Psychometric Research on Comprehension in Reading." In F. B. Davis (Ed.), *The Literature of Research in Reading with Emphasis on Models*. East Brunswick, N.J. (Box 372): Iris Corp., 1971.

Farr, Roger, Jaap Tuinman, and Michael Rowls. *Reading Achievement in the United States: Then and Now*. A Report Prepared for Educational Testing Service by the Reading Program Center and the Institute for Child Study. Bloomington: Indiana University, 1974 (ERIC).

Fries, Charles C. *Linguistics and Reading*. New York: Holt, 1963.

Gibson, Eleanor J., and Harry Levin. *The Psychology of Reading*. Cambridge, Mass.: The MIT Press, 1975.

Goodman, Kenneth S. "Reading: A Psycholinguistic Guessing Game." In H. Singer and R. B. Ruddell (Eds.), *Theoretical Models and Processes of Reading*. Newark, Del.: International Reading Association, 1970.

Gray, William S. "The Major Aspects of Reading." In Helen M. Robinson (Ed.), *Supplementary Educational Monograph No. 90*. Chicago: University of Chicago Press, 1960.

Hollander, Sheila K. "Reading: Process and Product." *The Reading Teacher,* March 1975, *28*(6).

Holmes, J. A. "The Substrata-factor of Reading: Some Experimental Evidence." In J. A. Figurel (Ed.), *New Frontiers in Reading*. New York: Scholastic Magazines, 1960, pp. 115–121.

Huey, Edmund Burke. *The Psychology and Pedagogy of Reading*. Cambridge, Mass.: The M.I.T. Press, 1908.

Kling, Martin, and Frederick B. Davis. *The Literature of Research and Reading with Emphasis on Models*. East Brunswick, N.J.: Iris Corp., 1971.

Lefevre, Carl A. *Linguistics and the Teaching of Reading*. New York: McGraw-Hill, 1964.

Mathews, Mitford M. *Teaching to Read: Historically Considered*. Chicago: University of Chicago Press, 1966.

Morrison, Coleman, and Mary C. Austin. "The Torch Lighters Revisited—A Preliminary Report." *The Reading Teacher*, April 1976, *29*(7).

Robinson, Helen M. "The Major Aspects of Reading." In H. Allen Robinson (Ed.), *Reading: Seventy-Five Years of Progress. Supplementary Educational Monograph No. 96*. Chicago: University of Chicago Press, 1966.

Singer, Harry. "Theoretical Models of Reading." In H. Singer and R. B. Ruddell (Eds.), *Theoretical Models and Processes in Reading*. Newark, Del.: International Reading Association, 1970.

Smith, Frank, and Kenneth S. Goodman. "On the Psycholinguistic Method of Teaching Reading." *Elementary School Journal,* January 1971, *71*, 177–181.

Thorndike, Edward L. "Reading As Reasoning: A Study of Mistakes in Paragraph Reading." *The Journal of Educational Psychology*, June 1917.

Chapter 2

Phonics:
Our Alphabet,
Phonemes, Methods

In Chapter 1, we focused on some basic principles of reading instruction. That introduction provided what some educational psychologists might call an *advanced organizer*; study skills experts could call it an *overview*. In this chapter, we will examine our alphabet and phonics more closely.

In the United States, we write and read primarily by means of an alphabet. An alphabet is a set of symbols which more or less represent speech sounds (see Figure 2-1). While our alphabet is of crucial importance in our communication, there are hundreds of millions of people in this world who do not write and read by means of an alphabet; instead, they use a system of *ideographs* or symbols which stand directly for an idea or concept. The ideographs are not related to speech sounds. In fact, a child in south China cannot talk to a child in north China because they speak different languages, but they can write letters to each other or read the same books.

Most of the scholars in the world feel that the alphabet is a wonderful invention because it simplifies attainment of literacy. Elementary teachers in China must spend many more hours in the school day teaching their children to read and write than do those who teach in countries where alphabets are used. An indication that alphabets continue to provide a favorable means for writing is the relatively recent introduction of alphabet systems in some areas of the world (Africa and many Pacific isles) where languages were first written down in the past century.

Phoenician	Early Greek	Latin	Modern
ʞ	A	A	A
ᐟ	Ɛ	B	B
ʔ	ʌ	C	C
⊿	Δ	D	D
⋧	Ⅎ	E	E
Y	F	F	F
I	I	..	..
..	..	G	G
⊌	B	H	H
⊕	⊗	..	..
ʔ	ϟ	I	I
..	..	..	J
ψ	K	K	K
ʅ	ʌ	L	L
⸞	ʌ	M	M
ʂ	N	N	N
∓	‡	..	..
O	O	O	O
ʔ	ʅ	P	P
h	..	..	..
φ	φ	Q	Q
ᖴ	P	R	R
w	ϟ	S	S
+X	T	T	T
——	U	V	U
..	..	..	V
..	..	..	W
..	+	X	X
..	..	Y	Y
..	..	Z	Z

Figure 2-1 This chart shows some of the steps in the development of our alphabet from the Phoenicians in 1500 B.C. through Greek and Latin to the present. *(Adapted from* Compton's Pictured Encyclopedia and Fact-Index, *E. F. Compton Company, Division of Encyclopaedia Britannica, Inc., Chicago, 1968.)*

Our alphabet is called the *Roman* alphabet because it first came to England with the Romans—before that, the peoples of what is now England did not have a developed written language. Since the Romans spoke Latin, it is also called the *Latin alphabet*. Figure 2-1 shows that the Roman alphabet had even earlier origins, and went through many modifications. This information is important as we begin to study phonics because it helps to explain why the Roman alphabet, which was meant for Latin, does not fit modern English too well.

VOWELS VERSUS CONSONANTS

In the Roman alphabet, there are two major classes of letters: vowels and consonants. This may sound very simple and basic, but do you know the difference between a vowel and a consonant? Look away from this page and see if you can formulate an answer in your mind. On a piece of scratch paper state as best you can why a vowel is a vowel or why a consonant is a consonant, what a vowel and a consonant are, and how they differ from each other.

It's not so easy, is it? You might have written that vowels are the letters A, E, I, O, U, and sometimes Y, which, while accurate, is not a definition. How do we define these major classes of letters? First of all, there are several speech or sound characteristics. Vowels always use the vocal chords; speech teachers would say that they are *voiced*, which means the vocal chords are used. Consonents may or may not use the vocal chords. For example, making the /s/ sound at the beginning of "Sam" or end of "cats" is made simply by whistling the air by your teeth. Your vocal chords are not used, and it is called an *unvoiced* sound.

Consonants also tend to shut off or constrict the breath. Note what happens to the airflow when you make the /p/ sound in "pin" or the /t/ sound in "top."

Vowel sounds can be sustained. The long /e/ sound at the end of the word "see" can be sustained indefinitely if you want to, but how can you sustain the /p/ sound at the end of "stop"? Consonants may or may not be capable of being sustained. The /m/ sound at the end of "Tom" can be sustained, but you can't sustain the /t/ no matter where it occurs.

Structurally, there is also an interesting difference. You must have one vowel sound —and only one vowel sound—in every syllable. In fact, that is one way of defining a syllable (you can't have two vowel sounds without having two syllables). You can have a one-letter syllable (for example, "po-li-o") and you can have a one syllable word (for example, "I," or "a" in the phrase "a book"). But there is no word in English which is just a single consonant, and there is no syllable which is composed of just consonants.

There is another important difference between vowels and consonants in the teaching of phonics. Most consonants have only one sound, whereas the vowels all have two or more sounds.

For dictionary definitions of alphabet, vowel, and consonant, see Figure 2-2.

Phonemes and Graphemes

Before we go on discussing phonics we need to introduce several terms from linguistics because they add a bit of precision to our discussion and will be useful to you in reading professional journal articles which use such terms.

al·pha·bet (al′fə bet′), *n.* **1.** the letters of a language in their customary order. **2.** any system of characters or signs with which a language is written: *the Greek alphabet.* **3.** any such system for representing the sounds of a language: *the phonetic alphabet.* **4.** first elements; basic facts; simplest rudiments: *the alphabet of radio.* **5. the alphabet,** a system of writing, developed in the ancient Near East and transmitted from the northwest Semites to the Greeks, in which each symbol ideally represents one sound unit in the spoken language, and from which most alphabetical scripts are derived. [< LL *alphabēt(um)*, alter. of Gk *alphábētos.* See ALPHA, BETA]

vow·el (vou′əl), *n.* **1.** *Phonet.* **a.** (in English articulation) a speech sound produced without occluding, diverting, or obstructing the flow of air from the lungs (opposed to *consonant*). **b.** (in a syllable) the sound of greatest sonority, as *i* in *grill.* Cf. **consonant** (def. 1b). **c.** (in linguistic function) a concept empirically determined as a phonological element in structural contrast with consonant, as the (ē) of *be* (bē), *we* (wē), and *yeast* (yēst). **2.** a letter representing or usually representing a vowel, as in English, *a, e, i, o, u, w, y.* —*adj.* **3.** of or pertaining to a vowel or vowels. [ME < OF *vouel* < L *rōcāl(is)* adj.; see VOCAL] —**vow′el·less,** *adj.* —**vow′-el·like′,** *adj.* —**vow′el·y, vow′el·ly,** *adv.*

con·so·nant (kon′sə nənt), *n.* **1.** *Phonet.* **a.** (in English articulation) a speech sound produced by occluding with or without releasing (p, b; t, d; k, g), diverting (m, n, ng), or obstructing (f, v; s, z, etc.) the flow of air from the lungs (opposed to *vowel*). **b.** (in a syllable) any sound other than the sound of greatest sonority in the syllable, as *b, r,* and *g* in *brig* (opposed to *sonant*). Cf. **vowel** (def. 1b). **c.** (in linguistic function) a concept empirically determined as a phonological element in structural contrast with vowel, as the *b* of *be,* the *w* of *we,* the *y, s,* and *t* of *yeast,* etc. **2.** a letter which usually represents a consonant sound. —*adj.* **3.** in agreement; agreeable; in accord; consistent (usually fol. by *to* or *with*): *behavior consonant with his character.* **4.** corresponding in sound, as words. **5.** harmonious, as sounds. **6.** *Music.* constituting a consonance. **7.** *Physics.* noting or pertaining to sounds exhibiting consonance. **8.** consonantal. [late ME *consona(u)nt* < L *consonant-* (s. of *consonāns,* prp. of *consonāre* to sound with or together). See CON-, SONANT] —**con′so·nant·ly,** *adv.* —**Syn. 3.** concordant, congruous, conformant. —**Ant. 6.** dissonant.

Figure 2-2 From *The Random House Dictionary of the English Language,* unabridged edition, Random House Inc., New York, 1966.

A *phoneme* is roughly what we have been talking about when we describe the sound a letter makes. Perhaps we sometimes call it a *speech sound.* A phoneme is the minimum speech sound needed to change meaning. In the classic example, the difference between "pin" and "pan" represents a phoneme change because meaning has changed. Not everybody says "pin" exactly the same way, so some of the little differences in accent or intonation are really *allophones*—they don't change the meaning but they might vary the sound slightly.

A *grapheme* is roughly the way you write down a phoneme. Often a grapheme is a letter. But let us give the linguistic definition of grapheme: "A grapheme is the minimum written symbol needed to change meaning." Hence, the written difference between "pin" and "pan" is that the middle letter is changed, and thus the meaning is changed. For the sake of clarity, and so that you will be able to read other books that use linguistic terminology, we will indicate phonemes as a letter or letters set off by slash marks, and graphemes by the capital letter or letters. For example, the sound that you hear at the beginning of the word "pin" is the /p/ phoneme, indicated by the grapheme, P.

As reading teachers we are concerned about the *phoneme-grapheme correspon-dence* which teachers usually call *phonics*. That is, it is called "phonics" if we go in the direction of *decoding* or looking at the printed symbols and saying the spoken word.

When we turn the process around and attempt to go in the opposite direction, or *encoding*, we call it *writing* or *spelling*. Spelling is sometimes called by its more classic name of *orthography*, which is the set of rules or customs that dictate which letters are used to correctly set down a word in writing.

As I stated earlier, English is written with the Roman alphabet. One of our prob-lems is that we do not have enough letters for all the English phonemes, so we construct more by using two letters to simulate a new letter. That is, two letters sometimes con-stitute one grapheme. For example, the phoneme at the beginning of the word "the" is spelled by the grapheme TH. The TH is not a *blend* of /t/ and /h/ but a completely dif-ferent phoneme or speech sound. The phoneme /th/ is just as much a separate and dis-tinct phoneme as the /p/, the /a/, or the /n/ in "pan." When two letters are used to make one grapheme, reading teachers call the grapheme a *digraph* (*di* means "two" and *graph* means "write"). Blends are two graphemes which make two phonemes. The S and the T in "stop" are both sounded, and they are a beginning consonant blend.

Now for a bit of review. A phoneme cannot be seen; it is a speech sound and is heard. A grapheme is the way you write down a phoneme; it may be one or more let-ters. You can't hear a grapheme.

In English orthography, one grapheme sometimes will have several phonemes. For example, the A in "pat" sounds different from the A in "mate," and the A grapheme in "all" sounds different yet. Occasionally, the opposite is true; that is, one phoneme will have several graphemes. For example, the /s/ phoneme in "sat" can also be spelled by the grapheme C, as in "city." These examples illustrate the kinds of problems in-volved in teaching phonics.

Consonant Phoneme-Grapheme Correspondence

Let us discuss consonants first because they are simpler than vowels, and more mean-ingful. They are simpler because there is a better one-to-one correspondence between the consonant graphemes and phonemes. They are more meaningful because the *dis-tinctive features* (elements that make the word different from other words) of written words are more bound up with consonants than vowels. Figure 2-3 shows a brief para-graph first with the consonants removed, and then with the vowels removed. You will note that the consonants carry much more of the *information* than the vowels. In fact, some languages (like Hebrew) can be written without the vowels (vowel symbols are added for children and adults learning to read the language).

Here is a simplified set of consonant principles. These constitute the bulk of what is taught in most elementary reading instruction.

Regular Consonants   These are represented by the following letters. They are pre-sented here roughly in their order of frequency of occurrence, which some people think is a good order in which to teach them.

T N R M D S L C P B F V G H W K J Y Z

Directions: Read down from the top.

Vowels Only

    _ _ i _ _ a _ _ a _ e i _ _ ei _ _ _ _ i _ _ e _ i _ _ _ o _ i _ _ e

_ e _ _ _ a _ _ _ o _ i _ e _ ou a _ e _ _ e _ ie _ _ e o _ _ ea _ i _ _

_ i _ _ ou _ _ o _ _ o _ a _ _ _ a _ _ _ ea _ i _ _ _ i _ _ ou _ _ o _ e _ _.

_ o _ _ i _ _ i _ u _ _ _ o _ _ _ _ i _ e _ o _ io _ ye _ i _ i _, _ ou _ ee _

_ o _ _.

Consonants

    Th _ s p _ ss _ g _ _ s b _ _ ng wr _ tt _ n _ n tw _ d _ ff _ r _ nt

w _ ys t _ g _ v _ y _ _ _ n _ xp _ r _ _ nc _ _f r _ _ d _ ng w _ th _ _ t

c _ ns _ n _ nts _ nd r _ _ d _ ng w _ th _ _ t v _ w _ ls. F _ r d _ ff _ c _ lt

w _ rds l _ ke p _ l _ _ m _ _ l _ t _ s, y _ _ n _ _ d b _ th.

Figure 2-3 Sample of a passage written with vowels only and with consonants only to illustrate which is easier to read.

Some Consonants Have Several Sounds

S The regular sound of the grapheme S is the sound it makes in the word "sat." A *regular sound* is usually the most common use. The second sound of this grapheme is like /z/, as in the word "has." S only makes the /z/ sound at the end of a word or syllable, never at the beginning. However, S also makes the /s/ sound at the end of some words ("this").

C The regular sound of the grapheme C is the /k/ sound as in "cat," and its second sound is the /s/ sound as in "city." With some degree of regularity, C makes the /s/ sound before I, E, and Y, and the /k/ sound before A, O, and U, but there are exceptions.

G The regular sound of G is its own sound that is heard at the beginning of the word "good," but it sometimes makes the /j/ sound, as before I, E, or Y ("ginger," "gym").

Y The grapheme Y is sometimes a consonant, usually when it appears at the beginning of a word, as in "yes." However, its consonant sound is really its second sound because most often it is a vowel. See the section on vowels which follows.

Consonant Digraphs Two letters (one grapheme) that represent one consonant sound (phoneme) are called a "consonant digraph." There are not very many of them; in fact, only about half a dozen occur with any degree of frequency.

CH The consonant digraph CH makes the /ch/ sound heard at the beginning of the word "chair."

SH The consonant digraph SH makes the /sh/ sound heard at the beginning of the word "shoe."

WH The consonant digraph WH makes the /wh/ sound heard at the beginning of the word "wheel." Some dictionaries describe this phoneme as a blend of /h/ and /w/ or /hw/ for some WH words and as only a /w/ for other WH words, but reading teachers usually consider it a /wh/ phoneme and ignore the difference. Part of the problem here is that American speech is changing, and many people do not sound the /h/ in WH words. If you are interested in testing your own speech, say a number of WH words like "white, while," etc., and see if you can detect an /h/ (blowing) at the beginning of the word. You might contrast your /wh/ (or /hw/) with the /w/ at the beginning of W words like "with, we," etc. For example, first say "when," and "we" while holding a finger in front of your lips; if you feel a noticeably greater amount of air coming out when you say "when," you are probably making a /hw/ sound—but many people use just a /w/.

TH The TH grapheme is really a bit complex because it has two distinct phonemes, the so-called voiced /th/ in a word like "that," and voiceless /th/ in "three." Say both words aloud and notice the use of your voice—vocal chords—in the first. The voiceless /th/ phoneme has been underlined to indicate that it is the second sound.

PH The consonant digraph PH is really a second way of spelling the /f/ phoneme; the regular way, of course, is with an F.

NG The consonant digraph NG is never used at the beginning of a word. It makes the /ng/ sound heard at the end of a word like "sing." In case you are wondering if NG really makes a unique phoneme rather than a blend, try observing your own mouth and tongue positions when you make an /n/ (as in "pin"), and an /ng/ (in "sing").

Letters Without Their Own Phonemes There are several letters which could be regarded as superfluous from a phonics standpoint because they have no sounds of their own.

X The letter x is usually used to make the /k/ /s/ blend heard at the end of a word like "fox," but once in a while it makes the /g/ /z/ blend in a word like "example." Its use at the beginning of a word like "x-ray" is of low frequency; in that instance it makes an /e/ /k/ /s/ syllable. In teaching phonics, you should use its more regular /k/ /s/ sound in words like "fox."

Q The letter Q is never used alone, but always as part of the QU digraph which makes a /k/ /w/ blend in words like "queen."

In discussing "superfluous" letters, we should perhaps include the C mentioned earlier, because it really has only a /k/ sound in some instances and an /s/ sound in other instances. (But it is also needed for the CH digraph.)

It is too bad that the Roman alphabet, which doesn't have enough symbols for all the English phonemes, has three (x, q, and c) that don't match specific phonemes.

Silent Letters Almost any letter can be silent in some instances. Several common instances of silent letters are:

C before K as in "back"
K before N as in "know"

W before R as in "write"
GH as in "night"

Since these examples occur almost as digraphs CK, KN, WR, and GH, they could be viewed as digraphs.

There are many other letters that can be silent—like the B in "climb"—but the most common silent letter of all is the E at the end of a word, as in "come." That silent E is sometimes used as a *marker* to indicate that the preceding vowel is long (the so-called *final E rule*) as in "made," but sometimes it just sits at the end of a word like "come" and doesn't contribute to the sound at all. A *marker* is a term used by linguists to indicate a letter or combination of letters that indicate something such as a particular sound.

Vowel Phonics Principles

Vowels are considerably more complex than consonants, because each vowel grapheme has more phonemes than the usual consonant. Or, another way of saying the same thing, is that the one-to-one phoneme-grapheme (letter-sound) correspondence is more frequently irregular. When a beginning reader looks at a vowel grapheme it is hard to know what sound it makes. However, there is some order in the chaos, and here are some principles or generalizations in approximate teaching order:

Short Vowels Teaching the short vowels first makes good sense because they have the highest frequency. Another way of saying this is that if you come across an A in an unknown word, and you don't know anything else, the probability is that it is a short A. Sometimes children (and even teachers) have trouble remembering the short sounds. A handy reminder is provided by this little sentence which has only short vowel sounds in it, occurring in the traditional alphabetical order of AEIOU: "At End Is hOt pUp."

In trying to sound out the short vowel sounds in isolation, the only one that is the least bit tricky is the short O; it has what some people call an "ah" sound.

Long Vowels The long vowel sounds are those heard in pronouncing the individual vowel letters of the alphabet. There are several so-called rules or generalizations which help the beginning reader to know when to make the long sound for a vowel:

The *Final E Rule* states that when the syllable ends in a consonant followed by a silent E, then the preceding vowel is long. Note the vowel sound shift from short to long in these pairs of words: "mad-made, hat-hate, us-use, not-note." However, as I pointed out earlier, this rule is not infallible; "come" certainly doesn't have a long O (it's a short U).

Long Vowel Digraphs are two letters (one grapheme) that represent the long vowel sound. Common examples are:

Long E	EA as in "eat"
	EE as in "see"
Long A	AI as in "fail"
	AY as in "day"

Long O   OA as in "coat"
                                    OW as in "own"

These vowel digraphs used to be taught as the "double vowel rule" but its generalization of "when two vowels are together the first is long and the second is silent" had so many exceptions that it was found that it was better to teach these six correspondences as digraphs, though some older phonics systems may still discuss the so-called "double vowel rule."

The Open Syllable Rule states that when a syllable ends in a vowel, the vowel is long, and when it ends in a consonant, the vowel is short. This is sometimes referred to as the "open syllable–closed syllable rule"; an open syllable is one that ends in the vowel, and the closed syllable is one that ends in a consonant. Some words that illustrate this are "mu-sic," "go," and "ti-ny." Obviously, one of the difficulties with this rule is that the child must know how to break a word into syllables before the rule can be applied. Therefore, it is not too useful for beginning readers. Another problem is that it has so many exceptions that some phonics systems do not believe in teaching it.

Schwa The schwa is the unaccented vowel sound heard at the beginning of a word like "ago." It is usually represented by the upside-down E (ə) in most dictionary phonetic spelling systems. The schwa sound is most difficult to teach because there are no good rules as to when it occurs. There is only one thing that you can depend upon technically, and that is that it must be in an unaccented syllable; hence, there must be another accented syllable in the word. The difference between a schwa sound and the short U sound is also a technical one; the schwa sound has a briefer duration or less emphasis. This awkward set of circumstances causes us to call the O in "come" a "short U" and the A in "about" a "schwa."

The schwa sound can be made by any vowel but most often is made by just three of them:

A in "about"
E in "happen"
O in "money"

Because the schwa is difficult to recognize if you don't already know the word, it is often excluded from phonics teaching systems for children. It is probably best taught by example words or as part of dictionary use. Unfortunately, it has a rather high frequency of occurrence. However, if a student is trying to sound out a word and substitutes a short vowel for a schwa sound, the child can often approximate the sound of the word (perhaps aided by context clues) and be able to recognize the word.

The schwa sound also often occurs as part of a final unaccented syllable. The syllable is taught as a unit or phonogram; for example, "happen," "lemon," "pencil."

Vowel Plus R When the letter R follows a vowel, the vowel is usually neither long nor short.

First of all, the digraphs IR, ER, and UR all make the same sound, as seen in the example words "sir," "her," and "fur." Different dictionaries handle these vowels in different ways—short U's, schwas, etc.—but the sound is just like the consonant plus an /r/.

When an A or an O is followed by an R, the situation is different. OR is rather uncomplicated in that it usually makes the sound heard in "for." But AR is a bit more complex in that it makes two different sounds as heard in the words "arm" and "vary." Both of these A sounds are a little difficult to teach because they are relatively infrequent. Some dictionaries mark the first with an umlaut or double dot over the /ä/ as in "arm," and a tilde over the /ã/ as in "vary." One help is that these As usually precede an R; however, the second sound is also sometimes spelled AIR, as in "fair."

Y Rule   The letter Y is most often a vowel. Its most frequent sound is the long E sound at the end of a word like "funny." You might remember that the letter E at the end of a word is usually silent; if you want to make the long E sound at the end of a word, the usual way is with a Y. This convention holds for words of two or more syllables.

The letter Y at the end of a one-syllable word makes a long I sound, as in "fry." This long I sound is also made by Ys at the end of syllables in the middle of a word, such as in the word "cycle."

Thus, Y is a consonant only at the beginning of a word, as in "yes." This is certainly its least frequent use, but it is somewhat more important than its low frequency would indicate because consonants, particularly at the beginning of a word, have a greater distinctive features value. This means they aid a student more in sounding out or recognizing the word than do medial vowels or consonants in other positions. Many phonics systems will teach the consonant Y first.

Diphthongs   A diphthong is something like a vowel blend. It is sometimes described as a sliding sound between two vowels. In fact, some phoneticians (linguists who specialize in speech sounds) consider diphthongs as two vowel phonemes or as a vowel plus a semivowel sound. But reading teachers almost always consider the vowel diphthongs as a unit, or perhaps we should say *a* digraph-phoneme correspondence. In any event, there are only two diphthong sounds, each of which has two ways to spell it. The /ou/ sound is represented by OU as in "out" and OW as in "how." The /oi/ sound is represented by OI as in "oil" and OY as in "boy." It is not a terribly important generalization, but OU and OI tend to be used at the beginning of a word, and OW and OY tend to be used at the end of a word. Either can be used in the middle of a word.

Double O and U̇-Ü   The double O digraph (OO) tends to have two different phonemes, as seen in the words "moon" and "book." These same sounds are also sometimes called the two-dot U /ü/ as in the word "rule" and the one-dot U /u̇/ as in the word "put."

Reading teachers sometimes call the OO in "moon" *long*, and the OO in "book" *short*.

In any event, the vowel phoneme in "moon" and in "rule" is the same /ü/, and the vowel phoneme in "look" and "put" is the same /ủ/.

Broad O The broad sound, sometimes represented by an O with a circumflex over it /ô/ in some dictionary phonetic spelling systems, is sometimes spelled with an O grapheme, but more often with an A followed by a U, W, or L. For example:

AU as in "auto"
AW as in "awful"
AL as in "all"
O as in "off"

Exceptions and Spelling Reforms

Even though we have covered quite a few consonant and vowel generalizations, there are more, but they are of much less importance. Several that we might mention are the /zh/ phoneme made by the second G in "garage" or the SI in "vision."

One moderately prominent vowel exception is that the EA digraph sometimes makes the short /e/ sound, as in "bread."

There are a number of instances where TI makes the /sh/ sound as in "action," but most of the time this occurs as part of the TION suffix and is taught as a phonogram.

You might well ask, "If there are so many different phoneme-grapheme correspondence rules and beyond these even more exceptions, why don't we revise the alphabet, or at least revise the spelling system?" The answer is that it has been tried many times and usually failed; not because any scholar couldn't make vast improvements, but because of a failure of society to make the change.

In almost every session of the United States Congress, bills have been introduced to initiate *spelling reform*, but they never get out of committee. Many similar proposals have come before the British House of Commons with a similar fate.

Nearly every generation sees some revival of the reform idea. For example, Benjamin Franklin devised a simplified spelling system. In 1898, the National Education Association spearheaded a serious spelling reform movement. Even today, there is a small but active Simplified Spelling Society.

Sometimes the cudgels of reform are taken up by newspapers like the *Chicago Tribune*, which, in the 1930s, singlehandedly started respelling many words, substituting "nite" for "night," for example. Even today we see advertisements that simplify the spelling of product names like "Day Glo."

Alphabet reform is, of course, a more serious revision, but it has been frequently attempted by introducing a new alphabet as a system of beginning reading instruction. The most recent system of prominence has been the ITA (Initial Teaching Alphabet), developed in England by Sir James Pitman, which was both a spelling and alphabet reform that made the phoneme-grapheme correspondence more regular for beginning readers. It was tried in many United States schools but has been dropped by most of them because it did not produce clearly superior results with beginning readers. The following sentence is written in ITA:

ᴡun morniŋ lucky wonteɖ tɷ gœ fiʃhiŋ.

Alphabet and spelling reform is also opposed by some language scholars who feel that our present system of spelling incorporates much useful information as to word origins and present-day meaning. As an obvious example, *homophones* (words with the same sound but different meaning and often different spelling, such as "blew" and "blue")[1] would be wiped out in most spelling reform systems. Thus, their meaning differences would have to be determined by context, as orthographically they would look the same (see Figure 2-4).

Some scholars feel that though a slight edge might be given to children who are taught with a more regular alphabet at the beginning stages, children who are taught with a more meaning-encoded orthography, such as English, are ahead in the more advanced stages of reading.

Homophones

Wood you believe that I didn't no
About homophones until too daze ago?
That day in hour class in groups of for,
We had to come up with won or more.

Mary new six; enough to pass.
But my ate homophones lead the class.
Then a thought ran threw my head.
"Urn a living from homophones," it said.

I guess I just sat and staired into space.
My hole life seamed to fall into place.
Our school's principle happened to come buy,
And asked about the look in my I.

"Sir," said I as bowled as could bee,
"My future rode I clearly sea."
"Sun," said he, "move write ahead.
Set sale on your coarse. Don't be misled."

I herd that gnus with grate delight.
I will study homophones both day and knight.
For weaks and months, through thick oar thin.
I'll pursue my goal. Eye no aisle win.

GEORGE E. COON

Figure 2-4 From *The Reading Teacher*, April 1976.

[1] Some dictionaries would call "blue" and "blew" *homonyms*, but other dictionaries would not, saying that homonyms would have to have the same spelling; however, all would agree to calling them homophones in any event. Homographs incidentally are words of the same spelling and different meaning like *"run* in a race" or "to *run* a store."

METHODS OF TEACHING PHONICS

It is the general plan of this book to concentrate more on "what to teach" in the earlier chapters rather than "how to teach"; however, it is very difficult to separate the two. Too much concentration on what to teach might make the chapters seem somewhat irrelevant, but there is little point in knowing "how to teach" but not "what to teach." Therefore, this section is intended to give you some ideas on "how to teach" the phoneme-grapheme correspondence you have been reading about.

First of all, the teaching of phonics skills is incorporated into nearly all basal reading systems (which we will study in Chapter 7), and the diagnosis of a student's phonics knowledge is incorporated into many standardized achievement tests, criterion referenced tests, and test management systems (which we will explore in Chapter 11).

It is hard to say what *the* typical way of teaching phonics is, but a typical way is to have the teacher explain one or more phoneme-grapheme correspondences, perhaps using examples on the chalkboard or with a chart, then follow up the explanation by having the students do exercises in a workbook. Figure 2-5 shows a phonics chart for

U   u

umbrella

up   run

us   much

under   just

until   cut

but   funny

Author's Comments: **U** is a vowel which has several sounds. The short sound of **U**, as in "up" is the most common and should be taught first.

Other sounds of **U** are: the "Long Open Syllable Rule" (#27), the "2-Dot" **U** (#71), and the "1-Dot" **U** (#72). **OO** sometimes makes the "2-Dot" **U** sound (#69), and sometimes makes the "1-Dot" **U** sound (#70).

U also appears in #60-UR, #64-AU, and #65-OU.

U   Vowel Sound: **Short**

Figure 2-5 Phonics chart used in teaching a short vowel sound. (*From* 99 Phonics Charts, *Dreier Educational Systems.*)

use in teaching the Short U sound, and Figure 2-6 shows a portion of a workbook which involves short vowel sounds. These are commercially prepared materials, but many teachers could put material similar to the chart on the chalkboard, then rewrite their own follow-up lesson on a ditto master, or perhaps incorporate some of the Short U example words into a spelling or handwriting lesson.

At the end of this chapter there are several dozen phonics teaching materials listed and annotated. Some of these materials can be seen in college curriculum materials' centers or in nearby public schools. Large assortments of curriculum materials are also shown at various meetings for educators. You can get more detailed information on most of the materials listed by simply writing the publisher and requesting it.

You will note that the listed materials include workbooks, filmstrips, overhead transparencies, games, spirit (ditto) masters, audiotapes, tests, charts, flashcards, picture cards, wipeoff (magic) cards, magnetic cards (audiocards), comic books, word wheels, and probably much more. Some of the materials are packaged in "kits" or boxes which contain various combinations of the above materials, usually with a teacher's manual.

The list of materials is certainly not exhaustive, and it does not purport to be a complete list of all the materials available, but it is a pretty fair sample. These, plus the materials listed in later chapters, will probably make up more than half the materials available at time of publication. However, curriculum materials is an ever-changing field, and every year many of the major publishers—and no small number of the minor publishers—have something "new" in phonics. This is one reason why teachers must

Short Vowel Rule: If a word (or syllable) has only one vowel and it comes at the beginning or between two consonants, the vowel is usually short.

Say the name of each picture. Draw a ring around its name.

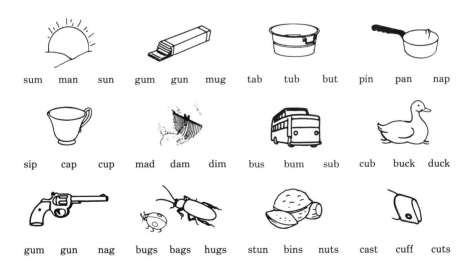

sum man sun	gum gun mug	tab tub but	pin pan nap
sip cap cup	mad dam dim	bus bum sub	cub buck duck
gum gun nag	bugs bags hugs	stun bins nuts	cast cuff cuts

Figure 2-6 Sample portion of a pupil workbook that teaches short vowels. (*From* Phonics Is Fun Book 3, *Modern Curriculum Press.*)

Phonics instruction can be aided by the use of charts, games, and work wheels. (Mike Q/Coronet Studios.)

know the phoneme-grapheme correspondences discussed earlier in this chapter. There might be some phoneme-grapheme correspondence lists (phonics content outlines) which are more extensive than others—or some which have slightly different correspondences included—but basically they remain the same.

In selecting phonics material to use, the teacher must examine the content— "which phonics skills are taught?" It is surprising what some of the well-packaged materials omit, and some even appear to have errors.

The other important factor that the teacher must consider in selecting materials is "how" the exercises are presented. Exactly what are the students expected to do? Do they draw lines or write letters? Are they learning only to recognize similarities, or are they expected to be able to make the sound when shown the last grapheme?

Even different sensory inputs are utilized in the various curriculum materials. Obviously, vision is the most-used modality, but some of the materials are multimodal and also present auditory information through teacher directions, audiotape-controlled drills, or audiocards (cards with a strip of magnetic tape across the bottom, so that when they are inserted into a card reader, the machine will "say" a word, phrase, or phoneme).

Old and New Phonics Methods: McGuffey and TV

To give you a little further insight into phonics teaching methods, it is interesting to look at two methods nearly a century apart. Figure 2-7 is from an 1879 edition of the famous McGuffey Readers, the most popular reading series in the middle of the last century.

As you can see, the teacher was instructed to have the children learn the sound that several letters made, and then combine these into words. You will note that Professor McGuffey quickly got the teacher to use these words as sight words, and suggested reading phrases as meaningful wholes.

McGuffey was really quite progressive, as he suggested teaching the alphabet *after* a few lessons had been mastered. A century earlier, the alphabet method was in vogue, and the first thing a child learned was the alphabet or "The ABCs." It is interesting that in many kindergartens today, teachers teach "The ABCs" as a first step in the learning-to-read process. Parents buy tons of coloring books and children's toys which purport to teach the alphabet before a child is sent to school.

Some educators have found that children who know the alphabet before entering first grade make better reading progress. There is, however, a confounding factor, since children who come to school knowing the alphabet also come from homes in which learning, in general, and reading, in particular, are held in high esteem. In nearly every first grade every year there are children who learn to read quite a few sight words— whole little books, in fact—before they "know their alphabet." It certainly isn't necessary to know the alphabet before starting to read, and its desirability is a matter of opinion.

Professor McGuffey utilized the medium of his day; namely, the printed word in book form. This century has seen the rise of a dramatically new type of media for teaching, in the form of television. There are some interesting similarities and contrasts between McGuffey's Readers and "The Electric Company" (a large and well-financed national television production seen in many homes and schools).

The Phonic Method: First teach the elementary sounds and their representatives, the letters marked with diacriticals, as they occur in the lessons; then, the formation of words by the combination of these sounds. For instance, teach the pupil to identify the characters a, o, n, d, g, r, and th, in Lesson I, as the representatives of certain elementary sounds; then, teach him to form words by their combination, and to identify them at sight. Use first the words at the head of the lesson, then other words, as, nag, on, and, etc. Pursue a similar course in teaching the succeeding lessons. Having read a few lessons in this manner, begin to teach the names of the letters and the spelling of words, and require the groups, "a man," "the man," "a pen," "the pen," to be read as a good reader would pronounce single words.

McGUFFEY'S

FIRST READER.

LESSON I.

dŏḡ   the   răn

ă   ŏ   n   d   ḡ   r   th

The dog.

The dog ran.

Figure 2-7 Some suggestions to the teacher from the famous *McGuffey's First Eclectic Reader* giving a brief description of the Phonic Method. *(From* McGuffey's First Eclectic Reader, *revised edition, American Book Company, New York, 1879. Still in print.)*

"The Electric Company" is a series of half-hour television shows which are aired regularly (daily in many areas) over both commercial and educational television stations. It is aimed at beginning readers in the elementary-school-age groups, but it is watched by a much wider segment of the population, from preschoolers to illiterate adults. Because of current awareness of the reading difficulties of many urban minority groups, "The Electric Company" uses urban settings and some stars of black or hispanic origin. "The Electric Company" is not the only television program that teaches reading skills, but it is a good and widely used example.

"The Electric Company" is also used in many schools, both in primary grades and in remedial reading situations. In fact, "The Electric Company" produces a teacher's guide so that the teacher may plan ahead with materials or lessons that coordinate with the content of the program. While "The Electric Company" teaches many facets of reading—such as comprehension, sentence structure, and basic sight words—one of its strong components is phonics. Phoneme-grapheme correspondences are handled in a simplified and dramatic fashion. Usually only one correspondence is emphasized. The OO grapheme, as in "moon," is taught with many sound (audio) presentations in a clever cartoon story utilizing a little character who is on the moon (see Figure 2-8, which shows storyboard illustrations from the program). In the presentation the viewer is literally bombarded with the /oo/ sound. Television has the benefits of a very dramatic and interesting multisensory presentation, but for the most part it has the disadvantage of not providing for any student response. If used in a school or in tutoring projects, a live instructor can follow up the TV lesson with student activities.

Both McGuffey and "The Electric Company," and nearly every other systematic method of teaching phonics, have a carefully unfolding master plan or list of phoneme-grapheme correspondences or phonic principles similar to those mentioned in this chapter. Figure 2-9 gives the phonic skills taught in both the McGuffey and "The Electric Company" teaching systems. The phonic skills in most modern basal readers or reading systems which are primarily books would perhaps have a little more detailed list of skills, but, in the main, there would be a lot of overlap with both McGuffey, "The Electric Company," and modern basal readers.

CONCLUSION

Phonics teaching methods will also be discussed in many other places in this book— such as the next chapter—as part of syllabification and word-attack skills, in discussions of basal readers, as part of testing of evaluation, and as part of supplementary materials and special approaches. This chapter is aimed primarily at future teachers of reading to provide an idea of what is taught (the content).

A good knowledge of phonics is also very useful in conducting spelling lessons, and in dictionary-use lessons.

The material at the end of this chapter includes some suggested learning activities that you can do on your own initiative or on assignment from your instructor. One of the suggested learning activities is to administer the Individual Phonics Criterion Test, found at the end of this chapter, to a student or adult. It will show you one way that

"The Electric Company" television series is designed to teach basic reading skills to beginning readers. (Henry McAllister/Carl Byoir & Associates, Inc.)

you can diagnose strengths and weaknesses of phonics skills. The Individual Phonics Criterion Test also will give you a list of 99 phoneme-grapheme correspondences which you can use as a suggested teaching order, or you can use the list for comparing various commercial phonics materials.

There is also a list of vocabulary and study terms to help you in reviewing the chapter through self-testing of the knowledge you have acquired. Part of learning any subject is learning the vocabulary of the subject. This is what you will be teaching your children, and this is what you should practice yourself. This list of vocabulary and study terms covers most of the new or technical terms used in the chapter, and it also provides a kind of overview or summation. You might try to formulate a brief definition for each term. If you can't, perhaps you need to reread parts of the chapter. The terms are roughly in order of presentation. Learning this many new terms is a bit difficult, but it will aid you in studying later chapters in this book, and in understanding other articles and books about reading and education throughout your career as an educator.

Explanatory Note for Phonics Test

The following test serves two purposes:

1. It gives you a listing on 99 phoneme-grapheme correspondences or phonics principles together with their commonly referred-to names ("short E," etc.) and an example word. This is a majority of phonics rules covered in most basal series and skills systems.

2. The Phonics Criterion Test is a useful tool that you can use in your classroom to diagnose phonics strengths and weaknesses of individual students. By using it a few times, you will quickly get an idea of how much phonics a child knows. By testing the student later in the year, you can determine how much has been learned.

Another in the same series, in which un-earthly creatures find "oo" on the moon."

Figure 2-8 Illustrations from the television program "The Electric Company," showing a dramatic and interesting introduction to the /oo/ sound as in "moon." *(Copyright 1971, Children's Television Workshop.)*

LONG VOCALS.

ā, as in āte.	ē, as in ẽrr.
â, " eâre.	ī, " īçe.
ä, " ärm.	ō, " ōde.
å, " låst.	ū, " ūse.
a̱, " a̱ll.	û, " bûrn.
ē, " ēve.	o͞o, " fo͞ol.

SUBVOCALS.

b, as in bīb.		v, as in vålve.
d, " dĭd.		th, " thĭs.
g, " gĭg̓.		z, " zĭne.
j, " jŭg̓.		z, " ăzure.
n, " nīne.		r, " râre.
m, " māim.		w, " wē.
ng, " hăng.		y, " yĕt.
l, as in lŭll.			

SHORT VOCALS.

ă, as in ăm.	ŏ, as in ŏdd.
ĕ, " ĕnd.	ŭ, " ŭp.
ĭ, " ĭn.	o͝o, " lo͝ok.

DIPHTHONGS.

oi, oy, as in oil, boy. | ou, ow, as in out, now

ASPIRATES.

f, as in fīfe.	t, as in tăt.
h, " hĭm.	sh, " shē.
k, " kīte.	ch, " chăt.
p, " pīpe.	th, " thĭck.
s, " sāme.	wh, " whȳ.

SUBSTITUTES.

a̱, for ŏ, as in whạt.	ȳ, for ī, as in mȳth.
ê, " â, " thêre.	e, " k, " eän.
ç, " ā, " fçint.	ç, " s, " çīte.
ĩ, " ē, " polĩçe.	çh, " sh, " çhāise.
î, " ĕ, " sîr.	eh, " k, " ehāos.
ȯ, " ŭ, " sȯn.	g̓, " j, " g̓ĕm.
ọ, " o͞o, " tọ.	ṉ, " ng, " ĭṉk.
ǫ, " o͝o, " wǫlf.	s̱, " z, " ăs̱.
ô, " a̱, " fôrk.	s, " sh, " sure.
ō̱, " û, " wō̱rk.	x̱, " g̱z, " ex̱ăet.
u̱, " o͝o, " fu̱ll.	gh, " f, " läugh.
u̱, " o͞o, " ru̱de.	ph, " f, " phlŏx.
ȳ, " ī, " flȳ.	qu, " k, " pïque.
qu, for kw, as in quit.		

The Electric Company Television Series

1. Consonants
   - b (as in bag)
   - c (as in cat and as in city)
   - d (as in dog)
   - f (as in fig)
   - g (as in got and as in gin)
   - h (as in hot)
   - j (as in jet)
   - k (as in kiss)
   - l (as in lot)
   - m (as in map)
   - n (as in nap)
   - p (as in pot)
   - qu (as in quit)
   - r (as in rot)
   - s (as in sit)
   - t (as in top)
   - v (as in vat)
   - w (as in won)
   - x (as in extra)
   - z (as in zoo)

2. Vowels
   - a (as in rat)
   - e (as in met)
   - i (as in bit)
   - o (as in hot)
   - u (as in cut)
   - y (as in dry and as in happy)

3. Consonant Blends (initial and final)
   Most frequently used:
   bl-, br-, cl-, cr-, -ct, dr-, -ft, gr-,
   -nd, -nt, pl-, pr-, sk-, -sk, sp-, -sp,
   st-, -st, tr-

1. Vowel Combinations
   - ai (as in bait)
   - ay (as in day)
   - ea (as in neat)
   - ee (as in see)
   - ie (as in die and as in thief)
   - oa (as in boat)
   - oi (as in boil)
   - oo (as in food and as in good)
   - ou (as in found)
   - ow (as in know and as in cow)
   - oy (as in toy)

2. Consonant Digraphs
   - ch (as in chop)
   - ph (as in phone)
   - sh (as in ship)
   - th (as in thin and as in this)

3. Controlled Vowels
   - ar (as in car)
   - er (as in fern)
   - ir (as in bird)
   - ur (as in burn)

4. Larger Spelling Patterns
   - -all (as in tall)
   - -alk (as in talk)
   - -igh(t) (as in high and as in night)
   - -ing (as in sing)
   - -tion (as in action)

Figure 2-9 Outlines of the phonics content of the McGuffey Readers and "The Electric Company" television series.

DREIER
EDUCATIONAL SYSTEMS

300 RARITAN AVENUE
HIGHLAND PARK, NEW JERSEY 08904
TELEPHONE (201) 572-2112

© Dreier Educational Systems, Inc. 1976

INDIVIDUAL PHONICS CRITERION TEST
Of 99 Phoneme Grapheme Correspondences
A Criterion Referenced Test
by Edward Fry, Rutgers University

Student's Name _____ Date _____

Examiner _____ Class _____

In phonics, as in everything else, a good teacher must know where the student is. This survey test will help you to discover which letter sounds your students know and which ones they need to work on. The test uses nonsense words because in this way we control the possibility that a student already knows a word as a sight word.

Don't try to test a student on all of the sounds at once. You will notice the test is divided into sections. We suggest that you test on only one or two sections at a time. In general, the sections are listed in order of difficulty. If a student does not do well on the first part, he will have difficulty with the other parts. How a student has been taught phonics will influence how he does on particular sections of the test, for example some children have not been taught the long open syllable rule or the schwa rule and can be expected to make errors in these sections.

HOW TO TEST: Ask the student to read the nonsense words aloud to you from one copy of the test. Have it folded so that he can see only the test words. The examiner should use a separate copy for scoring. Pay attention only to the grapheme being tested. Tell the student that these are not real words. Encourage him to try to sound them out. If a student makes an error, allow him a second chance (but not a third) on the same nonsense word. Do not tell him the correct answers. You may want to use the test with him again.

HOW TO SCORE: For each nonsense word, score only the letter-sound relationship (phoneme grapheme correspondence) that is being tested.

The asterisks by certain test word numbers indicate an explanatory note that will be found at the end of the test.

When a student pronounces the nonsense syllable correctly, put a "C" in the space next to it. If he makes an error, put an "X" in the space. You can administer this same test again at the end of the semester or year to show progress in phonics knowledge.

Fold At Dotted Line So Student Cannot See Example Word

EASY CONSONANTS

No.	Grapheme	Phoneme	Example			TEST WORDS		
1	T	Regular	Top		1	TAF _____	FOT _____
2	N	Regular	Nut		2	NAF _____	FON _____
3	R	Regular	Ring		3	RAF _____	ROF _____
4	M	Regular	Man		4	MAF _____	FOM _____
5	D	Regular	Dog		5	DAF _____	FOD _____
6	S	Regular	Saw		6*	SAF _____	FOS _____
7	L	Regular	Letter		7	LAF _____	FOL _____
8	C	Regular (K sound)	Cat		8*	CAF _____	COF _____
9	P	Regular	Pencil		9	PAF _____	FOP _____
10	B	Regular	Book		10	BAF _____	FOB _____
11	F	Regular	Fish		11	FAV _____	VOF _____
12	V	Regular	Valentine		12	VAF _____	FOV _____

SHORT VOWELS

No.	Grapheme	Phoneme	Example
13	I	Short	Indian
14	E	Short	Elephant
15	A	Short	Apple
16	O	Short	Ox
17	U	Short	Umbrella

LONG AND SILENT VOWELS

No.	Grapheme	Phoneme	Example
18	Y	Long E	verY
19	E	Silent	somE
20	A	Long, Final E	mAke
21	I	Long, Final E	rIde
22	O	Long, Final E	hOme
23	A	Long, Open Syllable rule	tAble
24	E	" "	wE
25	I	" "	Idea
26	O	" "	sO
27	U	" "	Use

DIFFICULT CONSONANTS

No.	Grapheme	Phoneme	Example
28	G	Regular	Girl
29	H	Regular	Hat
30	K	Regular	King
31	W	Regular	Window
32	J	Regular	Jar
33	X	KS sound	boX
34	Q	Qu makes KW blend	QUeen
35	Z	Regular	Zebra
36	Y	Consonant	Yacht

CONSONANT DIGRAPHS

No.	Grapheme	Phoneme	Example
37	TH	Digraph voiced	moTHer
38	TH	Digraph voiceless	THree
39	CH	Digraph	CHair
40	SH	Digraph	SHoe
41	WH	Digraph (HW blend)	WHeel

Fold At Dotted Line So Student Cannot See Example Word

TEST WORDS

13	FIM	_____	PIB	_____
14	CEP	_____	LEF	_____
15	LAV	_____	SAB	_____
16	BOD	_____	SOT	_____
17	FUT	_____	MUB	_____
18	VIPPY	_____	SETTY	_____
19	RUPE	_____	BINE	_____
20	BAFE	_____	NASE	_____
21	BIME	_____	LIPE	_____
22	POTE	_____	VOPE	_____
23	TA	_____	PA'DY	_____
24	FE	_____	HE'NOD	_____
25	LI	_____	TI'RAB	_____
26	MO	_____	LO'MIL	_____
27	FU	_____	BU'FAD	_____
28	GOF	_____	LIG	_____
29	HIB	_____	NIH	_____
30	KIV	_____	MIK	_____
31	WAF	_____	WEK	_____
32	JAV	_____	POJ	_____
33	MOX	_____	DAX	_____
34	QUOP	_____	QUAT	_____
35	ZIN	_____	RIZ	_____
36	YED	_____	YOL	_____
37*	THAP	_____	THIR	_____
38*	THAP	_____	THIR	_____
39	CHOT	_____	RACH	_____
40	SHAV	_____	KUSH	_____
41	WHEM	_____	WHAP	_____

No.	Grapheme	Phoneme	Example			TEST WORDS	
		CONSONANT SECOND SOUNDS					
42	C	S sound	City		42*	CIB _____	CEK _____
43	S	Z sound	eyeS		43*	FOS _____	BES _____
44	G	J sound	Gem		44*	GIME _____	LAGE _____
45	Y	Long I sound	mY		45	FY _____	CHY _____
		SCHWA SOUNDS					
46	A	Schwa	Again		46*	AG GOT́ _____	LOF́ FAN _____
47	E	Schwa	happEn		47*	EN LIṔ _____	TAB́ BET _____
48	O	Schwa	Other		48*	POT TAŔ _____	BAŹ ZON _____
		LONG VOWEL DIGRAPHS					
49	EA	Long E	EAt		49	BEAL _____	ZEAS _____
50	EE	Long E	bEEp		50	BEED _____	JEET _____
51	AI	Long A	AId		51	YAIG _____	MAIT _____
52	AY	Long A	dAY		52	TAY _____	CAY _____
53	OA	Long O	OAk		53	MOAV _____	WOAT _____
54	OW	Long O	OWn		54*	OWM _____	MOW _____
		VOWEL PLUS R					
55	OR	OR Sound	fOR		55	LORT _____	FORB _____
56	AR	AR Sound	ARm		56*	GAR _____	LART _____
57	AR	AIR Sound	vARy		57*	ZARY _____	GARE _____
58	ER	R Sound	hER		58	PER _____	TER _____
59	IR	R sound	sIR		59	ZIR _____	LIR _____
60	UR	R sound	fUR		60	HUR _____	DUR _____
		BROAD O					
61	O	Broad O	Off		61*		
62	AL	Broad O	All		62	RALM _____	SALL _____
63	AW	Broad O	sAW		63	TAW _____	AWZ _____
64	AU	Broad O	AUto		64	AUB _____	AUL _____
		DIPHTHONGS					
65	OU	OU Diphthong	OUt		65	OUM _____	OUD _____
66	OW	OU Diphthong	hOW		66*	ROWN _____	DOWT _____
67	OI	OI Diphthong	pOInt		67	HOIM _____	LOI _____
68	OY	OI Diphthong	bOY		68	MOY _____	LOY _____
		DIFFICULT VOWELS					
69	OO	2 dot U or Long OO	brOOm		69*	ZOOP _____	VOOZ _____
70	OO	1 dot U or Short OO	bOOk		70*	ZOOP _____	VOOZ _____
71	U	2 dot U	blUe		71*	SLUE _____	ZUNE _____
72	U	1 dot U	pUll		72*	MULL _____	FUSH _____
73	EA	Short E	brEAd		73*	ZEAD _____	REAT _____

Fold At Dotted Line So Student Cannot See Example Word

No.	Grapheme(s)	Phoneme(s)	Example			TEST WORDS	
			CONSONANT BLENDS				
74	PR	Blend	PRess		74	PRIZ _____	PRUT _____
75	TR	Blend	TRap		75	TROP _____	TRAT _____
76	GR	Blend	GRass		76	GRUE _____	GRIF _____
77	BR	Blend	BRass		77	BRAF _____	BRUT _____
78	CR	Blend	CRab		78	CRAT _____	CRON _____
79	DR	Blend	DRess		79	DRUN _____	DROT _____
80	FR	Blend	FRog		80	FRIT _____	FREM _____
81	ST	Blend	STar		81	STOK _____	FEST _____
82	SP	Blend	SPot		82	SPAD _____	LASP _____
83	SC	Blend	SCar		83	SCUB _____	SCOM _____
84	SK	Blend	SKate		84	SKOT _____	MISK _____
85	SW	Blend	SWim		85	SWAD _____	SWEED _____
86	SM	Blend	SMoke		86	SMOL _____	SMIZ _____
87	SN	Blend	SNow		87	SNOKE _____	SNUR _____
88	PL	Blend	PLease		88	PLAM _____	PLER _____
89	CL	Blend	CLiff		89	CLOB _____	CLIN _____
90	BL	Blend	BLock		90	BLIM _____	BLUT _____
91	FL	Blend	FLower		91	FLA _____	FLER _____
92	SL	Blend	SLide		92	SLUP _____	SLAN _____
93	GL	Blend	GLass		93	GLOR _____	GLIP _____
94	TW	Blend	TWin		94	TWIC _____	TWAM _____
			CONSONANT EXCEPTIONS				
95	PH	F sound	PHone		95	PHET _____	UMPH _____
96	KN	N sound	KNife		96	KNE _____	KNIM _____
97	WR	R sound	WRite		97	WRES _____	WRIB _____
98	NG	NG sound	siNG		98	FING _____	KONG _____
99	GH	Silent Blend	weiGH		99	BEGH _____	LIGH _____

Fold At Dotted Line So Student Cannot See Example Word

NOTES:

6. S may make either an s or a z sound. If the student uses the z sound for S as in eyes you may say, "The letter S makes another sound. Can you say that word in a different way?"

8. C most often makes the k sound before a, o, or u. The other C sound is listed in 42.

37–38. There are no firm rules for whether a TH is voiceless or voiced. Therefore, only one set of test words is given and the student is scored correctly if he gives either the voiced or the voiceless TH. If you wish, you may say after the student has pronounced the test words one way, "The letter combination TH makes two sounds. Can you say these words another way?"

42. C tends to make the s sound before i, e, or y.

43. There are no firm rules for when S makes the z sound, although it hardly ever occurs at the beginning of a word. If the student uses the s sound as in Saw you may say: "The letter S makes another sound. Can you say these words another way?"

44. G generally has a soft sound of j before e, i, or y but there are common exceptions such as Get, Girl, and Give. If the student should use the hard G sound, you may say, "The letter G makes another sound. Can you tell me what it is?"

46–48. In order to have the student produce the schwa sound, ask him to pronounce these test words with the underlined letters representing a stressed syllable. Children who have not been specifically taught the schwa rule can be expected to make errors in this section.

54 & 66. Since OW has 2 sounds if the student gives the diphthong sound for 54, ask for "the other sound" and visa versa for item 66.

56–57. The AR sound is not consistent. Either the sound mARy or fAR is correct. If the student pronounces the test words with one sound, you may say, "The letters AR can make two sounds. Can you say that word another way?"

61. There are no consistent rules as to when the grapheme O makes the broad O sound.

69–70. There are no firm rules for whether the OO sound is long or short. Therefore, only one set of test words is given. If you wish, you may say after the student has pronounced these words one way, "The letter combination OO makes two sounds. Can you say these words another way?"

71. If the student produces the long ū sound, this is not incorrect, but try to elicit the 2 dot u sound as well.

72. If the student produces the short ŭ sound, this is not incorrect, but try to elicit the 1 dot u sound too.

73. There are no firm rules for when the EA letter sound is short or long. Many words, such as rEAd or lEAd can be pronounced both ways depending on whether they are used as verbs or nouns. If the student uses the long sound of EA when reading the test words you may say, "The letter combination EA makes two sounds. Can you say these words another way?"

SUGGESTED LEARNING ACTIVITIES

1 Observe a phonics lesson being taught in a school or in a demonstration lesson. Note which correspondence are being taught; which rules, exceptions, and types of activities the children are being asked to perform. Be discreet, but try to find out one important thing: Did the students already know the correspondence before the lesson? Did they know it after the lesson?

2 Look up the section on "alphabet" in several encyclopedias and write a brief summary of the development of our alphabet. Include a chart or figure of the development of some of the letters.

3 Examine the phonics content of a basal reader system, or the phonics content of some supplemental phonics material, and see how it compares with the phoneme-grapheme correspondences discussed in this chapter or with the list of 99 correspondences in the Individual Phonics Analysis.

4 Watch one or more educational TV shows, such as "The Electric Company," and note the phonics or other reading principles being taught.

5 Administer the Individual Phonics Criterion Test to a pupil or another adult. Study the test carefully first, and read both the directions and the footnotes.

VOCABULARY AND STUDY TERMS

Alphabet
Ideograph
Roman alphabet
Latin alphabet
Vowel
Consonant
Voiced-unvoiced
Phoneme
Grapheme
Phoneme-grapheme correspondence
Allophone
Encoding-decoding
Orthography
Regular sound
Consonant digraph
Marker
Short vowel
Long vowel

Final E rule
Long vowel digraph
Double vowel rule
Open syllable rule
Schwa
Vowel plus R
Y rule
Diphthongs
Double O (long and short)
Broad O
Spelling reform
Alphabet reform
I.T.A.
Homonyms (various phonics teaching methods)
Audio card
Card reader
McGuffey
"The Electric Company"

LIST OF PHONICS CURRICULUM MATERIALS

The New Phonics We Use: Arthur Heilman; Rand McNally; six workbooks; **1–6**.
Speech to Print Phonics: Donald D. Durrell and Helen A. Murphy; Harcourt; kit; **K–1**.
Phonics Practice Program: Donald D. Durrell and Helen A. Murphy; Harcourt; kit; **2–3**.
Dolch Sounding Material: Edward Dolch; Gerrard; nine boxes.

Schoolhouse, "A Work Attack Skills Kit": SRA; kit; **1-3**.

The Readiness Stage, The Phonics Express, Phonics Explorer: SRA; kits; **K-3**.

Group Phonics Analysis: Edward Fry; Dreier; Test; **1-4**.

Individual Phonic Test: Edward Fry; Dreier; Test; **1-4**.

99 Phonics Charts: Edward Fry; Dreier; Book; **1-4**.

Word Attack Series: Shirley Feldmann and Kathleen Merrill; Teachers College; four workbooks; **2-4**.

Individualized Phonics: Macmillan; kit; **1-6**.

Phonics Crossword Puzzles: Kramer; McCormick-Mathers; four workbooks; **1-6**.

Patterns, Sounds and Meanings: Roberta La Coste; Allyn and Bacon; four workbooks, tapes; **1-4**.

Phonic Sets: Scholastic; two workbooks plus a game; **1-3**.

Phonovisual Method: Lucille D. Schoolfield and Josephine B. Timberlake; Phonovisual; workbooks and materials; **2**.

Phonics Comic: Word Probe: Cornet; 10 cassettes, 10 30-page comic books; **4-8**.

Words We Use: Benific Press; eight workbooks; **1-6**.

Reading Skills: Milton Bradley, Random House; four kits; **1-4**.

Instructional Fairs Task Force 2–Phonics: Donald L. Barnes and Arlene Burgdorf; Instructional Fair; 10 sets of plastic cards; **1-3**.

Phonics: Basic and Intermediate: Edward Fry; Learning through Seeing; 48 Filmstrips; **1-4**.

Basic Phonics: Learning Resources Co.; fifty audio card sets; **K-3**.

Phonics and Word Power: "My Weekly Reader" staff, Xerox; three paperback books; **1-3**.

First Steps in Reading, Second Steps in Reading: Grolier; Teaching machine program; **1, 2-R**.

Phonics Blends: Roberta Ross; Scott Education; 69 transparencies; **1 and 2**.

Learning with Laughter: Scott Education; 54 kits; **1-3**.

Reading Game Sound System: Bell and Howell; 11 sets of audio cards; **1-4**.

Phonics Activity Cards: Annette Taulbee; Frank Schaffer Pub.; **1-4**.

Phonics Learning Center: Frank Schaffer Pub.; kit; **1-5**.

Audit 100: Learning Systems; spirit master kit; **1-3**.

Reading Skills Development: LSI; kit with talking ink cards; **1-3**.

Telar-Teaching Essential Language and Reading: Edits; kit; **K-2**.

Minisystems in Reading: George Bond, Lois Nichols, and George Smith; Modern Curriculum Press; 100 tapes and activity sheets; **K-3**.

Get It All Together: Minnette Gersh and Janet Maker; Crabapple Productions; activity cards; **2-5**.

Friendly Tutor Reading Set: Creative Teaching Associates; 14 sets of electric board cards; **K-4**.

How to Create Reading Skill Centers: Educational Insights, Inc.; two boxes of activity cards; **1-6**.

REFERENCES

Aaron, Ira. "What Teachers and Prospective Teachers Know About Phonic Generalizations." *Journal of Educational Research*, 1960, *530*, 323-330.

Atkins, Ruth E. "An Analysis of the Phonetic Elements in a Basal Reading Vocabulary." *Elementary School Journal*, 1928, *20*, 596-608.

Bailey, Mildred H. "The Utility of Phonic Generalizations in Grades One through Six." *The Reading Teacher*, 1967, *20*, 413–418.

Betts, Emmett Albert. "Phonics: Three Word-Patterns and How to Use Them." *The Reading Teacher*, May 1974.

Bloomer, Richard H. "An Investigation of an Experimental First Grade Phonics Program." *Journal of Educational Research*, 1960, *53*, 188–193.

Bloomfield, Leonard. "Linguistics and Reading." *Elementary English Review*, 1942, *19*, 125–130, 183–186.

Burmeister, Lou E. "Usefulness of Phonic Generalizations." *The Reading Teacher*, 1968, *21*, 349–356.

Chall, Jeanne S. *Learning to Read: The Great Debate*. New York: McGraw-Hill, 1967.

Clymer, Theodore L. "The Utility of Phonic Generalizations in the Primary Grades." *The Reading Teacher*, 1963, *16*, 252–258.

Cordts, Anna D. "Analysis and Classification of the Sounds of English Words in the Primary Reading Vocabulary." Unpublished dissertation, University of Iowa, 1925.

Cordts, Anna D. "When Phonics is Functional." *Elementary English*, November 1963, 748–750.

Dolch, E. W. "Phonics and Polysyllables." *Elementary English Review*, 1938, *15*, 120–124.

Downing, John. "What Is Decoding?" *The Reading Teacher*, November 1975, *29*(2).

Durkin, Dolores. "Phonics Test for Teachers and Phonics Knowledge Survey." New York. Teachers College, 1964.

Durkin, Dolores. "Phonics: Instruction That Needs to Be Improved." *The Reading Teacher*, November 1964.

Durkin, Dolores. "Phonics, Linguistics and Reading." *The Reading Teacher*, December 1973.

Durkin, Dolores. *Phonics, Linguistics, and Reading*. New York: Teachers College, 1975.

Emans, Robert. "The Usefulness of Phonic Generalizations above the Primary Grades." *The Reading Teacher*, 1966, *20*, 419–425.

Emans, Robert. "When Two Vowels Go Walking and Other Such Things." *The Reading Teacher*, 1967, *21*, 262–269.

Fry, Edward. "A Frequency Approach to Phonics." *Elementary English*, November 1964, 759–765.

Fry, Edward. *Reading Instruction for Classroom and Clinic*. New York: McGraw-Hill, 1972.

Gates, Arthur. "Results of Teaching a System of Phonics." *The Reading Teacher*, March 1961, *14*, 248–252.

Gurren, Louise, and Ann Hughes. "Intensive Phonics vs. Gradual Phonics in Beginning Reading: A Review." *Journal of Educational Research*, April 1965, 339–346.

Hanna, Paul R., Richard E. Hodges, Jean S. Hanna, and Edwin H. Rudorf, Jr. *Phoneme-Grapheme Correspondences as Cues to Spelling Improvement*. Dept. of HEW (OE-32008), Washington, D.C.: U.S. Government Printing Office, 1966.

Hanna, Paul R., Richard E. Hodges, and Jean S. Hanna. *Spelling: Structure and Strategies*. Boston: Houghton Mifflin, 1971.

Heilman, Arthur W. *Phonics in Proper Perspective*. Columbus: Merrill, 1976.

Kottmeyer, W. A. "Phonetic and Structural Generalizations for the Teaching of a Primary Grade Spelling Vocabulary." As reported in Webster Publishing Company Research File No. 528-S and 529-S, St. Louis, Mo.: June 1954.

Lamb, Pose, "How Important is Instruction in Phonics?" *The Reading Teacher*, October 1975, *29*(1).

Mazurkiewicz, Albert J. "What Do Teachers Know About Phonics?" *Reading World* (formerly known as the *Journal of the Reading Specialist*, The College Reading Association), March 1975, *14*(3).

Moore, James T. "Phonetic Elements Appearing in a 3000 Word Spelling Vocabulary." Unpublished dissertation, Stanford University, 1951.

Morris, Joyce. "Sequence and Structure in a System with Problematic Sound-Symbol Correspondence." In John E. Merritt (Ed.), *New Horizons in Reading*. Newark, Del.: International Reading Association, 1976.

Piekarz, Josephine A. "Common Sense about Phonics." *The Reading Teacher*, November 1964, 114–117.

Ramsey, Z. Wallace. "Will Tomorrow's Teachers Know and Teach Phonics?" *The Reading Teacher*, 1962, *15*, 241–245.

Ruddell, R. B. "Reading Instruction in First Grade with Varying Emphasis on the Regularity of Grapheme-Phoneme Correspondences and the Relation of Language Structure to Meaning." *The Reading Teacher*, May 1967, *20*, 730–739.

Smith, Carl Bernard. "The Double Vowel and Linguistic Research," *The Reading Teacher*, April 1966, 512–514.

Smith, Nila B. "Phonics Then and Now." *Education*, 1955, *75*, 560–565.

Stone, David. "A Sound-Symbol Frequency Count." *The Reading Teacher*, 1966, *19*, 498–564.

Venezsky, Richard. "English Orthography: Its Graphical Structure and Its Relation to Sound." *Reading Research Quarterly*, 1967, *2*, 75–105.

Weintraub, Samuel. "A Critique of a Review of Phonics Studies." *Elementary School Journal*, October 1966, 34–41.

Winkley, Carol K. "Why Not an Intensive-Gradual Phonic Approach?" *The Reading Teacher*, April 1970, 611–617.

Chapter 3

Word Analysis:
Syllables, Phonograms,
and Other Units

The term *structural analysis* is used in many reading textbooks and basal series, and the elementary teacher should be familiar with it. There seems to be universal agreement that it includes such skills as breaking new words down into units somewhat smaller than the whole word so that they can be spoken orally or so that the meaning can be understood. As a result, the study of prefixes and suffixes is included. Syllabification skills and understanding compound words would also generally be included.

However, there seems to be some confusion, or at least difference of opinion, as to whether phonics is part of structural analysis. Some authors and reading series would maintain that phoneme-grapheme correspondence (phonics) is separate from structural analysis. Others would include phonics as part of structural analysis. Teachers must carefully examine books and materials labeled "structural analysis" to see just what is included.

In this chapter we will be discussing units of written language larger than a grapheme and smaller than a word. Thus, we are separating phonics from structural analysis for the purpose of concentrating on different-sized units, though you should realize that, in a real-life teaching situation, phonics and other word-attack skills are often intertwined.

A TOUCH OF HISTORY

In Colonial times, children learned to read by the alphabet method. That is, they first had to memorize the alphabet before there was any reading instruction. They then memorized several letters in combination. These letter combinations were sometimes called "syllables," but now we would call many of them "phonograms." The illustration of the *hornbook* (a wooden paddle on which is laid a single page covered with a thin layer of horn to keep grubby little fingers from soiling the print) shows the rapid progression from alphabet to "syllables" to whole-word prose in the form of the Lord's Prayer (see Figure 3-1).

The hornbook was used in the Middle Ages and came across the Atlantic with the Pilgrims. The next major development in reading instruction was the *New England Primer* in the 1700s, which again started with the alphabet but had much more teaching material (several pages) of syllables and a list of words containing one syllable, two syllables, three, four, and even five syllables (see Figure 3-2). The *New England Primer* also had the significant development of easy reading before plunging the poor child into the Lord's Prayer, adult poems, and Mr. Cotton's catechism. The easy reading section consisted mostly of couplets with rather strong admonitions:

He that neer learns his **ABC**
For ever will a Blockhead be.

In Adam's Fall
We sinned all.

In the 1800s, reading teaching materials greatly improved with such series of books as McGuffey's, but the importance of the syllable as a beginning teaching unit declined. McGuffey told teachers to use either the single-letter (or grapheme) phonics method or the whole-word method. However, in later lessons (the twenty-first lesson in the first primer), polysyllabic words are first introduced and are presented in a syllabicated form with diacritical marks. For example: Fań ny prét ty (prit-).

The great step forward of the McGuffey's over the *New England Primer* encompassed a vast increase of carefully selected easy reading material (six books versus one), the gradual increase in difficulty, the inclusion of teaching suggestions, and the more sophisticated and accurate phonic system. These same trends have continued, and modern reading systems reflect an even more careful vocabulary control, story difficulty control, elaborate directions for the teacher, and more accurate phonics system. The trend toward trying to interest the child continues, and there has been a vast increase in the amount of reading material available for children.

THE UNIT SIZE PROBLEM

The problem of unit size remains. A practical way of looking at the problem is: Do you teach "cat"

as single letters? C+A+T
as consonant and vowel plus a consonant? CA+T (The CA would be called a "helping phonogram" by some teachers.)

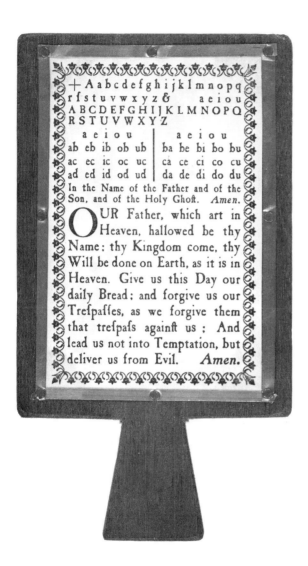

Figure 3-1 The hornbook is a small paddle of wood which has one page of print affixed to it which was covered with a plastic-like substance. It contained the alphabet, some syllables and the Lords Prayer. Hornbooks played a major role as curriculum material for beginning readers in the 17th and 18th centuries. *(Photo of a replica of a hornbook printed by Otto H. Miller at Todd's Printing Shop on Beacon Hill for The Horne Book, Inc., 585 Boylston Street, Boston, Massachusetts.)*

He that ne er learns his A, B, C,
For ever will a Blockhead be ;

The Great Capital Letters.

A B C D E F G H I K L M N
O P Q R S T U V W X Y Z.

The small Letters.

a b c d e f g h i j k l m n o
p q r s t u v w x y z &

Easy Syllables for Children.

Ab	cb	ib	ob	ub
ac	ec	ic	oc	uc
ad	ed	id	od	ud
af	cf	if	of	uf
ag	eg	ig	og	ug
al	el	il	ol	ul
am	em	im	om	um
an	en	in	on	un
ap	ep	ip	op	up
ar	er	ir	or	ur
as	es	is	os	us

An ALPHABET of Lessons for Youth.

A Wise Son makes a glad Father, but a foolish Son is the heaviness of his Mother.

B ETTER is a little with the Fear of the Lord, than great Treasure and Trouble therewith.

C OME unto Christ all ye that labour and are heavy laden, and he will give you Rest.

D O not the abominable Thing which I hate, saith the Lord.

E XCEPT a Man be born again he cannot see the Kingdom of God.

F OOLISHNESS is bound up in the Heart of a Child, but the Rod of Correction shall drive it from him.

G RIEVE not the Holy Spirit, lest it depart from thee.

H OLINESS becomes God's House forever.

I T is good for me to draw near unto God.

THE
SHORTER CATECHISM,

Agreed upon by the Reverend ASSEMBLY
of DIVINES at *Westminster.*

W HAT is the chief End of Man?
A. Man's chief End is to glorify
God and enjoy him forever.

Q. *What Rule hath God given to direct us how we may glorify and enjoy him?*
A. The Word of God which is contained in the Scriptures of the Old and New Testament, is the only rule to direct us how we may glorify and enjoy Him.

Q. *What do the Scriptures principally teach?*
A. The Scriptures principally teach what Man is to believe concerning God, and what Duty God requires of Man.

Q. *What is God?*
A. God is a Spirit, Infinite, Eternal and Unchangeable, in his Being, Wisdom, Power, Holiness, Justice, Goodness and Truth.

Q. *Are there more Gods than One?*

Figure 3-2 Sample pages from *The New England Primer.* This was a major reading text used with beginning readers in the 1700s. *(From* The New England Primer, *Boston, printed by E. Draper for B. Larkin, circa 1785. Reprinted by Ginn & Co.)*

as consonant plus vowel and consonant? C+AT (The AT would be called a "family phonogram" by some teachers.)

as syllables? CAT-TLE

as a whole word? CAT

as part of a phrase? THE CAT

as part of a sentence? THE CAT RAN

Unfortunately, educational research does not provide any conclusive answers as to which is the proper way to break down a word or which is the proper unit size. The problem is considerably more complicated than the search for a single proper unit size as though it were a stable constant good for all readers at all times. The question of unit size should be more properly considered in light of certain qualifications, such as: What is the best unit size to teach Johnny, who knows 50 words by sight and half a dozen phonics principles? Or: What is the proper unit size to teach Mary, who has fluent third-grade reading ability and who knows 2,000 sight words, 27 phoneme-grapheme correspondences, 75 syllables, and 15 common phonograms?

The famous USOE (U.S. Office of Education)-sponsored First Grade Studies, which were 21 coordinated studies, did not show conclusively whether phonics instruction, special alphabets (ITA), or whole-word (they called them "meaning emphasis") approaches were best for large groups of children. Even when the children's

SHORT VOWEL U   20

Name

Say the name of each picture. Write the vowel that you hear.

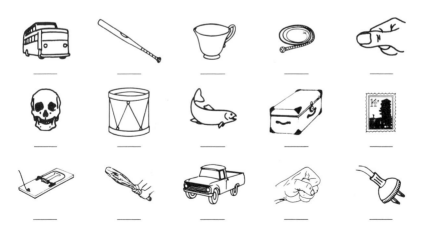

Figure 3-3 Part of a workbook page that teaches a phoneme-grapheme correspondence. Note the unit size here is one letter. *(From* Phonics Is Fun Book 3 *by Louis Krane. Modern Curriculum Press, Cleveland/Montreal, 1973.)*

reading achievement scores were looked at by intelligence (brighter-duller), or sex (boy-girl), no method emerged as superior. Under these circumstances, there is little justification for recommending any particular method or unit size as being "best."

As teachers, we should know at least a little about each of the different-sized units because many of them are incorporated into the major reading systems or basal readers that are used to teach the majority of the beginning readers throughout the world.

The Letter or Grapheme as a Unit

The purely alphabetical method of teaching is extinct—if it ever really existed. True, in past and present kindergartens, the alphabet is taught as simply a list of separate letters. This is often for the purpose of teaching writing or penmanship, though books of bygone centuries did attempt a type of phonics system based chiefly on the sound the individual letter makes. However, certainly, since the days of *McGuffey Readers* and Noah Webster's famous *Blue Back Spellers* in the middle of the last century, graphemes as teaching units have been widely used. The grapheme is a more stable correspondence (fewer exceptions) and nearly the only way to explain the sound of many words; for example, the beginning of the word "the" is with the grapheme TH. To try to explain the sound of "the" as beginning with the letter T only gets you into a lot of trouble.

Most modern reading systems include phonics and utilize graphemes as the teaching unit. However, as you will see in Chapter 7, systems vary in the extent to which they emphasize phonics or structural analysis. Although those systems that emphasize phonics might be called "phonics approaches," they usually include a variety of methods.

While some reading systems give instructions to the teacher to explain new words, grapheme by grapheme, others are leery of talking about graphemes or phonemes in isolation. These latter systems, such as those advocated by William S. Gray (and the Scott, Foresman readers of the 1940s and 1950s), told teachers to call attention to the sound heard at the beginning of a word. For example, the teacher would write the word "hit" and show how it differed from the sound heard at the beginning of a similar word, like "bit." To analyze new words, the child was taught to go from a known word, such as "hat." The teacher would point out that "hit" had the same beginning as "hat" and the same ending as "but," etc. In this way, single letter or single grapheme phonics was really being used, but the graphemes and phonemes were not used in isolation. To many, this seemed cumbersome, but millions of children learned to read using the old Scott, Foresman system, which was the largest selling basal reader series in the mid-1900s.

In defense of the *grapheme-in-context* method which I have been describing, there are many consonant phonemes which really cannot be pronounced in isolation; that is, without a vowel sound. For example, the consonant sound /p/ heard at the beginning of "pat" almost can't be pronounced without some schwa sound; the same might hold true for /k/, /t/, and many other consonant sounds. If the teacher chooses to talk about or teach single grapheme phonics, then consonants like /p/ shouldn't be pronounced with an exaggerated schwa or /u/ sound at the end. Some consonants, such as /s/ or /m/, do not need any schwa sound at the end.

The general rule in pronouncing phonemes in isolation is: Don't use any vowel sound at the end if it can be avoided; if it can't be avoided, do it as little as possible. For example, say "sss" /s/, not "suh" /su/.

Some phonics systems avoid the problem by never having the student pronounce a consonant without a vowel. Hence, the child is taught to say or memorize combinations like (use long vowel sounds) BA, BE, BI, BO, BU. Some then go on and have the child learn the consonant with the short vowel sound, broad sounds, etc. The child is then confronted with part of a reading lesson consisting of /bā/, /bē/, /bī/, /bō/, /bū/, /bă/, /bĕ/, /bĭ/, /bŏ/, /bŭ/ and /bô/, etc. If that isn't enough, the teacher can progress to the next consonant and teach /cā/, /cē/, /cī/, etc. One trouble with this system is, of course, that for every consonant there are fifteen or more vowel phonemes to combine it with, and if each of these are seen as a correspondence (separate sound symbol relationship) to be learned, the child must learn upwards of 200 correspondences, and this does not take into account variants or exceptions to basic rules. In contrast, there are only about forty-four phonemes in the system taught in Chapter 2, which is similar to most basal reading systems.

While we are concerned with numbers of correspondences with the variant spellings discussed, there are about ninety-nine correspondences covered in Chapter 2, that is, the forty-four phonemes are spelled by ninety-nine graphemes. For example, the phoneme (K) can be spelled with a C in "cat" or a K in "king," and the long A phoneme can be spelled with an A in "hate," an AY in "may," and an AI in "maid," etc.

It usually takes a child about three years to master this much phonics, though it might be "covered" in one or two years of reading instruction. Some children never learn this many correspondences, yet seem to be perfectly good readers. They analyze new words by using bigger units or by relying heavily on context. For example, if the child didn't know "raid," he or she would remember the "aid" sound from "maid."

You should also know that there is considerable difference in the total number of phonemes used in English, depending on which *phonetic* system is used. Note that we are using the term "phonetic" in its proper sense to refer to a system of speech sounds. The total number of phonemes in English might vary from the low thirties to the high forties. The phonic part of most reading systems would pick a number somewhere in the low forties. The way some linguists get low numbers (34 phonemes) is primarily by stating that many vowel sounds, certainly the diphthongs, but even some of the long vowels, are composed of two short vowel phonemes. Long A /ā/ would really be composed of a short E /ĕ/ and a short I /ĭ/. It isn't necessary for reading teachers to worry about this or to get involved in the controversies of phoneticians (which are many). But the teacher should be aware that such divergencies do exist.

If the reading teacher is interested in seeing a major phonetic system, the one most widely recognized, the International Phonetic Alphabet, can be found in some unabridged dictionaries and speech textbooks. It is used in describing speech problems by speech therapists in schools, and by linguists who write down different languages or dialects.

Blending

If the teacher chooses a phonics system which is essentially a single letter or single grapheme system, the problem of blending must be faced immediately. The symbols CAT might look neat in isolation, and theoretically all you have to do is put them together. But to a child who has been taught to sound out "cuh," "ah," "tuh," it might be quite a formidable job to see how these things go together and mean a soft, furry, little animal that drinks milk. This is, of course, the classic criticism of teaching phonics sound in isolation. It is devoid of meaning, and it is difficult to blend together the separated sounds to get a whole word. The argument in favor of phonics—or learning correspondences between individual phonemes and graphemes—is that by knowing a relatively few correspondences, the child can sound out or unlock thousands of new words.

To aid blending of isolated phonemes, the first thing to learn is to pronounce the consonant phonemes in isolation without a schwa sound (if possible). If this is not possible, you should emphasize the vowel as little as possible.

Some teachers have the child try to say the isolated phonemes over and over, faster and faster, in order to attempt to achieve a blended sound. This might have a scintilla of merit, but it is something less than perfect.

Another way is to get the child first to blend together just part of the word, such as seeing that the A and the T go together to make AT, then adding or blending the C sound. This method of first blending part of the word is really quite close to that which uses units called "phonograms," which we will discuss later in this chapter.

Blends

The unit called *blends* usually refers to consonant blends. These are groups of two consonants that occur together so frequently that they are taught as a unit. Since a blend is really two phonemes, like the BL in "black," it is not the same as a consonant digraph, like the SH in "shoe," which is one phoneme. Another term for a consonant blend is a consonant *cluster*.

Though you might think that any two consonants could be blended together, actually there is a relatively small number of combinations of consonants that are blended together at the beginning of a word or syllable. These beginning blends can be classified into three "families":

S Family ST, SP, SC, SK, SL, SW, SN, and SM
R Family PR, TR, GR, BR, CR, DR, and FR
L Family PL, CL, BL, FL, and GL

Like almost everything in phonics, there is an exception: TW is also a beginning blend.

Most linguists do not talk about blends, but just consider them as separate phonemes and separate graphemes. The concept of blends does have some utility to reading teachers, however, particularly as one of the important teaching strategies is to ask a child, "What sound does the word begin with?"

You will note that we have limited the discussion of blends to beginning blends. There are a limited number of ending blends which can occur only at the end of a word, like ND or NK ("end" and "ink"), and a few that can occur either place. Because their utility is not as great in a teaching situation, final consonant blends are not usually taught as blends (children can sound them out as individual phonemes). Most phonics teaching systems do not include terminal blends. However, just in case you would like to see a few of the more common terminal blends, here they are with example words:

ND	and blond	CT	act duct
NT	ant bent	LD	old mild
NK	ink bank	MP	jump lamp
NC(E)	once since	PT	kept slept
RT	smart hurt	LT	salt belt

There are even some consonant blends that have more than two letters; for example, the SCR in "scream." They are usually another blend or digraph with R; for example, THR, SHR, CHR, STR. But these are relatively rare; that is, they do not have a very high frequency, but they are taught in some basal series.

Phonograms

The next-sized unit that reading teachers use is called a "phonogram." A phonogram is a combination of two or more letters that represents one or more phonemes. It does not have any relationship to meaning. Its purpose is to help the beginning reader translate written language into spoken language. By this definition, a digraph or a blend can be called a phonogram. Usually, however, the term is reserved for some combination of vowel and consonant that is smaller than a word, and often smaller than a syllable.

Old-time reading teachers talk about two kinds of phonograms, "helpers" and "families." A *helper phonogram* is usually a consonant plus a vowel. For example:
Helper Phonogram "hi-"

> hit
> hid
> him
> hick

A *family phonogram* is more or less the opposite; namely, a vowel plus a consonant which takes a single consonant or a blend at the beginning. For example:
Family Phonogram "-at"

> hat
> bat
> sat
> spat

Teaching phonograms help students translate written language into spoken language. A family phonogram is a vowel plus a consonant which takes a single consonant or a blend at the beginning. *(Hugh Rogers/Monkmeyer)*

Phonograms, of course, can be more complicated, as we can see in the following family phonograms:

-ight	-ould
fight	would
sight	could
bright	should

The structural linguists have rediscovered the phonogram as a teaching unit, though, as usual, they have given it a new name. Teaching with phonograms like "hat," "cat," "bat," etc., is called "consonant substitution." So rechristened, it is now respectable to teach family phonics in some academic circles, whereas before, it was just using an old-fashioned reading teacher's method.

There is a large number of games, charts, audiovisual devices, and lessons in basal readers that focus on family phonics. A typical device, often made by the teacher, is a word wheel or chart with a strip of paper sliding through a slot to show changes in the beginning consonant or blend while the phonogram remains the same. Phonograms also are widely used in chalkboard lessons when the teacher or a student sees how many different words can be made from a particular phonogram.

Even some of the newest teaching materials, such as programmed instruction, utilize phonograms. Figure 3-4 shows a frame from a programmed reading book. One of the ways that *programmed instruction* differs from a more traditional workbook is that the student is given immediate feedback; that is, the correct answer is provided immediately after each response. In the example, feedback is given by having a slider cover the lefthand portion of the frame. After the student marks an answer, or sup-

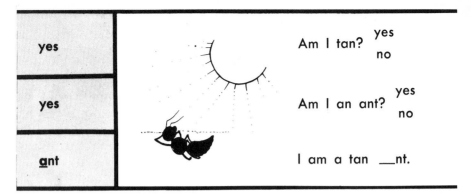

Figure 3-4 A frame from a programmed instruction book that teaches consonant substitution to beginning readers. *(From* Programmed Reading Book 1, *3rd edition, by Cynthia Dee Buchanan of Sullivan Associates, Webster Division, McGraw-Hill Book Company, St. Louis, 1973.)*

plies a missing letter or word, all that is necessary is to move the slider down to see if the answer is correct.

Syllables

The next-sized unit of writing that we should consider is the syllable. It is a little difficult to define a syllable, but a technical definition would be "a segment of speech produced with a single pulse of air." Like many things in language, the basic definition rests in spoken language. There might be a slight difference in some cases, but usually a written syllable is the letters used to spell that segment of speech.

Another useful way of partially defining a syllable is to say that it is a vowel sound with or without attached consonants. You can't have two vowel sounds in a syllable. If you wish to count the number of syllables in a word, you only need to count the vowel sounds. For example, "polio," though short, is really three syllables "po-li-o" because there are three different vowel sounds Conversely, "through" is a longer word, but only one syllable because there is only one vowel sound. You will note from the above examples that a syllable may contain only one letter if it is a vowel, or a syllable may be a vowel sound plus one or more consonants. Note also that two letters that are called "vowels"—the OU in "through"—only have one vowel *sound* and, therefore, the word has only one syllable.

Syllables are also a very useful unit for teaching reading and spelling. The *New England Primer* contained lists of words of one syllable, words of two syllables, words of three syllables, etc., up to five syllables. At the turn of the century, around 1900, a popular set of readers contained only words of one syllable in entire primers. At the present time, some basal readers or reading systems instruct the teacher to introduce new words separated into syllables.

Syllables are useful units for the reading teacher because they are interchangeable between words. Part of the general area of *word analysis* or *structural analysis of words* might include analyzing new words syllable by syllable.

Syllables also play an important part in phonics or code cracking. They often help explain why a vowel has a long sound or a short sound. This is usually done by teaching the student about open syllables and closed syllables.

An *open syllable* is a syllable that ends in a vowel. The rule states that in open syllables the vowel sound is usually long. For example: "me."

A *closed syllable* is a syllable that ends in a consonant. The rule states that in closed syllables the vowel sound is usually short. For example: "met."

Syllables also play an important part in spelling lessons. Many spelling books not only point out the syllable divisions of words being taught, but also have drills where students learn to spell the word syllable by syllable. If you have ever watched the champion spellers in the national spelling bee, they are very careful in pronouncing difficult words, almost syllable by syllable, before attempting to spell them.

Worth Osburn conducted research at the University of Washington, and identified the most common syllables in the initial position, the medial position, and in the final position. The numbers in Table 3-1 are the number of times that particular syllables occurred on the Rinsland Word List (a list of 14,571 common words used by children in writing). You might note that many of the syllables in the initial position are prefixes, and many of the syllables in the final position are suffixes. We will discuss prefixes and suffixes in a following section of this chapter. It is interesting to note that of the 14,571 words on the Rinsland list, approximately 4,500 of them are one-syllable words.

From the viewpoint of a teaching strategy, we can see the utility of teaching at least the most common syllables. For example, knowledge of the initial syllable "ex-" means that the student knows the beginning part of 141 relatively common

Table 3-1 The Commonest Syllables in the English Language adn Their Frequency of Occurrence on the Rinsland List of 14,571 Words

	Initial syllable	Frequency		Medial syllable	Frequency		Final syllable	Frequency
1	*re*-ceived	209	1	an-*i*-mals	277	1	go-*ing*	881
2	*in*-to	203	2	Jan-*u*-*a*-ry	161	2	start-*ed*	338
3	*a*-round	149	3	sev-*er*-al	131	3	moth-*er*	323
4	*de*-cid-ed	146	4	dec-*o*-rat-ed	107	4	on-*ly*	290
5	*con*-tains	145	5	af-*ter*-noon	81	5	hous-*es*	212
6	*ex*-cept	141	6	el-*e*-phant	79	6	va-ca-*tion*	210
7	*un*-til	99	7	pe-*ri*-od	75	7	ver-*y*	193
8	*com*-mon	95	8	reg-*u*-lar	72	8	pret-*ty*	95
9	*dis*-cov-ered	82	9	In-*di*-an	56	9	re-*al*	84
10	*en*-joy	81	10	won-*der*-ful	44	10	ta-*ble*	82
11	*an*-oth-er	68	11	car-*ni*-val	40	11	af-*ter*	75
12	*o*-pen	65	12	gym-na-*si*-um . . .	40	12	base-*ment*	73
13	*e*-ven	63	13	ar-*ti*-cle	40	13	sto-*ry*	69
14	*pro*-gram	58	14	ear-*li*-est	35	14	larg-*est*	65
15	*ac*-ci-dent	56	15	o-*ver*-alls	34	15	sev-*en*	48
	Total	1,660		Total	1,272		Total	3,038

FROM: "Teaching Spelling by Teaching Syllables and Root Words," by Worth J. Osborn. *The Elementary School Journal*, September 1954.

words. Knowing the final syllable "-ing", the student knows the final sound of 881 relatively common words. Knowing only part of a word can be a tremendous clue to unlocking it, especially since the reader usually has context clues and often additional phonic (grapheme) clues.

Syllabification Part of the problem in using syllables in reading instruction, or in teaching a child to use syllables as one method in word analysis, is this: "How does the student know which letters make up a syllable if he or she can't sound out the word in the first place?" There are several partial answers. First of all, if some common syllables have been taught, either in syllable teaching lessons or by presentation of a number of new words divided into syllables, the child might be able to recognize certain recurring letter clusters. We might call these *sight syllables*. The fifteen most common beginning, medial, and final syllables in the English language can be seen in Table 3-1.

A second way to divide words into syllables is to use some syllabification rules. Perhaps we should call them syllabification "generalizations" since there are many exceptions to the "rules." A further problem is that many of the syllabification rules were developed for purposes of word division such as is required by printers or typists when they have a long word at the end of a line of type. Thus, the rules were not always written with the beginning reader in mind; they often assume that the person already knows how to read the word. However, some syllabification rules are often included in basal reading systems or are part of some supplementary phonics or word analysis teaching materials. A list of syllabification generalizations can be found in Figure 3-5.

Accent A further problem in word analysis using the syllable unit is accent. This problem might be better defined as "Which syllable is stressed?" Many polysyllabic words—that is, words with more than one syllable—can be sounded out by the beginning reader, using either graphemes or syllables, getting the sound close enough so that the word can be recognized. Accent still presents a minor problem in pronunciations and word recognition. There is a vague generalization in English to the effect that if you don't know where to accent a polysyllabic word, you should accent the first syllable unless it is a prefix.

If you really want to know how a given word is accented, any dictionary will tell you. For purposes of the beginning reader, looking up unknown words is slow and cumbersome, but often very helpful. The dictionary not only shows accent and stress, but also a phonetic spelling (usually with diacritical marks). Getting students to look up new words in a dictionary is a very useful habit to instill. If you are teaching a primary grade, make every effort to have a dictionary developed for primary school use, as both adult dictionaries and some commercial (home) children's dictionaries are too confusing.

One important consideration in accent is that the vowel sound is much more consistent (following phoneme-grapheme correspondence rules) in the stressed sylla-

1. There are as many syllables as vowel sounds.
   For example: "boat"; "yes-ter-day"; "vi-o-let"
   a. Except that the final "le" picks up the preceding consonant to form a syllable.
      For example: "ta-ble"; "cir-cle"
   b. Except for the so-called syllabic l, m, and n which occur at the end of some words.
      For example: "pris-m"
   c. Two vowels together with separate sounds form separate syllables.
      For example: "vi-o-let"; "buoy-an-cy"
      Don't separate diphthongs like oi, oy, ou, ow, or digraphs like ea, ee, ai, ay, oo, oa, ow, or combinations al, aw, au, ar, or, er, ir, ur.
   d. It is probably useful to remember that the letter "e" at the end of a word is always silent when it follows a consonant and another vowel is in the word.
      For example: "come"; "hate"
   e. The letter "y" at the end of a word or in the middle of a word always makes a vowel sound and hence a syllable.
      For example: "my"; "ver-y"; "cy-cle"
      The letter "y" at the beginning of a word is always a consonant and doesn't make a separate syllable.
      For example: "yes"

2. Prefixes and suffixes tend to form syllables.
   For example: "go-ing"; "un-known"
   a. Suffixes which follow double consonants tend to pick up one of the consonants.
      For example: "get-ting"
   b. The suffix "ed" when preceded by a single d or t forms a separate syllable.
      For example: "plan-ted"; "mol-ded"
      However, most of the time "ed" does not form a separate syllable.
      For example: "played"; "helped"; "stopped"
   c. The suffix "s," of course, does not form a syllable because it has no vowel in it.
      For example: "runs"
   d. The suffix "y" tends to pick up the preceding consonant or blend.
      For example: "fligh-ty"; "rel-e-van-cy"; "spec-i-fy"

3. *A single consonant* between two vowels tends to go with the following vowel.
   For example: "bro-ken"; "be-gin"
   a. Except if the first vowel is accented and short.
      For example: "wag-on"; "hab-it"

4. If there are *two consonants* between two vowels, split them.
   For example: "pic-ture"
   Except if the consants are a blend.
   For example: "mi-grate"

5. Divide *compound words.*
   For example: "black-bird"; "mail-man"

Figure 3-5 Syllabification generalizations.

ble. The unstressed syllable frequently contains a schwa /ə/ sound. As you perhaps remember from the last chapter, the schwa sound can be made by any vowel letter.

AFFIXES

The last and final part of word analysis that we will discuss in this chapter is affixes. An affix is a letter or group of letters added to a base or root part of a word. If it comes before the root (or another prefix) it is called a *prefix*, and if it comes after the root (or another suffix), it is called a *suffix*. The *root* is also called the *stem* or *base*. For example, in "unobtainable" the "un-" is the prefix, the "obtain" is the root or stem, and the "-able" is the suffix. Both "un" and "able" are affixes. The word "unrewarding" has two prefixes. Some common prefixes and suffixes can be seen in Table 3-2.

Affixes are usually syllables, but not always; they are defined on a totally different base than a syllable. A syllable is based on speech sounds; in contrast, an affix is based on meaning. Another way of saying this is that a syllable is based on phonology, and an affix is based on morphology. Morphology is the study of units of meaning.

A *morpheme* is a meaning unit. The base unit of meaning in language is usually the word. Technically, a word is called a *free morpheme* because it can stand alone. A prefix is usually a *bound morpheme* because it can't stand alone. For example, "necessary" is a free morpheme, and if I put an "un-" in front of it, it changes the meaning, but the "un-" can't stand by itself. Its definition is not related to speech sounds. The "un" in "unnecessary" is a syllable, but the suffix "-s" in "runs" is not a syllable. Note that "s" in "runs" is a morpheme because it changes meaning. The "s" is also a bound morpheme because it can't stand alone.

Teaching Word Attack Skills

Affixes are frequently taught as part of vocabulary improvement. For example, the "un-" prefix means "not." "Unnecessary" means "not necessary" and "unsuccessful" means "not successful," etc.

However, here we are concerned with the use of prefixes as part of word analysis, or helping the new reader to unlock the sound of new words by the use of affixes. Reading lessons which do this are much like syllable teaching lessons. Several words with the same affix are presented, and the similar part—the affix—is pointed out. It helps if the student knows one or more of the words already. A new or strange word with the same affix then is presented to show the student that he or she already knows part of the new word. Figure 3-2 will give you a list of common prefixes, but most basal reading systems regularly include lessons on teaching affixes—both prefixes and suffixes. For example, even in the very earliest primers the suffix "-s" is presented to show the difference between "run" and "runs." Students are delighted to find that once they know "run," it is very easy to learn "runs," and that the same principle applies to "walk" and "walks."

Materials that teach word analysis or word-attack skills are usually contained in larger systems, or as part of materials which also teach phonics. For example, every

Table 3-2   The Commonest Prefixes and Suffixes in English

	Prefix	Meaning		Suffix	Meaning
1	in en im em	in, into, not	1	er or	action or process, something that does something
2	re	again	2	tion tions sion cion	action
3	a ad ap at	to, toward	3	ty	condition
			4	al	pertaining to
4	de dis	from, away from, apart	5	ble able ible	capable of being
5	ex e	out of, out from	6	ment	action or the result of action
6	con	together	7	full	full, complete
7	com col	together with	8	man	human, man
8	o op of ob	against, away from	9	ic ics	pertaining to
			10	ous ious	full of, like
9	pro pre	before, for	11	ence ance	action, state of being, relating to, state of, quality
10	al ar	pertaining to, like			
11	an	belonging to			
12	ac	pertaining to			
13	be	around, all over, act of being, action			
14	for	away, off			
15	di	doubly, to separate			

FROM: "Vocabulary Development by Teaching Prefixes, Suffixes and Root Derivatives," by L. C. Breen. *The Reading Teacher*, November 1960.

basal reading system and most spelling series include lessons on syllabification and affixes, and most also include information on blending.

There is no list of materials at the end of this chapter, but you should look again at the list of materials at the end of Chapter 2, as many of those materials also include lessons on word-attack skills. When we get to Chapter 4, many of the vocabulary improvement materials will include affixes. Also, some of the illustrations for tests in Chapter 11 contain word-attack materials.

YOUR LEARNING

It is very difficult to learn about the teaching of reading by just reading a textbook once, and this is why I have included three additional aids at the end of this and other chapters: (1) suggested activities to get you involved with lessons and materials, (2) a list of vocabulary and study terms that you can review by trying to define or discuss each of them briefly, and (3) references which can give you more information on some of the principles you have been reading about. Meaning and reinforcement of your learning is also enhanced by classroom lectures, discussions, demonstrations, and other activities. Many students also spend part of their learning time as observers in a public or private school setting, watching—and sometimes aiding—an experienced teacher working with live children in a classroom beset with its many influences and realities.

SUGGESTED LEARNING ACTIVITIES

1 Look at the teacher's manual and workbook of a basal reading series, and see how several word-attack or structural analysis lessons are taught. Basal reading can usually be found in a college curriculum library or a public school.

2 Look at some supplementary material that teaches structural analysis. See list at the end of Chapter 2 and locate materials as above.

3 Observe a teacher conducting a structural analysis lesson.

4 Make some of your own games, charts, workbook pages, or other material to teach structural analysis.

5 Get two different dictionaries, such as a *Thorndike-Barnhart* and a *Merriam-Webster,* and show where their pronunciation systems (or diacritical marking systems) are similar and where they are different.

6 Using the syllabification generalizations in Figure 3-5, try to divide every word on one page of a fifth-grade children's reader.

VOCABULARY AND STUDY TERMS

Structural analysis

Alphabet method

Hornbook

New England Primer

Unit size problem

First Grade Studies

Grapheme-in-context

Pronuncing individual phonemes

Number of phonemes

International Phonetic Alphabet

Blending

Arguments against phonics

Consonant substitution

Word wheel

Programmed instruction

Syllable

Open syllable

Closed syllable

Common syllables

Syllabification

Sight syllables

Accent

Affixes

Prefix

Blends	Suffix
Initial blend families	Root-stem-base
Ending blends	Morphemes
Three-letter blends	Morphology
Phonograms	Free morpheme
Helper phonograms	Bound morpheme
Family phonograms	

REFERENCES

Burland, Richard J. "Learnin' Words: Evaluating Vocabulary Development Efforts." *Journal of Reading*, December 1974, *18*(3).

Burmeister, Lou E. "Vocabulary Development Content Areas through the Use of Morphemes," *Journal of Reading*, March 1976, *19*(6).

Fries, Charles C. *Linguistics and Reading*. New York: Holt, 1962.

Hunter, Diana Lee. "Spoken and Written Word Lists: A Comparison." *The Reading Teacher*, December 1975, *29*(3).

Johns, Jerry L. "Dolch List of Common Nouns—A Comparison." *The Reading Teacher*, March 1975, *28*(6).

Lorge, Irving, and Jeanne Chal. "Estimating the Size of Vocabularies of Children and Methodological Issues." *Journal of Experimental Education*, 1963, *32*, 147–157.

Mills, Robert. "An Evaluation of Techniques for Teaching Word Recognition." *Elementary School Journal*, January 1956, *56*, 221–225.

Robinson, H. Alan. "A Study of the Techniques of Word Identification." *The Reading Teacher*, January 1963, 238–242.

Sabaroff, Rose. "Breaking the Code: What Method? Introducing an Integrated Linguistic Approach to Beginning Reading." *Elementary School Journal*, November 1966, 95–103.

Smith, N. B. "What Research Tells Us about Word Recognition." *Elementary School Journal*, April 1955, *55*, 440–446.

Spache, George D., and May E. Bagget. "What Do Teachers Know about Phonics and Syllabification?" *The Reading Teacher*, 1965, *99*.

Sparks, J. E. "The Development of Comprehension: A Curriculum for the Gifted Reader." In John E. Merritt (ed.), *New Horizons in Reading*. Newark, Del.: International Reading Association, 1976.

Stauffer, Russell G. "A Study of Prefixes in the Thorndike List to Establish a List of Prefixes That Should Be Taught in the Elementary School." *Journal of Educational Research*, 1942, *35*, 453–458.

Waugh, R. P., and K. W. Howell. "Teaching Modern Syllabification." *The Reading Teacher*, October 1975, *29*(1).

Winkley, Carol. "Which Accent Generalizations Are Worth Teaching?" *The Reading Teacher*, 1966, *20*, 219–224.

Chapter 4

Vocabulary:
Sight Words
and Vocabulary Building

In the preceding two chapters we have talked about parts of words. In this chapter we will discuss whole words, what they are, and how to teach them.

WHAT IS A WORD?

It might surprise you that the definition of a word is somewhat fuzzy, and that in some respects what is or is not a word is somewhat arbitrary. If you doubt this, try to define a word before you read any farther.

The Thorndike Barnhart dictionaries define a word as "a sound or group of sounds that has meaning." By this definition, a "squeal," in the right context, is certainly a word, yet you won't find it in a dictionary and you would have trouble writing it down. In that case, we had better look at that dictionary's second definition, "the writing or printing that stands for a word." Note that the primary definition is based on speech sound.

Written words as you see them on this page all have space around them so that they stand out. What happens in speech? Do words have space around them? If we look at a sound spectrograph, a special sound analyzing device that takes a spoken sound and turns it into a visible display on a television-type tube, we can literally *look* at speech.

The sound spectrograph can record speech so accurately that it is used by police departments in the apprehension of criminals. The voice of a suspect is taperecorded— say a telephoned bomb threat—then the suspect's voice is taped separately. When both sounds are played into a sound spectrograph, similar patterns or voice prints can be seen,much as in fingerprints, though voice prints are not as accurate or reliable as fingerprints for identification. No two people have exactly the same voice character- istics.

Now, what happens when we use this accurate instrument to look at a phrase or a sentence? Do we see separate words standing out? We do not. Phrases and sentences are a continuous flow of sounds (except for obvious pauses). To state it another way, there is no more distinct difference between words than between phonemes. From a point of view focusing purely on sound, one would have a difficult time defining a word.

Webster's New International Dictionary says, in part, that a word is "the smallest unit of speech that has meaning by itself." Like Thorndike Barnhart's, this is basically a semantic definition. It is similar to the definition of a free morpheme. It sounds all right most of the time, but let's look a little more closely. The word "cat" is a small unit that stands alone. If I add an "-s" to the word, making it "cats," the "-s" obvi- ously can't stand alone and have any meaning, so "-s" isn't a word. In the meantime "cats" does stand alone and is, therefore, a word.

Now comes the catch. Suppose we look at the phrase "a cat." If I look at it on a voice print it looks like one word. Suppose I apply the test of meaning? What does "a" mean? Well, it contributes slightly to the meaning; "a cat" means something a little different from "the cat." But the word "a" all by itself would be hard put to claim more meaning than the suffix "-s," yet one is called a word and one is not!

As you may recall from the last chapter, a word is similar and often identical to the linguist's definition of a *morpheme*. A morpheme is a unit of meaning. If it stands alone as in "cat," it is called a *free morpheme*. If it can't stand alone, as the "-s" in "cats," it is called a *bound morpheme*. The "-s" is a morpheme because it is a unit of meaning (the "-s" denotes the meaning of more than one). Hence, a morpheme is really the smallest unit of speech that has meaning.

Now, let us come to what I think is the most useful definition of all, at least for a reading teacher: "A word is what the dictionary says is a word." True, the other two definitions, one based on phonology and the other based on semantics, are indeed useful and basic; when it comes right down to it, however, most of us will use *author- ity,* or put another way, *convention.*

When modern English was emerging as a popularly written language, it received a great boost in stability when Samuel Johnson published his dictionary in 1755. Cer- tainly, Johnson had a lot to do with stabilizing spelling as, up to that time, alternate (often phonetic) spellings were quite acceptable among literate people. However, he also had something to do with stabilizing what is a word.

At this point, it would be useful to clarify the distinctions between authority and convention. An authority is presumably an expert (or a body of experts) who say that something is so. In teaching grammar, schools used to teach "prescriptive grammar," that is, they taught how words were to be used because some authorities said it was right. Modern linguists can be called "descriptive grammarians," that is, without making judgments as to what is right, they simply describe what is being done. Dictionaries follow both of these principles. They define word meaning, and often use, by how a word is being used by the public at large or by certain well-known authors.

The distinction between regular dictionaries and slang dictionaries is partly one of authority versus popular use. A complicating factor is the impermanence of slang.

Teachers are regularly faced with the problem of word use. A reading teacher, using the language experience approach—or making a story chart for all the children to read, based on stories that the children tell—is faced with the problem of what is a proper word to put in a story. There is a common assumption that older teachers will attempt to prescribe what is a proper word, and younger teachers will be more liberal or descriptive. But this certainly isn't always the case; often experienced teachers are more liberal than some young teachers who want to write down the story "correctly" (in Standard English dialect) to give the students a good model and impress the principal. The long standing controversy over "ain't" might illustrate the point.

In Chapter 13 we will discuss the problem of dialects and special populations, such as inner city children who speak in a dialect different from that used in most schools (the so-called Standard English dialect or Great American, as some phoneticians call it). Most textbooks are written in the Standard English dialect, but whether or not this is all the child should learn to read is a good question. Certainly, most words of all dialects are similar enough that learning to read the words in any English dialect has great transferability to any other dialect.

THE WHOLE WORD METHOD

Teachers frequently talk about the whole word method of teaching reading. Sometimes they contrast it with the phonics method or some other method. The whole word method is also called the *sight method* or the *look-say method.*

Very few teachers would use just the whole word method. Actually, they use a number of methods in combination, but what is the whole word method?

Basically, it is concentrating on the word as the instructional unit. The student is taught to recognize words without sounding them out, and sometimes without using context. Flashcards might be a pure example. The teacher drills the student on a small group of words, each of which is printed on a card. The teacher asks the child to read the word on the card that is held up. If the student doesn't know it, he or she is told the word and asked to repeat it. That card is put at the bottom of the pile, and the student is given another try when it comes up again. This is usally done with easy words that are well within the student's speaking vocabulary, so there is no problem of the student not knowing the meaning of the word. See Figure 4-1 for an interesting historical description of the whole word method.

Later, the new words learned are used in sentences on the chalkboard, in workbook exercises, in experience charts, in spelling lessons, and in reader stories.

In fact, many systems of basal readers are partly based on a gradual introduction of whole words. This structure can be seen in the last few pages of primary books where every new word that is introduced is listed, together with the page where it

Flashcards can be used to implement the whole word method. (Larry Smith/Black Star)

III. WORD METHOD.—Teach the pupil to identify at sight the words placed at the head of the reading exercises, and to read these exercises without hesitation. Having read a few lessons, begin to teach the names of the letters and the spelling of words.

IV. WORD METHOD AND PHONIC METHOD COMBINED.—Teach the pupil to identify words and read sentences, as above. Having read a few lessons in this manner, begin to use the Phonic Method, combining it with the Word Method, by first teaching the words in each lesson *as words;* then, the elementary sounds, the names of the letters, and spelling.

Figure 4-1   The word method as described in the suggestions to teachers in *McGuffey's First Eclectic Reader. (From* McGuffey's First Eclectic Reader, *Eclectic Educational Series, American Book Company, New York, 1879.)*

first appears. The series author keeps a careful record of every new word introduced in the page of every book for as long as three years. The first little preprimer might use as few as seventeen new words, then the second preprimer uses those seventeen words plus gradually introducing twenty more words, etc., on up through every reader through the third grade. See Figure 4-2 for a typical list of words at the end of a text.

Our School

PRIMER

New words: 95.   *Total vocabulary:* 158.

Our School is the primer of the Sheldon Basic Reading Series. It is designed to be read after the successful completion of the pre-primer program.

Our School introduces 95 new words and maintains the 63 words used initially at the pre-primer level. No more than 2 new words are introduced on a page, and no more than 6 new words in any one story. After introduction, each new word is repeated and systematically maintained throughout the remainder of the book.

Variants formed by adding *ed*, and adding or dropping *s* from known words are not listed as new words. Also not listed is the possessive form of the known word *Mary*.

5. school	23. Mr.	39. store
6. good-by	nurse	40. children
7. too	24. where	41. was
8. will	now	fun
9. . . .	25. . . .	42. . . .
10. are	26. . . .	43. liked
11. . . .	27. pet	44. . . .
12. this	28. hen	45. show
13. . . .	29. house	have
14. like	30. . . .	46. be
15. what	31. brown	47. . . .
but	32. egg	48. . . .
16. read	33. Miss	49. . . .
17. day	34. white	50. . . .
18. . . .	rabbit	51. am
19. ready	35. . . .	52. no
20. all	36. she	yes
21. . . .	37. laugh	53. do
22. . . .	38. box	54. . . .

Figure 4-2   Sample page from a traditional basal reader which illustrates the careful and systematic introduction of whole words as the underlying structure for the series. (*From* Our School by *William D. Sheldon, Queenie B. Mills, Merle B. Karnes, and Mary C. Rose. Allyn and Bacon, Boston, 1963.*)

143

The teacher's manual tells the teacher to introduce the new words for each lesson before the children are asked to read it. Often meaning and the phonic elements of the new words are discussed in the teacher's manual, and, in turn, told to the children, but the underlying structure of the series is the gradual introduction of new whole words.

Some users and authors of these basal series would be offended if they were labeled as a whole word method approach. They often prefer them to be labeled as "meaning emphasis" or "eclectic approaches," which is also partly true.

It is indeed interesting that some teachers talk about a basically phonic or grapheme center approach as being a "linguistic method." It is correct that some eminent linguists, such as Leonard Bloomfield and Charles Fries, used a basic phonic approach when they attempted to develop reading teaching methods, but there are other linguists who openly advocate basically a whole word approach in teaching beginning reading. The Bill Martin series is an example of a linguistically oriented approach which uses a number of word substitution patterns. For example: *What words can we put in the final position of this sentence?*

Mary had a _____. ball   toy   cat   mother

This appears to be based on the structural linguists' way of defining word class: "A noun is a type of word which fits in a noun position in a sentence and can be substituted with other words of a similar type." This is opposed to the traditional grammarian who would say that "a noun is a person, place, or thing." In any event, the words that are being put into the blank in this example sentence might be all of one form class, but they certainly do not have phonic elements in common. In many ways it is simply a whole word approach, i.e., the unit of instruction is the word. Thus a "linguistic method" of reading instruction does not have much meaning without further definition.

The whole word method of teaching reading usually involves repetition as one of the important teaching strategies. In simple terms, the new word is presented over and over again until the child learns it. In practice, some basal series actually count the number of times a word is used in the stories, and they make certain that each new word receives an adequate number of repetitions. It is partly this need for repetition that caused new words to be introduced so slowly and carefully. Though authors and editors were often ingenious, it sometimes resulted in stories that were a bit boring and monotonous in order to get in the desired repetition. Workbooks that accompanied and correlated with the basal readers also used the same *controlled* vocabulary, and suggestions in the teacher's manual for games and audiovisual presentations emphasized the same words.

No one knows just when the word method began, but it was used in 1657 (Comenius' *Orbis Pictus*) and was one of the methods advocated in the McGuffey series (see Figure 4-1). However, it is interesting to note that McGuffey also advocated combining the word method with the phonic method.

The method of teaching a whole word first, then breaking it down into phonic elements, is known as an *analytic approach*. This is opposed to the *synthetic approach* which was used in the *New England Primer*, often along with hornbooks which had the child first learn phonetic elements and later put them together to form words. Both methods are used today, but the analytic method is the most popular. Many of the modern reading systems introduce the whole word first, then instruct the teacher to break down the word into grapheme elements. Of course, when the teacher uses phonics or phonograms, and shows children how they can blend elements together to form a new word, a synthetic approach is being used.

Basic or Sight Vocabularies

Reading teachers often talk about basic or sight vocabularies. In some respects, the terms are interchangeable, and in other respects they are different.

A *sight vocabulary* for a child is all the words that can be recognized at sight, that is, without using any word-attack skills. Another way of saying the same thing is that the student recognizes the whole word. Traditional basal readers, which have as their basis the gradual introduction of new words, have as one of their major goals the development of a good and ever-increasing sight vocabulary.

The term *basic vocabulary* usually means a list of common words which are necessary for most reading. Frequently, these lists of common words are based on frequency counts. Two widely used lists are Edward Dolch's 220 Basic Sight Words and my own Instant Words. These lists were originally developed for remedial reading instruction, but now they are also used in many regular classrooms as supplements to the words introduced in the basal system.

Most basal reader systems also have their own specially developed vocabularies which they consider as basic. Both the Dolch list and the Instant Words have a high overlap with each other and with the vocabulary introduced in most basal readers. The Dolch list of 220 words contains no nouns, but there are 95 Dolch nouns that can be added. The Instant Words contain 600 words in order of frequency in groups of 25. The Instant Words are roughly graded so that the first 100 words are approximately first-grade words, the second 100 are approximately second-grade words, the third 100 are approximately third-grade words, and the second 300 are approximately fourth-grade words (see Figure 4-3). Dolch states that his 220 words are usually mastered by the middle of the third grade.

A high percentage of most basic vocabularies is *structure words* (also called *function words*). That is, they are words that hold the language together, like "a," "this,"

THE INSTANT WORDS

FIRST HUNDRED WORDS (Approximately First Grade)				SECOND HUNDRED WORDS (Approximately Second Grade)				THIRD HUNDRED WORDS (Approximately Third Grade)			
Group 1a	Group 1b	Group 1c	Group 1d	Group 2a	Group 2b	Group 2c	Group 2d	Group 3a	Group 3b	Group 3c	Group 3d
the	he	go	who	saw	big	may	ran	ask	hat	off	fire
a	I	see	an	home	where	let	five	small	car	sister	ten
is	they	then	their	soon	am	use	read	yellow	write	once	order
you	one	us	she	stand	ball	these	over	show	try	didn't	part
to	good	no	new	box	morning	right	such	goes	myself	set	early
and	me	him	said	upon	live	present	way	clean	longer	round	fat
we	about	by	did	first	four	tell	too	buy	those	dress	third
that	had	was	boy	came	last	next	shall	thank	hold	fell	same
in	if	come	three	girl	color	please	own	sleep	full	wash	love
not	some	get	down	house	away	leave	most	letter	carry	start	hear
for	up	or	work	find	red	hand	sure	jump	eight	always	yesterday
at	her	two	put	made	friend	more	thing	help	sing	anything	door
with	do	man	were	could	pretty	why	only	fly	warm	around	eyes
it	when	little	before	book	eat	better	near	don't	sit	close	clothes
on	so	has	just	look	want	under	than	fast	dog	walk	through
can	my	them	long	mother	year	while	open	cold	ride	money	o'clock
will	very	how	here	run	white	should	kind	today	hot	turn	second
are	all	like	other	school	got	never	must	does	grow	might	water
of	would	our	old	people	play	each	high	face	cut	hard	town
this	any	what	take	night	found	best	far	green	seven	along	took
your	been	know	cat	into	left	another	both	every	woman	bed	pair
as	out	make	again	say	men	seem	end	brown	funny	fine	now
but	there	which	give	think	bring	name	also	coat	yes	sat	keep
be	from	much	after	back	wish	dear	until	six	ate	stop	head
have	day	his	many		black		call	gave		hope	food

THE SECOND 300 WORDS (Approximately Fourth Grade)											
Group 4a	Group 4b	Group 4c	Group 4d	Group 4e	Group 4f	Group 4g	Group 4h	Group 4i	Group 4j	Group 4k	Group 4l
told	time	word	wear	hour	grade	egg	spell	become	herself	demand	aunt
Miss	yet	almost	Mr.	glad	brother	ground	beautiful	body	idea	however	system
father	true	thought	side	follow	remain	afternoon	sick	chance	drop	figure	lie
children	above	send	poor	company	milk	feed	became	act	river	case	cause
land	still	receive	lost	believe	several	boat	cry	die	smile	increase	marry
interest	meet	pay	outside	begin	war	plan	finish	real	son	enjoy	possible
government	since	nothing	wind	mind	able	question	catch	speak	bat	rather	supply
feet	number	need	Mrs.	pass	charge	fish	floor	already	fact	sound	thousand
garden	state	mean	learn	reach	either	return	stick	doctor	sort	eleven	pen
done	matter	late	held	month	less	sir	great	step	king	music	condition
country	line	half	front	point	train	fell	guess	itself	dark	human	perhaps
different	remember	fight	built	rest	cost	hill	bridge	nine	themselves	court	produce
bad	large	enough	family	sent	evening	wood	church	baby	whose	force	twelve
across	few	feel	began	talk	note	add	lady	minute	study	plant	rode
yard	hit	during	air	went	past	ice	tomorrow	ring	fear	suppose	uncle
winter	cover	gone	young	bank	room	chair	snow	wrote	move	law	labor
table	window	hundred	ago	ship	flew	watch	whom	happen	stood	husband	public
story	even	week	world	business	office	alone	women	appear	himself	moment	consider
sometimes	city	change	airplane	whole	cow	low	among	heart	strong	person	thus
I'm	together	being	without	short	visit	arm	road	swim	knew	result	least
tried	sun	care	kill	certain	wait	dinner	farm	felt	often	continue	power
horse	life	answer	ready	fair	teacher	hair	cousin	fourth	toward	price	mark
something	street	course	stay	reason	spring	service	bread	I'll	wonder	serve	president
brought	party	against	won't	summer	picture	class	wrong	kept	twenty	national	voice
shoes	suit		paper	fill	bird	quite	age	well	important	wife	whether

Figure 4-3 The Instant Words, a 600-word basic vocabulary, graded according to frequency and approximate grade level of difficulty. (*Copyright 1957 by Edward B. Fry.*)

"when," etc., as opposed to *subject matter words* (also called *content words*), like "dinosaur," "red," "love." It is almost impossible to write a sentence without structure words; they are in every type of story and writing. Subject words, on the other hand, vary considerably with the type of story. For example, a story about automobiles might have subject words like "gearshift" and "carburetor," but would certainly contain words like "the" and "of." However, a story about butterflies would probably not contain a "gearshift" and "carburetor," but would probably also contain "the" and "of" (see Figure 4-4).

The reason basic vocabularies are so important is that they make up such a high percentage of all reading material. For example, the list of Instant Words comprises over half of all written material. In other words, half of all the words in this book and half of all the words in an encyclopedia are from the list of these 600 Instant Words. In easier material, the percentage is even higher. One study showed that 63 percent of all the words used in several primary reading series, grades one through three, were from the first 300 Instant Words. Is it any wonder that we say children should be taught to recognize them "instantly"? They occur so often that if a child had to use word analysis skills on them, the train of thought would be broken and comprehension would suffer grievously. Besides that, if sounding out the Instant Words were required, the chances of knowing the subject words, which occur much less frequently, would be even less.

Since basic vocabularies are often used in remedial or supplemental instruction, it is usually necessary for the teacher who plans to use them to first find out how many the child already knows. This can be done by a simple oral reading test. For example, you could have the child read the first five words from each group of Instant Words. Since the groups are graded in order of difficulty, when the child starts missing words, you could have him or her read down the group column and check off the words not known, or, better yet, write out an individual flash card for each word not known. Either you or a student who knows the words could then help the student to learn the words. For classroom-size groups there are group tests. The Dolch Basic Sight Word Test (Garrard Publishing Company) correlates with the Dolch List, and the Instant Word Recognition Test (Dreier Educational Systems) correlates with the Instant Words. Or you can make your own group test using these word lists or the list from

1. Noun Markers — *a, the, some, any, three, this, my, few* . . .

2. Verb Markers — *am, are, is, was, have, has, had* . . .

3. Phrase Markers — *up, down, in, out, above, below, to, of* . . .

4. Clause Markers — *if, because, that, how, when, why* . . .

5. Question Markers — *who, why, how, when, what, where* . . .

Figure 4-4   Some examples of common structure words which are also called markers by some linguists. The other major class of words, called content words or subject words, is made up of nouns, verbs, adjectives, and adverbs. (*From* Linguistics and the Teaching of Reading *by Carl A. Lefevre, McGraw-Hill Book Company, New York, 1963.*)

your basal series. To do this, place five words in a line and call out one of them so that the child has to mark it. However, commercially prepared tests have some advantages. For example, the Instant Word Recognition Test is self-scoring (a carbon-paper type of second sheet records marks in a box if the correct response is made) and half the items are constructed so that a child knowing the initial sound cannot guess at the word and get it correct.

There are many ways to teach basic vocabularies. I have already mentioned making individual flash cards. The Dolch Words can be purchased on printed flash cards, both small (calling-card size) for individual work and large (3 x 6″) for group work. A "flash card" is literally flashed in front of the child (exposed for an instant) by turning it or moving it up from behind a blank card. The short exposure helps to attract attention and to emphasize the necessity for instant recognition.

Other ways of teaching basic vocabularies include:

1   Using a card reader. (A special card has the word printed on it, and across the bottom of the card is a strip of magnetic tape. When the card is inserted into the device, it "says" the word. The Instant Words are available on audio cards from Califone or local audiovisual dealers.)

2   Using games such as bingo or rummy with words instead of numbers in the squares.

3   Spelling and writing lessons using the words.

4   Filmstrips that flash the word (tachistoscope).

5   Easy reading stories (most easy stories contain a high percentage of basic words).

Most types of reading lessons teach "words" one way or another; so, to a large extent, many other sections of this book are about how to teach the child new words, including basic words.

VOCABULARY BUILDING

Vocabulary building is a higher-order word learning skill. In teaching basic words, it is assumed that nearly all of them are already in the child's speaking vocabulary, and that they can be used correctly in speech even if the pupil cannot give an accurate definition of them. However, in vocabulary building, the child often confronts the word for the first time. Often, the word is not in his or her speaking vocabulary. The meaning of it needs to be learned. Conversely, the child might be able to decode or say the word aloud because of adequate phonics skills or perhaps even pronounce it correctly as it has been heard before, but not have heard it often enough in meaningful context to have acquired the meaning.

Vocabulary building, therefore, is a type of reading instruction done much more in the upper elementary grades than in the primary grades. It is sometimes referred to by the phrase *word meaning.*

There are really two basic types of vocabulary building: direct word study and the subject matter approach.

One type of word study is the teaching of word meanings by having the students study *roots,* prefixes, and suffixes. In the last chapter we saw a list of common prefixes

Dragon Race

Each child in turn flips a penny. If it comes up heads, he moves his paper clip <u>two</u> spaces on the back of his own book and reads the word aloud. It the penny comes up tails, he moves <u>one</u> space and reads the word aloud. Whenever he misses a word, he returns his paper clip to the space he was on before the flip, and another player tells him the word. The first player who reaches END wins.

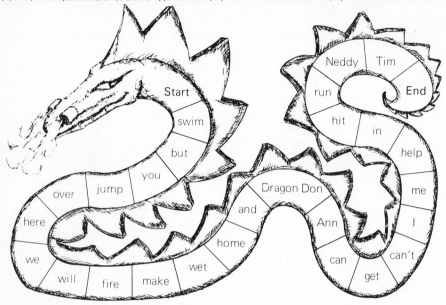

Figure 4-5 Sample board game for teaching sight words. (*From* Dragon Don and Tim, Storybooks for Beginners, *by Lee Mountain. Dreier Educational Systems, Highland Park, New Jersey.)*

and suffixes, together with their meanings. In Figure 4-6 we see some of the common roots from the same study.

Vocabulary building drills in many basal reading systems utilize the word root method of approach. This same approach is used in many other language arts learning materials, such as supplemental vocabulary building books, spelling books, and subject matter books (such as science books that use roots when introducing new words).

Dictionary use lessons also often include asking the students to look up the root as well as the definition. Dictionary use lessons might be specific or incidental; that is, the teacher may plan a lesson on how to use the dictionary, or may merely instruct students to look up words in the dictionary when they don't know a meaning. Students do not just naturally use a dictionary; there must be systematic and regular instruction from the teacher to develop dictionary use skills and habits.

The second major way of building vocabulary is the *subject matter approach*. To some extent, every subject matter lesson is a vocabular building lesson. To really teach the meaning of a word like "osmosis," a science lesson is needed. A student can get part of the idea or a bare outline of the concept by looking "osmosis" up in the dictionary, but to really understand the word, a good science lesson is needed. Thus, every lesson in every subject is a lesson in vocabulary improvement or reading comprehension. It has been said that one of the real benefits of a college education is

Greek Root Derivatives

Root Stem	Meaning	Example, English
graph (gram)	to write	barograph, graph, phonograph
syn (syl, sys)	together	synthesis, synthetic
(cir, circl, cycle)	ring	circle, circumference, cyclone
org, organ	organ	organ, organize
phon, phone	sound	phonetic, telephone
mon, mono	one	monotone, monotonous, monologue
tel, tele	far off	telephone, television
pol, poli	city	metropolis, politics
auto	self	automobile, automatic
phos (phot)	light	phosphate, phosphorus, photograph
(muse)	muse, to think	muse, museum, musical
para	beside	parallel, paraphrase
phys	nature	physics, physical
log	word, reason	logical, biology
dia	through	dia, diameter
(micro)	small	microbe, microscope
(pract)	to	practice, practical
chara	engraving	character, characteristics
hydra	water	hydrogen, hydromatic

Latin Root Derivatives

Root Stem	Meaning	Examples, English
fac, fact, fic, fy, fied, fash	to do, to make	face, fact, factory, benefit, feat, fashion, purify
sta, sti, stat, sist, st	to stand	station, status, insist, rest
pos, pose, pon, pound	to place	pose, post, opposite, opponent, compound
fer, ferre, lat, tol	to bear, to carry	coniferous, ferry, oblation, tolerate
reg, rect, reign, roy, rul	to rule	direct, regal, ruler, regular, royal
mit, mis, miss, mes, mise	to send	emit, mission, submit, surmise
tend, tens	to stretch	tend, tendor, tension
ced, ces, cess, ceed	to go, to happen	sede, session, secede
vid, vis, view, vise	to see	video, vision, visa, visit, advise
mov, mot, mob	to move	move, motivation, mobility
spect, spic or pic	to see	expect, spectacle, suspicion
ven, vent	to come	event, vent, convenience
ten, tent, tain, tin	to hold	tent, tentacle, tenant, attain, continent
par, para, pair	to get ready	apparent, prepare, repair
port	to carry	port, export, report, repair
cap, capt	to take, to head	cape, caption, captor, capital, capitol
duc, duct, duit	to lead	duct, conduct, conduit
quire, quis, quer, quest	to question, to ask	acquire, requisition, conquer, conquest
serv, serf	to serve	reserve, servant, service, serf
fin	to end	fine, finish, refinish
da, don, der, di, dote	to give	data, donate, add, pardon, render, antidote
part	to share, to participate	depart, particle, participate
signific, sign, less, fic	to indicate, to notify, to mark	significant, sign, signify
tra, tract, trait, treat	to pull, to draw	trace, traction, trait, retreat
gen, gener	cause to be, to begin	generate, Genesis, generation
lect	to choose	elect, re-elect, select
ag, act	to act	agent, act, action
pli, plic, ply	to fold	apply, complicated, duplicate, reply
ject	to throw	eject, dejection, project
press	to press	depress, press, impress
struct, stroy, stru	to build	construct, instrument, destroy, structure
vert, vers, verse	to turn	advertise, convert, reverse, verse
cid, cide	to fall, to happen	accident, decide, incident
cord, cour	heart	accord, concord, cordially, discourage
fort, force	strong	comfort, effort, force, fort

Figure 4-6 Common roots used in vocabulary building lessons. (*From* "Vocabulary Development by Teaching Prefixes, Suffixes and Root Derivatives," *by L. C. Breen, The Reading Teacher, November 1960.*)

that you learn how to read more difficult books. For example, one of the goals of this book is to improve your vocabulary in the subject matter of reading. This will help you to comprehend more advanced books and professional articles.

Subject matter learning of words is not limited to the sciences. It is just as important in literature, where many new and important words are used. You will not find any definition for a "myriad of stars" in an astronomy book, or a very satisfactory definition of "love" in a psychology course. All elementary teachers should, and most do, teach literature in elementary classrooms, either as part of reading lessons or as part of language arts. The discussion of literary terminology is an important part of such lessons.

Configuration

In the last two chapters we discussed a number of ways in which a child might be taught to recognize a new word if it were not known, through use of phonemes or phonograms, for example.

There is a type of whole word cue, called *configuration*, to aid in the recognition of new words. This deals with the shape of words. Note the different shapes of the following pairs of words:

"Dog" has a *descender* letter in the last position and "cat" has an *ascender*.

"If" is short, and "coming" is long.

Just as there is not definite research as to the size of the unit a child attends to in various stages of development of reading, there is no conclusive research as to how a word is perceived, or perhaps we should say, how the differences between one word and another or all others are perceived. However, word shape may be one of the perceptual cues used particularly by beginning readers, and some reading systems instruct the teacher to call attention to the different shapes of new words when introducing them at the primary levels.

Rebus

It is not much used now, but in the past some reading systems used a type of whole word substitution called a *rebus*. A rebus is merely a small picture inserted in the place of a noun (see Figure 4-7). It is used in primary reading material to overcome the limited vocabulary of the beginning reader. Rebuses cannot be used in place of most structure words, and are seldom used in place of verbs. They have the advantage of encouraging the child to read a whole sentence for meaning, and they have the advantage of giving the child practice in using structure words which occur frequently in all sentences.

One slight drawback is that sometimes children must learn to say what the rebus is—"dog," not "puppy" or "doggie"—and some educators feel as long as the child has

live live live live live

[Let all teachers of young children read the following article attentively—Ed.] My theory is, that words can be more easily remembered than letters, for two reasons. In the first place they are not such minute objects, and the faculty by which the forms are distinguished can therefore more readily perceive them; in the second place, every word that a child learns, will (if judiciously selected), convey a distinct image of a thing, or an act, to his mind, and can be more easily remembered than the name of a letter with which he can have no natural associations.

What is invaluable in this method is, that children are always happy to learn thus . . . it is altogether an unnatural one [effort] to learn writing signs to which nothing already known can be attached.

Figure 4-7 An example of rebuses used as noun substitutes in a beginning reader. (*From* Synthetic First Reader *by Rebecca S. Pollard, Western Publishing House, Chicago, 1889.*)

to learn this, the word might as well be learned (which is really reading, and in the long run much more useful).

In any event, rebuses are seldom included for very long in any reading system, and they are just one of the many approaches used in beginning reading instruction. The rebus, incidentally, may be found in ancient children's books as well as in modern CAI (Computer Aided Instruction).

Context Cues

One of the chief methods of getting children to learn unknown words is through the use of context cues. Basically, this method asks the child to look at the whole phrase or sentence, then to guess at the unknown word. For example, a boy knows all the words in the following sentence: "Birds fly and fish _____." He is asked to guess at the missing word. Probably he will use what is known as a *semantic cue*, that is, he will get the meaning of the sentence as a whole. If he is further able to apply a word analysis cue, such as knowing the sound of the beginning letter, such as "Birds fly and fish s———" he will have even more success in coming up with the right word; though, of course, context cues almost never give the student the exact word. The sentence might be: "Birds fly and fish sink." But that is not likely because children build up internal *patterns of frequency* of word usage. It is highly probable that the missing word is "swim" rather than "sink," and every user of English knows that.

Another interesting constraint on word usage (that aids anyone in using context cues) is the use of *syntactic cues*. Syntax is grammar or principles of word usage. There are only certain kinds of words that will fit in any specific position in a sentence. You can't have an adjective or an article in the last position of our example sentence. For example, in English you can't say "Birds fly and fish green" or "Birds fly and fish the."

Another way of defining *constraint* is by saying that the *degrees of freedom* are limited. The producer, speaker or writer, of the English language does not have unlimited freedom in choosing words. At times, choices are really quite limited. One cannot say: "Give me book." One can only say: "Give me a book" or "Give me the book." This illustrates a semantic constraint. Thus, out of the 250,000 or so words in the English language, there is a choice of only a few words that can be used in that particular position in that sentence. In short, the producer's degrees of freedom are one of several words, not 250,000 words. In other positions in the sentence, the choice is much wider, but in no instance is it unlimited, or limited only by the choice of words in an unabridged dictionary. There are about 250,000 words (main entries) in an unabridged dictionary.

A further constraint upon word use in a particular position is word frequency. In this case, constraint might better be perceived as probability. For example, in the sentence: "The animal that barked all night was a ———" the probability that the unknown word is "dog" is higher than the probability of its being "canine," although both are accurate and proper. Though a reader might know both words in speech, he or she is unlikely to attempt to use the low-frequency word "canine." There are also frequencies and probabilities for phrases as well as words.

This also applies to whole sentences. In reply to the question "How are you?" the probable reply is "I'm fine" rather than "I have polio." This illustrates the constraint of a frequency pattern.

Here, perhaps, we can see how closely reading is related to speaking, listening, writing, and all of the language arts.

The most common teaching technique utilizing context cues is to have the teacher explain, in a simplified fashion, how they work:

> If you don't know a word, read all the words on both sides of it in the sentence and see if you can guess what it is. Try several words and see if one seems better than another. Can you use any other cues to help you guess the unknown word? Do you know the beginning sound, or do you know a part of the word?

This might be called a context method of word attack, but note that there is a little word analysis in the last question. This can be done on the chalkboard before groups of students, or during a reading lesson when the student is reading along and becomes "stuck" at an unknown word.

The Cloze Technique as Context Training The cloze technique is a deceptively simple method used in teaching comprehension, testing student's reading ability, readability determination, and language research. It consists of asking the child to supply a missing word in a sentence or paragraph. In a typical cloze passage every fifth or tenth word is omitted, and a blank inserted. The student is asked to supply the missing word.

We will discuss its uses in testing and comprehension training later. Right now let's look at the cloze technique as a method of instructing the student in how to use context cues.

A passage from a reading text can be typed up with a blank in place of every tenth word. The student can be asked to guess at what the missing word could be. This could be done either orally—that is, the student reads the passage aloud and attempts to say the missing word—or it can be done silently, with the child reading the passage silently and writing the missing word. With beginning readers it is more likely to be done orally because their writing skills are often not as developed as their reading vocabulary.

HOW MANY WORDS DOES A CHILD KNOW?

This is a very difficult problem. However, it is a reasonable question for elementary teachers to ask because it might have some bearing on their future teaching activities and, in any event, they will learn a little bit more about the English language and dictionary use along the way.

If you ask the publishers of unabridged dictionaries how many words the books contain, they will answer something like this:

Webster's Third International Dictionary	450,000 entries
Random House Dictionary	260,000 entries
The World Book Dictionary	200,000 entries
Funk & Wagnalls' New Standard Dictionary	458,000 entries

However, an entry is not a "main entry," which is defined as the *alphabetical entry*. What these dictionary makers are calling an "entry" includes derived forms and subentries. If we look at only main entries, then Webster's, for example, contains only about 236,000 main entries.

These numbers might seem very large, perhaps impossible to teach, so let's look at what happens when we try to narrow down the number of different words in English. Harold DuPuy, in an interesting study for the government, attempted to find out how many basic English words there were, and how many of these were known by children.

Through a sampling procedure, the decision was made to count as basic words only those words that appeared as main entries in the four above-mentioned dictionaries, and to omit compound words, proper names, abbreviations, different spellings, and words that were classified as foreign, archaic, slang, or technical. The procedure also eliminated common variations of basic word forms, such as words formed with affixes, plurals, comparatives, adjectives, verb forms, etc. With these limitations, it was found that there were only 12,300 Basic Words in American English. This is quite a different number from the claimed entries of the big dictionaries, and begins to approach manageable teaching proportions.

However, when the study attempted to ascertain how many words children really know through use of a multiple choice test (which the children read), it was found that fourth graders knew about 2,704 words and sixth graders knew about 4,529 words. In a similar vein, Edgar Dale (in two studies: one with Jeanne Chall and one with Gerhard Eichholz) found that fourth-graders know the meanings of 4,302 words and sixth-graders know the meaning of 10,432 words.

In case you are concerned about the apparent discrepancy, let me hasten to assure you that how you define a word can make the difference of 50 percent, 100 percent, or even more. The DuPuy study defines a word, or rather what are different words, very narrowly (and each word as having only one meaning), whereas Dale considers different meanings as different words. For example, DuPuy would count "light" as one word, while Dale would count "light-not-dark" as one word and "light-lamp fixture" as a second word. Dale included "runaway, runabout," etc.

The size of a child's vocabulary, or the size of the English vocabulary, all depends on how you define a word. Are "run, runs, running" different words? How about "ran"? If you want to go into meaning, you get into even more trouble. If you say that a child knows the meaning of "run," he or she might be able to tell you or demonstrate knowledge of a meaning like "run around the school"—but what about "run" in a stocking, "run" on the stock market, to "run" a hotel, a rabbit "run," a salmon "run," or a drug "runner?"

There is another way of looking at vocabulary size, and that is to count usage or frequency rather than dictionary entries or children's word knowledge. One large computerized study, by John Carroll and others, counted 5 million words from reading passages used in grades four through eight including texts, novels, and encyclopedias. They found that about 87,000 different words were used. In this study no attempt was made to separate out homographs (same spelling for different meaning), but they did count as different words—for example, "run, Run, runs, runner, running," and about 14 other compounds and variant forms. Five million running words is a very large sample of texts, but whether you want to say that it contained 87,000 different words or only 20,000 different words probably depends on just how you define what is a different word.

The Carroll study also provided an interesting verification of the importance of teaching a high-frequency vocabulary, such as the Instant Words or the words in a basal reading series if they are based on frequency counts. Table 4-2 shows the 25 most common words ranked in order of frequency and their overall percentage

Table 4-1   Estimated Vocabulary Size By Grade

Grade 50th percentile	Number of Basic Words known	Approximate fraction of total (maximum possible vocabulary)
4	2200	
5	3100	1/4
6	3900	
7	4600	
8	5300	
9	5900	1/2
10	6400	
11	6700	
12	6900	
(H.S. grad)		
13	7500	
14	7900	
15	8200	
16	8400	
(B.A.)		
17	8800	
18	8900	
(M.A.)		
19	9000	
20+	9100	3/4
(Ph.D.)		

EXPLANATION: No estimate of vocabulary size is of any value whatsoever unless it is carefully defined. These figures are from DuPuy's norming of the Basic Word Vocabulary Test. The total population of words sampled was 12,300, which DuPuy determined were all the Basic Words in English. A Basic Word cannot be a derivative, a proper noun, archaic, technical, foreign, or a compound, and must appear in four major unabridged dictionaries. Vocabulary size was determined by a five-choice multiple-choice test of meaning using synonyms or descriptive phrases which the student read. Only the commonest meaning of the words was tested.

in the total of 5 million words of reading material. It is interesting that the five most common words ("the," "of," "and," "a," and "to") account for 17.5 percent of all the words used, and the first 25 most common words account for 32 percent of all the words in the fourth- through eighth-grade reading materials. At the other end of the frequency scale, of the 87,000 different words used, approximately 30,000 of them were only used once in 5 million words of reading material.

The Carroll study is an interesting verification of the efficacy of what many reading teachers have been doing for a long time; namely, teaching a basic or high-frequency vocabulary, such as the Instant Words (see Figure 4-3). A popular English series has presented a similar type of information in an interesting diagrammatic fashion (see Figure 4-8), which shows that the first 12 words make up about one-fourth of all running words and 100 words make up about one-half of all running words. Running words refers to the total number of words in a book or page; for example, this paragraph has about 116 running words.

Table 4-2   High-frequency Words from the Carroll Study

Rank	Words	Percentage	
1	the	7.3	
2	of	2.8	
3	and	2.6	
4	a	2.4	
5	to	2.4	
	Subtotal		17.5
6	in	1.9	
7	is	1.2	
8	you	1.0	
9	that	.9	
10	it	.9	
	Subtotal		23.4
11	he	.8	
12	for	.8	
13	was	.7	
14	on	.7	
15	are	.7	
	Subtotal		27.1
16	as	.6	
17	with	.6	
18	his	.5	
19	they	.5	
20	at	.5	
	Subtotal		29.8
21	be	.5	
22	this	.5	
23	from	.4	
24	I	.4	
25	have	.4	
	Total		32.0

SOURCE: John Carroll, Peter Davies, and Barry Richman's
American Heritage Word Frequency Book. New York: Houghton
Mifflin and American Heritage, 1971.

WORD TEACHING MATERIALS

All reading materials teach words. Just getting a child to read easy material is a word teaching technique; however, more formal instruction methods usually involve a basal reader series and various supplementary materials. We will study basal readers in Chapter 7, but controlling the introduction of new words and methods of teaching them are a strong point of most basal series. Supplementary materials, such as those listed at the end of this chapter, tend to fall into two categories: (1) those materials which teach sight recognition or basic vocabularies and tend to be for the primary grades; and (2) those materials that teach vocabulary meaning, including vocabulary building exercises using roots and affixes, and which are used more in intermediate grades and secondary schools.

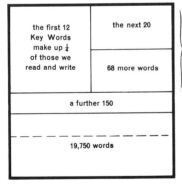

a and he
I in is
it of that
the to was

all as at be but are for had have him his not on one said so they we with you ₂₀

about an back been before big by call came can come could did do down first from get go has her here if into just like little look made make me more much must my no new now off only or our over other out right see she some their them then there this two up want well went who were what when where which will your old ₆₈

After Again Always Am Ask Another Any Away Bad Because Best Bird Black Blue Boy Bring Day Dog Don't Eat Every Fast Father Fell Find Five Fly Four Found Gave Girl Give Going Good Got Green Hand Head Help Home House How Jump Keep Know Last Left Let Live Long Man Many May Men Mother Mr. Never Next Once Open Own Play Put Ran Read Red Room Round Run Sat Saw Say School Should Sing Sit Soon Stop Take Tell Than These Thing Think Three Time Too Tree Under Us Very Walk White Why Wish Work Woman Would Yes Year Bus Apple Baby Bag Ball Bed Book Box Car Cat Children Cow Cup Dinner Doll Door Egg End Farm Fish Fun Hat Hill Horse Jam Letter Milk Money Morning Mrs. Name Night Nothing Picture Pig Place Rabbit Road Sea Shop Sister Street Sun Table Tea Today Top Toy Train Water ₁₅₀

This area represents 19,750 further words. Space does not permit the printing of these words.

This large square, outlined in heavy print, represents the vocabulary (approx. 20,000 words) of the ordinary person.

the first 12 Key Words make up ¼ of those we read and write | the next 20 / 68 more words — the total of these three sections shows that 100 words make up ½ of those in common use

a further 150

19,750 words

Figure 4-8 The diagram represents the 20,000 words in an average vocabulary. The frequency of use of the Key Words is indicated by area, and also to some extent by the size of the print used. (*From* Key Words to Literacy *by J. McNally and W. Murray, published by the Schoolmaster Publishing Co. Ltd., London.*)

Words are taught in almost every education medium imaginable; workbooks, filmstrips flashed tachistoscopically, **CAI** (Computer-Aided Instruction), games, charts, dictionaries, supplemental readers, content area books (science, math, etc.), and even comic books.

Word games are a means of effectively involving students in vocabulary building. (Mimi Forsyth/
Monkmeyer)

Frequently, teaching techniques involve some kind of activity on the part of the
child, such as saying the word, writing the word, matching the word with a meaning,
comparing the word with similar words, or using the word in a proper setting. The
teachers' manuals that accompany basal series show you many ways of doing this, as
do the manuals for the supplementary materials. Informally, teachers often enjoy
having discussions about new or different words with their class. They also take oc-
casions such as when a child asks about a word to discuss it with the child. The
discussions might center around meaning or the structural analysis of the word.

Learning about new words is not just a part of the reading lesson, but should be
a part of nearly every type of lesson—from physical education to physical science.
Words and information about words are taught in grammar lessons, spelling lessons,
penmanship lessons, and music lessons. School is, in part, a word learning factory.

SUGGESTED LEARNING ACTIVITIES

1 Work with a child and teach him or her five or ten previously unknown
words (note testing method on page 74). Try a variety of techniques—flash cards,
spelling, building sentences with the new words—and other methods suggested in this
chapter.

2 Analyze some sight word building lessons and some vocabulary building lessons that can be found in the teacher's manual of a basal series or some supplementary
materials. Note the list of materials at the end of this chapter. Perhaps you can visit

a school and see some lessons in progress. What element or techniques do you find in common? What kind of learning is the lesson trying to teach; recognition, meaning, use, etc.?

3 Carefully observe a child learning new sight words. Ask how he or she is trying to learn it (visual imagery, looking for similar elements in known words, repetition of use, multisensory hearing, seeing, writing).

4 Make some sight word or vocabulary building games using content from Figures 4-3 and 4-5.

VOCABULARY AND STUDY TERMS

Word (definitions of)	Subject matter words
Sound spectrograph	Content words
Samuel Johnson	Percent of basic words in written materials
Prescribed use	Methods of teaching words
Whole word method	Vocabulary building
Sight method	Word meaning
Look-say method	Word study
Flash cards	Dictionary use
Method of basal texts	Subject matter approach to vocabulary building
Meaning emphasis	Configuration
Linguistic method(s)	Rebus
Word class	Context cue
Controlled vocabulary	Semantic cue
Origins of word method	Syntactic cue
Analytic approach	Patterns of frequency
Synthetic approach	Constraint
Sight vocabulary	Context method
Basic vocabulary	Cloze technique
Basic sight words	Vocabulary size problems
Instant Words	Percent of high frequency words in written materials
Structure words	Variety in word teaching materials and lessons
Function words	

LIST OF VOCABULARY CURRICULUM MATERIALS

Dolch Sight Materials: Edward Dolch; Garrard; nine boxes; **1–3.**[1]

The Grolier Creative Reading Program: two small indexing phonographs, records, lesson cards; **1.**

Reading All Around You: Xerox; three paperbound books; **1–3.**

The Ginn Word Enrichment Program: Theodore Clymer, Thomas Barrett, and Lou Burmeister; Ginn; seven paperbound books, tapes; **1–3.**

Extending Reading Skills: Hargrave and Beck; McCormick-Mathers; three workbooks; **6–9.**

Plus 10 Vocabulary Booster: William Kottmer, Audrey Claus and Ruth Dockery; Webster/McGraw Hill; 22 cassettes and kit; **4–8.**

A B C Serendipity: Albert G. Miller; Bowmar; six books; **4–6.**

---

[1] Numbers following description indicate approximate grade level. See appendix for publishers' addresses.

Word Mastery Series With Puzzles and Games: Scholastic; three paperbound books; **1-6**.
Instant Word Recognition Test: Edward Fry; Dreier; Test; **1-4-R**.
Wordpacers: Charles W. Slack and Dell Duncan; David Montgomery, Random House; kit; **4-7**.
Oxford Vocabulary Workshop Series: Jerome Shostak; five workbooks; **4-8**.
Tachistoscopic Reading: Edward Dolch; Singer Education; Filmstrips; **1-7**.
Wordcraft 1 Vocabulary Program: Burgen Evans; six filmstrips, three cassettes, student study manual; **4-6**.
Instant Words and Instant Word Phrases Tachisto-Filmstrip Programs: Edward Fry; Learning Through Seeing; 48 filmstrips; **1-6**.
Instant Words, Instant Word Phrases, Audio Card Program: Edward Fry; Califone International; 600 word audio cards, 864 phrase audio cards; **1-4**.
Vocabulary Development Series: Learning Resources Co.; 11 sets of audio cards, activity sheet; **1-3**.
Vocabulary Activity Cards: Frank Schaffer; **2-5**.

REFERENCES

Carroll, John B., Peter Davies, and Barry Richman. *Word Frequency Book.* New York: American Heritage, 1971.

Dale, Edgar. *Bibliography of Vocabulary Studies.* Columbus: Ohio State University, 1949.

Dale, Edgar, "Vocabulary Measurement: Techniques and Major Findings." *Elementary English,* 1965, *42,* 895–901.

Dale, Edgar, and Gerhard Eichholz. *Children's Knowledge of Words: An Interim Report.* Columbus: Bureau of Educational Research and Service, Ohio State University, 1960.

Dale, Edgar, and Joseph O'Rourke. *Techniques of Teaching Vocabulary.* Palo Alto, Calif., Field, 1971.

Dale, Edgar, and Taher Razik. *Bibliography of Vocabulary Studies (5th ed.).* Columbus: Ohio State University, 1973.

Dolch, E. W. "A Basic Sight Vocabulary," *Elementary School Journal,* 1936, *36,* 456–460; *37,* 268–272.

DuPuy, Harold J. *The Rationale, Development and Standardization of a Basic Word Vocabulary Test.* Department of HEW. Rockville, Md.: National Center for Health Statistics, Publication No. HRA 74-1334, April 1974. (For reference to test used, see Chapter 11.)

Fry, Edward. "Developing a Word List for Remedial Reading." *Elementary English,* November 1957.

Harris, Albert J., and Milton D. Jacobson. *Basic Elementary Reading Vocabularies.* New York: Macmillan, 1972.

Harris, Albert J., and Milton D. Jacobson. "Basic Vocabulary for Beginning Reading." *The Reading Teacher,* January 1973.

Harris, Albert J., and Milton D. Jacobson. "Some Comparisons Between the Basic Elementary Reading Vocabularies and Other Word Lists." *Reading Research Quarterly,* 1973–74, *9*(1), 87–109.

Horn, Ernest. *A Basic Writing Vocabulary—10,000 Words Most Commonly Used in Writing.* Iowa City: State University of Iowa, 1926.

Kucera, Henry, and W. Nelson Francis. *Computational Analysis of Present-Day English,* Providence: Brown University Press, 1967.

Rinsland, Henry D. *A Basic Vocabulary of Elementary Children,* New York: Macmillan, 1945.

Thorndike, Edward L., and Irving Lorge. *The Teacher's Word Book of 30,000 Words.* New York: Teachers College, Columbia University, 1944.

Chapter 5

Comprehension: Skills and Teaching Methods

We can now turn to the most important element of the entire reading process—comprehension. To show its central importance, here is a definition of "reading": *Reading is the process of getting meaning from written symbols.*

In other words, *getting the meaning,* or *comprehending,* is the process of reading. Without getting meaning, you can't really call it reading.

ORAL READING: HOW IMPORTANT IS IT?

Some people might say that you can "read" orally without comprehension, or at least without much comprehension; however, this couldn't properly be called reading. The dictionary provides some assistance in this quandary by giving the meaning definition first choice, and the "act of rendering into speech something written" as the second definition.

In any case, when adults read—or for that matter, when children read—they are usually reading silently for comprehension. It is a wonder that so many elementary teachers haven't caught on to the importance of comprehension. If asked, they will of course say that comprehension is important, but if you examine their reading lessons, you will often see that, in practice, oral reading is assigned a greater importance, or is regarded at least as of equal importance.

Oral reading has a long and honorable history. Before the introduction of television, radio, and gramophones, it was a common family entertainment for someone to read aloud while others listened. The skill of reading aloud correctly and fluently was highly praised. It was painfully obvious who could do it well and who did it poorly. The local schoolmaster who did not turn out good oral readers was soon relieved of his post, and there was no NEA or AFT to suggest that his rights were being violated. Modern reading systems usually have a much better balance tilted in favor of silent reading comprehension, but old values change slowly in the education business. Let us hope that the generation of teachers who are reading this book will be able to see what kind of reading modern children and adults really do, and structure their lessons accordingly.

There are some merits in oral reading lessons. They tend to demonstrate the close correlation between the written language and the spoken language. Already knowing the spoken language is a great help in learning to read. Children who are born deaf, for example, do not learn to speak (without very special training), yet they can be taught to read. However, congenitally deaf children frequently do not become fluent adult readers; they achieve basic literacy but seldom much more. Of course, the normal distribution curve applies here, and there are brilliant exceptions.

Oral reading lessons also give the teacher some feedback as to the child's progress in word knowledge, and—by intonation—some insights into comprehension. It also gives the listening child an association between the spoken word and the printed word. Thus, there are benefits to be derived from oral reading; overemphasis can be harmful at worst, and an inefficient use of time at best. It can be harmful because it can put a limit on rate and a de-emphasis on comprehension. The reason it limits rate is that speaking speed is slower than silent reading speed; the typical high school graduate speaks at 150 words per minute, and reads silently at 250 words per minute.

THE PHRASE AND SENTENCE UNIT

Before we really delve into comprehension, we will return to the unit size theme that we have been following in Chapters 2, 3, and 4. In those chapters we looked at the letter, grapheme, syllable, word, etc. The next logical units of instruction are the phrase and sentence.

Like other reading methods, use of these units is not new. We do not know when phrase and sentence reading methods started, but they were suggested in 1657 by Comenius (who also suggested the word method), and actually used in the schools of Binghamton, New York, about 1870-1890. George Farnham published a book entitled *The Sentence Method of Reading* in 1895, and a number of reading series were heavily influenced by this method in the early 1900s.

The basic concept of the sentence method is that the whole sentence is presented because it is a "unit of thinking." If the sentence is the natural unit of language, then it is natural in reading as well as in speaking.

In teaching the sentence, the teacher first presents the whole sentence, and the child learns to read it by repetition. Later, the sentence is broken into word units, and the student learns to read the words in isolation or in other combinations. Finally, the words are "analyzed" into phonetic elements.

This *analytic method* can even be carried further. Some teachers present a *whole story*. They discuss background for the story, then give the children a whole little story to read. Analytic lessons follow, where words and phonetic elements are pointed out.

The whole process seems to become a little circular when the reason for analyzing the story or sentence into words and phonetic elements are given. Children should learn words and phonetic elements so that they can attack new words or new sentences, and thereby put together or figure out what the new sentence is. Thus, the analytic method becomes the *synthetic* method. It seems that it doesn't make much difference where in the circle you start to teach reading, or which point you wish to emphasize, within reason, because soon you get around to teaching the other size units. If you start reading lessons with phonic elements, you soon get to teaching whole words, phrases, and sentences, and if you start with words or phrases, you usually move on to teach graphemes.

Study Figure 5-1 to get the overall picture of unit size plus analytic and synthetic progression.

OBJECTIVE AND SUBJECTIVE COMPREHENSION

It is all right to say that comprehension is important, but just what is it? This question can be answered in a relatively simple fashion and in a relatively complex fashion.

One of the simplest analyses of comprehension is a two-part division into objective and subjective.

Objective comprehension is simple, factual, literal comprehension. If a story says that there are ten cows in the barn, the comprehension question might ask, "How many cows are there in the barn?" Unfortunately, many of the comprehension questions posed by the teachers, and a good number of the comprehension questions found in commercially prepared comprehension drill books, are of this simple objective nature.

There is nothing wrong with pointing out to the child the necessity for objective comprehension in reading, as long as you are also careful to point out that there is much more to comprehension.

Subjective comprehension comprises all the higher comprehension skills. For example, a subjective comprehension question might ask, "Are the cows contented?" The story might have told that the cows are being fed, that they were warmer than when they were outside in the rain, but nowhere would there have been a sentence or phrase saying "the cows are contented." It would be up to the reader to infer that the cows were contented.

Subjective comprehension includes such things as mood, tone, conjecture, inference, extension, interpolation, and criticism. It calls on the reader's background store of information to a much greater degree than objective comprehension. Since it is less objective, it is more debatable. Answers to subjective comprehension questions are not always clearly "right or wrong." They involve judgment. Readers with different backgrounds might have differing answers.

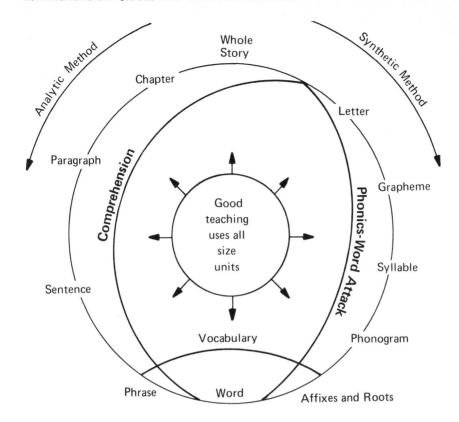

Throughout history, and to some extent even in modern times, teachers of reading have started beginning reading instruction with each of these sized units of written language. When they proceed clockwise, they are following a *synthetic* approach, and when they proceed counterclockwise, they are following an *analytic approach*. Regardless of where they begin, most reading systems get around to all the other unit sizes from either or both directions (analytic or synthetic). Frequently the difference is which size unit they emphasize most, but also they tend to be known by the unit that they use in the beginning—for example, "It is a phonics approach" or "it is a whole word method," but, on closer examination of good reading systems, it becomes obvious that all other units are also taught.

Figure 5-1 Graphic unit sizes used in teaching reading.

Subjective comprehension might be the most important part of the message. A girl reading her boyfriend's letter about all the things happening to him on a summer trip might not be a very good reader if she can't figure out whether she will have a boyfriend next fall. A diplomat reading a communique from a foreign ambassador would not be very effective if only the objective content of the text was comprehended.

The impact of a humorous story or a written joke is certainly lost if the reader doesn't laugh, and a love story with no emotional impact might be better put aside for an economic text. Stockbrokers read for economic trends, engineers for efficient functions, and drama critics for touches of greatness. All of these involve subjective comprehension.

Teachers can begin encouraging the development of subjective comprehension by the way they talk about, and discuss, even beginning reading lessons. Certainly, in upper elementary grades, subjective comprehension should become the major objective of most reading lessons.

Reading Teachers' Comprehension Analysis

Reading teachers and authors of reading materials usually have a developed analysis of comprehension skills embracing more than the factors of objective and subjective comprehension. They frequently would have a list of comprehension skills that might look something like this:

Getting the facts
Noting sequence (time line)
Identifying the main idea
Perceiving relationships
Drawing conclusions
Making inferences
Extending interpretation beyond stated information
Recognizing the author's intention
Restating the material
Summarizing the material
Reacting emotionally

There are probably as many lists of reading comprehension subskills as there are authors. Everyone has a different one, so don't be disappointed if you can't find *the* list of comprehension skills. However, certain subskills, such as "getting the main idea" or "time sequence," appear on most lists.

This lack of exact agreement on comprehension subskills also extends to basal readers or reading systems. In Figures 5-2 and 5-3 we see the skills list for basically the primary grades (grades one through three) for two major systems, the Harper & Row *Design for Reading* and the Scott, Foresman *Reading Systems.* In comparing the two, the first thing you might notice is that they don't even agree on calling the skills by the same general title. Harper & Row calls their list "Comprehension Skills," while Scott, Foresman calls their list "Critical Reading and Study Skills," yet both include "Main Idea," "Inference," "Detail," etc. While there are differences in use of terminology, there is general agreement as to the importance of comprehension. Given that general agreement, however, there are different notions as to what constitutes comprehension, and less than perfect agreement as to how it should be taught.

The foregoing lists of subskills for comprehension were taken mostly from primary reading examples, that is, the first three years of elementary school. What about the intermediate grades, which we will loosely define as grades four through six (or even sometimes eight)? Lists of skills for these grades do not differ much from primary lists; however, there might be more emphasis on the so-called higher skills, which are loosely defined as *critical reading*.

Comprehension Skills
  Aims
  Characterization
  Classification and seriation
  Comparison
  Conclusion
  Detail
  Empathy
  Evaluation
  Following directions
  Forecasting
  Foreshadowing
  Generalization
  Inference
  Judgment
  Library and research
  Literary style
  Main idea
  Mental imagery
  Outlining
  Personal reaction
  Previewing
  Recall
  Relationships
    Analogous
    Cause-effect
    Part-whole
    Place-space
    Size
    Time
  Sequence
  Skimming
  Summarizing

Figure 5-2 Comprehension subskills from the Harper and Row *Design For Reading.*

Critical reading places more emphasis on discerning fact from opinion, and even spotting contradictory opinions, than it does on just getting the facts. In critical reading, you can judge an author based on what you know about a subject before you even started reading. Critical reading also helps you to unmask an author's motives so that you can ascertain whether you are getting a cogent argument or a sales pitch. The critical reader should be aware of slanted opinions, instances where facts that don't agree with a point of view are deleted, and hidden motives of the author.

Literary criticism is perhaps even more subtle, because it often involves an individual reader's taste. What pleases one reader might not please another.

Another important upper-level comprehension skill is the ability to *follow directions.* For a young child, this might mean getting a note and locating a hidden piece of candy in the room without asking any assistance. For an older child, it might mean putting together a complicated mechanical toy. Being able to do something directly from written material is indeed a satisfying type of comprehension drill for both the pupil and the teacher. Following directions in printed form might not be the most common

Critical Reading and Study Skills

Recognition of main idea and supporting details
Recognizes main idea of picture, sentence, paragraph, selection
Recognition and use of organization of ideas
Classifies words and information; lists and charts ideas; uses
    lists and charts for purpose of comparison; describes pro-
    cesses; organizes ideas on basis of time or place, by types
    of literature, from different sources
Recognition of story problem and solution
Recognition of elements of plot structure
Recognizes time and place of story action
Recognition of elements of style
Recognizes repetitive refrain, rhyme, personification, flashback,
    foreshadowing, point of view, figurative language
Recognition of characteristics of different types of literature
Recognizes modern fantasy, realistic fiction, informational
    article, folk tale, poetry, fable, essay, drama, biography,
    historical fiction, myth
Recognition of purposes for reading and ways of reading for
    different purposes
Reads to enjoy a story; reads for information; reads to answer
    questions, to verify responses, to check details; reads to
    follow directions; reads orally; rereads for various purposes;
    previews; skims
Recognition of traits and motives of characters
Recognizes emotional reactions, traits, and motives of story
    characters
Recognition of author's delineation of characters
Recognizes delineation of characters through description, con-
    versations, actions, and thoughts
Recognition of author's purpose
Recognizes author's purpose to inform, entertain, explain, or
    persuade
Recognition of illustrator's purpose
Use of ideas gained from reading to make inferences, to make judg-
    ments, to draw conclusions
Recognition and use of reference aids and tools
Uses table of contents, glossary, annotated bibliography, diction-
    ary, encyclopedia, thesaurus, library card catalog
Use of graphic and tabular aids
Uses simple maps (neighborhood, state, national, world), biographi-
    cal time charts)
Location, selection, and evaluation of information from different
    sources for different purposes

Figure 5-3 Comprehension subskills from the Scott, Foresman *Reading Systems*.

type of reading, but it is often essential. Activities from following a recipe to filling out an income tax form are all based on this important reading comprehension skill.

The lists of comprehension skills are based mainly on the experience of the authors in the field, and on their synthesis of other authors' opinions. However, Frederick Davis attempted a more scientific approach to discovering comprehension skills by doing a factor analysis of many types of comprehension items found in reading comprehension tests. He discovered nine "clusters" or groups of items which statistical analysis found to be of a similar type. These clusters, which are also called "variables," are listed in Table 5-1. It is interesting that the list is not greatly different from many of the other lists. You might like to study it carefully, however, as it will give you a little different slant on just what we are talking about when we say "reading comprehension."

Table 5-1 Nine Operational Skills of Comprehension in Reading Among Mature Readers

Variable	Description
1	Word knowledge, as measured by recognition of vocabulary items
2	Ability to select the appropriate meaning for a word or phrase in the light of its particular contextual setting
3	Ability to follow the organization of a passage, and to identify antecedents and find references in the passage
4	Ability to select the main thought of a passage
5	Ability to answer questions which are answered directly in the passage
6	Ability to answer questions which are answered in the passage, but not in the words in which the question is asked
7	Ability to draw inferences from the passage about the content of the passage
8	Ability to recognize the literary devices used in a passage, and to apprehend its tone and mood
9	Ability to determine the writer's purpose, intent, and point of view; i.e., to draw inferences about the author

More formal lists of reading or educational skills are also called *taxonomies*. Probably the best-known general education taxonomy is Bloom's Taxonomy. It attempts to classify most school learning content into two large "domains," the *Cognitive Domain* (thinking) and the *Affective Domain* (feeling). The cognitive domain is further divided into six major sections: knowledge, comprehension, application, analysis, synthesis, and evaluation. These six sections are further subdivided into many subsections, and sample test items for each are given. I have tried to apply these to reading comprehension in my remedial reading text. A better-known effort at building a taxonomy for reading comprehension was done by Thomas Barret. If you are interested in exploring this topic further, see the references at the end of this chapter.

METHODS OF TEACHING

How Do You Teach Comprehension with Basal Readers?

There are probably as many ways to teach comprehension as there are comprehension subskills and creative teachers. The usual way of teaching reading comprehension is to ask questions after the pupil has read the material. The questions may be oral or written.

An example of teaching comprehension during a basal reading lesson can be seen in Figure 5-4. In this figure, which is taken from the *Ginn Reading 720* series, a sample page from the story, "The Elves and the Shoemaker," is shown, together with questions that the teacher can ask to find out if the children understood the story. Unfortunately, all of these questions are rather simple factual questions of the type frequently asked by teachers. Figure 5-5, which tells the teacher how to conduct a discussion at the end of reading the whole story, illustrates a better level of questioning. It might be further noted that the teacher is instructed to ask detailed questions, such as in Figure 5-5, only in the first half of the story on a page-by-page basis. The pupils are then instructed to read the entire second half of the story, five pages, silently, followed by the discussion in Figure 5-5.

Figure 5-4 also provides an example of a *prereading question*. One of the important strategies that a teacher can use in teaching comprehension is to focus the pupil's attention on comprehension. Fortunately, it is at least partially true that pupils tend to learn what we tell them is important. If the teacher is continually telling the pupils that comprehension is important by use of a prequestion, then, again, by use of postquestions, the pupil might begin to get the idea that comprehension is what reading is all about. Some authors call this type of lesson a *Directed Reading Activity* or DRA. Chapter 8 has a more detailed discussion of DRA.

However, not all comprehension instruction is strictly questioning. For example, after the students have completed reading "The Elves and the Shoemaker," the *Reading 720* manual shows the teacher how to have some follow-up seat work using phrases from the story. Figure 5-6 shows what is termed a *classification type lesson*. Another way of looking at it is to call it *phrase comprehension*. But whatever you call it, it certainly involves reading comprehension, and it is typical of the kind of comprehension lesson elementary teachers conduct. Figure 5-7 shows a workbook activity illustrative of those which accompany most basal reading series, with reading comprehension drills.

How Do You Teach Comprehension With Supplementary Materials?

The vast majority of American schools use some type of basal reading system, and *all basals contain a variety of comprehension lessons*. However, most classroom teachers also supplement the basal reading system with some type of comprehension lesson. By far the most common type of lesson is to have the student read a short passage silently and then answer questions about the passage.

These short reading passages and their accompanying questions come in a variety of forms. One of the most common is a small paper bound booklet, such as those in the trusty old *McCall Crabb Standard Test Lessons*, which are a series of booklets that cover the intermediate grades. These booklets were originally published in 1926. but they are still used in many schools. One of their strengths is their gradation—each booklet is assigned an approximate grade level but, within the booklet, each paragraph and set of following questions will yield a grade level score depending on the number of questions the student can answer correctly.

Before Reading

What happens when the little old man opens his shop for the day?

After Reading

How did the people who came into the shop feel about the shoes? What did they give the little old shoemaker? What did the old man do with the money? Why didn't he make more shoes with the leather he bought?

That day people came into the shoemaker's store. They liked the new shoes, and they gave the shoemaker money for them.

Late that day the old man went out to get more leather to make more shoes. When he got back, he didn't have time to make the shoes.

So the shoemaker went to bed.

195

Figure 5-4 Sample pages from the *Ginn Reading 720,* Teachers' Edition. (*Copyright Ginn and Company, a Xerox Company.*)

Discussion of Purposes

Have pupils identify the parts of the story that they particularly enjoyed. Ask if they noticed that anything kept happening over and over, or that any phrase was repeated several times. For example, the occasion and events of the elves' visits are repeated. The elves are rewarded with seven identical pairs of shoes and seven identical coats.

Continue by asking such questions as: Why were the elves called "the helpers"? Why did the elves say they would not return? Were the elves being unkind by not returning? Why not? Have you ever heard about or read about other imaginary little people or animals who were helpers?

Then have pupils suggest reasons for the long-lasting popularity of "The Elves and the Shoemaker." Some individuals may already know the story; ask how they first became familiar with it.

Figure 5-5 Sample pages from the *Ginn Reading 720*, Teachers' Edition. (*Copyright Ginn and Company, a Xerox Company.*)

Comprehension Activity

Specific Objective

On the chalkboard write The logs at the top of one column and The sun at the top of a second column. As you say each of the following words and phrases, have pupils tell you under which heading to place each expression: very, very big, far away, blaze, like a ball of fire, come from trees, give daylight, fell down, for building houses, many.

Then have the children fold a sheet of lined paper in half vertically. At the top of the left column, have them write The elves. At the top of the right column, have them write The shoemaker. List the phrases below on the chalkboard and instruct the children to read each phrase and then write it under the proper heading. Note that sometimes a phrase can be correctly written under either heading and when this occurs, the children may write the phrase under both headings.

lived in a little old house	stayed up all night
liked to make shoes	had no coats
had no money	had no shoes
wanted to get leather	made little shoes
went to bed	thanked the elves
made seven pairs of shoes	thanked the shoemaker
jumped about and sang	were not seen again

Figure 5-6 Sample pages from the *Ginn Reading 720*, Teachers' Edition. (*Copyright Ginn and Company, a Xerox Company.*)

To evaluate ability of pupils to recall story details, distribute copies of the following exercise.

Directions: Pick the words that belong in the blank.

The shoemaker	The elves
Indian boys	One Indian boy
The white horse	The wolf

1. _____ went to bed.
2. _____ fell down into the canyon.
3. _____ made some red shoes.
4. _____ saw the white horse in the sky.
5. _____ wanted to eat the sheep.
6. _____ wanted to run wild in the desert.
7. _____ needed leather for shoes.
8. _____ did not say a thing.
9. _____ are such little people.
10. _____ ride and ride.
11. _____ ate the sheep.

Figure 5-7 Sample pages from the *Ginn Reading 720*, Teachers' Edition. (*Copyright Ginn and Company, a Xerox Company.*)

Another convenient form in which comprehension drills are published is the "kit" or "laboratory" form. One of the most common is the *SRA Laboratory* series, which has a box full of graded passages and accompanying questions, each printed on a folded piece of cardboard (making a four-page pamphlet). The strong feature of the SRA Labs and similar materials is that they have many fine gradations of story difficulty. They are attractively color-coded and have a self-correction feature in that the student is instructed to correct answers after completion of the exercise. There is one SRA Lab (box full of cards and accompanying student record books) for each elementary grade. Other kits cover a grade spread of several grades. The labs are designed so that each child can work at his or her own level; hence, they have a kind of individualization built in. SRA does not have a monopoly on the "lab" or "kit" idea, and there are a number of other interesting boxes full of carefully graded comprehension selections; many of them are listed at the end of this chapter.

As we have seen, there are workbooks written to accompany basal readers which have comprehension drills. However, you should be aware that there are also other series of workbooks designed to teach comprehensions skills that are entirely independent of any series. In other words, they are strictly supplementary or also intended for remedial instruction. Some of these supplementary workbooks also come in printed "ditto master" form—the teacher orders a box full of printed ditto master sheets, each one similar to a workbook page, then duplicates as many copies of the page as needed. This is particularly useful where the teacher wishes to individualize instruction and have just one copy, or a few copies of a particular page, for certain children.

Some of the better known supplemental workbooks are the *McCall Crabb Standard Test Lessons in Reading, The Gates Pearson Reading Exercises, Reading for Meaning, Stone-Grover-Anderson New Practice Readers, The Reader's Digest Reading Skill Builders.* These are all soft-bound general interest elementary level booklets which contain relatively short passages or stories followed by specific and general comprehension questions. A popular comprehension drill series is the Barnell Loft *Specific Skill* series by Richard Boning, which teaches seven skills:

Getting the main idea
Using the context
Following directions
Working with sounds
Drawing conclusions
Getting the facts
Locating the answer

There are six books, Level 1–6, for each of the skills.

Another interesting type of supplementary comprehension lesson can be found in various supplemental reading series, such as the *American Adventure Series, The Deep Sea Adventure Series,* and *The Checkered Flag Series.* These hardcover books come in a variety of reading levels covering the elementary years, and provide stories of high interest for poor readers in upper grades. However, they are used in many regular elementary classrooms. Many have comprehension questions for each chapter or section.

Comprehension Lessons Using Texts of Other Subjects

Though we have been talking about reading materials specifically designed to teach reading comprehension, elementary teachers should not overlook the many excellent comprehension drills in textbooks on other subjects. For example, social studies texts frequently have excellent comprehension questions at the end of various lessons. They are put there to see if the student has mastered the content of the chapter, but from a reading teacher's point of view, they are really comprehension questions.

In fact, use of texts from different subject areas tends to point out slightly different reading comprehension skills desired in different curriculum areas. Science books, for example, require a little different kind of comprehension than do novels. Written problems in arithmetic call for yet another type of reading comprehension.

THE PLACE OF TEACHING COMPREHENSION IN THE SCHOOLS

Educators at all elementary grade levels place a heavy emphasis on the importance of teaching comprehension. In a nationwide survey, Mary Austin, Coleman Morrison, and others found only slightly more emphasis on comprehension in grades 3 through 6 than in grades 1 and 2, but at all levels teachers and supervisors reported "considerable" emphasis on comprehension (see Table 5-2). Furthermore, they found that teaching comprehension is important all the way from first through twelfth grade. You might be interested in what these excellent observers of the reading teaching process had to say about successful reading comprehension teaching:

> First, the teacher herself had in mind definite goals of instruction and provided specific activities to develop specific comprehension skills. Children were led to find central ideas, to note essential details, and to recognize significant relationships among these.
>
> Her questions actually required more extended answers than a simple yes or no. She made certain that questions were worth answering, and then asked them thoughtfully rather than mechanically.
>
> Second, the teacher made certain that reading was associated with concrete or vicarious experiences whenever possible. Believing that the ability to interpret and visualize what is read depends upon previous experiences, she set up activities and visual aids in the classroom. These were supplemented by short trips in the community and group discussions, all of which enabled the children to interpret what they read in the light of their own knowledge. In this way she attempted to bridge the gap between their own experiences and any unfamiliar concepts in their reading material.

Third, schools were providing planned, sequential programs of skills development. Programs to develop comprehension skills systematically from kindergarten on through junior and senior high school levels were seen as part of the movement toward better articulation between elementary and secondary education. A number of school systems already have prepared, or are in the process of preparing, reading and language arts courses of study which extend from pre-first through twelfth grade. Obviously, comprehension skills cannot be learned "once and for all" at any one grade level. (Austin et al.; see below.)

Table 5-2   Relative Amount of Reading Time Devoted to Developing Comprehension Skills by Grades as Reported in 795 Questionnaires

Amount of Time	Percentage of Respondents at Grade Level		
	(1 and 2)	(3 and 4)	(5 and 6)
Considerable	77.0	81.4	80.5
Moderate	17.2	13.1	13.0
Little	2.5	0.6	1.6
None	0.4	0.4	0.3
No answer	2.9	4.5	4.6
Total	100.0	100.0	100.0

Source: The First R, The Harvard Report on Reading in Elementary Schools by Mary C. Austin, Coleman Morrison, Mildred Morrison, Edward Sipay, Ann R. Gutmann, Katherine E. Torrant, and Charles Woodbury. New York: The Macmillan Company, 1963. (The study was sponsored by the Carnegie Corporation.)

Austin and Morrison have also produced their own list of comprehension skills, which is interesting for its brevity and clarity. Read it carefully, as it will give you a good idea of the reading comprehension skills included in the majority of reading comprehension lessons throughout the elementary years:

(1) grasping the general idea of meaning of a passage; (2) interpreting facts accurately; (3) identifying the sequence of ideas and events; (4) reading a conclusion or generalization; (5) following directions; (6) evaluating ideas for relevancy and authenticity; and (7) recognizing the mood, tone, or intent of the author.

Dolch's Comprehension Steps

One of the giants of the reading methods field in the last generation was Edward Dolch at the University of Illinois. He was most famous for the clarity with which he taught remedial teachers, and his book, *A Manual for Remedial Reading* (Garrard Press, 1945), is a classic.

Dolch's steps (methods) in comprehension have an interesting kind of relevance today because they would be appropriate for use with inner city or disadvantaged children, though they were developed for remedial readers. The steps, of course, are of value in regular classrooms as well.

His first step was to develop the ability to *repeat what is read*. In some oral reading situations, a child can read a passage and then be unable to relate what has just been read. An even more discouraging situation occurs when the child reads a passage silently and then cannot repeat, even in parrot fashion, what was written. Because of such problems, Dolch's first concern was to enable simple recall of material just read. If a child failed in his task, he or she was asked to reread the exact same passage. Dolch found, in fact, that in some cases, it might be necessary to repeat the reading, paragraph by paragraph, over and over again. While being kind and not fatiguing a child, the idea of what should be done should be made clear. Sometimes dramatic changes will take place in just a few paragraphs. Dolch advised beginning with short, easy units and then working up to textbooks.

Second, the child should be taught to *select the important things* in the passage. The first step might be called "retelling," and it should not be overemphasized. As the child makes gains in ability to retell, guidance should be provided to enable retelling of the more important things. Adults certainly can't and don't remember everything they read. They select and remember only the most important things. Children should be taught to do likewise. Children of lower learning ability, of course, have difficulty with this type of comprehension, but most can master it to some degree. In any event, it is an important goal of reading instruction toward which the teacher must strive.

Finally, Dolch states that comprehension means *thinking about*. What he means here is that it is the individual's reaction that is one of the most important parts of reading comprehension. Put in modern slang—"Does it turn you on?" A student who

Dolch's comprehension steps include having the child relate what has been read in oral reading. *(Dennis Stock/Magnum Photos)*

can read a book and get excited about space travel or assembling geodesic domes has mastered an important element of comprehension. Two important parts of generating this type of reading excitement are the skill with which a teacher can get a discussion going on the topic and the teacher's knowledge of interesting reading material at the proper level of difficulty.

Develop Comprehension by Practicing Reading

What is the absolutely guaranteed simple way to teach comprehension? "GET CHIL-DREN READING AND KEEP THEM READING." In these seven words, you have the essentials of a developmental reading program. You don't need lists of skills. You don't need workbook pages, boring drill questions, or phonics. What you *do* need is motivation and a good variety of reading materials. Home and school and other children can help with the motivation, and a library can help with the reading materials.

Some imaginative schools engage in a process called USSR, which stands for Uninterrupted Sustained Silent Reading. Every day for half an hour the entire student body of a school reads silently. USSR is not confined to students, however. The principal takes the phone off the hook, the secretary, the nurse, the janitor—everybody reads. The teacher must read; he or she can't correct homework or run the ditto machine. The kids read anything and everything, sprawled on the floor or seated on the radiator, but they must be absolutely quiet and they must read. They can read about tiger taming or horse racing, but usually something lengthy rather than brief blurbs.

While USSR sounds like a simple idea, such processes are not always so easy to pull off. To get all those kids reading requires excellent motivation and, in some instances, subtle discipline. A good knowledge on the part of the teacher about children's reading materials is required. The principal has a monumental job in supplying a good variety of books and in aiding teachers in little spots where the system might tend to break down. Not the least of the principal's efforts might be in defending the teacher and children from outside interruptions. If you start USSR in your school, it might work better at first if you use shorter periods.

In the United States, we are fairly effective in reading instruction. It is hard to get accurate figures, but there is at least some evidence that children are reading better today than ever before. Norms on some nationally standardized reading tests are at a higher level of difficulty now than 20 years ago and 40 years ago, for example. But it is doubtful that we are doing a better job of developing lifetime reading habits. Getting children to read for long periods of time helps to develop this type of habit. And children will not do sustained reading if they do not comprehend. So, get them reading and keep them reading. While other types of reading instruction should be used as well, encouragement and motivation to read, with the provision of a variety of reading materials, is certainly valuable.

SUGGESTED LEARNING ACTIVITIES

1 Take a passage from a subject matter textbook in the middle grades and try to write some comprehension questions using as many of the Davis variables as possible. (See Table 5-1.)

2 Analyze a set of comprehension questions found in a workbook, or other comprehension drill material, using the categories or topics found on one of the lists in this chapter. You might try one of the basal reader lists or the Austin-Morrison list.

3 Observe a teacher conducting a comprehension lesson. What skills are being taught? Is it interesting? What materials were needed?

4 Try teaching your own reading comprehension lesson to one child using Dolch's three steps.

5 Evaluate some commercially prepared material. Are different skills taught in kits, supplemental readers, or comprehension drillbooks?

VOCABULARY AND STUDY TERMS

Reading definition
Oral reading: historical importance
Oral reading: good and bad points
Sentence method
Unit size
Analytic method
Synthetic method
Objective comprehension
Subjective comprehension
Comprehension skills list
Critical reading
Following directions
Davis list of variables
Typical basal comprehension lesson
Typical supplementary comprehension lesson
Kits or laboratories
Comprehension teaching materials
Use of subject matter texts.
Dolch's three comprehension steps
Get a child reading
USSR

LIST OF COMPREHENSION CURRICULUM MATERIALS

Readers Digest Skills Builders; paperback books, cassettes; **1-6**.[1]

Readers' Workshop; Reader's Digest; two kits; **3-9**.

McCall-Crabbs Standard Tests Lesson in Reading; William A. McCall and Liah Mae Crabbs; Teachers College; five paperbound books; **3-7**.

Gates-Peardon Reading Exercises; Arthur I. Gates and Celeste C. Peardon; Teachers College; 13 paperback books; **2-6**.

Lessons For Self Instruction in Basic Reading Skills: Edward Fry, Lawrence Carillo, Grace Carol Bostwick and Miles Midlock; Dreier; 16 program instruction booklets and tests; **3-4**.

[1] Numbers following description indicate approximate grade levels. See appendix for publishers' addresses.

Specific Skills Series: Richard A. Boning; Barnell Loft; 53 booklets; **1–6**.
Read, Study, Think: "My Weekly Readers," Xerox; five paperbound books; **2–6**.
SRA Reading Laboratories; Don H. Parker and Genevieve Scannel; SRA; kits; **1–6**.
Schoolhouse; Comprehension Patterns; SRA; kit; **3–6**.
Reading for Understanding; SRA; kit; **3–8**.
SRA Pilot Library: SRA; kits; **3–9**.
Reading Comprehension Series: Scholastic Books; four paperbound books; **3–6**.
Supportive Reading Skills: Richard A. Boning; Dexter and Westbrook, Ltd.; over 100
    booklets; **1–6**.
Encounters: Reality in Reading and Language Series: Cambridge Book Co.; Eight 96-
    page books; **3–8**.
Mission: Read: Educreative Systems; four kits; **3–8**.
Instructional Fairs Task Force 1–Comprehension and Vocabulary Development Series:
    Donald L. Barnes and Arlene Burgdorf; Instructional Fair Inc.; 14 sets of cards;
    2–8.
Reading with a Purpose: Cornet Instructional Media; 10 cassettes, 30 student response
    books; **4–8**.
Reading Attainment System: Grolier; two kits; **3–6**.
Archie Graphics Reading Kit: Instructional/Communications Technology Inc., (order
    from local dealers); kit comic books; **3.5–5.5**.
Reading Comprehension Activity Cards: Frank Schaffer Publisher; **2–5**.
Programmed Reading Comprehension: John E. George, Ann Bengfort, and Linda
    Prugh; National Tutoring Institute; six books; **1–6**.
Minisystems in Reading: George Bond, Lois Nichols, and George Smith; Modern Cur-
    riculum Press; 78 tapes and activity sheets; **4–7**.
How to Be A Super Sleuth: Minette Gersh and Janet Maker; Crabapple Productions;
    activity cards; **4–6**.
Be a Better Reader: Nila B. Smith; Prentice-Hall; five books; **4–8**.
Sullivan Reading Comprehension System: M. W. Sullivan; Behavior Research Labo-
    ratories; several dozen booklets and materials; **1–6**.

REFERENCES

Amble, Bruce R. "Reading by Phrases." *California Journal of Educational Research*,
    1967, *18*, 116–124.
Auckerman, Robert C. *Approaches to Beginning Reading*. New York: Wiley, 1971.
Austin, Mary C., and Coleman Morrison. *The First R, The Harvard Report on Reading
    in Elementary Schools*. Macmillan, New York, 1963.
Barrett, T. C. "Taxonomy of Cognitive and Affective Dimensions of Reading Com-
    prehension." In H. M. Robinson (Ed.), *Innovation and Change in Reading Instruc-
    tion*. Chicago: University of Chicago Press, 1968. (Sixty-seventh yearbook of the
    National Society for the Study of Education.)
Bloom, B. S., et al. *Taxonomy of Educational Objectives. Handbook 1: Cognitive Do-
    main*. New York: McKay, 1956.
Calder, C. R., and S. D. Zalatimo. "Improving Children's Ability to Follow Directions."
    The Reading Teacher, December 1970, *24*, 227–231.
Cleland, D. L. "A Construct of Comprehension." In J. A. Figurel (Ed.), *Reading and
    Inquiry*. Newark, Del.: International Reading Association, 1965. (Conference
    Proceedings, Vol. 10).

Cleland, Donald L. (Ed.). *Reading and Thinking*. Report of 17th Annual Reading Conference. Pittsburgh; University of Pittsburgh Press, 1961.

Davis, Frederick B. "Fundamental Factors of Comprehension in Reading." *Psychometrica*, 1944, *9*, 185–197.

Davis, Frederick B. "Psychometric Research on Comprehension in Reading." *Reading Research Quarterly*, Summer 1972, *7*, 628–678.

Davis, Frederick B. "Psychometric Research on Comprehension in Reading." In *The Literature of Research in Reading With Emphasis on Models*. East Brunswick, N.J. (Box 372): Iris Corporation, 1971.

Davis, F. B. "Research in Comprehension in Reading." *Reading Research Quarterly*, 1968, *4*, 499–545.

Dawson, Mildred A. (Comp.). *Developing Comprehension Including Critical Reading*. Newark, Del.: International Reading Association, 1968.

Dolch, Edward. *Manual for Remedial Reading*. Champaign, Ill.: Garrard, 1954.

Evans, Howard M., and John C. Towner. "Sustained Silent Reading: Does It Increase Skills?" *The Reading Teacher*, November 1975, *29*(2), 155–163.

Henderson, Richard L., and Donald Ross Green. *Reading for Meaning in the Elementary School*. Englewood Cliffs, N.J.: Prentice-Hall, 1969.

Herber, Harold L., and Joan B. Nelson. "Questioning is Not the Answer." *Journal of Reading*, April 1975, *18*(7), 512–517.

Holmes, J. A., and H. Singer. *Speed and Power of Reading in High School*. Washington, D.C.: U.S. Government Printing Office, 1966. (Cooperative Research Monograph, No. 14.)

Kingston, A. L. "A Conceptual Model of Reading Comprehension." In E. P. Bliesmer and A. J. Kingston (Eds.), *Phases of College and Other Reading Programs*. Milwaukee: National Reading Conference, 1961.

McCracken, Robert A. "Initiating Sustained Silent Reading." *Journal of Reading*, May 1971, *14*(8), 521–525 and 582–583.

Robinson, H. M. "The Major Aspects of Reading." In H. A. Robinson (Ed.), *Reading: Seventy-Five Years of Progress*. Chicago: University of Chicago Press, 1966. (Supplementary Educational Monographs, No. 96.)

Roeder, Harold H., and Nancy Lee. "Twenty-five Teacher-Tested Ways to Encourage Voluntary Reading." *The Reading Teacher*, October 1973, *27*, 48–50.

Russell, David H., *Children's Thinking*. Boston: Ginn, 1956.

Spache, G. D. "What is Comprehension?" In E. P. Bliesmer and R. C. Staiger (Eds.), *Problems, Programs, and Projects in College-Adult Reading*. Milwaukee: National Reading Conference, 1962.

Wheat, Thomas E., and Rose M. Edmond. "The Concept of Comprehension: An Analysis." *Journal of Reading*, April 1975, *18*(7), 523–527.

Part Two

Readiness and Methods

Chapter 6

Readiness:
Tests, Factors, Activities

Reading readiness is an interesting and, as we shall see, a controversial concept. Viewed on the simplest level, the problem with reading readiness occurs somewhere around kindergarten or first grade when the teacher looks at Johnny and says, "Is he ready to learn to read?" This question assumes that there is some point at which Johnny is ready, and that before that point he was not ready. The teacher has been encouraged to think that way because of long-standing practices and some old research studies. In the early 1930s, Carlton Washburn, working in the Winnetka schools, did a study of reading readiness, and determined that a child had to have a mental age of about six and a half years old in order to learn to read. This study helped to establish a nearly universal policy that a child had to be about six years old in order to enter first grade. It is a curious fact that the British—who teach the same language—never heard of that study, and proceed to teach their children to read at age five. The Russians, on the other hand, don't find children ready to read until age seven.

Stanley Wanat, formerly Director of Research for the International Reading Association, has pointed out that there seem to be two basic conceptions of just what reading readiness is. One is the view that it is a series of subskills that the student must have in order to be able to learn to read. These subskills have such names as "visual-motor coordination," "letter recognition," "auditory perception," and a half-dozen or so more, depending on which test you look at or which set of materials you are using. The subskills theory is rather educational in nature in that its followers believe that a child who is not ready can be taught these skills and be made ready by proper education. Many major reading series publishers produce workbooks and teachers' manuals to aid teachers in teaching these subskills.

The opposing view of reading readiness holds that there is no point at which a child is "ready," but rather that reading instruction can begin at almost any age or stage of development, although, of course, older or brighter children will learn faster with less repetition and effort. Proponents of this view also hold that it is necessary to modify the kind of reading instruction based on the age and development of the child. For example, they might hold that the old Washburn study (finding that an age of six and a half was necessary for a child to learn to read) was correct when using the materials and methods which were being used in the Winnetka schools at that time.

Though admittedly a selected sample, I have seen a number of Rutgers graduate students teach their own four-year-olds how to read using Lee Mountain's little book, "How to Teach Reading before First Grade," which will be discussed later. These children had few or no formal "readiness activities."

In a major challenge to the traditional readiness age concept, the Denver schools initiated a large-scale program of teaching kindergarteners to read. They were successful, and there were no ill effects such as emotional problems, vision problems, etc. The early readers were better readers in the primary grades; but by the intermediate grades, there was very little difference between those who learned to read in kindergarten and those who waited until first grade.

There seems to be little point in arguing whether or not a child can learn to read before age six. Dolores Durkin, at the University of Illinois, and other investigators have found plenty of evidence that many children can. One could argue that it is not a good idea because eventually the child learns to read, and there isn't much difference in reading ability by upper elementary for early starters. For example, you might argue that it is not worth the effort to teach reading to younger children. Or, in a similar vein, that it might be better to teach young children something other than reading.

However, despite some controversy over the necessity or utility of the concept, reading readiness is tested and taught in most school districts.

READING READINESS TESTS

Tests designed to determine reading readiness vary considerably in content. For example, in analyzing eight readiness tests, Downing and Thackray found that all eight used a test of visual discrimination, six used tests of vocabulary, three tested motor skills, two used tests of reproduction of patterns and shapes from memory, and two made use of tests of relationships. Others tested ability to recall a story, ability to remember ideas in sequence, pronunciation, rhyming of words, auditory discrimination, handedness (preference for right or left hand), and eyedness.

Five well-known readiness tests are:

Clymer-Barrett Prereading Battery
Gates-MacGinitie Reading Test—Readiness Skills

Harrison-Stroud Reading Readiness Profiles
Metropolitan Readiness Tests
Murphy-Durrell Reading Readiness Analysis

These tests were studied by Robert Rude, and he found the following 12 skills tested:

1 Vocabulary knowledge (child is shown picture and asked "Which thing do we put on?")

2 Listening comprehension (child is read a story and questions are asked)

3 Letter recognition (child is shown a series of letters and asked which letter is B)

4 Numerical concepts (groups of numerals are shown and child is asked which number is three)

5 Visual-motor coordination (a series of dots are shown and child is asked to connect the dots)

6 Rhyming (words are read to the child, who is asked "Do these two words sound alike?")

7 Phoneme correspondence (pairs of pictures are shown and child is asked which pictures begin with the same sound)

8 Rate of learning (child is asked to learn a sample set of words)

9 Sound discrimination (child is asked whether "pin" and "pen" sound alike)

10 Blending sounds together (/f/ and /at/ make what word?)

11 Word reading (mark a written word read by teacher)

12 Visual matching of forms (□ is like 0 △ □)

Though there is apparently some overlapping or similarity in the subskills measured in various reading readiness tests, it is apparent that there is something less than universal agreement as to what skills are necessary in order to learn to read. The Gates-MacGinitie has seven subtests, and the Murphy-Durrell has only three; none has all 12. Some of the 12 skills are not directly related to reading readiness. For example, "number concepts" can be used to test a skill that might be useful, might be related to general intelligence, and might be related to socioeconomic status—but is it necessary for beginning reading?

Incidentally, the number concepts subtests have a relatively high correlation with later success in reading, as does "knowing the alphabet." However, "correlation is not causation." In general, children from middle- or upper-class homes tend to know the alphabet or numbers because they have been taught them or had greater exposure to them than have children from lower-class homes. It may be that socioeconomic status is a major determinant of later reading success, and that merely teaching the child the alphabet won't insure or even help later reading success. There is a high correlation between success in reading and socioeconomic status, as we shall see in Chapter 13.

Figure 6-1 contains some sample items from a readiness test.

Many reading authorities have questioned the predictive validity of reading readiness tests. For example, George and Evelyn Spache (1973) state:

MAKING VISUAL DISCRIMINATIONS
ATTENTION SPAN UNCONTROLLED

Put your finger on the blue box at the top of the page, here.... Draw a line under the word in the little box, just as you did before.... Now, slide your finger along the long box and look at each word. Now, draw a line under one word in the long box that is like the word in the little box....

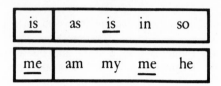

USING THE CONTEXT

9. (**Hold up a copy of the test and point, as you say:**) Point to the green box at the top of the page, here. Find a house, telephone poles, and a fence.... Listen: To get out of the yard, Don's dog had to jump over something. One picture in the box shows what his dog had to jump over. Draw a line under it.... (**Give no further help.**)

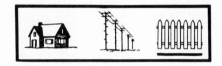

MAKING AUDITORY DISCRIMINATIONS

8. (**When the page has been turned correctly, say:**) Point to the big green box at the top of the page, here. Find a comb, a fork, and a coat.... Draw a line under the comb.... Now, draw a line from the comb to the other thing in the box whose name begins like comb.... (**Give no further help.**)

Figure 6-1 Sample items from the Harrison-Stroud Reading Readiness Profiles, published by the Houghton Mifflin Company.

Most readiness tests do not yield very accurate predictions of later reading success. Their correlations with reading are usually about .50 to .60, a relationship which gives a prediction of 25 to 30 percent better than sheer chance. Is it surprising that careful teacher observations and judgment often yield predictions just as accurate as any readiness test?

Mental Age for Readiness

Some educators have sought to determine readiness by use of an IQ test which yields a single factor of MA, or mental age. This presumably shows a state of total mental development or "capacity to learn." However, IQ tests have the same low predictive validity problems as readiness tests. Note that here we are talking about using IQ tests with children at the kindergarten or first-grade level for the purpose of determining reading readiness. With older children who have been exposed to instruction for a few years, IQ tests have somewhat greater predictive validity. This will be discussed in Chapter 11.

Readiness Teaching Materials

Most basal reading series have reading readiness workbooks and other materials that are scheduled to be used in kindergarten or the beginning of first grade with some or all of the children. Presumably, if they are to be used with only part of the children, these would be the children who had scored low on a readiness test. However, some schools use the materials on all children under the theory that they are useful. Other schools do not use formal (commercial workbook) readiness activities, not finding them necessary or being convinced that the teacher can do the same thing with informal or teacher-designed activities.

As you might suspect, readiness workbooks tend to contain many of the same types of skills found on readiness tests. Some typical listings of readiness skills can be seen in Figures 6-2 and 6-3. These are skills that are found in readiness books that accompany basal reading series. They are taught in consumable and nonconsumable booklets. The consumable booklets are similar to workbooks except, instead of writing words, the children color pictures or make marks such as underlines, circles, or connecting lines to indicate comprehension of the task. The nonconsumable booklet may be hard- or softbound (flexible cover), and it usually has more elaborate use of color. By definition, these are not to be written in or marked by the child so that they can be used several years by different students.

The teacher's manual is probably even more important for the readiness books than for the regular reading books, as a heavy burden of instruction is carried by the teacher. The teacher's manual contains stories to be read to the class or a smaller group, directions on how the child should mark the consumable workbooks, objectives of the lesson (such as discriminating between shapes), and auditory exercises in which the teacher calls out pairs of similar or dissimilar words.

Occasionally, beginning teachers have trouble distinguishing readiness books from preprimers since they both are usually small softbound booklets with colorful covers and vague titles. However, there is an important distinction that is apparent as soon

Level 1 (Readiness)

WORD RECOGNITION

Develop ability to recognize names, forms, and sounds of letters and to match names and forms with their sounds.
Develop ability to discriminate between initial sounds.
Develop perception of rhyme.
Recognize the schwa sound as heard in the word a.
Practice visual discrimination among various objects and letter forms.
Develop ability to match letters to initial sounds in words.
Work with the inflectional ending s to form plurals.

WORD MEANING

Learn to recognize a few words:
   a, can, I, like, little, Mom, my, play, school, see.
Practice completing sentences through identification of pictures.

STUDY SKILLS

Work with alphabetical order and simple categorizing activities.

LITERARY APPRECIATION

Discuss pictures, poems, and stories.

INTERPRETATION

Learn left-to-right progression in reading and writing.
Recognize and work with capital and lowercase letters and punctuation.
Develop listening skills, noting the effect of intonation.
Develop ability to recognize words and sentences through picture clues.
Practice completing sentences and rhymes and develop a basic recognition of sequential order.

CRITICAL THINKING

Develop ability to think logically and interpretively.
Recognize that many words have opposites.

LANGUAGE DEVELOPMENT

Practice telling stories and giving descriptions.
Work with simple sentence, poem, and story composition.

Figure 6-2 A list of readiness skills in the *Young America Basic Reading Program*, authored by Leo Fay and others. (*Lyons and Carnahan and Rand McNally.*)

LEVEL	ORAL LANGUAGE EXPERIENCES	THINKING PROCESSES	COMPREHENSION

READINESS:
LET'S LOOK
WORDS TO READ
Pictures to Read
Informal Reading Readiness
Teacher's Guide
3 Paperback Poetry Books:
  Poems and Verses to Begin on
  Poems and Verses about Animals
  Poems and Verses about the City
	Telling about personal experiences
	Listening to poetry and literature
	Playing language games
	Naming objects
	Dramatizing
	Following spoken directions
	Auditory perception of:
	  rhyming words
	  initial consonants (6)
	  endings: -s, -er, -ing
		Classification of pictured objects
		Sequence with pictures
		Awareness of words and their functions of naming and describing
		Interpretation of photographs	

STUDY SKILLS	PHONIC ANALYSIS	STRUCTURAL ANALYSIS	SIGHT WORD RECOGNITION
Turning page Top to bottom progression			Visual discrimination of forms and shapes Visual and kinesthetic discrimination of forms, shapes, letters, words Matching forms, shapes, letters, words Left to right progression 10 sight words

Figure 6-3 A list of readiness skills from the *Scope and Sequence Chart* of the *Chandler Reading Program*, authored by Lawrence W. Carrillo and published by Noble and Noble.

as you open the book and look at several pages—readiness books do not contain any words, while preprimers contain short stories to be read by the child. There is a slight exception to this "no-words" rule for distinguishing readiness books—a few of them do use words for discrimination exercises (that is, the child is asked to tell whether two words are the same or different)—hence the readiness book might have some words in it, but these are not for the purpose of having the child read them.

There are numerous supplementary readiness materials that are either related or unrelated to the basal series. These include listening records, all picture trade books, blocks and cards for design building, filmstrip stories, and anthologies of children's stories to be read by the teacher to the children. Figure 6-4 shows part of a sequencing exercise from a classroom newspaper which, besides teaching the concept of story sequence and beginning numbering, can be used for oral discussions (which most teachers deem an important part of the readiness program).

Television shows, such as "Sesame Street," also provide supplementary readiness and beginning reading lessons that are used both in the home and in school. Children's Television Workshop issues teachers' manuals that suggest preparation and follow-up activities for telecast "Sesame Street" program series. Information on how to get these manuals can be obtained from your local broadcasting station.

FACTORS AND ACTIVITIES

Vision

One of the factors frequently mentioned in readiness tests, materials, and lessons, is vision and various associated terms, such as *visual discrimination.*

It is important to distinguish between visual acuity and visual perception. *Visual acuity* is purely a physical phenomenon. Technically, it can be defined as getting a clear image on the retina (the lining of the inner eyeball). If a child does not have good visual acuity, the common remedy is glasses (corrective lenses).

Visual perception involves use of the brain for reaction and interpretation of the visual image. We perceive a girl to be pretty, a thundercloud threatening, or—in certain situations—we perceive two lines to be of unequal length when in fact they are exactly the same.

The test for *visual acuity* is frequently conducted by the school nurse, in the form of a Snellen Chart or a telebinocular. The *Snellen Chart* is the typical eye examination chart with the large letters on top and subsequent lines of letters decreasing in size. Each eye is tested separately at a distance of 20 feet. This tests for acuity at far point. If a lens is added, it can also be used as a screening for problems at near point. Far-point vision is used when a child looks at the chalkboard, and near-point vision in reading a book. The *telebinocular* and similar devices contain stereoscopic lenses, screen at both far point and near point, and screen for binocular coordination.

Notice that the word "screen" is used. These tests are not the same as eye examinations done by a physician or an optometrist; rather, they are gross measures used to refer a child for a more thorough examination which, incidentally, does not always result in the child being given glasses.

Visual Discrimination—Sequencing, Numbering Pictures in Order. Direct children to look at the pictures. Say: *What is the bear doing in the first picture? in the second? in the third? Look at the pictures again. If you were numbering these pictures in order, which picture would come first? Print the numeral 1 in the circle in the first picture. Which picture would come next? Print the numeral 2 in the circle in the second picture. Which picture would come last? Print the numeral 3 in the circle in that picture.* Let pupils learn to tell each picture story in sequence.

Figure 6-4 Sample reading readiness exercise from a school newspaper. (*From* "My Weekly Reader: The Children's Newspaper," *Edition 1, Volume 53, Issue 3, September 24, 1975, Xerox, Education Publications, Columbus, Ohio.*)

Visual acuity screening might be considered an important first step before beginning reading instruction. Some schools routinely do this. Unfortunately, some schools do not; they wait until a teacher refers a child for apparent vision problems. Teachers are not good at picking out vision problems, so a screening of all children is recommended.

Whether or not a screening examination is given, here are some signs of poor vision that the teacher should watch for:

Squinting
Holding the book abnormally close
Redness in one or both eyes
Closing one eye
Rubbing eyes
Having to get closer to the chart or board
Avoiding any kind of task requiring near-point vision

If any of these signs is observed over a continuing period, referral should be made to the school nurse or a vision specialist.

Another area of vision which can cause problems is poor *binocular coordination*. This can be detected by a telebinocular or other screening test. Such a condition results in one eye turning in or out either all the time or part of the time (when tired, for example). This type of problem can cause a disinterest in any near-point task, including reading. It can often be corrected by a vision specialist by surgery, by corrective lenses, or by eye exercises. Note that we are talking about eye exercises for binocular coordination problems only, not acuity problems. Incidentally, cross-eyedness (no binocular coordination) or one-eyedness (blind in one eye) are not vision problems that affect reading. A constantly cross-eyed child, or a child blind in one eye, can learn to read as easily as a child without these handicaps. However, partial sight or a tendency toward cross-eyedness can cause a reading problem.

Visual perception is another vast area which involves use of the brain in interpreting, using, understanding, selecting, and—in some fashion—dealing with visual images. It is very doubtful that there is such a thing as generalized perception training, or that training perception in one area results in improved perception in another area. In terms of readiness, this means that it is highly questionable that teaching children to discriminate between a square and a triangle will help them to discriminate between an "A" and a "B." Learning tends to be specific; and if you want them to know the difference between an "A" and a "B," then you should give them some "A" versus "B" lessons. Better yet, teach words, and teach them the difference between "apple" and "banana." Then they will really be learning visual symbols that are used in reading.

Visual discrimination is a term used in many readiness tests and materials. It almost always refers to perception rather than acuity. Visual discrimination tasks ask the child to pick out similar and dissimilar abstract shapes or realistic objects.

Another visual skill sometimes taught in readiness programs is *left-to-right progression*. The theory behind these types of exercises is that, since the eye must move from left to right along a line of print when reading, left-to-right training is a necessary prereading skill. There seems to be little evidence for this, and there are many cases of children receiving none of this type of training who start reading with no harmful effects.

Hand-eye coordination is another skill sometimes tested and taught. Children are taught to connect rows of dots, or numbered dots, or complete geometric figures. It is doubtful if normal children need this. Such exercises may be useful for brain-damaged children; but, with normal children, the training can be more specifically related to reading by teaching them to write words.

Eye movements during reading can easily be observed by simply looking at a person's eyes. The eye makes a number of short stops or *fixations* while moving along a line of print. Children in first grade make about two fixations per word, while high school seniors and adults make a little less than one fixation per word. There is a steady progression from grade to grade. As the person learns to read, the number of fixations decreases. Occasionally, the eyes make a backward movement or *regression* while looking again at a word, and this is normal, especially if the word is unfamiliar. At the end of a line of print, there is a large return sweep to the beginning of the next line. There are some audiovisual devices such as tachistoscopes (flash exposure devices) and controlled reading devices which purport to train eye movements. These devices often increase motivation and may be interesting ways to present reading material, but it is doubtful they can train eye movements while reading, and most reading authorities consider eye-movement training unnecessary.

Hearing

In hearing, a receptive sense like vision, there is also a distinction between acuity and perception.

Hearing acuity is the ability to know if a particular sound exists. The test for acuity is usually a pure tone audiometer. This is an electronic device that generates a sound in a particular frequency (pitch) at varying degrees of loudness. For example, using earphones in a quiet room, a person with normal hearing should be able to hear a low note of 125 cycles per second at the loudness of 10 decibels. If the sound has to be made louder, say to 20 or 30 decibels, before it can be heard, it is likely that there is hearing loss or partial deafness.

Inability to hear the sound at any reasonable loudness would be called "deafness" in that frequency. If the inability persisted throughout most of the range of pitches covering the human speech range (from 100 up to approximately 8,000 cycles per second), then the child would be unable to hear or understand speech. If a child never hears speech except with special training, he or she never learns to talk, a condition that is sometimes called "dumbness." In the old days, many persons were "deaf and dumb" (could neither hear nor speak); but with special modern techniques, many deaf and partially deaf persons are taught to speak, and—if not hear with a hearing aid—at least learn to lip-read.

Even a partial hearing loss in the speech range can cause both speech problems and hearing problems. Slurred speech or inappropriate tone (speaking too loud) is often a sign of hearing loss. Hearing problems also cause inattentiveness of students in school because they either can't hear or get tired of straining to hear. Some letter sounds, like the /s/, for example, are high-frequency sounds; if they are never heard, they are not included in the person's speech. This also causes trouble with phonics lessons.

It is a good idea to have the hearing of every child checked before beginning reading instruction. If for some reason this isn't or can't be done, then referrals should be made if hearing loss is suspected. Sometimes the school nurse gives hearing tests, and sometimes it is the speech correctionist. Most speech correctionists are trained in audiometry (hearing testing) because of the close relationship between speech problems and hearing problems. Speech problems are often caused by a hearing loss.

Auditory perception involves interpretation, understanding, or use of the sound. Perception involves thinking and memory. I can hear someone speak Chinese, but I can't perceive what he or she is saying; I can't understand Chinese; I have no bank of memory cells filled with auditory Chinese words against which to compare the sounds that I am hearing; I have no meaning associated with the sounds; and I would even have trouble distinguishing between some Chinese words because my auditory perception is trained for English.

Reading readiness tests and teaching materials sometimes have subskill areas in auditory perception. Students might be asked if they hear the same sound at the beginning of "pill" and "Bill." Seen as a possible prephonics lesson, this might have a touch of merit; but, like vision perception training, it is not certain that this is a necessary subskill for reading or that there is any generalization of auditory training between /p/ and /b/ and any other phoneme pair. In other words, it is highly doubtful that it is possible to train a general skill called "auditory perception." You can train a child that "sit" and "bit" are two different words, but unless he or she comes from an abnormally poor or foreign background, he or she will already know that. Since first-grade children are still learning to speak and listen to different words, both pronunciation and listening confusions regularly occur. This may be due not to poor auditory perception, but simply to the fact that language skills are not fully developed. Hence elementary teachers at all levels need to help children pronounce new and unfamiliar words, and they need to help them hear distinctions between similar sounding words; but this is language learning rather than training in auditory perception.

No matter how much you train a child to understand English phonemes, he or she will have trouble with perceiving Chinese phonemes because auditory perception is cultural rather than general. Incidentally, this is one of the problems with children who learn to speak English as a second language; if the phoneme is not used in their native language, they have much trouble saying and hearing it is English. Spanish does not have the phoneme /j/, which causes characteristic problems with Spanish-speaking children. German-speaking children would have other phoneme problems, but not /j/. The Japanese language does not contain the /w/ sound, so it is quite possible for a child to have perfectly normal auditory perception in Japan yet have problems on moving to America.

Listening Comprehension

Listening comprehension, which is sometimes called *auding,* is a skill which involves the comprehension of language. It might be likened to reading comprehension. In fact, the subskills of auding are nearly the same as for reading comprehension: getting the main idea, noting sequence, remembering details, critical listening, discerning fact from opinion, etc. Testing or drilling in listening comprehension usually involves listening to a passage, then answering verbal or written questions about it. Auding obviously involves both auditory acuity and auditory perception.

Listening comprehension is often taught throughout the elementary and, sometimes, high school years, but it is included in some reading readiness programs. It is an important communication skill that certainly can't be mastered at the prereading stage, but it may be beneficial to start there. Like reading comprehension, it involves "thinking," knowledge of the subject, intelligence, sensitivity, and experience. In fact, good listening—like good reading comprehension—really involves the total educational process. To be able to really understand a politician's speech might require a college course in economics plus a good knowledge of world affairs and domestic politics. It might also involve subjective feelings about whether the speaker is stretching the truth, whether proposals are realistic, and whether only one side of the story is being told to unduly influence the unsuspecting.

Language Activities

All readiness programs include various language activities. Listening comprehension might be one of them (readiness teachers usually take a less formal approach, and talk about story-telling time—when they read stories to the children and often discuss the story with them). Another language activity involves having the children tell stories. The children's stories might be their own creations, or they might be based on memory of a story told to them or a TV program they saw. This is an important language arts exercise; and since all the language arts are interrelated, it is undoubtedly beneficial.

Kindergarten and primary teachers often have a large number of language activities, including plays, listening games, telephone use lessons, language experience charts, show and tell (where the pupil brings something from home and tells the class about it), and discussions and plans for a school day or a trip. Language activities include teaching the children something about literature, both contemporary and classic. Poetry can be fun, and it can teach a lot about rhyming (see Figure 6-5).

Speech

Language readiness activities also involve helping the child to use proper forms of expression. Just what is proper has been examined recently with the many discussions about "black dialect." Linguists tell us that all of us speak a dialect: Southern, Western, Great American, New England, etc. They tell us that all are adequate forms for expression. They are all equally complex (including black dialect). However, a dialect means that there is mutual intelligibility; that is, a speaker of one dialect can understand another dialect with very little effort. Students with the heaviest black dialect don't have any trouble understanding most TV programs. Whether a teacher wishes to try to change a child's dialect is partly a cultural and social value problem.

Incidentally, most written English is a dialect (nobody really speaks that way unless reading from a text) so everybody learns to read a dialect different from what he speaks. If you doubt this, try tape-recording one of your lessons or one of your professors. When you type it up word-for-word, you will see that it doesn't come out in sentences that would be "proper" for written English. If it is a less formal situation,

A dog asked a snake who seemed chummy
If, when crawling, he got his chin crummy.
Said the snake, looking sad,
"On the chin it's not bad,
But it's terribly rough on the tummy."

— Edward S. Mullins

Figure 6-5 Listening drills can be a lot of fun if you select the right material. (*From Limericks by Irving Wasserman, published by Houghton Mifflin Company, Boston. This limerick is also in their Listening Library. It was originally published by Platt and Munk Publishers in* The Big Book of Limericks *by Edward S. Mullins.*)

say a phone conversation with a friend, the syntax difference is even greater, and vocabulary use is notably different.

Dialect should not be confused with speech problems. The most common speech problems with young children are the *articulatory disorders* or delayed development, such as the inability to make certain phonemes ("Gi*b* it to me" or What *f*ing?") either all or some of the time. Speech development specialists tell us that it takes until age six before certain speech sounds (some blends such as sl- or -nd) are made by 75 percent of the children, and there is a host of sounds that usually aren't made until age five. For students just a little slow in speech development, there are many deficient speech sounds evident in the primary years. Usually the classroom teacher or an alert parent can correct these by calling attention to them. If the teacher wishes to be even more helpful, some simple pronunciation tests and follow-up training can be given to the children. One training technique is to have the teacher and child both face a mirror and have the child watch the position of the lips and the placement of the tongue of the teacher and himself. Another activity done by some kindergarten and primary teachers is to have the child learn poems or sayings which include the defective speech sound. Extreme caution should be exercised so that, by calling the child's attention to defective pronunciation, you are not opening up a cause for ridicule by other pupils.

Stuttering and stammering are speech-flow problems and are best left to the speech correctionist. The best thing that the classroom teacher can do is to ignore the difficulty and not place the child in situations where the stuttering can cause embarrassment. If left alone, these problems will often disappear, but a trained speech correctionist should be consulted.

Though phoneme production is not always complete by entering-school ages, it is a remarkable fact that syntactic development is fairly complete. Children who have not yet learned to read are able to handle surprisingly complete sentences, conditionals, subordinate clauses, conjunctions, etc. That is, they can usually understand complex sentences when spoken, and often use them in speech. A study by Wendel Johnson shows that at age five, 25 percent of the children cannot pronounce eight relatively common phonemes; and at age six, 25 percent of the children cannot pronounce the /j/ sound in the final position. Most consonant blends (beginning and ending) cause trouble for 25 percent of the five-year-olds, and some blends even cause trouble for six-year-olds. Teachers should not be alarmed when they discover incomplete phoneme production in young children, as it is normal in a large percent of children; however, they should gently try to help the child to pronounce and hear phonemes that are not being used properly.

Both speaking and listening vocabularies continue to grow through the educational years. Teaching about word meaning is a process that can well begin at the readiness stage. However, poor vocabulary development should not be a cause for withholding reading instruction. While children with better speaking vocabularies probably learn to read more easily, there are a number of other factors—such as motivation, peer values, and physical health—which enhance such students' reading abilities. In any case, teachers should encourage vocabulary development from kindergarten right through graduate school.

Table 6-1 Earliest Age at Which 75 Percent of Children Correctly Use Phonemes

Age 5	
Phoneme	**Example**
v	*v*oice
th (voiced)	*th*is
th (voiceless)	*th*ing
s	*s*at
z	i*s*
sh	*sh*oe
zh	gara*g*e
ch	*ch*air
Age 6	
j	jud*ge*

Source: Based on Wendel Johnson's *Diagnostic Methods in Special Pathology*. New York: Harper & Row, 1963.

Socialization

One of the factors sometimes taken into account by teachers in judging whether or not a child is "ready" to learn to read is a factor called *socialization.* This means how well the child interacts with other humans or institutions and fits into the classroom. Some children arrive at school shy and withdrawn, afraid to open their mouths or express themselves even in drawing. Others come to school confident and expressive. Still others are used to being the center of attention in a permissive home; they don't see why they can't talk anytime they feel like it, or why they can't get up and run around when the urge hits them. Some kindergarten teachers think one of the main benefits of kindergarten is to teach children how to behave in school; to draw out the shy ones, and to corral the wild ones.

Beyond general deportment, socialization might include such skills as using pencil, paper, and crayons, handling books, and developing a longer attention span for such activities as story listening and getting along with classmates.

Some teachers would call children who are low in socialization "immature," and not ready to read. In extreme cases, they force such children to repeat kindergarten and prolong the "readiness" period or put them into a "junior first grade" in which reading instruction is delayed up to a half a year or more.

There is not much concrete evidence that delaying reading instruction for socially immature children helps them learn to read any better; it may, in fact, hold them back. Many first-grade teachers have found both extremely shy and obstreperous children in their top reading group. There are, of course, children who have emotional problems; in these cases, the school psychologist can perhaps help more than some extra work in a readiness workbook.

In 1963, Austin and Morrison, in a survey of reading practices, found that over a quarter of the school systems in the United States did not have kindergartens; so the need for socialization and other kindergarten-type activities is not universally recognized as necessary. This same trend has continued. For example, more recent evidence from the National Center for Education statistics shows that during the school year 1972-1973 there were 2,552,000 children in kindergarten; and the next year, 1973-1974, there were 3,407,000 children in first grade. In other words, 25 percent of the first-graders did not go to kindergarten.

Parent Help

In the 1930s, 1940s, and 1950s, the attitude of the educational profession toward parental involvement in teaching children seems to have been "hands off." "Let us educate the child; above all, don't do any formal instruction like teaching him or her how to read." In the 1960s and 1970s, the attitude seems to be swinging completely around to one recognizing the need for help at home. Parents are being told by teachers how to help their child with both reading readiness skills and actual reading skills. This is an interesting development in light of education practices in Colonial America, when some schools would not accept children who hadn't already learned to read at home.

Almost all educators *encourage parents to read stories* to their children. This has a number of benefits, such as getting children interested in stories, showing the association between the printed words and a story, and developing auding or listening comprehension.

Parents can have an important impact on their children's reading skills. (*Burk Uzzle/Magnum*)

There are a number of books on the market to help the parent who wants to teach reading to a preschooler (see Figure 6-6). Here are some excerpts from one of them in case you wonder how such an approach begins:

To start the first step of early reading instruction all you need are some unlined three-by-five cards and a black crayon or felt-tip pen. Write the word *Mommy* on one of the cards . . . say to the child, "What do you call me?" . . . Then say, "Yes, I am Mommy, and this is the word *Mommy*" as you put the card around your neck. Have your child look at the word, touch the card, and repeat *Mommy* after you . . . reward the child with praise when he looks at the card and repeats *Mommy* . . . when your teaching begins to take, move on to the second word, *Daddy* . . . .

In this first story book you will use only the words that your preschooler can already read—the words *Mommy, Daddy, telephones,* and the child's own name. To make this first book, staple or tie together five sheets of paper . . . On the next three pages of the book, print in letters at least half-an-inch high these three sentences, one sentence to a page:

Mommy telephones Daddy.

Daddy telephones _____
                    (child's name)

_____ telephones Mommy.
    (child's name)

Figure 6-6   Illustration from a parents' book on teaching reading to young children. (*Source:* How to Teach Reading Before First Grade *by Lee Mountain, Dreier Educational Systems, Highland Park, New Jersey.*)

The book then goes on to how to develop longer stories, simple phonics games, building a sign-word vocabulary, using games to teach, and library use.

Background Experiences

Background experiences provide a reality base for the somewhat abstract symbols of written and spoken language. For example, if the students are going to hear (or, later on, read) a story about frogs, a pet frog brought to class or a walk to a nearby pond will provide background experience.

Not all parents are willing to go so far into reading instruction, but most will help the whole readiness process by giving their children special background experiences. Schools also frequently provide special background experiences for kindergarten and primary children.

Trips of all kinds add a measure of reality to stories and later reading: walking trips to the fire station, bus trips to the zoo, and parent-conducted trips to nearby cities. There are all sorts of things children need to see and experience; city children need to see farms, and rural children need to see cities. Most children need to see museums, ballets, factories, ships, and airplanes.

There are many experiences to be gained around the home or school. Children need to learn to handle tools, cook, care for animals, grow things, sew, and perhaps decorate their own room or corner. With only a little imagination, each of these can be a real learning activity, and with slightly more imagination, the child can be shown how reading can enrich, foster, or develop each of these activities. Letting the child see that the radish seeds do sprout in the number of days printed on the back of the seed package might be an excellent prereading lesson. Such things as this develop a thirst for wanting to know how to read.

Alphabet Learning

The idea that a child should learn the alphabet before beginning reading instruction has been around so long that its origin is obscure. It was prevalent in Roman times, and the hornbooks used by the American colonists stressed learning the alphabet as a prerequisite to reading. Modern reading specialists like Donald Durrell have stressed the importance of learning the alphabet because alphabet knowledge skill on readiness tests correlates relatively well with later reading achievement. Toys for preschoolers frequently contain alphabet learning or familiarization. Traditional children's building blocks contain the alphabet as do many other young children's coloring books and play materials.

However, despite the common sense of learning the letters before learning words, there are many children who learn to read without knowing the alphabet; in fact, this happens in every first grade every year. Apparently the only people who do not believe this have never spent much time in a first grade as an observer. Parents are sometimes horrified that their child can read a whole preprimer and still not be able to name all the letters of the alphabet. Apparently what is "common sense" to adults is not always common sense to children.

Learning the alphabet before learning to read is unlikely to be harmful in any way as long as it is taught in an interesting fashion and doesn't foster a dislike for things academic. However, it obviously isn't a necessity to know the alphabet before learning to read. At present, many children learn much of the alphabet before entering school by watching educational TV programs such as "Sesame Street."

Handwriting In most schools the alphabet is really taught during handwriting lessons, and this is an excellent place for such learning to occur. In teaching formation of each letter, the teacher talks with the child about it. Attention is focused on the individual letters. Letters are added together to form words; thus, spelling lessons, which are necessarily letter-by-letter, are begun. Reading is not necessarily a letter-by-letter process. Eye movement studies show that even the youngest readers' eyes do not focus (fixate) on each letter; they make fixations every several letters or, on the average, about twice per word for beginning readers.

At the readiness level of school instruction, drawing pictures or copying geometric shapes is often taught to enhance readiness for handwriting. But many teachers start directly to teach the child to write letters, believing that this encompasses such things as hand-eye coordination, small motor skills development, visual discrimination, and, last but not least, letter learning. This view of teaching the readiness-level child to write letters goes along with the "specific learning" theory: That is, if you want a child to learn to draw triangles, you provide for practice in drawing triangles; but if you want the student to learn to write letters, you teach him or her to write letters. Learning studies provide the evidence that it is more efficient to teach directly what you want the person to know.

At the readiness level of instruction, many teachers start directly teaching children to write letters. (*Mike Q/Coronet Studios*)

Physical Health

Though it is not often mentioned as a readiness factor, general physical health is an important factor in learning efficiency. Sick children and malnourished children are not good learners. It takes effort to learn. Awareness and attention span are related to good health. In extreme cases of malnutrition—such as are found where famine exists and, unfortunately, in a few poverty areas of the United States—irreparable brain damage occurs. There is some evidence that poor nutrition (bad diet) can cause school learning problems. Some United States schools have found it beneficial to give children food in the morning, and again at lunchtime.

Exercise is important to growing bodies (or bodies of any age, for that matter); hence, physical education, if not considered a readiness activity, is an area which should not be neglected, either formally or informally, with children of any age.

Health education, including nutrition education, is not a strong subject in most schools; but a few schools are developing this important area. Many schools are not reluctant to send home homework for the child, or to suggest learning experiences for the parent to give the child, but they are somehow reluctant to inform the parent about good health practices which may have an effect on such things as learning to read.

SUMMARY AND CONCLUSIONS

The readiness concept is controversial. There are widely divided opinions on the use of readiness tests, on the use of readiness materials, on the skills that can be taught, on the skills that are necessary, and on the age at which reading should begin.

Those who favor the use of tests feel that there is some point at which a child is ready to learn to read, and that tests help to determine this point. However, advocates of readiness tests also attach importance to such information as the teacher's opinion on socialization or general maturity of the child. Those opposed to the use of readiness tests feel that there is no particular point at which is child is "ready," but that reading instruction can begin at most any age if the teacher is willing to modify teaching techniques and is willing to accept slow progress from very young or immature children. However, not all of the nontesters would argue in favor of teaching reading early (at some point prior to first grade), despite evidence that it can be done.

Readiness test users by and large feel that there are certain subskills that should be taught as part of the readiness program, and these subskills are often reflected in the reading materials of basal reading programs. However, there is considerable disagreement as to which subskills are important, and poor agreement among major reading readiness tests as to which subskills should be included. Some authorities also question the predictive validity of readiness tests.

On the more positive side, most educators would favor improving all of the language arts skills, such as listening to stories or even the more formal auding (listening comprehension), and approve of the benefits of developing oral expression.

Enriching the child's background experience is also noncontroversial. Parent help is seen as helpful—and perhaps essential—in the general education and physical health areas.

However, disagreement seems to arise over the benefits of testing or teaching auditory and visual perception factors. Most would agree as to the importance of visual and auditory acuity. However, those favoring perception often do not test for acuity. Likewise, there seems to be dispute over the necessity of testing or teaching the alphabet and various motor skills such as left-to-right progression or visual-motor coordination. Advocates of these controversial areas feel that they are necessary sub-skills, and, when properly developed, make the teaching of reading easier or more successful. Opponents feel that they are unnecessary and that other things should be done. What other things? Well, you could teach reading or you could teach Spanish, or mathematical concepts, or social studies experiences, or geography, or botany, or quite a few other things that young children don't know. It is possible that our kindergartens and primary grades overemphasize reading readiness and reading activities to the exclusion of other subject areas.

The age at which to begin reading instruction is similarly controversial. Those in favor of early reading point out that it gives greater reading achievement at least in the early years of elementary school. Those in favor of delaying reading instruction until first grade, or even the latter part of first grade, claim that by intermediate grades the children catch up anyhow, and that, by starting early, too much pressure is put on the child, which can harm overall development.

Perhaps a result of these many conflicts about the importance of readiness can be seen in the statistics which show that approximately 25 percent of the children in United States public schools do not attend kindergarten but start right in with first grade.

SUGGESTED LEARNING ACTIVITIES

1 Write out a list of some imaginative and creative "background experiences" suitable for a child in kindergarten or first grade.

2 Observe a kindergarten or the first part of first grade where some reading readiness activities are in progress. How many different skills or concepts can you see being trained? Refer to the skills lists in this chapter for both tests and basal series.

3 Give yourself a reading readiness test. Get a copy of a readiness test and the examiners manual, in a school or in a college curriculum library, and administer the test to yourself item by item so that you can see what the child experiences and how the scoring process operates.

4 Start to build up a file of interesting listening experiences. You should include listening discrimination, auding (listening comprehension), interesting stories, poems, and samples of writing that can be used for enrichment or class discussion. You can make the file on cards for easy reference. Put on each card how to conduct the lesson, sample material, and references to commercial material. You can get ideas from reading methods texts, teachers' manuals of basal series, supplementary materials, and observing and talking with other teachers.

5 Watch the school nurse or other specialized personnel give a vision test and a hearing test.

VOCABULARY AND STUDY TERMS

Age for readiness
  U.S.–Winetka
  British
  Russian
Readiness is subskills
Readiness is related to method
Kindergarten reading in Denver
Readiness tests
  Subtests include:
    Visual discrimination (matching); vocabulary; motor skills; reproduction of patterns; memory; pronunciation; rhyming; auditory discrimination; listening comprehension; letter recognition; numerical concepts; visual-motor coordination; phoneme correspondence; rate of learning; sound discrimination; blending; word reading
Mental age as predictor
Readiness Materials
  Workbooks, TV (Sesame Street), story anthologies, blocks and manipulative materials, records, filmstrips, picture books
Visual perception
Visual acuity
  Snellen chart
  Telebinocular
  "Screen"
  Signs of poor vision

Binocular Coordination
  Crosseyedness
Visual dscrimination
Hand–eye coordination
Eye movements
  Fixation
  Regression
  Tachistoscopes
Hearing
  Hearing acuity
    Audiometer
    "Deaf and dumb"
    "Hearing loss (effect on speech)
  Auditory perception
Auding
Language activities
  Listen and tell stories
Speech
  Dialect
  Articulatory disorders
  Stuttering and stammering
Socialization
  No kindergarten
Parent help
  Read stories
  Teach reading
Background experiences
Alphabet learning
Handwriting
Physical Health

LIST OF READING READINESS CURRICULM MATERIALS

NOTE: Most basal series listed at the end of Chapter 7 also have reading readiness materials. You can determine this by looking at the "level" and if there is a "K" it means readiness materials are included.

Dolch Readiness Materials: Edward Dolch; Garrard; workbooks, book, game, pad, cards; **K-1**.
Sesame Street Pre-Reading Kit: Shirley C. Feldmann, Elisha J. Bartlett, Linda Lerner, and Linda Roberts; Addison Wesley; kit books, cassettes, filmstrips, games; **K-1**.

(NOTE: Information on where to get lesson plans for Sesame Street TV programs can be obtained through the station doing the broadcasting. Children's Television Workshop is the publisher of those materials, not Addison Wesley.)

Early Learning Modules: Reader's Digest: kits, blocks, cards, charts, books; **K**.

First Step to Reading—Second Step to Reading: Xerox; books; **K-1**.

Zips Readiness Program: Xerox; books; **K**.

Reading Readiness: Ethel S. Maney; Continental Press; spirit masters; **K**.

Rhythm to Reading: Lucille Wood; Bowmar; book record sets; **K-1**.

PRSD Pre-Reading Skills Development Program: University of Wisconsin, Richard Venensky, Encyclopaedia Britannica; two kits, cards, games, practice sheets; **K-1**.

Try. Manolake, Weltman, Scain, Waldo; Nobel; materials and books; **K**.

Reading-Thinking Skills: Ethel S. Maney; Continental Press; transparencies; **K-1**.

Goal: Language Development: Merril B. Karnes; Random House; kit, cards, posters, puppets; **K**.

Goldman-Lynch Sounds and Symbols Development Kit: Ronald Goldman and Martha Lynch; American Guidance; kit, puppets, cassettes, posters, cards, workbook; **K-1**.

Singer Readiness Program: James A. Gallagher; Singer Education; filmstrips; **K-1**.

Introductory Vocabulary Series: Learning Resources; audio cards, activity sheet; **K-1**.

Ready, Set, Read!: Courtney Cazden, Margaret Golick, Sam Rabinobitch, and Minna Russ; Learning Resources; 8mm film loops, activity sheets; **K-1**.

Wordworld: Wilson Lane, Floyd Sucher, and Judith McCay; Economy; tape and booklets; **K**.

Here Comes Howie: Bell & Howell; language master cards and activity sheets; **K**.

REFERENCES

Almy, Millie. "Children's Experiences Prior to First Grade and Success in Beginning Reading." Contributions to *Education*, No. 954. New York: Teachers College, Columbia University, 1949.

Brzeinski, Joseph E., and Gerald E. Elledge. "Early Reading." In Robert C. Aukerman (Ed.), *Some Persistent Questions on Beginning Reading*. Newark, Del.: International Reading Association, 1972.

Chall, Jeanne S., Florence G. Roswell, and Susan H. Blumenthal. "Auditory Blending Ability: A Factor in Success in Beginning Reading." *The Reading Teacher*, 1963, *17*, 113-118.

Cramer, Ronald L. "Reading to Children: Why and How?" *The Reading Teacher*, February 1975, *28*(5).

Downing, John, and Derek V. Thackray. *Reading Readiness*. London: University of London, 1971.

Durkin, Dolores. *Children Who Read Early*. New York: Teachers College, 1966.

_____, Dolores. "A Six Year Study of Children Who Learned to Read in School at the Age of Four." *Reading Research Quarterly*, 1974-75, *10*(1), 9-61.

Durrell, Donald D., and Helen A. Murphy. "The Auditory Discrimination Factor in Reading Readiness and Reading Disability." *Education*, 1953, *73*, 556-560.

Food and Nutrition Board. *The Relationship of Nutrition to Brain Development and Behavior*. Washington, D.C.: National Academy of Sciences, National Research Council, 1973.

Gates, Arthur I. "The Necessary Mental Age for Beginning Reading." *Elementary School Journal*, 1937, *37*, 497–508.

Grant, W. Vance, and C. George Lind. *Digest of Educational Statistics*. Washington, D.C.: National Center for Education Statistics, U.S. Department of Health, Education and Welfare, 1974.

Groff, Patrick. "Reading Ability and Auditory Discrimination: Are They Related?" *The Reading Teacher*, May 1975, *29*(8), 742–747.

Malmquist, Eve. "An International Overview of Primary Reading Practices." *Journal of Reading*, May 1975, *18*(8), 615–624.

Mountain, Lee. *How to Teach Reading before First Grade*. Highland Park, N.J.: Dreier Education Systems, 1970.

Ollila, L. O. "Pros and Cons of Teaching Reading to Four- and Five-Year-Olds." In Robert C. Aukerman (Ed.), *Some Persistent Questions on Beginning Reading*. Newark, Del.: International Reading Association, 1972.

Paradis, Edward, and Joseph Peterson. "Readiness Training Implications from Research." *The Reading Teacher*, February 1975, *28*(5).

Robinson, Helen M. "Perceptual Training–Does It Result in Reading Improvement?" In Robert C. Aukerman (Ed.), *Some Persistent Questions on Beginning Reading*. Newark, Del.: International Reading Association, 1972.

_____, "Visual and Auditory Modalities Related to Methods for Beginning Reading." *Reading Research Quarterly*, Fall 1972, *8*, 7–39.

Rosborough, Pearl M. *Physical Fitness and the Child's Reading Problem*. New York: Exposition Press, 1963.

Rosen, Carl L., and Fred Ohnmacht. "Perception, Readiness, and Reading Achievement." In Helen M. Smith (Ed.), *Perception and Reading*. Proceedings of the 12th Annual Convention. Newark, Del.: International Reading Association, 1968.

Rude, Robert T. "Readiness Tests: Implications for Early Childhood Education." *The Reading Teacher*, March 1973, *26*, 572–80.

Spache, George D. "Outcomes of Visual Perception Training." In John E. Merritt (Ed.), *New Horizons in Reading*. Newark, Del.: International Reading Association, 1976.

Spache, George D., Michaela C. Andres, H. A. Curtis, Minnie L. Rowland, and Minnie H. Fields. "A Longitudinal First Grade Reading Readiness Program." *The Reading Teacher*, May 1966, *19*, 580–584.

Spache, George B., and Evelyn B. Spache, *Reading in the Elementary School*. Third Edition. Boston: Allyn and Bacon, 1973.

Wanat, Stanley F. "Reading Readiness." In B. Spolsky (Ed.), *Current Trends in Language Teaching*. Unpublished manuscript. 1975.

Chapter 7

Basals:
Reading Systems
and Individualized Reading

We have been discussing phonics skills, whole word methods, comprehension, and a number of elements of successful reading programs. In this chapter we will see some methods of combining these skills into a total package or system which the classroom teacher can follow from day to day, and through which the child progresses year by year. We have already looked at a comprehension lesson from a basal reader in the last chapter and at the phonics skills in Chapter 2, so some of the elements are familiar to you. This chapter will tell you more of the overall plans found in the commercially published reading series that are used in most schools.

One solution to the problems encountered in the classroom in teaching reading skills is provided by the basal reading series, or "reading systems," as some publishers are now calling them. Beginning teachers usually follow one of these series and its accompanying instructions in the teacher's manual rather closely, but more experienced teachers often add their own variations, particular emphasis, or even combinations of several systems.

In the latter part of this chapter I will discuss one method of individualized instruction so that you can contrast it with the more traditional basal method. However, many other methods of "individualizing instruction" are discussed in other chapters.

HISTORICAL READERS

Before focusing on basal readers, let's briefly recapitulate the development of reading methods in the United States. In Colonial times the hornbook plus the *New England Primer* was used. After memorizing the ABCs, students were given very little in the way of easy reading materials; usually they went directly into adultlike reading of the Lord's Prayer and catechisms. In the early 1800s, Webster's "blue back" spellers included some gradations of easy stories, but they were neither very long nor very carefully developed. The McGuffey readers, popular from around 1850 to 1900, represented a significant advance in providing substantially more reading materials for young and beginning readers, and actually had a graded series of books (though the books did not represent grade levels). This trend continues in that now we have very carefully graded sets of books for teaching beginning reading. The modern series are graded not only in terms of general reading difficulty, but often in several other areas as well, providing a careful introduction of basic vocabularies as well as a careful introduction of phonic or linguistic skills.

TRADITIONAL BASAL READERS

Probably the way you learned to read, and the way most young adults in the United States learned to read, was with a traditional basal reader. What I am calling a "traditional basal reader series" is the kind of series of reading books, stretching from kindergarten readiness through sixth or eighth grade, that has been widely used in American schools from the 1920s up through the present time. Of course, today's series are better developed and have more elements and supplementary aids than those used in the 1920s, but the traditional ones still follow the same patterns, and have successfully taught millions and millions of children to read.

The series of books is called "basal" because it forms the basis of instruction. The books are the chief materials used in reading instruction, and the teaching methods that they suggest in the teachers' manuals are often the major reading teaching method used by the classroom teacher. Furthermore, a basal series has an overall plan for the systematic introduction of a large number of reading skills as the child progresses upward through the grades. We saw some of these specific skills lists in the phonics and comprehension chapters. You obviously can't teach all these skills at once, so which ones are introduced first? Which skills next? Should some skills be repeated—or, as the authors of basal series like to say, "be reinforced"—in the upper grades?

The basal series, then, in addition to providing materials and methods, provides a curriculum plan for reading instruction from grades 1 through 3, or 1 through 6, and in some instances even wider ranges like K through 8. These plans for skills introduction across grades can be seen in *scope and sequence charts* which are put out by most major reading series publishers. You can examine them in curriculum libraries, in school district supervisors' offices, at exhibits of books at teachers' conventions, and sometimes even in the teacher's manuals of the series. Often they are printed on one large piece of paper measuring some 2 by 3 feet, and they are a little boring to read, but they do show some of the care and planning that have gone into the preparation of the series. They also show how the reading curriculum in any one grade relates to all other grades; for example, they show how the second-grade reading curriculum relates to the third-grade reading curriculum. However, the skills are woven into the material. From the standpoint of the teacher, the *three main elements of basal reading series* (sometimes called *core elements*) are: (1) the books for children to read; (2) the accompanying workbooks that supplement the child's books, as well as teaching additional skills; and (3) the teacher's manual that assists the instructor in use of the books and workbooks. The teacher's manual also supplies enrichment and motivational suggestions that are particularly appropriate for a given grade level. Supplementary materials include charts, records, cards, games, books, writing exercises, and many other materials which aid learning but which are not absolutely necessary to progress through the series.

Readiness Books

Basal series usually begin with one or two reading readiness books or workbooks. We discussed the nature and the problems of reading readiness in Chapter 6, but for the purposes of our current discussion, I should point out that readiness books provide activities that are aimed at getting a child ready to read; that is, to develop skills such as visual discrimination, motor coordination, auditory perception, and (often) familiarization with the alphabet. Reading readiness materials do not contain words to be read in story form for meaning. You can easily tell a readiness book from a preprimer or any other reader by simply glancing at the pages and seeing if words in story form are present.

Readiness books may be hardbound, but more often they are softbound (paper or soft cloth covers). They may be in workbook form, so that children can write in them, or they may be made so that the child is not supposed to write in them. In this latter case, there is usually an accompanying "write-in workbook" or a set of ditto masters from which the teacher can make worksheets for the children to mark on, color, or cut up.

Readiness books are used in kindergarten and sometimes the first part of first grade. Their use is slightly controversial, and some school systems do not use them at all. Some educators do not feel that readiness workbooks are an integral part of the basal system, but most basal systems have them because many other educators want them.

First-Grade Readers

Basal reading systems provide an abundance of materials for the first grade. Many text authors and school systems consider first grade *the* grade for teaching reading.

The first book that the child learns to read is called a *preprimer*. It is a small softbound book of 20 to 40 pages that begins with a very easy short story consisting of perhaps 4 pages and 3 different words. The story line is carried by the pictures and supplemented by discussion by the teacher. The following story in the preprimer is usually slightly longer and includes several new words in addition to the three words

Millions of children learned to read with Dick and Jane in the old Scott, Foresman basal series. (*Mike Q/Coronet Studios*)

taught in the first story. This pattern continues, with the child learning 15 to 30 words in the first preprimer. Following this, there are one or two more preprimers that build on the vocabulary already taught. It should be noted that we are describing here a whole-word beginning approach.

The workbooks that accompany these preprimers give the child additional practice in recognizing and using words in different sentences and situations. Soon, if not right away, some phonics skills are taught (Which words have the same beginning sound? What letter makes that sound?). Meaning is stressed by the teacher's discussion questions before and after the reading and in workbook exercises. (Figures 5-4 and 5-5 illustrate the kind of questions suggested.)

Basal series differ in the number of preprimers they include, varying from one to four, but typically there are three. Upon completion of the preprimers, children next read a *primer*. It is usually a hardbound book and substantially longer than preprimers; it might contain 50 to 100 pages and looks more like a regular book that older children read. It, too, is accompanied by a workbook and teacher's manual. Primers, preprimers, and most primary materials are liberally illustrated, usually with full-color illustrations.

After the primer comes the *first reader*. It is also a hardbound book, and usually a little longer than the primer. It, of course, also has a workbook and a teacher's manual.

Not all children in the first grade complete the first reader. In fact, it would not be unusual for some students to still be in the preprimers at the end of first grade. Others may read better than average in the first grade and may benefit from use of upper-level materials. Children progress at different rates. That children's levels of achievement vary is not necessarily a result of poor teaching or inadequate instructional materials. Recognizing differences and abilities, teachers try to do their best with each child.

Traditional Grouping Teachers using traditional readers frequently organize their classrooms into three groups: fast, average, and slow. In the latter half of first grade, it would not be unusual to have one group in preprimers, one group in primers, and one group in first readers. The groups should be fairly flexible so that children can be transferred as their skills improve.

Reading groups can also be organized on the basis of different skills, like phonics or spelling. Arithmetic groups might have yet different children in the fast and slow groups.

The use of basal readers does not necessarily mean that only three reading groups can exist in the classroom. Some teachers use four groups and some use two. There are even special instructions with some basal series that tell the teacher how to undertake individualized instruction using basal materials.

Basals are primarily designed for use by the classroom teacher; however, they can be used in special reading teaching situations like remedial reading or supplemental instruction. We will take up grouping problems in Chapter 12, and individual differences in Chapters 11 and 13.

Supplementary Materials We have been discussing just the three core elements of a basal reading series: the child's book or "reader," the workbook, and the teacher's manual. There is a number of supplementary or ancillary materials that often accompany the basal system. Most series, for example, provide word cards that contain (one word to a card) each of the words taught in the texts in first grade. As new words are introduced, the teacher puts the words up in a card rack. Later, the cards can be arranged to make sentences or phrases. However, this type of lesson can be provided through use of the blackboard or teacher-made cards.

At certain points in the curriculum—upon completion of a book such as the primer, or at the end of the year—curriculum development tests can be used. These are sometimes called "check tests," "criterion-referenced tests," "progress tests," or "diagnostic tests." Their aim is to tell the teacher whether the child has acquired the reading skills that were taught in a particular segment of the program. They often suggest whether the child is ready to go on or if some reteaching of some or all of the skills is necessary.

Workbooks often come in the form of duplicating or spirit (ditto) masters. These spirit masters sometimes contain exactly the same material as the workbook, but sometimes they are different and are additional or supplementary. Spirit masters cost less initially than workbooks which the children write in and then discard. However, if the cost of buying paper and the teacher's time are considered, they may not be more economical.

Stories or poems to be read by the teacher to the children are other popular supplementary materials. Some publishers produce stories or poems on records or tapes.

Readers for Grades Two and Three

In the upper primary grades, second and third, the basal series assumes a different format. For the second grade there are two fairly large books (more pages than a primer or first reader) for the children, and each is accompanied by a workbook and teacher's manual. Likewise, there are two even longer books for the third grade, with workbook and teacher's manual. Traditional books are usually identified by the symbols 2_1, 2_2, 3_1, and 3_2, with the subscript indicating the first or second half of the year. Newer series use letter or other designations (see Table 7-1).

The workbooks and teacher's manuals usually stress numerous reading skills. If, for example, the basic structure of the series is a controlled vocabulary, then the skills stressed in workbooks are meaning (comprehension) and word-attack skills, which would include phonics. Progress tests to be given after the completion of each text diagnose areas of strengths and weaknesses in knowledge of sight words, comprehension, and word-attack skills.

Though publishers still provide supplementary materials for use in these grades, they are not quite as voluminous as those available for first-grade classes. Second- and third-grade supplementary materials might take the form of charts or overhead transparencies illustrating word-attack principles (such as syllabification) or word usage (such as homonyms), or they might be in the form of games that teach short vowels. Supplementary reading materials frequently include additional reading booklets or full-sized books. It might not be obvious in first grade that the word cards are supplementary, but in the upper primary grades, the overhead transparencies are more obviously supplementary, even though they are made to correlate exactly with the basal reader lessons.

Readers for Intermediate Grades

The intermediate grades are traditionally thought of as grades 4, 5, and 6. At this level, a subtle shift takes place from "learning to read" to "reading to learn." In the primary grades most of the reading skills are at least introduced. Most of the phoneme-grapheme correspondences have been covered and they are reviewed in the intermediate grades. Authors of the basal readers often use the word *reinforce* when they review a previously taught skill, the concept being that the skill is strengthened with additional practice, examples, and information.

In the primary grades, it is important that the child learn how to read almost anything. Hence, basal readers teach such universal skills as basic words and comprehension. The stories in some readers are not too substantial, though recently there has been a trend to get good children's literature into even primary grades. However, in the intermediate years, reading is used as a tool, and both reading books and reading lessons assume a smaller part of the elementary curriculum. Publishers of the more traditional basal series produce only one reading book for grades 4, 5, and 6. Each, of course, has its accompanying workbook and teacher's manual.

Table 7-1   Reader Level Translation Chart

	Traditional basal reading series books	American Book Read System	Scott, Foresman Reading Systems level	Random House Reading Program basic units*
Kindergarten	Readiness book(s)	First, second, third step	1	
Primary				
First grade	Preprimer 1	A	2	
	Preprimer 2	B		
	Preprimer 3	C		
	Primer	D	3	
	First reader	E	4	
Second grade	2_1	F	5, 6	
				Yellow
	2_2	G	7, 8	Grades 2 and 3
Third grade	3_1	H	9, 10	
	3_2	I	11, 12	
				Red
Intermediate				Grades 3 and 4
Fourth grade	4	J	13, 14, 15	
				Blue
Fifth grade	5	K	16, 17, 18	Grades 5 and 6
				Green
Sixth grade	6	L	19, 20, 21	Grades 5 to 7
				Tan
				Grades 6 to 8
Junior high				
Seventh grade	7			Olive
Eighth grade	8			Grades 7 and 8

*Random House units (boxes of 50 books) cover wider grade levels, but those grade levels indicated are the areas of concentration for each color-coded box.

The elementary curriculum does not require less reading in the intermediate grades. It requires more, but the additional reading is done in different textbooks in areas such as science and social studies. Reading in the intermediate grades is often supplemented by reading in trade and reference books not directly associated with any text.

It is not surprising that, at this level, the reading lessons often concern themselves with study skills such as library use or book usage (use of indexes, tables of contents, dictionaries, etc.).

Word-attack skills, while reinforced in the intermediate grades, are also often taught as part of writing, spelling, or language arts lessons.

In the intermediate grades, books in areas such as science and social studies are used. (*Photo Trends*)

Vocabulary building undergoes a similar shift. In the primary grades, vocabulary learning was often learning sight words or using word-attack skills to unlock a written word that was already in the child's listening or speaking vocabulary. In the intermediate grades, vocabulary building often involves learning word meanings and learning to recognize words that are new to the child.

Readers for Junior High Grades

For the purposes of this discussion about readers, the junior high grades are grades 7 and 8. The traditional basal reader series include one reader or reading book for each of these grades. The seventh- and eighth-grade books of a basal reading series are merely upward extensions of intermediate grade books. However, junior high readers are not widely used. Many basal reading series do not even have seventh- and eighth-grade books.

There are several reasons for the disuse of junior high readers. One is educational; since children learn at different rates, the spread in abilities is much greater in upper grades than in lower grades. A seventh-grade book may be too difficult for one-third of the class and too easy for another third. The same problem exists in all grades, but it is even more pronounced at junior high levels.

The second reason for disuse of junior high readers is organizational. Many junior high schools are departmentalized, with different teachers for different subject areas— e.g., a science teacher, an art teacher, a social studies teacher, etc. The person responsible for reading is often the English teacher, who will most likely use an English textbook rather than a reading textbook.

From the standpoint of supervision, the junior high schools are often under different supervisors and administrators; hence, there is often a different overall curriculum plan. A series selected by the elementary supervisor, faculty, or administration might not be continued in grades 7 and 8. Less importance is placed on continuity of skills development from grades K through 8, which is one of the few strong points that seventh- and eighth-grade basal readers have.

There is another consideration, and this is the most regrettable of all: *except for remedial reading, reading as a subject is simply not taught in junior high schools.* This isn't true in all districts, but it is unfortunately true in the majority.

In any case, where reading is taught to all or most pupils in the junior high, either as a separate course or as part of the English curriculum, texts and materials other than a basal series are frequently used. Some of these materials are discussed in Chapters 8 and 9, and some of the phonics comprehension and vocabulary materials already listed apply to grades 7 and 8. As for reading plans, both individualized reading (see pp. 145 to 147 at the end of this chapter) and test management system (see Chapter 11) apply.

READING SYSTEMS

The term *reading system* will be used here to indicate modern approaches to the total reading program that are used instead of a basal reader series. However, in some instances a modernization of a basal series might be called a "reading system."

Certainly, a basal reader series can be called a "system" in the conventional sense of the word. It integrates and articulates a large number of ideas together with a system of delivery, namely, the books and materials. However, a basal series is rather closely tied to the idea of grades, first grade, second grade, etc., and, along with that, the idea of teaching in groups, even though the group might be somewhat smaller than the full class.

Reading systems usually have a sequential development pattern of *levels* which are not openly designated as equivalent to grades, and which often have much more provision for individualization.

Let's begin by looking at a system that departs relatively little from the traditional basal series. The Read System by Roy Kress, Marjorie Johnson, and John McNeil,[1] published by American Book Company, has almost exactly the same pattern of children's books, workbooks, and teachers' manuals found in most traditional series in grades K through 6. However, instead of calling them a preprimer or a 2_1 book, they are designated level A, level F, etc. (see Table 7-1 for a correlational chart). The mere relabeling of book names might seem like a trivial thing, but it does help to take away the stigma of using a first-grade book in second grade. Good schools have been using basal readers according to children's needs and abilities for a long time, but there still are too many schools or teachers who only want to use a second-grade book in second grade and a third-grade book in third grade. By removing grade-level designations, it makes it easier for teachers, pupils, and parents to accept the use of a wider range of books in any one classroom.

[1] Contributing authors to the Read System are Tom Whitman, Herman Roberts, Marion Cutler, Paul Hutchins, Pose Lamb, Elsie Black, and Millard Black.

The Read System also differs from traditional series in its greater emphasis on progress tests, called "checkup tests," and screening activities for placement. There are more systematic provisions for reteaching with phonics kits and comprehension kits (boxes providing a multitude of specific skill exercises). The Read System still uses group instruction for basal-type reading lessons, but it is somewhat more individualized with its provision of skills tests and specific instructional activities.

A more radical departure from a traditional basal series is the Scott, Foresman reading system called "Reading Unlimited," developed by a large team of authors and the Scott, Foresman staff.[2]

The most distinctive feature of the Scott, Foresman system is its large number of *components*. A component is a book, workbook, test, or other teaching aid. There are literally dozens of large and small booklets, practice pads, tests, and other items. In contrast to the Read System, levels do not closely parallel traditional basal designations (see Table 7-1). Another difference is that difficulty progression is not determined primarily by vocabulary difficulty (as is traditional in basal series) or by phonics difficulty (an even more traditional alternative to the whole word method of progression). Rather, the Scott, Foresman difficulty progression is more syntactic. That is, what makes level 3 more difficult than level 2, for example, is that the former uses more advanced grammatical constructions, though some attention is paid to vocabulary difficulty and concept (meaning) difficulty.

Given these differences, one important similarity between the Scott, Foresman reading system and basal series, as well as the Read System, is that the teacher's manual is explicit in its instructions. It tells the teacher, step by step, which component to use and how. (See Figures 5-4, 5-5, and 5-6 in Chapter 5.) Like most other teacher's manuals, additional or enrichment activities are suggested, and teachers using this system, like teachers using the traditional basals, soon learn to depart from the exact steps in the manual through their own creative innovations or adaptations for individual situations.

In addition to the teacher's manual for each level, a special set of booklets (the teacher's edition) is provided with an overprint of pertinent directions and questions repeated from the teacher's manual, so that the teacher can hold a book like the child's and not continually refer back to the somewhat larger manual. The workbook in this system is called a "studybook," and directions for its use are in the teacher's manual (see Figure 7-1). A set of exercises similar to those in the workbook is provided on pads, so individual pages can be torn off and given to the child—this same material can also be obtained on spirit masters.

The pads (or spirit masters) also contain special letters to parents which can be sent at the appropriate time, enabling the teacher to get the parents involved in the education process. Fostering this trend of home assistance, special economical editions of some of the pupil's booklets are given to the child to take home and keep.

In addition to all of this, there are tests for each level and record-keeping sheets.

[2] Scott, Foresman authors are Ira Aaron, Sterl Artley, Kenneth Goodman, Charlotte Huck, William Jenkins, John Manning, Marion Monroe, Wilma Pyle, Helen Robinson, Andrew Schiller, Mildred Beatty Smith, Lorraine Sullivan, Samuel Weintraub, and Joseph Wepman.

Making inferences   Level 6
(Grade 2)

American Indian Names

Sometimes the names of Indian children are chosen because they remind people of an interesting animal.

This little boy watched a beaver building a house in the water. Then the little boy tried to make a beaver house in a puddle. What do you think his mother named him?

Flying Fish ☐   Gray Squirrel ☐   Small Beaver ☐

Sometimes the names of Indian children are chosen because they do something that people remember.

When this little boy was small, he was very curious. He asked questions about everything. What do you think his mother named him?

Eagle Wing ☐   Many Questions ☐   Running Horse ☐

Sometimes their names are chosen because of an animal that is seen nearby.

When this girl was little, her mother used to watch some red deer. The mother liked to look at these beautiful animals. What do you think her mother named her?

Blue Fox ☐   Beautiful Deer ☐   White Swan ☐

Figure 7-1   Sample Scott, Foresman studybook (workbook) page.

Another type of component that Scott, Foresman labels "core," but which many other systems would call "supplementary," is a set of books for each level to be read to the child. Many educators would agree that one of the most valuable experiences you can provide for a beginning reading child is to let him or her listen to stories and thus gain a sense of syntax, vocabulary, and appreciation for literature. This listening to stories might be called *listening training* or *auding*. Auding is a receptive language arts skill using the ears as reading uses the eyes. It is a valuable learning activity for the child that can be done in the home, in kindergarten, and in all elementary grades.

INDIVIDUALIZED READING

If you have taken a child through a primary learning-to-read system, such as is found in the first three years of a basal reader system, what approaches are appropriate in the intermediate grades? You could continue in the basal series or you could use an individualized reading program.

Individualized reading is a method of reading instruction which relies on each child selecting a different book according to interest and ability level. The book is read silently with a little help from the teacher. After reading the book, there is an individual child-teacher conference in which the teacher discusses the book to find out if the child has understood and enjoyed it. The teacher attempts to discern what types of comprehension skills have been used and sometimes to determine if the child has facility with word-attack skills. The teacher then suggests some follow-up activities and helps the child select the next book. Records are kept of both the child's progress and activities. The system requires an interesting selection of books with appropriate levels of reading difficulty, and a teacher who is both creative and well informed about children's books.

An example of a commercially packaged, individualized, reading system and selection of books is the Random House Reading Program. This program has six basic units, each of which is comprised of a box of 50 children's *trade books*. A trade book is the kind sold in the bookstores and found in most libraries. In other words, the units include books for children that are not textbooks, readers, or reference books. Each unit is coded by a different color and contains books spanning a range of about four or five years, as well as 10 or more books in a concentrated span of one and one-half or two years. See Table 7-1 for the concentrated span of reading difficulty level for each of the basic units.

Since these 50 books are regular trade books, the didactic (teaching) part is comprised of five cards that are located in a pocket inside the front cover.

In the beginning, the teacher of an individualized program helps the child select a book that is interesting. Each box contains a selection including "biography, science, stories about real boys and girls, fun and fantasy, action and adventure." Since these are on different grade levels, some teacher guidance is necessary. It is also helpful to have more than one basic unit per classroom; for example, a fifth grade might have both red and yellow units (which would give a good range of both easy and difficult books). In selecting a book, the child can look at the illustrations and try reading part of it.

Before reading the book, the child is taught to use the five cards. The first card is the *survey card*. This card eases the book selection process by telling the pupil to look at the spine, the title page, the illustrations, etc. The *vocabulary card* contains a list of above-grade level words used in that book. The child is instructed to look these words up in the dictionary, try pronouncing them, etc. (presumably with some assistance by the teacher). This card also includes some vocabulary building information, like prefixes and synonyms. Both the survey and vocabulary cards require responses which can be made on a *pupil worksheet*. The student can then check the correctness of his or her answers on the *answer key card*.

The child is then directed to read the *detail card* before reading the book; however, the detailed questions on the content of the book usually are not answered until after completion of the book. The pupil may choose to answer the detail questions in the course of reading, using the same worksheet—one worksheet is provided for each book.

After reading the book, the child answers the questions on the *comprehension card*. These questions are aimed at different comprehension skills than are the questions on the detail card, and focus on such skills as main idea, inferring purpose, evaluating, and a host of critical reading skills.

The final card in the book pocket is the *activity card*, which suggests some follow-up and optional activities, sometimes involving small-group work or reading a similar type of book.

When the child has completed reading the book and recorded on the worksheet all the answers to the questions on the cards, there is a conference with the teacher. The teacher's guide to the unit contains summaries of the story in each book and some comprehension questions that lead to discussion and pinpoint different comprehension skills. The teacher might help the student get started on some of the activities suggested on the activity card, or may discover weaknesses in certain comprehension skills and provide a bit of individualized instruction by giving the student drills from the special *skillpacer unit*. In other words, if a child is able to answer all the teacher's questions, he or she can proceed to the selection of another book, but if the child is unable to answer some questions, several lessons from the skillpacer unit are given.

The teacher keeps a *folder* for each pupil containing a worksheet for each book the child has read; thus, a record is maintained of accomplishments. In addition, the teacher has available some diagnostic information on reading skills, as there is a space on the worksheet to record the correctness of the child's answers. The *teacher's guide* contains general information on administering the system (classroom management) and story summaries with questions for each book.

The Random House Reading Program may be a bit formalized for what has been called "individualized reading" for many years, but along with other individualized systems, it does contain the following basic elements:

1 Children select books that interest them (perhaps with a little teacher guidance.)

2 Most children are reading different books at different levels.

3 There are individual teacher conferences which develop motivation and check on comprehension, plus suggested future activities.

4 The progress is self-paced.

5 The teacher maintains individual records of progress.

It is not necessary to use an individualized reading program as the main reading program; individualized reading can supplement any reading program. It might be helpful, but it is not necessary, to have a set of commercial materials such as the Random House Program, or others listed at the end of this chapter. Individualized programs have been carried out for years, using classroom or school libraries. Some advocates of individualized reading maintain that there should be a minimum of three books per pupil in the classroom library. If this informal system of classroom or school libraries is used, it poses a real problem for the teacher who has to discuss the content of each book after a child has read it. Some experienced teachers do get to know the content of a large number of books over a span of several years, but other teachers just ask general questions.

Allowing complete self-selection by the child has advantages and drawbacks. On the one hand, it is often highly motivating to the child; on the other hand, some children get in a rut and read only one type of story. Austin and Morrison report visiting an individualized program where one boy had read 10 books—nine of them on sports.

Some users of individualized reading ask their students to keep a list of unfamiliar words so that they can question the teacher when they get a chance or at a scheduled conference. Not all individualized programs have conferences only after completion of a book. Some teachers schedule individual conferences periodically; sometimes a teacher can get around to all pupils once a week for three to 10 minutes. Unfortunately, however, observers of individualized programs report that, in some cases, conferences are held at monthly intervals.

If children write some kind of report after reading the book, other language arts can be related to the reading program. For example, some teachers keep a list of misspelled words for the child's individualized spelling list.

Some educators feel that use of an individualized reading program, more than basal series or other reading systems, requires an excellent master teacher, particularly if it is not a formalized, individualized reading program with some systematic check of skills development. But there is no denying that such programs go right to the heart of the most pressing reading problem—developing interest in sustained reading.

POSTSCRIPT

This chapter has centered heavily on materials. In mentioning the American Book Read System, the Scott, Foresman Reading Unlimited, and the Random House Reading Program, the intention is not to recommend them above others, but rather to tell you about several widely used programs. There are many more. At the end of this chapter you will find a list of other basal reading systems and individualized reading programs. I do not claim that it is complete, as there are so many reading teaching materials on the market that it is almost impossible to produce a complete list. If you ever did achieve a complete list, one month—or certainly one year—later, it would be out of date. However, the list at the end of the chapter probably comprises a clear majority of materials used in both the more traditional basal reading programs and the individualized programs. There are two main ways a student of reading can get to know materials; one is to sit down and study them—read the children's stories, read the teacher's manuals, try out the workbook pages—the other is to see them in action being taught in a classroom. The best way to get to know a system will come later in the classroom where you actually use a system with a class of children.

All of the major publishers have salesmen and consultants who are good at explaining their company's materials. You can talk to these people at book exhibits and when they visit schools. They sometimes put on lectures in schools or college classes describing the materials, and a consultant occasionally will put on a demonstration lesson in a school.

Teachers are frequently involved in textbook selection committees, so judging the merit of various series is a skill that should be developed. Read over the criteria in Figure 7-2, and you will see some of the questions that can be asked about a reading system. They will also help you in learning about a new system.

Interest

Would the story content interest the pupils?

Are the activities interesting?

Are the artwork and illustrations relevant, artistic, and not offensive to any group?

Skills

Compare the phonics, word-attack, and comprehension skills with several other lists that you like.

Are higher skills taught, such as speed, study skills, reference? (Use several lists.)

One way of finding out which skills are taught is to look at the scope and sequence chart, but you must then look at the teacher's manuals to see if the skills listed on the scope and sequence chart can really be found in the teacher's manuals and workbooks in the proper amount and that they are taught in a meaningful and worthwhile fashion.

Literary Merit

Are the stories and poems good?

Are the students put in touch with good children's literature—either in the books themselves or in suggested activities?

Is there a good variety of material type?

Teachability

Are the teacher's directions clear and useful?

Is the material organized so that there is little confusion?

Can the children use the materials without an overdependence on the teacher?

Would the children really learn if the directions were followed?

Are there useful supplementary materials?

Figure 7-2 Some criteria for judging a basal series. (Figure continued on next page.)

Range of Student Abilities

Does the system provide adequately for the type of students in your school?

Does it provide for individual differences?

Is the readability of the stories on the right level?
(Don't just take the publisher's word for this; use a readability formula and/or try it out on some typical students.)

Does it provide for students who fail or need extra help?

Evaluation

Do the teacher's manuals, workbooks, and other materials provide for frequent and accurate feedback on the student's progress?

Are there more formal testing programs either as separate tests or as part of drill activities?

Is there any record-keeping system for progress?

Authorship and Publisher

Are the authors known and respected in the reading field?

Does the publisher have a good reputation for quality, content, service, and durability of materials?

Cost

What is the initial (first-year) cost?

What is the replacement cost (second-year or five-year cost)?

How does the cost compare with similar systems?

Even if it costs more, is it worth it?

Effectiveness

Is there any evidence (journal articles, reports, etc.) that the series does indeed teach reading?

Can you visit other schools using the series, talk to teachers, see test results?

Figure 7-2 Some criteria for judging a basal series (continued).

SUGGESTED LEARNING ACTIVITIES

1 Study a well-known basal reading system in your curriculum library in a school district. Look at both the core material and the supplementary material. Try to answer some of the questions in Figure 7-2.

2 Witness a basal reading program in action. Try to observe lessons on several different levels; reading readiness, beginning reading, and the intermediate level.

3 Conduct a sample reading lesson, or at least tell how you would do it. Study the teacher's manual. Prepare questions for students. Have words or phrases to put on the chalkboard. Select workbook drill and supplementary activity.

4 Look at an individualized program. Exactly what activity would the teacher and child undertake before, during, and after reading one book?

5 Prepare your own comprehension questions and follow-up activities for a children's trade book.

VOCABULARY AND STUDY TERMS

Titles of historical readers
Traditional basals
Scope and sequence charts
Core elements
Supplementary materials
Readiness goals
Readiness materials
First-grade materials
Traditional grouping
Number of books, grades 2–6
Learning to read versus reading to learn
Reinforcement of skills
Different skills for intermediate readers
Reading "system"
Levels
Components
Similarities and differences between traditional and modern systems
Auding
Individualized reading materials
Trade book
Individualized reading methods (elements)
Criteria for judging series

LIST OF BASAL READING SERIES (SYSTEMS)

Houghton-Mifflin Reading Series: William K. Durr, Jean M. LePere, and Vivian O. Windley; Houghton-Mifflin; basal series; **K–6.**

Reading 720: Theodore Clymer, Consultants William Blanton, Milton Jacobson, Ken Johnson, Rodger Shuy, and Paul Torrance; Ginn, Xerox; basal series; **K–6.**

Open Court Correlated Language Arts Program: S. A. Bernier and Louise Gurren; Open Court; basal reading and language arts series; **K–6.**

The Young America Basic Reading Program: Leo Fay; (Lyons and Carnahan) Rand McNally; basal series; **K–8.**

The Macmillan Reading Program: Albert J. Harris, Mae Knight Clark, Marion Gartler, Carl Roman, and Marcella Benditt; Macmillan; basal series; **K–6.**

The New Macmillan Reading Program Series R: Carl B. Smith and Ronald Wardaugh; Macmillan; basal series, skills reservoir; **K–6.**

The Book Mark Reading Program: Margaret Earley, Marion Young Adell, Robert Canfield, Elizabeth Cooper, Robert Karlin, Nancy Santeusanio, Thomas Schottman, Sara Srygley, and Evelyn Wenzel; Harcourt, Brace; basal series; **K–6.**

Basic Reading: Lippincott; basal series; **K–6.**

Reading Unlimited (Scott, Foresman System Revised): Ira Aaron, A. Sterl Artley, Kenneth S. Goodman, William A. Jenkins, John C. Manning, Marion Monroe, Wilma J. Pyle, Helen M. Robinson, Andrew Schiller, Mildred Beatty Smith, Lorraine M. Sullivan, Samuel Weintraub, and Joseph M. Wepman; Scott, Foresman; basal series; **K-6**.

Keys to Reading: Theodore L. Harris, Mildred Creatmore, Louise Mattoni, and Harold B. Allen; Economy; basal series; **K-8**.

The Holt Basic Reading Systems: Eldonna Everetts, Lyman Hunt, Bernard Weiss, and Joseph Renzulli; Holt; **K-6**.

The Read Series: Marjorie Sedden Johnson, Roy A. Kress, John D. McNeil, Tom Whitman, Hermese Roberts, Marion Cutler, Paul Jerry Hutchins, Pose M. Lamb, Elsie Black, and Millard Black; American; basal series; **K-6**.

Design for Reading: Mabel O'Donnell, Byron H. Van Roekel, Eldonna Everetts, Mary Jean Kluwe, J. Louis Cooper, Daisy M. Jones, Walter B. Barbe, William Hannan, Ned D. Markseffel, David L. Shepherd, Rita A. Ragger, and Wilbert S. Schaefer; Harper & Row; basal series; **K-8**.

The Bank Street Readers: Bank Street College of Education, Macmillan; smaller basal; **K-3**.

Merrill Linguistic Reading Program: Wayne Otto, Mildred Rudolph, Richard Smith, Rosemary Wilson, Betty Yarbrough, Margaret Clark, Miriam Fuller, Adelaide Holle, Loraine Hull, Conrad Katzenmeyer, Elaine Markley, Dixie Lee Spiegel, and Ginger Van Blaricom; Merrill; basal series; **1-6**.

The Palo Alto Program: Theodore E. Glim; Harcourt, Brace; primary reading program; **(K) 1, 2,** and **3**.

Sounds of Language Readers, Revised: Bill Martin Jr. and Peggy Brogan; Holt; smaller basal series; **K-8**.

SRA Basal Reading Program: Donald Rasmussen, Lynn Goldberg, Thelma Thurstone, Thomas Bever, Thomas Creswell, Harry Levin, Raven I. McDavid Jr., Judson Newberg, Peter Rosenbaum, and Ida Waters; SRA; basal series; **K-6**.

The New Open Highways: Ira Aaron, A. Sterl Artley, William A. Jenkins, Alfonso R. Ramirez, Helen Robinson, Andrew Schiller, Mildred Beatty Smith, Ida Johnson, John Manning, Joseph Wepman, Lorraine Sullivan, and Marion Monroe; Scott, Foresman; remedial reading program; **K-8**.

Chandler Reading Program: Lawrence W. Carrillo and Donald Bissett; Nobel; small basal series; **K-3**.

SRS: Dorothy Kendall Bracken; Jones-Kenilworth; small basal series; **1-6**.

Let's Read: Clarence L. Barnhart; Clarence L. Barnhart Inc.; small beginning reading program; **1-4**.

Sullivan Reading Program: M. W. Sullivan; Behavioral Research Laboratories; basal series; **1-6**. (Note: another program by Sullivan is listed under "Programmed Instruction" in Chapter 8.)

The Phoenix Reading Series: Marion Gartler and Marcella Benditt; Prentice-Hall; small series (underachievers); **4-6**.

LIST OF INDIVIDUALIZED READING CURRICULUM MATERIALS BASED ON STUDENT SELF-SELECTION OF BOOKS

Personalized Reading Center: Virginia Jones Benedict; Xerox; grade-level kits, trade books, records, games, spirit masters; **3-6**. *Plus* reading, scholastic books, five kits, 25 books, cards; **2-6**.

Yearling Individualized Reading Program: Noble; kits, titles, cards, Yearling Skills Center, tests, worksheet; **3-6**.

Glasure Reading Involvement Program (GRIP): Glasure, Hertzburg; kits, trade books; **2-6**.

Individualized Reading Unit: Scholastic Books; six kits, paperback books, cards, worksheets; **1-6**.

One to One: A Practical Individualized Reading Program: Prentice-Hall; cards, two kits, book guide (designed to work with books found in the library); **1-4** and **4-6**.

Book Bin: Morton Botel; Learning Ventures (Bantam Books); books, cards; **4-8**.

Random House Reading Program: S. Allen Cohen and Flora Nell Roebuck; Random House; six kits, books, cards, worksheets, skill pacer box; **3-8**.

Houses of Books: Benefic Press; four kits, books, record charts; **1-5**.

Reading: Beginning, Patterns, Explorations: Morton Botel, John Dawkins, and Alvin Granowsky; D. C. Heath; kits, books, spirit masters, tests; **K-3**.

REFERENCES

Ammon, Richard. "Generating Expectancies to Enhance Comprehension." *The Reading Teacher*, December 1975, *29*(3).

Armstrong, Mary K. "First Grade Lift-Off with Library Books and Lots of Energy." *The Reading Teacher*, May 1974, 778–780.

Askland, Linda C. "Conducting Individual Language Experience Stories." *The Reading Teacher*, November 1973, 167–170.

Blakely, W. Paul, and Beverly McKay. "Individualized Reading as Part of an Eclectic Reading Program." *Elementary English*, March 1966, *43*, 214–219.

Bond, Guy L., and Robert Dykstra. "The Cooperative Research Program in First-Grade Reading Instruction." *Reading Research Quarterly*, Summer 1967, *2*, 5–142.

Bruton, Ronald W. "Individualizing a Basal Reader." *The Reading Teacher*, October 1972, *26*, 59–63.

Duker, Sam. *Individualized Reading: An Annotated Bibliography*. Metuchen, N.J.: Scarecrow Press, 1968.

Dykstra, Robert. "Summary of the Second-Grade Phase of the Cooperative Research Program in Primary Reading Instruction." *Reading Research Quarterly*, Fall 1968, *4*, 49–70. (a)

_____. "The Effectiveness of Code- and Meaning-Emphasis Beginning Reading Programs." *The Reading Teacher*, October 1968, *22*, 17–23. (b)

Hall, Mary Anne. "Linguistically Speaking, Why Language Experience?" *The Reading Teacher*, January 1972, 328–331.

_____. *Teaching Reading as a Language Experience*. Second Edition. Columbus, Ohio: Merrill, 1976.

Herrick, Virgil E., and Marcella Nerbovig. *Using Experience Charts with Children*. Columbus, Ohio: Merrill, 1964.

Jacobs, Leland. "Individualized Reading is Not a Thing." In Alice Miel (Ed.), *Individualizing Reading Practice*. Practical Suggestions for Teaching, No. 14. New York: Bureau of Publications, Teachers College, Columbia University, 1958.

Kendrick, William M., and Clayton L. Bennett. "A Comparative Study of Two First Grade Language Arts Programs—Extended into Second Grade." *The Reading Teacher*, May 1967, 747–755.

Kidder, Carole L. "Choosing A Basal Reading Program." *The Reading Teacher*, October 1975, *29*(1), 39–41.

Lee, Dorris M., and R. V. Allen. *Learning to Read through Experience*. New York: Appleton-Century-Crofts, 1963.

Pyrcza, Fred. "Passage-Dependence of Reading Comprehension Questions: Examples." *Journal of Reading*, January 1975, *18*(4).

Spache, George D., and Evelyn B. Spache. *Reading in the Elementary School*. New York: Allyn and Bacon, 1973.

Stauffer, Russell G. (Ed.) *The First Grade Reading Studies: Findings of Individual Investigations*. Newark, Del.: International Reading Association, 1967.

Stauffer, Russell G., and W. Dorsey Hammond. "The Effectiveness of Language Arts and Basic Reader Approaches to First Grade Reading Instruction." *The Reading Teacher*, May 1967, *20*, 740–746.

Sucher, Floyd. "Use of Basal Readers in Individualizing Reading Instruction." In J. Allen Figurel (Ed.), *Reading and Realism*. Newark, Del.: International Reading Association, 1969.

Veach, Jeanette. *Individualizing Your Reading Program*. New York: The Ronald Press, 1966.

Vilscek, Elaine C., Donald L. Cleland, and Liosanne Bilka. "Coordinating and Integrating Language Arts Instruction." *The Reading Teacher*, October 1967, *10*.

Witty, Paul A., and others. "Individualized Reading—A Summary and Evaluation," *Elementary English*, October 1959, *36*, 401–412.

Chapter 8

Methods:
From Directed Reading
to Audiovisual

In the first part of this book we discussed some underlying principles of reading instruction. Then we showed how these principles were put together in major systems like basal series and individualized reading. Later, we will consider some very practical problems like grouping and evaluation. In this and the following chapter we return to teaching methods in the form of supplemental materials and higher skills.

There is certainly some overlap between some of the supplemental methods and those suggested as part of a basal series, or those that might be incorporated into other procedures such as a test management system. But it just so happens that many of the methods suggested as part of a basal series can also be used independently or with other materials. For example, the Directed Reading Activity is at the core of many basal systems; yet, it can be used with science books or social studies texts. It is reviewed here so that the elements are sharpened and can be applied elsewhere when a basal teacher's manual is not guiding you.

The reading field is rich in its abundance of materials. The so-called "supplemental materials" that accompany basal readers are only a minor part of the wealth of supplemental materials available. In this chapter, I will acquaint you with many more.

DIRECTED READING ACTIVITY

The Directed Reading Activity, sometimes abbreviated to DRA, is a typical "reading lesson" used in many basal reading systems. It can, however, be used as a reading lesson in the "content areas" such as mathematics, social studies, or science. This discussion can also help you to see the elements in the basal series you use. Although various series differ, and there are slightly different elements, DRA frequently includes the following activities suitable for use without a basal series.

Prereading Activities

Stimulate Interest A discussion by the teacher which attempts to stimulate interest in the story topic is basic to most prereading activities. If the story is about horses, a picture of the teacher on a horse would engender interest. The teacher might ask if any of the children have ever ridden on a horse or taken care of one.

Discuss Plot In addition to talking about the topic or subject, the teacher might lead the discussion on the type of story or plot. If it is a mystery or suspense story, then the discussion might be about other mystery stories, TV programs, or movies.

Introduce New Words The prereading session should include an introduction of new or difficult words. In basal reading series for the primary grades, the teacher's manual will often tell the teacher which words are "new" or haven't been introduced before. In the upper grades, the teacher might pick out new or difficult words either with the help of the teacher's manual or by using independent judgment.

Pick Out Essential Words Even if the words are not new or difficult, the teacher might pick out words for prereading discussion that are essential or key to understanding the story. A child might be able to read a word as a sight word, but might not be familiar with how the word is used in the context of a particular story.

Apply Word-Attack Skills Sometimes when introducing new words, the teacher will apply word-attack skills. He or she will put the new word on the chalkboard, or use a word card provided by the publisher, and help the children to sound it out using syllables, phonemes, phonograms, or a combination of all three. The purpose of this word-attack introduction is not to have a whole word-attack lesson, but rather to show how previously introduced word-attack skills can be applied to new words. It is an excellent way to review some word-attack skills in a very practical way.

Emphasize a Type of Comprehension Finally, the teacher might pose questions in the prereading session which emphasize the kind of comprehension skills in which the children need practice. If the teacher is interested in having the children get the main idea, one type of question would be appropriate; if the focus is on details or time sequence, other types of questions could be posed. In most basal reading series, there are suggested questions for the teacher to use in the prereading session. However, experienced teachers usually use these only as a guide which they supplement or re-work to make more relevant for their particular classes. Basal reading series usually have a master plan for systematic teaching of various comprehension skills. Teachers can also use informal observations or information from previously given tests to sug-gest what type of comprehension should be emphasized.

Use Page or Story Segments The prereading activities described here are some-times used page-by-page throughout a story. A longer and more formal part of the prereading activities would *precede the whole story;* shorter prereading activities *would precede segments of the story* or individual pages. In other words, sometimes the teacher might discuss content or ask questions before the reading of each page, but other times he would do it just once before the whole story was read.

Teach Graphs or Illustrations A part of some prereading activities is a discussion of the pictures. Particularly in preprimers or primers, a good bit of the content or story line is carried by the *illustrations* or *graphs.* Teachers can point out significant features of the illustrations that aid the child in understanding the story. A discussion of the pictures can also serve to stimulate interest.

Reading Activities

Silent and Oral Some basal reading authors are most insistent that children read the story silently before it is read orally. Other authors are not concerned about this, in some cases directing the teacher to have the children read orally immediately after the prereading activity. In any event, both silent and oral reading frequently follow the prereading activities.

Read with Purpose When silent reading comes first, the teacher encourages the student to read with the purpose of answering specific questions discussed by the teacher. In some cases, more general purposes are stated, such as to get the mood, to see what is funny, to compare the story with their own experience, or to relate to other parts of the book. The students might then hold a discussion, and the teacher might direct them to reread parts of the story to verify points that are made.

Oral Reading Groups Oral reading is a staple part of the typical Directed Read-ing Activity. In the traditional classroom, this is done in small groups, each usually about a third of the class, comprised of students with similar reading ability. These groups are often called by names, such as the "Red Birds" and the "Blue Birds"; but by whatever name they are called, everybody, including all the children, knows that they are the top, middle, and low reading group. In the typical primary classroom, the groups are about a half a grade apart (even though ability ranges are wider). In the intermediate grades, they are about a year apart (even though ability ranges are certain to be much wider).

Round Robin During oral reading in the small group, children take turns reading aloud. This is sometimes colloquially referred to as "round robin" or the "barbershop method" because the teacher continually calls out "next." In the teacher's manuals, oral reading might be called "guided reading." It is guided because the teacher has set some purposes, and helps by supplying words that the student can't read or by giving the child who is stuck on a word suggestions on word attack, such as "What sound does it begin with?"

Phonics and the Whole Word Method In part, telling the student the word he or she can't read is the "whole word method," and telling the student to use word-attack skills is the "phonics method." Most teachers vary between the two, depending on the situation. Sometimes the teacher wishes to emphasize comprehension and not interrupt the flow of the story, so the whole word is supplied. At other times, the teacher sees the student's inability to read the word as an opportunity to show that word-attack skills are helpful.

Context Cues Another alternative to supplying the word and requesting the use of word-attack skills is to tell the child to use *context cues*. This is done by asking the child to look at a few words ahead and a few words behind the unknown word to see if the child can guess the word. This guessing can be aided or verified partially by some use of phonics. If the child knows the beginning sound of a word but can't sound it all out, then a combination of context cues plus the beginning sound can help him guess the word. Adult readers, incidentally, use context cues frequently when they don't know the meaning of a word or when they don't know a word in print.

Oral Reading Is Diagnostic Oral reading is diagnostic in that it gives the teacher immediate feedback about the words missed, the kinds of errors made, and some insights about the student's comprehension. The alert teacher can learn something about the child's interest, knowledge of sight words, ability to apply word-attack skills, and use of context cues. Oral reading not only gives the teacher information about the child's reading ability and general word knowledge, but it also gives the teacher a chance to guide the children into using valuable reading aids like word-attack skills and context cues.

Don't Overuse Oral Reading One potential problem with oral reading is that, if overused or done poorly, it can be very boring. Students can lose interest if they have to sit and wait for their turn to read while others stumble through the text. However, even listening can be a learning experience if the reading text is selected correctly; then there are new words in the text for most of the children. Silently reading along with the child who is reading orally, and associating the spoken word with the printed word, is a valuable learning experience.

Some reading authorities would argue that the oral reading of other children is presenting a poor model for a child to follow, and that students should only read aloud individually to the teacher. They could listen to the teacher or a professional reading the story on a tape recording while they follow along in the text, but this assumes that the child will pay attention to the tape. The group oral reading lesson has as one of its benefits the active attention of the teacher, who tries to see that every child is attending to the story.

Some reading authorities oppose extensive use of oral reading in small groups. However, this method has helped millions of children learn to read. But, like any other method, some teachers overemphasize it. Opponents claim that much classroom time is wasted by too much oral reading and that silent reading should be emphasized more.

If oral reading is done first, the teacher will then frequently instruct the group to read the whole story silently. When this is done, the teacher should be available to aid children who have difficulty with specific words. If silent reading is done first, then oral reading may be done only on selected parts.

Postreading Activities

Postreading Discussion   After the reading part of the lesson, the teacher frequently has another discussion about the story. This discussion might center around the children's ability to answer the questions posed in the prereading phase of the lesson. The postreading discussion is often a valuable comprehension-building activity. The teacher might ask individual children comprehension questions, such as: "Why did the girl fall into the brook?" "Was Mother happy?" "Was the ending as you expected it to be?" Note that the teacher should strive for questions which call for more comprehension than just recalling the facts. "How many cows were there?" is a low-level type of questioning. It is all right to sometimes see if the students are getting the facts or the specific details, but more critical or thought-provoking questions should be used most of the time.

Rereading of Parts   When there is disagreement between two or more children on an answer, a good suggestion is to have the pupils reread parts of the story to substantiate the answer. Children often like to catch each other in mistakes, and verification of concepts is a good type of comprehension-building activity. When dealing with critical reading or the more subjective questions, there is often no "right" answer; all answers are a matter of opinion. It is good for children to learn this, also. Both Chapter 5 on "Comprehension" and Chapter 11 on "Evaluation" contain classifications of various types of comprehension skills which you can use.

Workbook Use   Postreading activities include a number of types of activities other than discussion. One of the most frequent is use of the workbook that accompanies the basal series. The workbook use is often directed by the teacher's manual. Workbook activities are vocabulary building, word attack, and comprehension-type lessons. The comprehension lessons often correlate exactly with the story just read in the reader. They use the same new words or give added repetition and explanation for new words. Students are often drilled on the same skills focused on by the teacher in discussing the story.

Word-attack skills, including phonics, are systematically introduced throughout the series. Some series have heavy early first-grade phonics emphasis, and other series delay phonics somewhat and stretch it out through the primary grades.

Workbooks, sometimes called "activity books," are widely used. They are an integral part of most basal reading series, and supplementary workbooks designed for incidental use are widely used in addition to the basal workbooks. They are used because they systematically cover a predetermined list of skills both for initial presentation and for repetition or reinforcement. They are often interesting and keep the child actively involved in the learning process; however, they may be boring and tedious. The teacher must be aware of which workbooks are boring for which children on which lessons, and must seek other learning activities for them. Workbooks provide a record of each child's accomplishment and sometimes include formal tests of mastery of specific skills or knowledge of new vocabulary.

Since no method of teaching is free of criticism, workbooks have come in for their share. Critics of workbooks point out that they sometimes involve rote (mechanical learning) and do not provide for individual differences. They may develop skills in isolation and, if overused, may monopolize too much time.

Follow-up Activities Postreading activities also include numerous creative follow-up lessons, such as those dramatizing part of a story, or using the story content or vocabulary as a springboard for writing stories or drawing pictures. The stories in the readers may engender interest in some topic which can lead to suggested further reading in other texts or in library books. The teacher's manual will often suggest follow-up activities, but creative teachers can frequently think of many more.

Oral Reading

I have mentioned oral reading as part of the Directed Reading Activity or typical basal reader lesson; however, both during the DRA, and independent of it, the teacher might wish to have oral reading lessons. The first caution is not to "overdo" oral reading. Adults seldom read aloud. Hence, the real type of reading we should teach in school is silent reading. In secondary schools and colleges, oral reading is taught in the drama or speech department as a performing art. Silent reading for comprehension, on the other hand, is a daily necessity. If not overemphasized, reading aloud is useful in teaching elementary students. With that caution in mind, let's look at some oral reading techniques.

As I just pointed out in the DRA section, oral reading is diagnostic; that is, it gives the teacher excellent feedback on the child's knowledge of words and some insights on word-attack skills and facility in using context cues. However, if diagnosis is the chief purpose, then individual reading to the teacher is better than using a group reading situation.

Fluency Fluency, as opposed to word-by-word reading, is something most teachers strive for. Fluency means a smooth flow and proper intonation while reading the sentence. Linguists sometimes refer to *sentence tunes,* which means proper use of pitch and juncture. *Pitch* is the rising and falling of the voice, such as raising the voice at the end of a question. *Juncture* has to do with the almost imperceptible pauses between words or phrases which contribute to intelligibility. Extreme lack of juncture is a speech problem called *cluttering.* Old-time reading texts had many specific directions on sentence tunes, and modern linguists also study pitch and junctures as part of the communication process. Traditionalists considered pitch and juncture as part of *elocution,* or the art of speaking properly before an audience. See Figure 8-1.

The Rising Inflection is an upward turn, or slide of the voice, used in reading or speaking; as, Are you

prepared to recite your *léssons?*

The Falling Inflection is a downward turn, or slide of the voice, used in reading or speaking; as,

What are you *dóing?*

In the falling inflection, the voice should not sink below the *general pitch;* but in the rising inflection, it is raised above it.

The two inflections may be illustrated by the following diagrams:

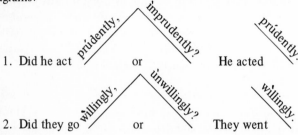

1. Did he act *prudently,* or *imprudently?*   He acted *prúdently.*

2. Did they go *willingly,* or *unwillingly?*   They went *wíllingly.*

Figure 8-1 Sentence tunes, or pitch, as taught in an old reader. (*From The New School Reader, fourth book by Charles W. Sanders, Ivison, Blakeman, Taylor & Company, New York, 1880.*)

Reading teachers properly perceive fluency as part of comprehension. Students who read a sentence in a very "flat" manner often do not understand it well, or at least are not comfortable reading at this level. In Betts' terms this might be one indication of reading at the frustration level. Betts' levels of reading difficulty (independent, instructional, and frustration) during oral reading will be discussed in Chapter 11 as part of "Informal Reading Inventory."

Another oral reading problem encountered by reading teachers is *word calling.* This means reading each word as though it were isolated. Again, this is a fluency problem and can be related to poor comprehension.

When word calling or poor sentence tune is observed, the first thing the teacher should do is to question the reading level of the material. It may be too high for the child. If not, then instruction may proceed using some kind of modeling proedure. The teacher or another child reads the sentence fluently with good tune, and the child imitates it. Use of a tape recorder is also helpful in dealing with the problem. Tape-record both the child having problems and a correct model, and let the child hear himself in comparison with the model. Repeated practice with the tape recorder often brings remarkable improvement.

Choral Reading   Choral reading is another standard technique used to improve oral reading. In choral reading, a group of children read in unison. Weaker students can follow the lead of superior students, and hence it is partly a modeling procedure. It is also a way of getting repetition of new words. Students who are having trouble learning new words see and hear the word (associate) one more time. Choral reading of some selections and poems can be akin to singing, and creative classrooms sometimes put on performances of choral reading for other members of the class, the school, or PTA groups.

Plays   Another excellent method of involving children in oral reading activities is to have them read plays or radio scripts. Donald Durrell and B. Alice Crossley have authored a book of plays for elementary classroom oral reading practice entitled, *Thirty Plays for Classroom Reading, Grades 4-6*, published by Plays, Inc. (8 Arlington Street, Boston). Other plays useful in oral reading can be found in the list of materials at the end of this chapter. The school librarian or teachers interested in drama are good sources for recommendations of more books or plays. Having the children read the play into a tape recorder makes it more fun and gives them excellent feedback. They enjoy hearing themselves perform, and they frequently will follow along in the book while listening and correct their own mistakes. Other children can then use the tape as a listen-while-reading activity. They often enjoy hearing the voices of their friends.

Make Word Lists from Oral Errors   To improve the efficacy of an oral reading lesson, make lists of the words each child misses or needs help in pronouncing. When a child is finished reading, the sheet of paper is given to the child to study. The teacher might ask the student to practice writing the words and locating them in the story just read. After the child feels that he or she has mastered them, they are read to the teacher, or the teacher can ask the child to bring them to the reading group the next day and read them. Teachers, particularly teachers of primary-age children, find that the children sometimes lose their sheet of paper; a good trick is to use a sheet of carbon paper so that the teacher has another copy. The teacher's carbon copy can be kept in the child's file folder and becomes a valuable individualized study list or spelling list. If you can do this, don't get exasperated if you find the same words cropping up on a child's list over and over again, just go right on teaching them; that's part of the job.

SIGHT WORD BUILDING

One of the functions of basal series is to teach sight words (or *recognition vocabulary,* as it might sometimes be called). Oral reading is another way of teaching recognition vocabulary; however, there are a number of other methods of teaching the recognition of words.

Many basal readers have the vocabulary printed on *flash cards.* These cards are usually about 4 by 8 inches, with one word printed on them in large type. When used as flash cards, the teacher holds up the card with the back (blank) side to the reading group, then quickly shows (flashes) the word by flipping the card over for a second. The children try to call out the word. This is a pure sight-recognition task as there is no possible time to use word-attack skills or context cues

The same card can be used as a *sentence building card*. The children or the teacher can line the cards up along the chalkboard, or in a pocket chart, to form phrases or sentences. Children sometimes enjoy moving the cards about to make different sentences, and enjoy seeing how the sentence differs with just the changing or adding of one card.

Some workbook pages are aimed at building sight vocabulary by having the children write the words or use them in a variety of circumstances, such as matching, seeing the word in different kinds of type, or altering the word by adding bound morphemes. The workbook might be part of the basal series or it might be part of a supplementary workbook. In fact, the same kind of exercise might be on ditto sheets or on separate plastic-coated cards (which the child can write on with crayon which can later be wiped off).

Sometimes children enjoy making their own individual set of flashcards from lists of words that they have missed in oral reading, or new words that are introduced in the basal series, or words that turn up as "unknown" on criterion referenced tests of basal vocabularies.

Correlating spelling lessons with new or needed words is a standard technique which gives the child much additional practice in seeing the word and studying its parts.

Last but not least, just the act of reading is practice in using and developing a sight word vocabulary. Easy silent reading is one of the finest ways to improve a sight word vocabulary.

Vocabulary Improvement

The term *vocabulary improvement* is most often used when a child is being taught the meaning of new words. In building a sight or recognition vocabulary, it is usually assumed that the child knows the meaning of the word, that it is part of his or her listening or speaking vocabulary. Vocabulary improvement usually implies that the child learns the meaning of a word, or one particular meaning of the word in any form, not previously known. Children have much larger listening vocabularies than speaking vocabularies; larger speaking vocabularies than reading vocabularies; larger reading vocabularies than writing vocabularies.

Vocabulary improvement is done much more extensively in the upper grades than in the primary grades. While it is an important part of reading instruction, it is, or should be, a very important part of lessons in most other subjects. For example, one of the goals of this book is to help you master the vocabulary of reading (that is one reason for the "Vocabulary Study Terms" at the end of each chapter). In teaching science, or social studies, or art, or any subject, it is important to use the proper vocabulary and to teach the child to read the words of that subject and to know their meanings. The word "slip" has one meaning in common language, a different meaning in pottery making, another quite different meaning in girls' clothing, a fourth meaning for sailors, etc.

Where can a teacher find vocabulary improvement materials? There are numerous sources. For example, some of the postreading activities of the *Readers Digest Skill*

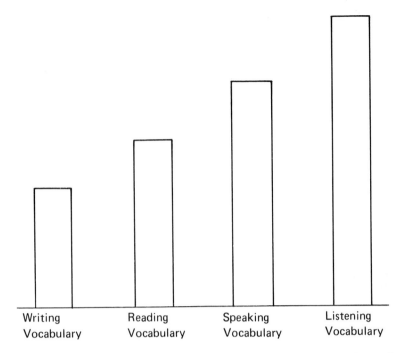

Figure 8-2 Bar graph showing the relative sizes of listening, speaking, reading, and writing vocabularies of elementary children.

Builders have vocabulary-building exercises. Some pages of workbooks, both supmentary and basal, have vocabulary building. Spelling series often contain some vocabulary building. Classroom dictionaries, such as the *Thorndike-Barnhart* dictionaries, have dictionary use lessons in the front of each copy, and some of these have excellent suggestions for vocabulary improvement. Richard Boning has a graded series of exercises, entitled "Reading Hononyms," as part of the Dexter and Westbrook *Supportive Reading Skills.* Many subject-matter texts in science and mathematics have vocabulary building aids ranging from glossaries to specific mention of word meanings in the text. The SRA laboratory cards often contain vocabulary-building exercises. See the list of materials at the end of this chapter for many more.

In addition to the many commercial materials, teachers develop their own lessons. Asking a child to keep a list of words that she doesn't know while she is reading is an old standard. The teacher then discusses the student's word list with her. This discussion is probably better than just telling her to look the words up in the dictionary, because it is more personal and motivating. However, a dictionary can also be used with the child's individual vocabulary building list. Teachers often have class discussions on word meanings and sometimes do this systematically using common roots or words with similar derivatives.

Probably one of the most important factors in students' vocabularies is the teacher's attitude toward learning word meanings. If the teacher shows a genuine interest in word meaning—by discussion, by looking words up in the dictionary, and in carefully explaining new words in context—the child will learn to value word meanings.

Word-Attack Materials

In this section I will not distinguish between phonics and other word-attack skills such as affixes or syllabification. The amount of commercially available materials in this area is almost staggering. You can teach phonics with charts, filmstrips, games, workbooks, programmed instruction, ditto pages, basal series, spelling lessons, and audio cards. Without any particular attempt to evaluate them or recommend one over the other, here are some of the methods teachers use with commercially prepared and self-made materials.

Word wheels which substitute part of a word have been around for decades. They are really part of the old system we have seen in the McGuffey Readers with initial consonant substitution; can, fan, ran, man, etc. By rotating a paper disk with a hole in it, the initial consonant can be made to change. The same mechanical word part substitution can be done with cards which have fold-over smaller cards (see Figure 8-3).

A number of workbooks and ditto master sets teach phonics skills exclusively; *Phonics We Use* and the Merrill Skill text are among the better-known phonic workbook series. Using workbooks can be expensive, especially if the student only needs one or two exercises in the whole book. A way around this is to buy sets of ditto masters and run off only the number of pages needed for those students who have demonstrated weaknesses in phonics skills; the teacher can then teach the skills needed.

Many word-attack skills are taught in parts of the curriculum not labeled "reading." For example, syllabification or using proper suffixes might be part of a writing lesson or part of a language arts or grammar lesson. Phoneme-grapheme correspondence (phonics) is regularly part of many spelling lessons. In fact, some whole spelling series, by such authors as William Kottmeyer and Paul Hanna, have a strong phonics base. It is often reinforcing for the child to have phonics or syllabification taught in some context other than reading. It is an interesting experience when you see a child realize that something taught at one time in one context is applicable at another time in another context.

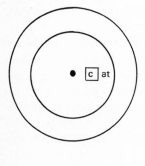

Word Wheel

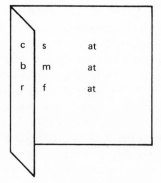

Foldover Cards

Figure 8-3   Illustration of word wheel and foldover card.

TEACHING COMPREHENSION

We have already discussed many ways of teaching comprehension in Chapter 5, which was wholly devoted to comprehension, and in Chapter 7, which discussed the basal series. In Chapter 11 we will discuss the testing of comprehension skills. However, there are many more ways. For example, one of the Croft skill packs has small booklets with half a dozen workbook-type pages devoted to reading comprehension.

Another excellent type of comprehension-teaching materials is the set of questions at the end of each short chapter in various supplemental readers, such as the *Checkered Flag Series,* the *American Adventure Series,* or the *Deep Sea Adventure Series.* These supplemental series cover the elementary reading levels and have especially high interest for reluctant readers or older children who are reading at a lower grade level. For example, a sixth-grader who can only read at a second- or third-grade level need not feel the least bit embarrassed reading from these series, as they are not aimed at the interest level of younger children; in fact, such themes as auto racing, deep sea diving, and the Old West frontier appeal to a very wide range of ages. Some of these series (such as the *Checkered Flag*) also have audio tape cassettes so that the child can listen to the tape while reading for an interesting individual or group activity (see Figure 8-4). The comprehension questions for each chapter of these series can be used for oral discussion or written response; both are good ways to teach comprehension.

The Science Research Associates (SRA) is probably best known among reading teachers for its SRA Laboratories, which were originally developed by Don Parker. These boxes are full of folded cardboard sheets, each making up a four-page lesson which usually contains a short story followed by some comprehension questions and some word-attack skills. The students are given a workbook which tests to determine what level they should be working on; then each child starts selecting lessons at the appropriate color-coded level (Mary is in green, Sammy is in brown, etc.) After the student reads the story, he or she answers the questions in the workbook, then goes back to the kit and gets the answer card to correct his or her own written answers. The student works through all the cards on one level (color), then proceeds to the next higher level. On the lowest levels, grades below three, the levels are about two-tenths of a year apart. At the upper levels they are six months and a full year apart. The lessons are not graded too accurately, but at least they are a serious attempt to provide multilevel materials for use in a single classroom. A few teachers use the SRA laboratories instead of a basal reading series, but the SRA labs are used primarily as a supplement. Teachers like them because they provide both easy and difficult materials, for children of different abilities, that can be used simultaneously. You can have a child with sixth-grade ability sitting alongside a child with second-grade ability, both working at their appropriate level (color). Another feature of the SRA labs is that they are self-correcting. Of course, the teacher has to check up on the children regularly to see that they are indeed working at the correct level and that they are using the lessons properly (not looking at the answer key first). Some of the lessons, particularly the word-attack sections, need a bit of teacher explanation, and brief discussions of incorrect comprehension answers are helpful and motivating. Like most other types of lessons, the SRA labs can be used too much and can become boring. Table 8-1 shows the range of SRA labs available and the approximate reading levels they cover.

Figure 8-4 *The Checkered Flag Series* by H. A. Bamman and R. J. Whitehead. (Addison-Wesley Publishing Company, Inc., School Division, copyright 1968.)

Another interesting SRA product is the *Junior Reading for Understanding,* a kit which contains 400 different cards, each with 10 short unfinished paragraphs and a choice of conclusions. Many teachers and students find this an interesting and different comprehension training method.

Table 8-1 SRA Reading Laboratory Ranges

Reading laboratory	Reading level range	Possible classroom grade*
1a	1.2 – 3.5	1
1b	1.4 – 4.5	2
1c	1.6 – 5.5	3
2a	2.0 – 7.0	4
2b	2.5 – 8.0	5
3a	3.5 – 11.0	7
3b	5.0 – 12.0	8

*The possible classroom grade is merely a suggestion; the teacher should use kits in which the range of reading levels most nearly matches the children's abilities. For example, the teacher might want to use the SRA lab only with the slow children in the class, and thus should choose a lab with lower reading levels.

PROGRAMMED INSTRUCTION

Teaching materials have undergone vast changes in the past 200 years. In Colonial times, children had the hornbook—a paddle containing the alphabet, a few syllables, and the Lord's Prayer. They then used the *New England Primer,* which quickly moved from alphabet jingles to psalms. In the middle 1800s, the McGuffey and other reading texts came in series of half a dozen short but roughly graded books. Readers developed in the earlier half of this century, but the new innovation was the workbook. We are now in a period of multiple materials, including books from basal series, supplementary readers, and graded trade books, plus numerous devices, such as cards and audiovisual materials.

An innovation of the 1960s was programmed instruction. This movement attempted to combine testing ("start where the child is" or "teach him what he needs next"), specific objectives, and individually paced self-correcting principles. It is based on the techniques and learning principles of Sidney Pressy, in the 1920s, and B. F. Skinner, in the 1940s. One way in which programmed instruction differs from textbook exercises is that the feedback (self-correction) is immediate after each response. Purists would not consider the SRA materials programmed instruction or programmed learning because the student answers 10 or more questions before any self-correction is done. They would say that the feedback is neither immediate enough nor specific enough. Frequently, a student who corrects a workbook page gets a score like 70 percent correct. This is not good learning feedback—it is more important that he knows that he couldn't find a short /i/ immediately after he tried, and furthermore, he should be told what a short /i/ is right then and there, not five minutes or one day later.

There is probably no single element in programmed instruction that couldn't be found elsewhere, but the combination of them is unique. While each of the elements have historical atnecedents, modern programmed materials differ significantly from materials used by Colonial or Civil War-era teachers.

The following elements can be used elsewhere in your teaching, and you will see them in many commercially prepared materials.

Specific Objectives Are a Prerequisite What do you want the child to know? Some educators are particularly concerned that the objectives be *behavioral objectives*. This means that the child exhibits behavior that can be observed. Though the term isn't used, much the opposite of a behavioral objective is a *cognitive objective*.

Examples of these two types are:

A *behavioral objective* might be "given the graphemes A E I O U, a child can orally make the short sounds."

A *cognitive objective* might be "the child understands simple written directions."

Note that the behavioral objective is much more specific, stating exactly what behavior can be observed. Programmed instruction can use either type of objective, but there is a tendency toward behavioral objectives. The field is split, however, with some definitely advocating behavioral objectives while others permit the use of cognitive objectives. The idea of specifying objectives did not originate with either Skinner or Pressey; earlier educationists like W. W. Charters, and others in the scientific education movement of the 1920s, were concerned with better teaching objectives.

Small Units Programmers want the material in relatively short sections for easy step-by-step learning, which provides for frequent reinforcement (rewards for learning).

In programmed instruction, the small unit is often called a *frame,* and might consist of a sentence or two of material plus provision for some type of response. In the Sullivan programmed reading materials, the response required might be the circling of a "yes" or a "no," or it might be to fill in several missing letters or words which demonstrate reading comprehension, or the proper use of a word-attack skill. The Sullivan materials might be called "small step" because there is not much to read before making a response. Another aspect of small step is that the "cognitive distance," or amount of material to be learned, is reasonably small. See Figure 8-6.

The other type of programmed instruction material, which for the sake of clarity we will call "large step," requires more reading. Note Figure 8-5 for the Lessons for Self-Instruction; a whole paragraph must be read before a multiple-choice response is made by turning to the page or frame indicated alongside each choice.

The response can be written (sometimes called "corrected response"), which requires the student to *recall* the answer, or the response can be multiple-choice, which requires that the student merely *recognize* the correct answer. Research has shown that recognizing (selecting from several choices) is easier, or requires less mastery of the material, than a recall answer, where the student must come up with the answer from memory.

Feedback The next element of programmed instruction is the immediate *feedback*, which is given frame by frame or response by response. In the case of the *Sullivan Programmed Reading Program,* the student gets immediate feedback by moving

This is another lesson on facts that you learn in- **21**
directly. You will again have a question about the
paragraph you have been studying. Read it again, if
you wish.

> The earthworm is very small, but it
> helps people. It lives in damp ground.
> The earthworm burrows through the soil
> and eats it. It brings soil from under the
> ground to the surface. In this way, the
> earthworm acts like a plow. It loosens
> the soil and lets air in. That is good for
> plants. Our food is better because the
> earthworm works in the ground.

The paragraph tells things directly. It also tells
things indirectly.

Below are three statements. The information in
one of them is given in the paragraph. You are to
find that statement.

> Farmers do not like the
> earthworm.   (No. 27)

> The earthworm is a mammoth
> creature.   (No. 33)

> The earthworm makes the soil
> more fertile.   (No. 37)

Which statement contains information that is also
in the paragraph?

Farmers do not like the earthworm.   **27**

 No. This information is not contained
in the paragraph. You could not learn
it from anything said in the paragraph.
You could learn, indirectly, just the opposite. A
farmer likes anything that is good for plants. What
the earthworm does is good for plants. Therefore,
farmers like the earthworm.

Return to No. 21. Remember: You are looking
for a statement with information indirectly contained
in the paragraph. Read the two other choices.

Figure 8-5 Sample frame from a larger-step, programmed instruction booklet using a simple
branching sequence and multiple-choice response. This is teaching comprehension at approximately fifth-grade level. *Note:* The two other choices on pages 33 and 37 are part of this frame,
but are not reproduced here. Students mark a record of all choices on a separate student record
sheet. [*From* Lessons for Self-Instruction in Basic Skills (LSI), Reading Interpretations II, Know
What You Read Level C–D, *by Gracecarol Bostwick (Consultants Edward Fry and Lawrence
Carrillo), California Test Bureau, a division of McGraw-Hill Book Company, Monterey, California, 1965.*]

a slider down the inside margin of the page, which exposes the correct answer (hopefully after the student has written the answer on the page). See Figure 8-6.

In the case of the lessons for self-instruction, the student gets immediate feedback by turning to the frame corresponding to the choice she has made. When she gets to the frame of her choice, she is greated by a smiling or a frowning little face plus some reasons explaining the smile or frown.

Some programmed instruction is done by teaching machines. These operate on programmed instruction principles, and give feedback by red or green lights or by simply not progressing to the next frame until the student presses the right choice key.

Feedback can be of several types:

1   Right or wrong, yes/no, green light/red light
2   Wrong, but here is the right answer
3   Wrong, but here is why you are wrong

Figure 8-6 Sample page of small-step programmed instruction using linear sequence and constructed responses. Note use of phonetically regular words. This illustration is at the first-grade level. *From* Programmed Reading (3rd ed.) *by Cynthia D. Buchanan, Sullivan Associates, Webster Division, McGraw-Hill Book Company, St. Louis, 1973.*

The Sullivan programmed reading books tend to tell the student either (1) yes or no, or (2) here is the right answer. The lessons for self-instruction tend to give "why" the answer was right or wrong.

Another criterion for "size of step" is the percent of correct answers a student gets. Small-step programs arrange the materials so that the student is correct a large percentage of the time (low error rate). The large-step type of program is not so concerned with low error rates, but is based on the notion that the student can learn by making mistakes and having them corrected. Hence, one is more in favor of following small steps, and one is more in favor of trial-and-error learning or large steps.

Behavior Modification Some educators advocate *rewarding*, or as Skinner would say, *reinforcing;* learning by giving the child a token after he or she gets a specified number of correct answers. Tokens can later be traded in for prizes like dolls or going to recess early. This system of using tokens is sometimes applied to other methods of learning outside of programmed instruction, and is called *token economies* or *behavior modification.* The basic idea is that you control behavior by rewarding (reinforcing) the desired behavior and ignoring no behavior or undesired behavior. Teachers have long used some aspects of behavior modification by praising students for good behavior. Teachers may also use more formal systems, like putting a gold star on a chart opposite the child's name for each book read or each comprehension drill answered perfectly. The difference between the teacher's gold star system and modern behavior modification is in the specificity and immediacy of the reward, but the basic idea is similar.

The use of negative reward or punishment is not used in programmed instruction, nor is it used much in modern schools. Both programmers and educators find that there are less emotional and value judgment complications if punishment is avoided. Most of the time, behavior can be shaped with positive reinforcement or rewards. Punishment was a significant feature of schools of Colonial times (and even up to the early parts of this century), but society has changed in the ways of controlling children's learning behavior. The old dunce cap hasn't been used for a while, but valedictorians are still "in."

Program authors would argue that programs often are highly motivational because the student is continually getting feedback. Being told he or she is correct has the effect of positive rewarding.

Sequencing Proponents of programmed instruction claim that it focuses on proper learning sequence to a far greater extent than do most instructional materials. They even claim that the sequencing can be more objectively determined by looking at the student's responses. If the student starts making a lot of errors, there is something wrong; the program is not teaching. Maybe the steps are too large, and more information must be given before those particular responses are made. Note that they don't blame the student when learning doesn't occur. It is the fault of the program author, or the fault of the teacher for using a program that proceeds too rapidly or is inappropriate. Perhaps reading teachers could learn something from this attitude whether or not they ever use programmed instruction materials.

Another interesting factor in sequencing is that some programs are *linear;* after frame 1 comes frame 2, then frame 3, etc. Every student goes through the program in the same sequence. The student might work faster or slower, but doesn't skip anything.

The other type of sequencing is *branching,* where the student who misses an answer is given more information (or even shuttled onto a remedial loop), to return to the main program sequence after demonstrating mastery in some skill. The Sullivan materials tend to be linear, and the lessons for self-instruction tend to be branching. When computers are used in programmed instruction, the branching can be rather elaborate. Some test management systems and basal reading series have a kind of branching concept built into them by cycling students who do not learn back into additional instructional material.

Individualized Instruction   Last but not least, programmed instruction has some factors that are implied but rarely directly stated. It is similar to some kinds of individualized instruction. Pretests, if passed, given an indication that the student does not need to go through the material. Since students go through a program on an individual basis, they can progress at their own rates; there is not a group to keep up with (this is good in that some students need to go slower, but poor in that they might not get the motivation group learning often engenders).

In many systems of programmed instruction, there is a record made of learning activities (answers to questions in frames) through which the teacher can check student's progress.

Programmed Instruction in the Curriculum   Programmed instruction has been used in many subject areas, from telling time for elementary children to teaching the weather code to airline employees. In reading, it has been used chiefly to teach comprehension, phonics, and vocabulary.

As you look over other instructional materials, systems, and methods used in teaching reading, you will find some of these elements of programmed instruction in all of them. For example, some school districts have their curriculum guides written in behavioral objectives, and advocate audiovisual devices which require responses, or test management systems that require specific objectives and mastery. The teaching machine or programmed instruction movement has had an influence on several major trends in education, but programmed instruction materials account for only a relatively small amount of instruction time. Programmed instruction in book format is more popular than when the same principles are embodied in a teaching machine or computer (CAI – Computer Assisted Instruction).

Perhaps the most valuable thing programmed instruction has done for reading, or any education area, is the insight it has given teachers to the application of a number of important learning principles, such as:

Specifying objectives
Pretesting before teaching
Student involvement (activity)

Immediacy of feedback

Specificity of feedback (exact step missed)

Types of feedback (right versus wrong; why wrong)

Learning in small units

Branching

Need for clarity (so student can respond correctly)

A systems approach (set goal, careful sequence of steps to get there, individualized record keeping)

Reward or success as a motivation factor

Individualized instruction (each student on a different topic or different rates of progress or different branches)

DIFFERENT ALPHABETIC APPROACHES

As you saw in Chapter 2, there is less than a one-to-one phoneme-grapheme correspondence; that is, each letter in our alphabet does not have one, and only one, sound. For anyone learning to read, it would certainly be easier if each letter had only one sound. The notion of simplifying the alphabet is not recent. In 1644, an Englishman names Hodges was an advocate of a modified alphabet, as was Benjamin Franklin in this country in 1768, and numerous people since then have made similar proposals. Most recently it occurred to Sir James Pitman, an Englishman and grandson of Isaac Pitman, the developer of the shorthand system. Isaac Pitman, incidentally, developed a modified alphabet for children to learn to read by in 1844.

Initial Teaching Alphabet

Sir James Pitman started a noble experiment in the British schools with something called the "Augmented Roman Alphabet." Because its purpose (to aid in teaching reading) was misunderstood, the name of Sir James' system was changed to the Initial Teaching Alphabet, or ITA.

The ITA "augments" our regular alphabet by adding a number of characters. Long vowels in ITA have their own symbol, which looks much like a letter "e," added to and touching the vowel letter (see Figure 8-7). In addition to the added characters, there is a spelling reform; for example, "said" becomes "sed." However, the changes provide compatibility. Persons fluent in regular English writing (which ITA people refer to as "TO," for Traditional Orthography) can read ITA with no instruction. It seems a little odd at first, but fluency is obtained with very little practice. Try it yourself.

While common sense might tell us that a one-to-one letter-sound correspondence should produce better readers, large-scale research studies, comparing students taught with and without ITA, did not find much difference. ITA advocates still claim a slight superiority, but the vast majority of reading experts in both the United States and Britain claim that if there is any difference at all, it is so slight it is not worth bothering about. However, conversely, there is no evidence that it harms children or that there is any significant difficulty with transition into TO, which occurred in about the upper second or third grade in most ITA systems.

sωn ∫hɛɛ met jack, bob and bill.

"lωk at us!" ∫hæ sed. "∫his iꞩ fun!"

∫he littl œld wωman tωk bob'ꞩ tin can stilts.

it woꞩ fun tω wauk on ∫hem!

∫hɛɛ gæv ∫hem back and went on.

10

Figure 8-7 Sample page of a children's reader printed in ITA (Initial Teaching Alphabet) which gives a more regular phoneme-grapheme correspondence by the use of a modified alphabet and simplified spelling. It has been used in a number of British and American schools for beginning reading instruction. (*From Book 4,* Early to Read, ITA, *Albert Mazurkiewicz and Harold Tanyzer, Pitman, New York, 1963.*)

The height of both experiments and ITA use occurred in the second half of the 1960s. ITA is still being used in the 1970s, but in far fewer schools.

Many ITA studies did show that children writing in ITA did write longer and (according to some) better stories, but they wrote them under the special condition of the teacher saying, "Don't pay any attention to your spelling as you will have to change spelling systems in a year or two anyway." It is possible that children taught in TO and given instructions to disregard spelling would write longer stories, too.

Some linguists point out that in spelling or alphabet reforms, such as the ITA, it is possible to lose morphemic information; for example, "principle" and "principal" would be spelled the same. Another factor is that, after the primary years, phoneme-grapheme correspondence plays a very small part in the reading process.

Incidentally, there is no solid evidence that ITA was especially beneficial to any particular group, such as boys or girls, bright or dull, younger or older children. One beneficial effect of ITA use was that it helped teachers renew their own enthusiasm about teaching reading and taught them a lot about phonics.

Other Alphabet Modifications

There have been numerous other alphabet modifications, but none has been tried out on as large a scale as ITA. Some have special purposes; Unifon, for example, has phonetic regularity, but the letters are strangely shaped so that some types of computers can more easily read the print. Words in Color used letters of different color to indicate different sounds. Words in Color did not print textbooks with colored letters, but rather had a series of charts which had drill words and parts of words ("ta," "ut," "tu"). The children had drills on the charts, then read books in black ink.

I tried an experiment using diacritical marks on letters to give them phonetic regularity, yet maintaining the same basic word form and spelling. While it worked as well as ITA and TO, the system had no real advantages. The Diacritical Marking System, DMS, survives today only as a teacher training device or aid in explaining new words. However, a few teachers use the DMS to teach their children phonics and to give them a better understanding of dictionary phonetic systems. It also has some use in introducing new words. This isn't exactly a new idea, as McGuffey used diacritical marks in introducing new words and, in 1894, Edward Ward printed whole primers using a diacritical marking system.

Simplified-spelling systems have met a fate similar to that of alphabet reformers; however, there are even today small, active simplified-spelling societies in Britain, and some active individuals in the United States. Simplified spelling certainly makes a lot of sense, but it seems impossible to get the English-speaking world to change the present orthography now that there are so many books in print and so many people literate under the present system. The problem is that the people who really need a simplified system, the children and the illiterate adults, have no political power. Simplified spelling systems would save money, as books and newspapers would take less space printed in simplified orthography, but these savings are not major enough to overcome the inertia of the present system. The objections of some linguists (about losing morphemic information) might also be a factor.

AUDIOVISUAL READING MATERIALS

When you think about reading materials, you nearly always think of printed materials on paper, such as books, newspapers, magazines, or even workbooks. However, there is a large variety of ways to present reading lessons in other than the traditional print media. Here are a few of them:

Television
Video cassettes
Film
Filmstrips (with and without sound)
Slides
Overhead transparencies
Card readers
Records and tapes
Charts
Wipe-off cards
Games

Television Some studies show that children spend more time per year watching television than they spend in school. A few critics see television as incompatible with, or hostile to, reading; however, there is no firm evidence for this. Book sales are higher than ever before, standardized scores on reading achievement tests are higher now than in preceding decades, and there is some evidence of a decrease in the number of adult illiterates. There is also some evidence that television can facilitate reading. Programs such as "Sesame Street" and "The Electric Company" are watched by millions of children. "Sesame Street" emphasizes reading readiness instruction with just a bit of beginning reading, and "The Electric Company" was originally aimed at urban poor readers in the middle elementary ages; however, it is watched by all types of children in ages from preschool to junior high. Many schools have supplemental reading instruction, either using these programs during school time or in keying some supplemental lessons to programs watched at home. At least one publisher, Addison Wesley, has developed some reading books and materials to correlate with "The Electric Company," and other manufacturers have developed dolls and toys based on these shows. Figure 6 in Chapter 2 shows a sample of a TV lesson in phonics.

Video Cassettes This relatively new way of playing back TV shows, in the classroom and at the teacher's convenience, operates much like a record player or tape recorder except that it plays back both the picture and the sound through a TV monitor. Some schools have cassette equipment which will also record, so that teachers or classes can make their own TV programs.

There are newer technological developments on the horizon which will enable the recording of TV shows on something like a phonograph record, which should substantially lower the cost. As the cost comes down, it will be more feasible for classrooms to have television-type reading instruction in the classroom for the whole class, small groups, or even individuals. The teacher will have to decide for whom, when, how much time, which program, what content, etc. Those who fear that television or some automated device will replace the teacher simply haven't studied the many variables.

Large-group instruction, which in the case of television means thousands or millions of children at one time, has some advantages in that very carefully planned instruction can occur; production costs can be in the many thousands of dollars for a half-hour show. But mass instruction often needs to be individualized to be effective. As we all know, television can waste a lot of time. At its best, it can be very effective, and at its worst . . . ; teacher judgement will always be needed.

Films Films are a medium much like television, but they are used on a much less regular schedule. Broadcast television tends to have many more daily or weekly series with only an occasional "special," but in films, it is the reverse. Most films used in the schools are special-topic type films selected for one-time use. There are a number of films about reading for teacher training, and a few for children. For example, the movie version of a current novel or a classic book is shown before the students are required to read it in class. Incidentally, bookstores and libraries report that children frequently request a book after seeing a movie or television version.

Direct reading instruction by film has been used more at upper levels; for example, there are a number of films aimed at increasing the reading rates of secondary students and adults.

Filmstrips These provide a variety of reading instruction approaches. One common type is designed like a series of illustrated charts, and is used for such things as phonics instruction. Another common type presents words and phrases to be flashed tachistoscopically. A tachistoscope ("ta-kiss-toe-scope") is any device that flashes a visual image in less time than it takes to make an eye movement (one-fifth of a second). A tachistoscope frequently uses a filmstrip projector (with a specially prepared filmstrip) that has a shutter for controlling a very brief exposure time. Tachistoscopic presentations often hold high interest for regular and special education children.

Sound Filmstrips These are regular filmstrips accompanied by a record or audiotape cassette. A narration is programmed to accompany each frame (picture) of the filmstrip. Some sound filmstrips fit special projectors in which the filmstrip automatically advances at the proper time in the audio narration. Reading programs for sound filmstrips can teach any part of reading, though they most frequently are used to present stories such as are found in trade books. In reading readiness sound filmstrip programs, the illustration is shown and the narrator tells the story. For more direct reading instruction, the filmstrip can show the printed words while the narrator reads them. Reading exercises akin to workbook-type drills are presented auditorily and visually.

Overhead Transparencies Large sheets of clear plastic, usually about 8 by 10 inches, on which words and illustrations are printed, are called "overhead transparencies." They are projected on a screen or the chalkboard by an overhead projector so that the teacher faces the group while the group sees the projected image behind the teacher. This medium has several advantages. One advantage is that the teacher can easily point to parts of the chart, or even add to it by writing on the transparency with a grease pencil. Another advantage is that the plastic sheets can easily be stored in file folders, each taking up no more room than a sheet of paper. Several companies put out combination overhead transparency-ditto-master workbooks for such subjects as phonics and reading comprehension. The teacher can run the ditto masters on a ditto machine (purple ink) so that each child can have a workbook-type page. For group instruction, the teacher can project the overhead transparency of the exact page and even fill it in. Students can first try to make their response on their own individual worksheets, then by group discussion the teacher can help them decide which is the best answer. Filling in the transparency with a grease pencil enables the children to see, as well as to hear, the answer. Transparencies need not be limited to workbook page content; some are well-prepared charts used in initial presentations of such topics as syllabification and phoneme-grapheme correspondences. Any teacher who has tried to store several sets of reading charts will appreciate the convenience of overhead transparencies.

Charts Made of good old ink on heavy paper, charts are not outmoded by transparencies and other projected visual devices because they, too, have several valuable and unique characteristics. A chart is useful in a group explanation, but it is also often left exposed so that the child can refer back to it during the day or for the next few days. Projected images, such as overhead transparencies, are usually turned off and put away immediately after the lesson. Charts are also more "touchable" than projected images. It is not a good idea to touch any film screen, particularly if it is a beaded-glass screen, but children and the teacher can hold their hands under a word, or point directly to an illustration. It is also possible to leave several charts exposed at one time, whereas projectors are able to show only one frame or transparency at a time.

Reading charts are used more at the primary level than in intermediate grades, and the charts are often on a chart rack which is at eye level for little children, again contributing to the feeling of closeness. Some basal reading series have a series of charts in a "big book" which is an exact replica of a preprimer. Other popular series of charts recapitulate phonics rules and are often used in remedial or supplementary reading as well as regular classrooms.

Charts are probably the most common medium for teacher-made or student-made audiovisual devices. In Chapter 10 we will discuss the importance of charts in the language experience approach where children dictate a short story and the teacher writes it on a chart. An interesting instructional procedure is to have children draw illustrations of various phoneme-grapheme correspondences on charts; for example, one child makes a picture of a pig, and writes the word "pig" under it emphasizing the "p," while another child makes a picture of a phoneme emphasizing the "ph," etc. These individual phonics charts are then tacked all around the top of the chalkboards for semipermanent display. The teacher refers to them when a child is "stuck" on a word while reading. Another important use can be when the children are allowed to look at them during writing lessons or a spelling "test." The set of phonics charts acts as a phoneme-grapheme (sound-symbol) dictionary.

Card Readers Exemplified by the Bell and Howell "Language Master" and the Califone Card Reader Model 4400, card readers are audio devices which read cards. The student inserts a printed card into the machine, and the machine "says" the word or phrase printed on the card. The machine doesn't "read" the printed word, but passes a strip of magnetic tape (pasted on the bottom of the card) past a tape recorder head. The audio output can be through a speaker for small-group listening, through an earphone for individual use, or through a group of earphones when the teacher prefers silence in the classroom. The Instant Words and other basic vocabularies are available on cards (Califone), as are phonics and language acquisition cards.

The tape at the base of the card is really two-track, and the other track can be used for recording. The teacher can instruct the child to say the word as he or she passes the card through the machine. By pushing a button and passing the card through the machine a second time, the child can hear the correct word being spoken on the instructor's track. On the third pass through the machine, the child can hear his or her initial response, compare it with the instructor's, and see if he or she was correct.

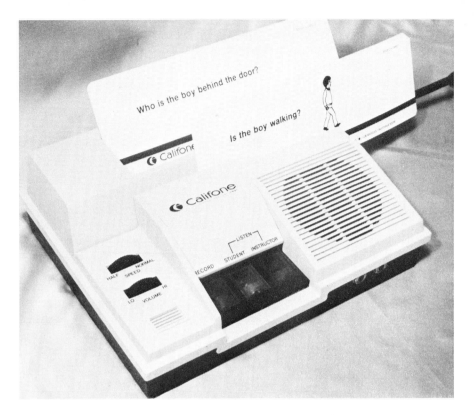

A card reader. When a student inserts an audio card, the word or phrase printed on the card is heard via speaker or earphones. The two-track system allows the student to record his or her own voice. (*Califone International*)

Most machines have a special feature which allows the teacher to make cards by recording on the instructor track and writing or pasting a picture on the cards.

With a special set of earphones which includes a microphone, the student can have *audio active* earphones; this means that the earphones pick up and amplify the student's own voice. Audio active mode is used in special education and for speech correction more than for reading instruction, but it does increase the feedback to the student and adds a dimension of intensity.

Most card readers allow the student to record his or her own voice on the card as described above, but a few are only "readers" with no recording possibility. These machines are simpler, more durable, and cheaper. They also can be used for special purposes, such as using one track for English and one track for Spanish, which helps bilingual students to hear the written word in both languages. It helps teach Spanish-speaking children to read English or English-speaking children to read Spanish.

Programs or sets of card readers teach many things besides sight words or foreign languages. There are phonics programs, reading readiness programs, vocabulary building programs, and phrase or sentence comprehension programs. These programs may be independent, or they may be part of a basal reading series.

Phonograph Records and Tapes Though audio only, records and tapes may be coordinated with visual devices such as workbooks or projected images. Pure *listening training* is viewed by some as part of reading instruction, and by others as part of language arts. Listening training might be viewed as akin to reading comprehension—where the student listens to a story, then answers questions about it—or it might be related to readiness, where the student tries to sharpen perceptive skills by noting the difference between a /b/ and a /d/ in isolation or in context of a pair of words like "big" and "dig."

Records and tapes are used to give directions for all manner of reading exercises, many of them similar to those found in workbooks. They are also used to present stories auditorily so that the student can read along. For example, the *Checkered Flag* series of supplementary readers has tape cassettes in which an actor reads the exact story to the student. The student can just listen and look at the pictures, or attempt to read along with the actor. Some learning psychologists might call this *modeling,* and others might see it as *guidance* which should be done before *trial and error.* In this instance, trial and error would be reading aloud independently. The student could even attempt to do choral reading (simultaneously) with the tape, or could try to read a little bit ahead of the tape, with the tape helping if he or she stumbled. The taped voice also has the benefit of giving proper intonation of sentence tunes. Proper spacing between words, "juncture," is also facilitated by modeling.

Listening to a story on a record while reading the words is good associational learning, matching visual and auditory symbols. (*George Ceolla/Black Star*)

Wipe-off Cards These cards have workbook activities or comprehension drills printed on them, but they differ from ordinary cards in that they are coated with plastic. When a student writes on them with a grease pencil or crayon, they can later by wiped clean.

Teachers sometimes make their own wipe-off cards by putting specially selected workbook pages, or their own typed or handwritten exercises, in a clear plastic envelope or folded sheet of plastic (such as can be purchased in a stationery store for term-paper covers or catalog sheet protectors). Commercially prepared wipe-off cards can be purchased in sets in many school supply stores. Teachers often file commercially made wipe-off cards, as well as their own, according to specific skills. For example, if a child needs a bit of help in "short O," then the teacher has several sheets the child can work on. They are excellent for individualization or remediation, and have the advantage that they are not consumed.

Games Games are standard classroom and individual teaching tools. The famous Dolch Games have been used in classrooms for decades because they teach specific skills in phonics and basic vocabulary. (See "List of Materials," Chapters 2 and 4.) Of less value are various "trade" word games, such as "Scrabble," because the skills they teach or utilize are more general. Many companies make Bingo-type games and Old Maid–type games which teach various reading skills. Properly used, games are excellent teaching devices; improperly used, they are a waste of time. Proper use means that they are teaching a specific skill which the child needs to learn, or at least one in which reinforcement is needed. Improper use is to have children playing a game just so that they will be quiet. Creative teachers often make their own games, which generally fall into one of five categories:

Board-type: shake dice and move a marker along a track.
Spinner: may be like board-type, or may read direction or word indicated by the spinner.
Deck of cards: for Rummy, Fish, or Concentration.
Bingo-type: put marker on square called out by teacher; cards are all different; student tries to get first solid row filled.
Crossword-type: uses letters to form words such as crossword puzzle, "Scrabble," or has word embedded in matrix of letters.

Flash cards Not quite a game, but almost in that general category, are the various sizes and kinds of flash cards or word wheels which expose one word or grapheme at a time for group or individual instruction. A typical way of using a set of flash cards would be to first select the cards, or make your own from basal reader lessons or words that many children have difficulty in learning. Then flash the card (expose briefly by flipping) to the group, and have the students take turns calling out the word. If the student succeeds, he or she keeps the card. If the child fails, the next student gets a chance. Students who keep the most cards, "win."

Students also sometimes enjoy working alone with individual flash cards, sorting them into "know" and "don't know" piles. Then the teacher or a student monitor checks up on the "know" pile by asking the student to read them, and follows up by helping the child to read some words in the "don't know" pile. Of course, if the cards are made for a card reader, they can be put into a card reader and the teacher or monitor can be dispensed with.

Word cards or alphabet cards can also be used to have the pupil build (write) phrases or sentences.

Nearly all of the above devices can be used as part of a set of behavioral objectives, or as part of, or supplementary to, a basal reader system. Often criterion referenced tests discover needs in reading skills that can be taught by these audiovisual devices.

SUMMARY AND CONCLUSIONS

It is difficult to distinguish between supplementary methods and basal methods. This is particularly true since the field of reading is shifting more toward individualized methods. Basal readers attempt to provide a complete reading program with their core materials of readers, workbooks, and teacher's manuals, but they also provide many supplementary materials such as flash cards, charts, games, additional reading supplies, and audiovisual aids. However, many other companies also provide additional supplementary materials not connected with basals.

An additional complication ensues when we find many teachers not using a basal series, or perhaps using several basal series plus a wide variety of materials. When this happens the teacher generally must follow some other plan, such as a school district curriculum guide or a skills or test management system. As this occurs, materials that used to be called "supplementary" tend to become the main line or primary source of teaching materials.

Any given material or method can be looked at from two different ways: (1) *as content,* such as teaching short vowels or basic vocabulary; and (2) *as a method,* such as a workbook page or a card page. In the first part of this book we looked at the content of reading. Then we began to look more at method, such as basal series and audiovisual methods and materials. Since it is difficult to talk about content without methods, or methods without content, there has been some mixing of the two. At the end of the phonics chapter there was a list of materials primarily devoted to the teaching of phonics and word-attack skills. However, you will also find phonics being taught in all the basal readers, with some of them having phonics as an initial major emphasis. In this chapter you will find many of the same skills taught in the methods discussed and in the materials listed at the end of the chapter. However, the primary emphasis of this chapter has been to point out teaching methods and types of materials in a more general way.

The interesting thing about teaching reading is that you really have to know everything at once. You need to know the content, methods, and materials, for getting it across. This chapter has tried to point out some more ways of getting it across. There is invariably some overlap. Oral reading is part of using a basal reading series, but here it was discussed in more detail—as an entity in and of itself—with additional information on pitch and juncture, and additional methods like choral reading and the use of plays.

We have certainly discussed word-attack skills, vocabulary, and comprehension, but in this chapter we were looking more at the methods of teaching these skills. The list of supplementary curriculum materials, at the end of the chapter, gives more commercial aids arranged by type or method of teaching.

Programmed instruction is not a major teaching method in the public schools, but it is important because of two factors: (1) it encompasses many of the teaching methods found in other materials, and by looking at them from a fresh viewpoint we can better understand other materials and classroom teaching practices; and (2) it is a viable method that is being used today and may be used more in the future, in the form of programmed instruction booklets, teaching machines, or computer-aided instruction. Some of the principles discussed, like "type of response," "type of feedback," "error rate," and "rewarding," have broad implications for all of your teaching.

Special alphabets like the ITA are interesting because of their uniqueness and logic, at least from one point of view (phoneme-grapheme regularity). However, they are also frustrating because of their failure to produce clearly superior results, and because of possible other complications like loss of morphemic information that is useful to more mature readers. However, all teachers should have at least some familiarity with modified alphabets and simplified spelling. The ideas are part of the history of teaching reading, and they seem to have an amazing resiliency.

Last, but not least, we took a look at a wide variety of types of materials used in the teaching of reading, from television to flash cards. The machine manufacturers often ask, "Why should the classroom be less automated than the family home?" Our homes have freezers, crock pots, microwave ovens, television, push-button phones, stereo receivers, and record players, plus many more things, from electric hedge clippers to blenders. Classrooms are beginning to add card readers (it has been estimated that there are approximately 500,000 in existence) and videotape cassettes. Teachers need to see these materials and methods in light of their reading programs. It is also well to remember that some of the older methods, like charts and records or tapes, still have a solid place in the reading program.

SUGGESTED LEARNING ACTIVITIES

1   Listen to a child read some material that is difficult. Listen for problems in fluency, pitch, and juncture. Will rereading the same or easier material improve fluency?

2   Get an example of a workbook page that teaches sight word vocabulary or vocabulary building, and some other type of instructional media (flash cards, games, or audiovisual). Show how these might reinforce each other.

3   Try working some pages of a programmed instruction material. Copy or mark examples of the following words to show that you know what they mean: frame, response, feedback, objective.

4   Give a demonstration of, or plan some curriculum material for, use of some type of audio emphasis—devices such as a tape recorder. phonograph, card reader, or sound filmstrip.

5   Analyze a skills kit that teaches comprehension or some other reading skills. What types of questions are included? How is feedback given? How extensive are the contents?

VOCABULARY AND STUDY TERMS

Directed Reading Activity (DRA)
  Prereading activity
      Interest
      New words
      Essential words
      Word-attack skill
      Comprehension skill
  Reading activity
      Silent or oral
      Round robin
      Context cues
      Oral overuse
  Postreading activity
      Discussion – comprehension
      Workbook use
      Follow-up activities
Oral reading
  Diagnostic
  Fluency, sentence tune
  Pitch and juncture
  Word calling
  Choral reading
  Plays and radio scripts
  List of errors
Silent word building
  Recognition vocabulary
  Flash cards
  Sentence building cards
  Workbook pages
  Correlate spelling lessons
  Easy reading
Vocabulary improvement
  More in upper grades
  Subject areas
  Workbooks, spelling, dictionaries
Word attack
  Many different media
Teaching comprehension
  Supplemental series, kits
Programmed instruction
  Specific objectives (behavioral)
  Small units, steps, frames
  Response – recall or recognize

Feedback — type of feedback
Error rate
Reward — reinforcement
Behavior modification — token economy
Punishment — negative reward
Sequencing — linear or branching
Pretest
Individualized rate
Record of activity
Different alphabets
  ITA
  Use and effectiveness
Audiovisual materials
  TV
  Video cassettes
  Films
  Filmstrips
  Sound filmstrips
  Overhead transparencies
  Charts
  Card readers (audio-active)
  Records and tapes
  Wipe-off cards
  Games
  Flash cards

LIST OF SUPPLEMENTARY CURRICULUM MATERIALS*

Many other supplementary materials are listed elsewhere in this book; for example, there are many phonics materials at the end of Chapter 2, and word materials at the end of Chapter 4.

Supplementary Reading Series and Materials

Early Reading Program: P. Platt and B. Witner; Addison Wesley; seven books; **1-2**.[†]
Cambridge Reading Work-a-Text: Cambridge Book Co.; 22 paperbound work texts; **K-6**.
Story Books for Beginners: Edward Fry and Lee Mountain; Dreier; four paperbound books; **1-6**.
Cornerstone Readers: H. A. Bamman, C. A. Collins, M. A. Dawson, G. E. Newman, G. A. Ransom, E. Stowe, and C. P. Thompson; Addison Wesley; five paperbound books; **1-6**.
Monster Books: Ellen Blance and Anne Cook; Bowmar; 13 softbound books; **1**.

*A list of publishers' addresses can be found at the end of the book
[†] Bold numbers indicate suggested grade levels.

Communications Skills Programs, SWRL: Ginn; paperback books, tests; **1-2**.

Reading Perspectives: Joanne Robinson Mitchell and Anne Libby Ryle, D. C. Heath & Co., seven hardbound books, **1-6**.

Individualized Reading Skills Program: Sylvia Gibb and Eila Talpiamen; SRA; four books; **2.5-3.5**.

Guidebook to Better Reading: Rambeau and Rambeau; Economy; readers; **1-6**.

High Interest, Controlled Vocabulary Readers: Addison Wesley;

    Checker Flag Series, eight books; **2.4-4.5**.

    Time Machine Series, eight books; **2.5**.

    The Jim Forest Readers, 12 books; **1.7-2.3**.

    The All American Series, eight books; **4.4**.

    Wild Life Adventure Series, eight books; **2.6-4.4**.

    Deep Sea Adventure Series, 12 books; **1.8-5.0**.

    The Morgan Bays Series, eight books; **2.3-4.1**.

Supplemental Readers: Benefic Press;

    Animal Adventure Readers, 12 books, audio; **1**.

    Butternut Bill, eight books, audio; **1**.

    Cowboy Sam Series, 15 books, audio; **1-3**.

    Tom Logan Series, 10 books, audio; **1-3**.

    Cowboys of Many Races, seven books, audio; **1-5**.

    Dan Frontier, 11 books, audio; **1-4**.

    Alley Alligator Series, five books; **1-3**.

    Sailor Jack, seven books; **1-3**.

    Treat Truck, eight books; **1-3**.

    Button Family Adventures, three books; **1-3**.

    Moonbeam, 10 books; **1-3**.

    Space Age, six books; **1-3**.

    Helicopter Adventure, six books; **1-3**.

    Horses, six books.

    Inner City, five books; **2-4**.

    Space Science, fiction, six books; **2-6**.

    World of Adventure, eight books; **2-6**.

    Mystery Adventure, six books; **2-6**.

    Racing Wheels, 12 books; **2-4**.

    Sports Mystery, 12 books; **2-4**.

    Target Today, four books; **1-4**.

    Invitation to Adventure, nine books; **1-6**.

    Oral Reading and Linguistics, eight books, audio; **1-6**.

Adapted Classics and Special Series: Fearon;

    Pacemaker Classics; **2**.

    Pacemaker Story Books, 27 titles; **2**.

    Pacemaker True Adventures, 11 titles; **2**.

    Adventures in Urban Reading; four titles.

    American West Series, three titles; **4**.

    Fearon Racing Series, five titles; **4**.

Workbooks, Spirit Masters, Skill Kits

Crossword Puzzle Books: Scholastic Book; six spirit master books, **1-6**.

Creative Reading Enrichment Masters: Instructional Fair Inc.; six spirit master workbooks; **K-3**.

Milliken Teaching Aids: Milliken Publishing; several dozen spirit master books, overhead transparencies, wipe-clean card books; **K-8**.

Instructor Curriculum Materials: Instructor Publications; charts, spirit masters, flash cards.

Power Reading: William T. Blanton, James L. Laffey, Edward L. Robbins, and Carl B. Smith; Winston Press; three kits, test, lesson plan cards, worksheets, assessment cards; **1-12**.

Individualized Directions in Reading: Paul Daniels, Gilbert Schiffman, Karen Fondessy, Karen Stull, and Elizabeth Kelly; Steck-Vaughn; four kits, tests, worksheets; **1-6**.

Listen, Look, Learn: E.D.L.; skills sheets, flash cards, tachistoscope, controlled reader tapes, books, workbooks, filmstrip, games; **1-6**.

Reading Essentials Series: Ullin W. Leavell, William L. Gardner, Adda Mae Sharp, Lester R. Wheeler, Viola D. Wheeler and Betty Davis Via; Steck-Vaughn; nine workbooks; **1-8**.

Bowmar Language Stimulus Program: Bowmar; a kit, books, cards; **3-6**.

Spectrum of Skills: Macmillan; 18 workbooks; **2-8**.

Reading Practice Program: Harcourt-Brace; kit cards, tests, spirit masters; **3-9**.

Building Reading Skills: Hargrave; McCormick-Mathers; six workbooks; **1-6**.

Primary Reading Skills Program: McCormick-Mathers; three kits, spirit masters; **1-3**.

Reading Step by Step: Lois K. Miller; Continental Press; spirit masters; **1**.

Filmstrips

Singer Pre-Primer Program: James A. Gallagher; Singer Education; 25 filmstrips; **1**.

Singer Projection Reading Program: Singer Education; 125 filmstrips, books; **1-3**.

SVE Filmstrips: Singer Education Division; filmstrips; **K-6**.

Beginner Book Filmstrips: Random House; filmstrips, six cassettes or records; **K-2**.

Reading Technology: Mind; sound filmstrip cassettes, worksheets; **1-3**.

Reading Adventures: Walt Disney Educational Media; eight filmstrips, cassettes, book sets; **4.5-5.5**.

Reading Skills Development Laboratory: Psychotechnics; system includes tachistoscope, tapes, reading materials, **1-6**.

Cassettes and Materials with Audio Components

Reading Improvement Series: Clara Jo Bridges; Learning Resources; cassettes, activity sheets; **1-3**.

Milton Bradley's Language Programs: Milton Bradley; five kits, five cassettes, response sheets, cards; **2-6**.

Imperial Tape Centered Reading Programs: Impearial International Learning Corp.; audio tape, cassettes, response booklets; **K-6**.

Clues to Reading Progress: Adrian Sanford and Kenneth Johnson; Educational Progress Corp.; cassettes, booklets; **2-5**.

Audio Reading Progress Laboratory: Educational Progress Corp.; kit, audiotapes, books; **1-8**.

Up Beat: Alvin Granowsky; D.C. Heath; kit, 78 paperbound readers, four cassette recorders; **1-3**.

Walt Disney Read Alongs: Walt Disney Educational Media Co.; storybooks, records, and cassettes; **K-3**.

Target Reading Skills Program: H. A. Bamman, M. A. Dawson, B. H. Hancock, R. P. Hilder, M. F. Hiyama, J. J. McGovern, and M. Poe; Addison Wesley; audio tape kits, spirit masters; **1–6**.

Highway Holidays Series: Joe Stanchfield; Bowmar; books, workbooks, cassettes; **3–6**.

Individualized Cassette Learning Package: Media Materials; kit, cassettes, booklets, tests; **K–6**.

Score Reading Improvement Series: Instructional Dynamics, Scott Education; cassettes, books; **4–8**.

Step-Up Reading Boxes with Sound: Children's Press; books, cassettes; **1–3**.

Reading Incentive: Ed and Ruth Radlauer; Bowmar; books, filmstrips, spirit masters, cassettes; **3–4**.

Story-Go-Round: Noble; books, cassette, paperback; **K–3**.

Words in Motion: Gail Schiller; Macmillan Publishing; kits, cassettes, spirit masters; **4–6**.

Programmed Instruction

Programmed Reading: Cynthia D. Buchanan; Sullivan Associates, Webster, McGraw-Hill; 23 programmed instruction booklets; **K–4**.

Lessons for Self Instruction in Basic Skills: Edward Fry, Lawrence Carrillo, Wayne Rosenoff, and Gracecarol Bostwick; California Test Bureau; 16 programmed instruction booklets; **4–9**.

Audio Cards

Card Reader Programs: Edward Fry, Erwin Pearlman, and Ralph Pearlman; Califone; audio cards; **1–5**.

Language Master: Bell and Howell; audio cards; **1–12**.

Tutorette, Audio Card Programs: Audiotronics; audio cards; **K–3**.

Plays

Plays for Reading: Esther Mack, James Feldman, and Jack Richards; Educational Progress; kits, 22 different plays; **4–6**.

Story Plays: Douglas Rector and Margaret Rector; Harcourt, Brace; kit, 40 plays; **2–4**.

Plays for Echo Reading: Donald D. Durrell and Loraine A. Dimila; Harcourt, Brace; kit, record, play booklets; **2–5**.

Playbooks for Problem Readers: Joan Matus and Howard Schwath; Xerox; paperback booklets; **3.5–4.5**.

Games and Wipe-off Cards

Reading with a Smile: Audrey Ann Burie and Mary Anne Holtsche; Acropolis; book; **K–6**.

Milton Bradley Materials: Milton Bradley; cards, word wheels, games, charts; **K–6**.

Try This and Try This Too: Nancy Santeusanio and Dorothy Batty; Harcourt, Brace; kits, cards; **1–2**.

Developmental Reading: Paul S. Amidon & Assoc.; tests, work sheet, cards, books, games; **1–6**.

Book Clubs

Weekly Reader Paperback Book Clubs: Xerox; book club selection plan for paperback children's trade books; **K-6**.

Firefly Book Club: Reader's Digest; purchase books in group; **2-3**.

REFERENCES

Adams, Ann H., and Cathy B. Harrison. "Using Television to Teach Specific Reading Skills." *The Reading Teacher,* October 1975, *29*(1).

Atkinson, Richard C., and John D. Fletcher. "Teaching Children to Read with a Computer." *The Reading Teacher,* January 1972, *25,* 319–327.

Becker, George J., and Joan F. Curry. "What Do You Do When the Machines Break Down?" *Journal of Reading,* March 1976, *19*(6).

Clay, Marie M., and Robert H. Imlach. "Juncture, Pitch, and Stress as Reading Behavior Variables." *Journal of Verbal Learning and Verbal Behavior,* April 1971, *10,* 133–139.

Criscuolo, Nicholas P. "Six Creative Reading Programs." *The Reading Teacher,* March 1975, *28*(6).

Davis, Dorothy Voight. "Book Clubs in the Middle Grades." *Journal of Reading,* November 1975, *19*(2).

Dolan, Dan. "Developing a Participation Guide for a Play." *Journal of Reading,* January 1975, *18*(4).

Fry, Edward. *Teaching Machines and Programmed Instruction.* New York: McGraw-Hill, 1963.

Johns, Jerry L., and Linda Lunt. "Motivating Reading: Professional Ideas." *The Reading Teacher,* April 1975, *28*(7).

Ladley, Winifred C. *Sources of Good Books and Magazines for Children: An Annotated Bibliography.* Newark, Del.: International Reading Association, 1970.

Lamb, Pose. "Reading and Television in the United States." In John E. Merritt (Ed.), *New Horizons in Reading.* Newark, Del.: International Reading Association, 1976.

Manzo, Anthony V. "Guided Reading Procedure." *Journal of Reading,* January 1975, *18*(4).

Mason, George E. *Extra Stimulation in Intermediate Grade Reading.* College Reading Association, April 1968. ED 029–752.

Mountain, Lee H. "The Book Reporter's TNT: Talks Need Tapes." *Journal of Reading.* March 1976, *19*(6).

Rosen, Ellen. "Readability Analysis of SRA Power Builders." *Journal of Reading,* April 1976, *19*(7).

Spache, George D. *Good Reading for Poor Readers.* (Rev. ed.) Champaign, Ill.: Garrard, 1974.

Stauffer, Russell G., and Max M. Harrell. "Individualized Reading-Thinking Activities." *The Reading Teacher,* May 1975, *29*(8).

Swalm, J. E. "A Comparison of Oral Reading, Silent Reading, and Listening Comprehension." *Education,* 1972, *92,* 111–115.

Wagner, Guy, Max Hosier, and Joan Gesinger. *Word Power Games.* Riverside, N.J.: Teachers Publishing, 1972.

Chapter 9

Higher Skills: Critical Reading, Study Skills, Rate, and Literature Selection

This chapter will contain many of the reading skills often thought of as applying chiefly to secondary school students; however, there is no reason why they cannot also be used in the elementary school, particularly during the intermediate years. Most reading skills form a continuum; you don't teach them once at one grade level, then never teach them again. Comprehension needs to be taught in first grade, in sixth grade, and again in college. Study skills might have a bit more application with older students, but I have seen some very creative and clever flowcharts made by primary children.

As a child progresses through elementary school, reading instruction tends to shift from "learning to read" to "reading to learn." This is evident in many ways. For example, look at the number and kind of textbooks purchased. In first grade, most of the textbooks are basal reading series. In grade six, there may be one basal reading text or, in some schools, none. However, in the sixth grade and junior high, there are almost certain to be texts in arithmetic, science, social studies, spelling, and English or literature. In addition to regular texts, students are asked to read widely in reference works, biographies from the library, newspapers, and numerous other print sources for their assignments in science, social studies, and literature.

This chapter will apply some previously discussed reading skills to reading material in other areas of the curriculum, and it will introduce additional skills and techniques in such areas as rate and critical reading.

READING AND THE CONTENT AREAS

Upper-grade teachers frequently use the term "reading in the content areas," which basically means applying comprehension skills and other reading skills to reading other than the basal reader. Most basal reading systems will systematically cover most of the skills, but they often apply them chiefly to their own textbooks. It is then up to the classroom teacher or the content teacher (science teacher, social studies teacher, etc.) to show students how to apply reading skills in content textbooks.

In this section I will refer to "content teachers," and will apply this term to the regular classroom teacher when teaching a subject area, such as arithmetic or science, as well as the specialist teacher of arithmetic or science. This chapter will refer to skills mentioned in other chapters and remind you that they can easily be applied to content reading. In distinguishing between content texts and basal readers, I do not mean to imply that there is no content in basal or supplementary readers; many, in fact, contain excellent children's literature and interesting selections from science, history, and other subjects. But the focus in basal readers is on reading skills, whereas the teaching of subject matter is the focus in content texts. In teaching content or "reading to learn," the following are some reading skills or lesson suggestions for "content" or "reading to learn" areas of the school curriculum:

1 *The Directed Reading Activity* (DRA) discussed in the last chapter can certainly be applied to most content reading. You might review that part of Chapter 8 which describes prereading, reading, and postreading activities with the thought in mind of applying it to your history or science reading lesson (pages 155–159).

2 *Vocabulary building* is an important part of most content-oriented reading lessons. You might read again that section of Chapter 4 on vocabulary building—both the section on roots and prefixes of new words, and the section on the subject matter content of new words. Certainly, one major function of a teacher in any subject matter area is to help students understand how a word is being used in context. Different subjects use the same word to mean different things. Both prereading activities and postreading discussions and comprehension drills should include instruction in vocabulary unique to that subject.

3 *Graph reading* is a term which might include all kinds of nonverbal reading, including reading maps, schematic drawings, tables, and charts. These skills are taught in most basal series, but they are such a vital and integral part of many content areas (such as mathematics, science, and social studies), that graph reading must be specifically taught for each subject. Incidentally, a Directed Reading Activity for a graph or map makes an excellent lesson. Graph reading has all the accoutrements of reading, including vocabulary, reading for detail, reading for main idea, author's intent—in fact, most comprehension skills.

4 *Comprehension* is, of course, the ultimate purpose of reading in the content areas. You might want to review Chapter 5, particularly the section on "Reading

Teacher's Comprehension Analysis," where a list of comprehension skills is presented. Focusing on those skills, such as "Getting the Facts," "Noting Sequence," "Identifying the Main Idea," etc., the teacher can develop meaningful questions following the reading of a passage in science or social studies. Comprehension skills can also be used as guides for the content teacher who wishes to have a class discussion following the reading of a chapter.

You should be able to apply most of the skills mentioned in the comprehension chapter to most content areas. For example, the ability to follow directions is a skill regularly used in word problems in mathematics. Mathematics word problems use certain very specific words, like "divisor" or "percent," which are crucial to performing certain kinds of operations. Following directions in science might require equal skill in accurate reading, but the vocabulary and concepts may be quite different. This is why students need reading lessons for following directions in mathematics, science, and nearly every other subject. Cooking directions (recipes), carpentry directions, and bicycle repair directions are all excellent subject matter for lessons. Many of the other topics discussed in this chapter, like "Critical Reading," which follows, are often included as part of the topic of reading in the content areas.

CRITICAL READING

Critical reading is, of course, part of the broader topic of comprehension, but it is a type of reading that is often particularly associated with reading in content areas and with higher reading skills. A critical reader is one who can discern fact from opinion; one who can pick out the author's purpose in writing the passage even though it is not directly stated; one who can tell what arguments are used as proof of a contention, and—perhaps by knowing more about the subject than is stated in the passage—can get many inferences. In many ways, the definition of a critical reader is simply the definition of a good reader.

Critical reading is closely related to other important areas of education, such as logic, grammar, and the classification of knowledge. In short, it is related to the total education of a student. One of the main purposes of an elementary education is to enable students to become critical readers.

A major purpose of critical reading instruction is to enable the pupil to understand that the written word is not derived from some ultimate authority, but is rather the work of one or more authors. Children and, unfortunately, even adults, sometimes feel that a printed word is somehow "sacred" and not to be questioned. However, even when such august authoritative sources as various major encyclopedias are examined, it can easily be shown that there are different opinions on such facts as George Washington's childhood or the population of a state. Hence, a critical reader asks for proof, footnotes, references, sources, cross validation. If a child reports a fact, ask him how he knows it. If he has read it, ask him how the author knows it. Keep asking "how," again and again. It engenders thinking skills that make for critical readers.

Sometimes fact versus opinion can be determined simply by reading the article. Drills of this nature are excellent. Give the students a reading assignment and ask them to list the facts versus the author's opinions. When you hold a discussion on the answers, you will be exposing the students to the thinking needed for critical reading. What they should quickly see is that facts and opinions are usually intertwined, and this must be shown over and over again in every subject.

Propaganda Analysis

A part of critical reading instruction might be the use of propaganda analysis. In 1937, toward the end of the Depression and the beginning of World War II, when the European dictators were strong, an Institute for Propaganda Analysis was formed in the United States for the detection of propaganda. Its intent was to provide help in unmasking the devices used by authoritarian governments to control the population. Reading teachers quickly saw the value of propaganda analysis in promoting excellent critical reading. You can have interesting discussions with your class using these principles. You can have your students read newspapers, listen to TV, or tear out advertisements from magazines to illustrate the following eight devices.

1 *Name calling* is the device which seeks to influence people against an individual or group by using a derogatory term based on race, religion, political belief, or some other broad category. Inferring that an organization is "red" or "pinko" tends to paint with a broad brush and suggests a host of bad things that may or may not be true. Calling a black man a "nigger," a girl a "bitch," or a politician a "crook" is a name-calling generalization which conveys a negative emotional set and prevents critical or fair thinking about the individual or subject. Name calling is typically based on a single instance, fact, or characteristic, and its intent is to damn all areas of a total person.

2 *Glittering generalities* are statements which might have some shreds of truth, but which, when examined, do not always bear up. They are intended to convey an impression, influence your thinking, or perhaps stop your thinking about a subject. You have heard many of them in informal conversation, and sometimes seen them in print: "All politicians are crooks," "mothers-in-law are disliked," "such-and-such race or nationality is dumb," "education courses are useless," "students from that part of town cause trouble." More insidious are the manufactured generalities based on only a few facts: "We have the best automobile because it has the best brakes," "You shouldn't swim in the ocean because once a shark bit a person," or "A drug that helps a few people in a specific situation should be taken by everyone." Students need to be aware of the use of generalities, and their limitations.

3 *Card stacking* means telling only the facts on one side of the argument without revealing the other side or counterarguments. In a debate, or in many life structures, it is perhaps too much to ask someone trying to persuade you to give both sides. A salesman selling something, a politician asking for a vote, an enthusiast for a particular cause or belief might indeed be pardoned if they give only one side; however, the critical reader should recognize what is happening. Knowledge of the card-stacking principle should help in the critical evaluation.

4 *Testimonials* are a persuasion device as old as apple pie. Newspaper advertisements of the past century were filled with testimonials for patent medicines: "Mrs. G.W. of Podunk Junction took Dr. Fako's Patent Remedy and now she writes that she is totally cured of all female disorders and fallen arches." You might laugh or be amused at this, but look carefully and you will still see widespread use of testimonials in advertising, political campaigns, and articles that attempt to put over or persuade you of some idea. "I like blank because . . ." is still a great persuader. "I believe it," or "I use it" are still with us in letters to the editor, newspaper editorials, and even in signed articles in intellectual journals. The trouble with testimonials is that they are just that—the opinion of one person—and as often as not, they are not well substantiated. The Food and Drug Administration has pretty well stopped testimonial-type advertising for medicines, but you will still see testimonials at all levels of our culture in all fields.

5 *Plain folks* is the kind of emotional persuader which attempts to get you to go along with an idea or person not because of anything related to objective fact, but because of some simple tangential relationship. A politician who hides his Cadillac and takes off his coat and tie to eat corn on the cob with the locals, or soft drink advertisements which illustrate average people enjoying the beverage, are using the plain folks principle. However, you will find plain folks in many types of written prose: The harried classroom teacher is sympathized with in the writings of the new audiovisual device manufacturer, and the union newspaper is certainly written by someone who understands the bread-and-butter issues.

6 *Prestige identification* is a device which seeks to *transfer authority* from one situation to another. A man who knows how to hit home runs, or a woman who knows how to act very well, both smoke "El Ropos" or wash their underwear with "Hydrochloric Acid." What home-run hitting or acting have to do with smoking or washing is anyone's guess, but perhaps you will feel just a little bit more prestigious if you, too, smoke "El Ropos." In teaching students about propaganda devices, it is well to point out to the students that although someone may be an expert in one field, that fact alone does not justify the assumption that the person is expert in other areas. A movie star may or may not know anything more about soap or politicians than you do. Like other propaganda devices, prestige identification or transfer of authority seeks to influence you by using a device that is not related to the merit of the issue.

7 *Bandwagon* is the "everybody's doing it" phenomenon. Join the winning side. Use Item X because all your neighbors do. You are just a little bit out-of-date if you don't use the new XYZ reading series. The Blank method of testing, or remedial reading, or . . . is sweeping the nation; on the coast, practically everyone is switching to it. People who jump on a bandwagon are sometimes surprised that there are so few people on it, and even more surprised when the bandwagon stops. Point out to your students that there should be better reasons for adopting an idea, or buying something, than the suggestion that everyone else will get there ahead of you.

8 *Red herring* is a common factor in many of these propaganda devices. It is an emotional device dragged across the train of thought in order to stop further logical inquiry. Critical readers are able to recognize these devices and go on thinking.

An example of a "red herring" might be a politician's support of legalized gambling on the supposed basis of the crying need for extra funds for education, while his real purpose is to get a gambling ordinance approved for his friends; or a company's pointing out the possibility of a worldwide shortage of its product (while prices are

Name Calling
"They are the *enemy*."

Transfer of Authority
"The baseball hero uses it."

Glittering Generalities
"We all know it's true."

Bandwagon
"Everybody is doing it."

Testimonials
"My grandmother told me so."

Red Herring
"Look over there." (While I do this.)

Plain Folks
"I'm just one of you guys."

Figure 9-1   Learn to recognize common propaganda tricks.

being raised or inferior quality substituted). It is the logical equivalent of the magician's stock-in-trade—move the right hand very fast with a brightly colored handkerchief while the left hand slowly and carefully places the disappearing object into a nearby unusual pocket.

STUDY SKILLS

All too often reading teachers fail to look at the reading process as part of learning. When you read a printed page to comprehend it, you are really trying to "learn" what is on the page. Learn for how long? Long enough for instant pleasure, or long enough to be able to answer a set of questions immediately after reading, or long enough to be able to recall the main ideas next week or next year? It is long-term recall after reading that is the concern of study skills.

A student might have excellent reading comprehension if he or she laughs at a joke or cries at a death scene, but in these instances the "retention of the details" or "main idea" of the story are completely inappropriate concepts. The author merely wanted to "move" the reader, and having done that, both the writing and reading task were accomplished. However, in much school- and job-related reading, long-term retention is required.

How can you teach for long-term retention? If I rephrased the question to "How can you teach study skills?" you might not be interested. There is some type of conventional wisdom—or conventional nonsense—that study skills are taught only at the secondary level. Not so. Study skills, or reading for retention, or "learning by reading," must be taught in the elementary school, even from the first grade, though the emphasis will be in the upper grades.

You can teach "study skills," as we shall call this area, many ways.

Establish Purpose Part of most Directed Reading Activities is to establish the purpose of reading; sometimes state your purpose as wanting the students to know the materials next week. In teaching reading in the content areas, you can occasionally give a reading assignment with the stated purpose that students must be able to remember the main idea and most of the details at a much later time with no further rereadings in the meantime. Real purposeful reading comes from the reader. The student's *intention* is a powerful factor in learning. Offer a student five dollars to remember what he has read, and see what it does for his memory. If the student can see a reason for retaining what is to be read, it is more likely to become part of long-term memory.

Rereading We would be kidding ourselves if we did not acknowledge that rereading an article or chapter improves recall, both immediate and delayed. Mere repetition helps in remembering most tasks, but additional insights and improved comprehension often occur on the second or third reading. Rereading a chapter is a standard method used by college students; it is not the only study skill they should use, but it is a good one, and one that younger students should become acquainted with.

SQ3R Francis Robinson at Ohio State made famous a simple little formula which is used in many study skills courses and is even incorporated in some elementary reading curriculum materials like the SRA laboratories. The SQ3R formula incorporates a number of learning principles, and it can be taught fairly easily, but to become really effective and utilized by the student, a fair amount of supervised practice with it is essential.

Each part of SQ3R stands for a procedure: S = survey, Q = question, R = read, R = recite, and R = review. The process works like this:

First you tell the students to *S*urvey the chapter; turn the pages, read the subheads, skim a little to get the gist, find out if the chapter is 10 or 50 pages long, find out if it covers the next 20 years or 75 years of history, or if it covers all kinds of frogs or just bullfrogs.

Second, you tell the students to make up some *Q*uestions about the chapter. Sometimes they can make subheads into questions, and sometimes they can find a few topic sentences or paragraphs which will give questions that set the stage for later meaningful reading. The questions are written by the student.

Third, you ask the students to *R*ead the chapter so that they can answer additional questions about it. Note at this point how the SQ3R method differs from simple rereading as a study method. At this point in the SQ3R method, the student has gone through (or at least turned all the pages of) the chapter twice before even beginning to read it. Robinson attempted to get an overview before reading, and established some definite purposes (the questions).

Fourth, the student *R*ecites. This might take the form of written answers to his or her questions and the adding of a few more pertinent questions; it might take the form of two students working together with one student asking a question and the other answering. It might take the form of a written or oral summary. Here the method is utilizing interpersonal reaction, active involvement, and using what was learned.

Finally, the last step in the process is to *R*eview the chapter at a later time. This might take the form of rereading the whole chapter, rereading the written questions and answers, or rereading pertinent parts of the chapter.

Note Taking This type of study skill is similar to what students frequently do in a college course. As a reading study skill, students read with a pencil and paper at their side, and jot down notes on pertinent parts of the text or facts that they feel they should remember. Poor note taking means that the notes are not later useful because:

Good note taking actively involves the student and aids in study and review. (*Christopher G. Knight*)

1 The student might have written too much, making the notes no more useful in studying than rereading the chapter.

2 The student wrote too little, and there is not enough information in the notes to pass the exam.

3 Notes were on inappropriate parts or inconsequential details.

Good note taking involves thinking and understanding the passage. It is useful because it causes the student to be actively involved and can save a lot of time in later studying or review. Often the mere act of just taking notes aids retention of the material even if later studying is not done.

Summarizing Summarizing is much like note taking except that instead of taking notes as one reads, there is an attempt to restate the major points of the chapter in one or two concise paragraphs. Summarizing is usually done at the end of reading, but it may be done utilizing or incorporating notes made while reading. Years ago this was called *précis* (pronounced "pray-see") writing. It is still an excellent way of teaching reading comprehension and an excellent study skill.

Outlining Instead of writing down statements, the student attempts to find an overall structure of the chapter with main ideas and supporting details, or major points which are buttressed with minor points. Outlining format is typically different from note taking in that it uses indentation and both capital and small letters or numerals such as:

1 XXXXXXXXXXXXXXXXXXXXXXXX
   a xxxxxxxxxxxxxxxxxx
   b xxxxxxxxxxxxxxxxxxxxxx
   c xxxxxxxxxxxxxxxxxxxxxxxxxxxxxxxxxx
      (1) xxxxxxxxxxxx
2 XXXXXXXXXXXXXXXXXXXXXXXXXXXX
   a xxxxxxxxxx
      (1) xxxxxxxxxxxxx
      (2) xxxxxxxxxxxxxxxxx

Classifying Relating to outlining, classifying may cause the student to take ideas or facts from different parts of the chapter and group them together. Outlining and note taking tend to follow the author's order of presentation. Classifying tends to make the author's categories, or even categories from outside the author's writing, to make titles under which facts or concepts are written. We have seen classifying-type directions in some reading comprehension drills, "List the reasons you thought the hero was unhappy" or "Which of the antiques found would have been used in a kitchen, and which in the workshop?"

Underlining Underlining can be a very useful device in studying and review. It can be misused, however. First of all, it is certainly not fair to damage library books or books that don't belong to you. But if you own the book, underlining is not a bad study technique. Properly done, underlining can aid your comprehension by *getting you actively involved, and it can greatly facilitate later review or reference.* However, like poor note taking, too much, too little, or wrong underlining is a waste of time and misleading. Merely the mechanical underlining of parts of the text does not put the information into the brain. Furthermore, if underlines somehow helped comprehension, the printer could automatically underline everything and we would all have better comprehension. Incidentally, underlining has a modern twist called *highlighting* in which a felt-tipped pen with light-colored ink is used to go over the selected word or phrase, making it stand out against a yellow or pink background.

Graphic Representations   These can be very valuable as study devices in specific instances. Making a *time line* can materially contribute to the comprehension of a chapter or chapters in history. Making a *genealogy chart* can facilitate the comprehension of a novel. Making a *sociogram* can show relationships between groups or individuals in many social studies areas. Furthermore, there are all sorts of *flowcharts* and *schematic drawings* which can help a student's understanding of written prose. Sometimes these are supplied by the author as part of the text, but more often, the student will have to make his own—and the mere making of a drawing is a great facilitator of both comprehension and retention.

Scanning   This particular type of reading skill must be in the skills repertoire of every literate person. It is the type of "reading" one does when looking up a name in a telephone book or searching for data in an encyclopedia. It is a narrow, single-purpose type of "reading" in which everything is excluded except the object of the scan. Speed is an integral part of the scanning process. The whole reason for scanning is that it saves time—you don't want to take time to read an entire encyclopedia article, you just want to find out how long it takes a chicken egg to incubate. Teachers should frequently have scanning drills as part of reading lessons and as part of using text and reference books in all subject matter areas. Students love to compete with each other in seeing who can locate a name or date or fact first. However, teachers should not use just group competition in teaching scanning (or anything else); there must be drills and exercises in which the student gets adequate practice, experiences of success, and feedback on self-improvement.

Reference Books   As sources of information for students, these are excellent. Lots of children and adults love to pore over the *Guinness Book of World Records,* and a good number of heated out-of-class arguments are settled by world almanacs. It is a major part of study skills to know how to use reference books and have at least a brief acquaintance with the contents of major ones. *Roget's Thesaurus* improves themes, and dictionaries improve spelling and word use. As a student gets interested in specific subject areas, he or she should be given lessons in using the reference books of that field. Student dictionaries and school encyclopedias usually have specific curriculum and use lessons for the "how to use" section printed in the forematter; these have excellent lesson suggestions.

Library The library is one of the ultimate reference tools. Elementary teachers regularly take their students to both school and public libraries, and this should probably be done several times a year, every year. It should be done as part of structured lessons with lectures and student activity drills on using the card catalog, locating trade books, finding and utilizing reference books, etc. The library should not be used as a dumping ground or a study hall, but as a reference tool and a source for locating reading pleasure.

RATE OF READING

Improving reading rate is usually thought of as being a subject for adult reading improvement, or at least for secondary schools; however, improving reading rate has been quite successfully done in elementary schools. Marion Kimberly, when a graduate student at Rutgers, found that successful rate training could be done all the way down to second grade.

One of the problems is that *speed reading,* as rate training is often called, may have a bad connotation because some commercial organizations have promised more than they could deliver. Using the word "reading" in a usual sense, very few people, and perhaps nobody, can be taught to "read" at 2,000 words per minute. They can perhaps learn to *skim* at 2,000 words per minute, and this will be discussed later. However, this does not mean that all rate training is bogus or that significant gains in rate cannot be made by most people. Many people can learn to double their reading rate when trying hard on relatively easy factual material with little or no loss in comprehension. This is a very desirable skill. Elementary children can also learn to make significant rate gains. For example, it is not unusual for a student in the fourth grade

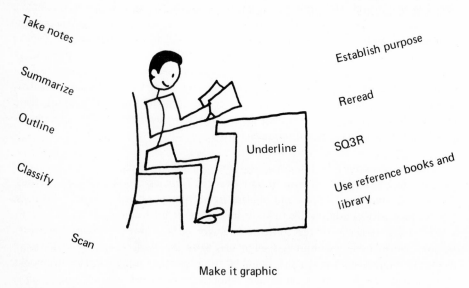

Figure 9-2 Study skills.

to be reading between 90 and 125 words per minute on materials of third- or fourth-grade difficulty. With rate training he might learn to read at 200 words per minute when trying, and when the materials are relatively easy for him.

Many authorities in speed reading talk about *flexibility*. This means the ability to read fast when you want to or the situation calls for it. When studying for a test you usually don't read fast; in fact, you should probably use a study skill because you are involved in a learning-retention process. At other times, the "density of ideas" or amount of new information is so great that slower rates are necessary. However, there are many times when improved rate is desirable. Reading newspapers, some books, letters, etc., does not call for study-skill type reading or a slow rate. Students who do not have flexibility in rate tend to have one speed (and it is usually slow). If you read everything at the same speed, you probably are not a very efficient reader. Business executives often learn to their great distress that there isn't enough time in the day to read, at an inflexible rate, everything they are supposed to. Training for faster rate and flexibility should begin in the elementary school.

How do you improve rate? The basic process is to give a series of timed drills followed by comprehension questions. Usually records are kept both of reading rate in words per minute, and of comprehension scores. The teacher exhorts the students to read a little faster each drill. Sometimes there are special lessons in skimming, and sometimes there are audiovisual devices that encourage faster reading by flashing phrases or controlling the rate of exposure of printed material. The timed drills usually extend over a period of weeks. For example, the elementary teacher might give a timed drill three times a week for eight weeks. The drills should be relatively short, 100 to 500 words, and, of course, they should be at a level which is fairly easy for the individual student.

Since drills are often individual, in the sense that students might all start together but are reading against their own previous rates, there is no reason why students with different reading levels can't be reading different-level materials at the same time. Comprehension questions are usually scored by the student with the aid of an answer key. The students can time themselves using a stopwatch, or the teacher can write the time on the chalkboard every 10 seconds after starting the class. The student then writes down the time that he or she finishes.

The teacher, besides encouraging each student to read a little faster each time, should also keep a careful watch on the speed-comprehension balance. Students with a low rate but consistently high comprehension should be encouraged to read faster, while students who have poor comprehension should maintain their present rate (not decrease rate) and concentrate on comprehension. It is not unusual for students who first increase their rate to lose some comprehension. With continued time drills, however, comprehension balance can usually be restored.

A rate increase of only 25 percent without loss of comprehension is a desirable outcome, and greater increases are frequently possible. When increasing rate (speed reading) is combined with instruction in study skills, the student begins to get the idea of flexibility. But the teacher should talk about rate flexibility often and in connection with content reading.

Skimming

Skimming is a special type of rapid reading in which comprehension is intentionally sacrificed for very rapid rate. Skimming is further characterized by omissions. In other words, when skimming, a student does not "read" all the material. Skimming rates are frequently twice as fast as regular reading at its fastest.

In regular reading, the student might sometimes get a lower comprehension rate, especially when trying to read fast, but he or she certainly doesn't intend to sacrifice comprehension. In skimming, however, lowered comprehension is directly implied. The student skims just for main ideas and a few of the facts. He might leave out (not read) whole halves of paragraphs if he feels that he has the main idea of the paragraph.

Both skimming and scanning drills should be part of regular elementary reading instruction. Scanning drills are often best done in groups, with the teacher throwing out such challenges as, "Where does it say that . . . ?" or "Who can find . . . ?"

Skimming drills are usually individually timed and are silent. In fact, skimming drills can be done on the same type of exercise that you use in regular timed drills— a passage is read while the students time themselves, followed by comprehension questions. Any kind of passage can be used, such as the *Reader's Digest Skill Builders* (grades 2 to 6), the *SRA Better Reading Book I* (grades upper 5 to 7), etc. Sometimes skimming drills can cover relatively long passages or whole chapters.

Teachers can make their own timed reading drills by selecting passages from text-books or supplementary materials. Just be sure that it is easy reading for the student. Look at the student's test score and do a readability formula on the material, or ask a student of similar ability to read part of it aloud. You can use multiple choice questions, short answer questions, or a cloze passage with every tenth word deleted. One caution is that all drills, both teacher-made and commercially prepared, are "drills"; they are not tests. You can't expect the comprehension questions of different drills to be equally difficult. This means that comprehension scores will go up and down from drill to drill. A student may get 60 percent one day and 80 percent correct the next day, merely as a function of uneven difficulty. However, longer spans of time show comprehension trends more clearly. Try averaging together a week's comprehension scores to get a more stable growth pattern.

During any kind of silent reading, including timed drills, the teacher should discourage vocalization (lip movement or saying the words to oneself). Vocalization holds down speed. It is also a sign of reading at the frustration level. If merely telling the student not to do it doesn't work, try lowering the reading level.

The same procedure should be used for finger pointing; tell them not to do it. If it continues, give them easier material to read. In most silent reading, students should use only their eyes; not their lips, their fingers, their neck muscles (turning the head), or any other type of body activity.

If you are interested in more details on how to conduct reading rate improvement, at any level, you can look at my book, *Teaching Faster Reading*.

LITERATURE SELECTION

We have spent most of our time on "how to teach reading," with emphasis on the most important principles and skills involved. This book is not intended to be a book on "what to read." Choice of literature for elementary readers, however, is extremely important. Most colleges and universities have courses in children's literature which are taken by many future elementary teachers, either as undergraduates or as graduate students.

Frequently, elementary teachers have their own private list of books that "work" with children of a given age or with children with certain interests. Elementary teachers should strive to build up such personal lists of books, and it helps if they have read some of them recently so that they can discuss them with students.

If you can't take a course in children's literature, and you don't know where to start looking for interesting children's books, here are a few reference works that will help facilitate your selection of appropriate books:

George Spache's *Good Books for Poor Readers* (Garrard Publishing Company) lists many children's trade books categorized by interest groups, such as "Cowboys," "Mexico and Mexican-Americans," "Mystery." Each book listed has an interest level and a readability level reported.

Nancy Larrick's *Parent's Guide to Children's Reading* (Bantam paperback or Dutton hardcover) is written for parents, but is extremely useful for elementary teachers. It talks about the world of children's reading, and mentions and annotates literally hundreds of books.

Two classic college textbooks in children's literature, which discuss principles and provide many valuable teaching suggestions as well as titles, are May Hill Arbuthnot and Zena Sutherland's *Children and Books* (Scott, Foresman), and Charlotte Huck and Doris Kuhn's *Children's Literature in Elementary School* (Holt, Reinhart and Winston).

There are also many booklists. Interesting ones are published regulary by major city public libraries, and special-purpose lists appear regularly in the *Language Arts* (formerly *Elementary English*) journal and other publications of the National Council of Teachers of English. More exhaustive lists can be found in the reference sections of most libraries; for example, the Wilson Company's *Children's Catalogue*, Bowker Company's *Growing Up With Books*, and Bro-Dart's *Elementary School Library Collection*. The latter has worked out a readability formula for a large percentage of the books listed; it also ranks books in order of importance by recommending which should be a "first purchase."

Finally, one of the most effective sources of finding interesting books is by talking to children who read and librarians who check out books. They can tell you what sparks reading interest in your own neighborhood. Teachers probably do a better job in teaching children how to read than they do in getting children to read and developing lifelong reading habits. If more teachers could develop a personal interest in children's literature and encourage the reading of books, it might have some effect on children's reading activities, both inside and outside of school.

SUMMARY AND CONCLUSIONS

This chapter discussed many of the higher reading skills that are usually thought of as applying primarily to secondary or college reading instruction. However, in reading— as in mathematics and many other fields—what once were thought of as college-level concepts have progressed to the high school and even to the elementary school.

This makes the instruction of reading both more interesting and more challenging for the elementary teacher.

With a good grounding in the basic reading skills of comprehension and vocabulary building, it is easy to see how these skills might apply to reading in the content areas. Critical reading and propaganda analysis are really extensions of basic reading comprehension. Study skills, while also related to comprehension, add a new dimension of "learning how to learn" or practical applications of educational psychology.

Reading rate improvement, long solely in the province of adult and college education, is beginning to move into the elementary school. Properly done, without ridiculous emphasis or goals, it is a very valuable skill. Furthermore, it is not hard to teach.

SUGGESTED LEARNING ACTIVITIES

1 Make at least two different kinds of graphic representation that could be used as a comprehension or study aid. For example, take a passage from a history or science book and make a timeline, genealogy chart, flowchart, or schematic drawing which illustrates the main idea or interrelationship of the parts.

2 Clip current magazines or newspapers to provide examples of five of the propaganda analysis skills.

3 Study a chapter at least three different ways (such as SQ3R, outlining, and summarizing) to see which method is most suitable for you and for the type of chapter—OR—teach several study skill techniques to another individual or group; help them to apply the skills to one particular subject.

4 Write out a lesson plan for a reading lesson in the content areas. Include DRA, vocabulary building, and comprehension skills.

VOCABULARY AND STUDY TERMS

Reading in the context areas
  Directed reading activity
  Vocabulary building
  Graph reading
  Comprehension skills
Critical reading
  Fact from opinion
  Author's purpose
  Inference
Propaganda analysis
  Name calling
  Glittering generalities
  Card stacking
  Testimonials
  Plain folks
  Prestige identification
  Bandwagon
  Red herring

Study skills
  Long-term retention
  Establish purpose
  Rereading
  SQ3R
Note taking
  Not too much, too little, inappropriate
  Summarizing
  Outlining
  Underlining (highlighting)
  Graphic representation
      Timeline, flowchart
  Scanning
  Reference books
  Library use
Rate improvement
  In elementary school
  Flexibility
  Timed drills and comprehension
  Skimming
Literature selection
  Spache, Larrick, anthologies
  Journals, catalogs
  Talk to children

LIST OF STUDY SKILL AND HIGHER READING SKILL CURRICULUM MATERIALS*

Dictionary Skills: Scott Education; transparencies; **4–6**.†
Using the Dik-she-nehr-re: "My Weekly Reader," Xerox; four paperbound books; **3–6**.
Library Instruction: Scott Education; transparencies; **4–8**.
Content Readers: Reader's Digest; paperback readers; **2–6**.
Learning to Use the Library: "My Weekly Reader," Xerox; paperback books, sound filmstrips; **3–6**.
Table and Graph Skills: Xerox; four workbooks; **3–6**.
Maps Skills for Today: Xerox; five workbooks, spirit masters; **2–6**.
Know Your World: Xerox, 28 classroom newspapers per year; **2.5–3.5**.
Better Reading Books: Elizabeth A. Simpson; SRA, three hardbound books for speed improvement; **5–10**.
Careers: A Supplemental Reading Program: Diane Gess and Robert C. Miles; Harcourt, Brace; three kits, story folders, activity cards; **4–6**.
Our Constitution and What It Means: William D. Kottmer; Webster, McGraw-Hill; one workbook, **6–8**.
Studies Skills for Information Retrieval Series: Don Barnes and Arlene Burgadorf; Allyn and Bacon; four workbooks; **4–8**.

*A list of publishers' addresses can be found at the end of the book.
†Bold numbers are suggested grade levels.

Maps Skills Series: Scholastic Book; three paperback books; **1–6**.

Go–Reading in the Content Areas: Scholastic Book; books, spirit masters; **4–8**.

The Mag Bag: Random House; kit, 10 different popular magazines, cards; **5–9**.

Aware: Barbara Harrison; Random House; kit, cards, books, cassette, scent samples, Braille card, cards; **4–8**.

Reading, Thinking and Reasoning Skills Program: Don Barnes, Arlene Burgdorf, and L. Stanley Wenck; Steck-Vaughn; **1–6**.

What's Happening?: Associated Press and Curriculum Concepts, Westinghouse Learning Corp; kit cards, newspaper activity book; **4–8**.

Getting into Literature: Educational Insights; comic-type booklets; **4–6**.

Insights about America: Educational Insights; kits of cards (comic format); **4–6**.

REFERENCES

Allington, Richard L. "Improving Content Area Instruction in the Middle School." *Journal of Reading*, March 1975, *18*(6).

Arbuthnot, May Hill, and Zena Sutherland. *Children and Books*. (4th ed.) Chicago: Scott, Foresman, 1972.

Bickley, A. C., Billie J. Ellington, and Rachel T. Bickley. "The Cloze Procedure: A Conspectus." *Journal of Reading Behavior*, Summer 1970, *2*, 232–249.

Braam, Leonard. "Developing and Measuring Flexibility in Reading." *The Reading Teacher*, January 1963, *16*, 247–254.

Brown, James I. "The Techniques for Increasing Reading Rate." In John E. Merritt (Ed.), *New Horizons in Reading*. Newark, Del.: International Reading Association, 1976.

Buswell, Guy T. "Relationship Between Rate of Thinking and Rate of Reading." *School Review*, September 1951, *49*, 339–346.

Donald, Sister Mary. "The SQ3R Method in Grade Seven." *Journal of Reading*, October 1967, *11*, 33–35, 43.

Eanet, Marilyn G., and Anthony V. Manzo. "REAP–A Strategy for Improving Reading/Writing/Study Skills." *Journal of Reading*, May 1976, *19*(8).

Fry, Edward. *Teaching Faster Reading*. Cambridge, England: Cambridge University Press, 1963.

Gans, Roma. "A Study of Critical Reading Comprehension in the Intermediate Grades." *Contribution to Education*, No. 811. New York: Teachers College, 1940.

Harris, Albert J. "Research on Some Aspects of Comprehension: Rate, Flexibility, and Study Skills." *Journal of Reading*, 1968, *12*, 205–210, 258.

Harris, Theodore L. "Experimental Development of Variability in Reading Rate in Grades Four, Five, and Six." USOE Cooperative Research Project, No. 1775. Madison: University of Wisconsin, 1965.

Huck, Charlotte S., and Doris Y. Kuhn. *Children's Literature in the Elementary School*. New York: Holt, 1968.

King, Martha L., Bernice D. Ellinger, and Willavene Wolf (Eds.). *Critical Reading*. Philadelphia: Lippincott, 1967.

Lake, Mary Louise. "Improve the Dictionary's Image." *Elementary English*, March 1971, *48*, 363–366.

Lees, Fred. "Mathematics and Reading." *Journal of Reading*, May 1976, *18*(8).

Rankin, Earl F. "How Flexibly Do We Read?" *Journal of Reading Behavior*, Summer 1970–1971, *3*, 34–38.

Robinson, H. Alan. "Reading Skills in Solving Social Studies Problems." *The Reading Teacher*, January 1965, *18*, 263–269.

Sanacore, Joseph. "Locating Information: The Process Method." *Journal of Reading*, December 1974, *18*(3).

Stauffer, Russell G. (Ed.) *Dimensions of Critical Reading*. Proceedings of the Annual Education and Reading Conferences, Vol. 11. Newark, Del.: University of Delaware, 1964.

Stauffer, Russell G., and Ronald Cramer. *Teaching Critical Reading at the Primary Level*. Reading Aids Series. Newark, Del.: International Reading Association, 1968.

Smith, Helen K. "Evaluating Progress in Recreational Reading." In John E. Merritt (Ed.), *New Horizons in Reading*. Newark, Del.: International Reading Association, 1976.

Tanyzer, Harold, and Jean Karl (Eds.). *Reading, Children's Books, and Our Pluralistic Society*. Newark, Del.: International Reading Association, 1972.

Whitehead, Robert. Children's Literature: *Strategies of Teaching*. Englewood Cliffs, N.J.: Prentice-Hall, 1968.

Chapter 10

Writing:
Language Experience
Approach, Readability

We have been discussing reading instruction through the use of extensive published material. Most basal series are expensive and elaborate. They have dozens of books, teachers' manuals, workbooks, supplementary books, charts, audiovisual aids, and dozens of other bits and pieces of material.

We will now discuss a method of teaching reading that does not require any special materials. Pencils and paper, and sometimes a chalkboard or a large sheet of paper for making a chart, and crayons or some kind of art supplies are helpful. But you don't have to have any books, kits of preprinted cards, tests, teachers' manuals, sets of phonics rules, lists of high-frequency words, or syllabification rules. You don't have to know what a grapheme is, and you don't have to know the child's IQ or cultural background. Not only that, but it is a method of teaching reading that is probably just as effective as any other method.

THE LANGUAGE EXPERIENCE APPROACH

The language experience approach is a method of teaching reading in combination with writing—not just handwriting (penmanship), but creative story writing. The basic idea is to get the children to write their own stories and read them back to themselves and to each other. Sometimes they read each other's stories silently.

Let's look at some of the techniques of implementing this method. First of all, it requires a creative teacher who has already motivated the class, reading group, or individual child. Teachers who successfully use the language experience approach often start by having the child first express the story in picture form. They give the child a blank sheet of paper, or a special piece of children's writing paper that has the top half blank and the bottom half with light-blue writing lines, and ask the child to draw a picture of something that interests him or her. The directions might be somewhat structured, asking for a picture of a vacation, a dream, a trip to the zoo, a favorite TV program, a modification of a children's story, something that is frightening, the future, a sports incident, or a school happening. After the child presents the picture, the teacher asks the child to tell about it, and then to write about it. The telling (oral presentation) might take place in front of a small group. The writing might require considerable help from the teacher, a teacher's aide, or another student. The teacher tries to guide the student into using sentences that are more or less proper sentences, and to assist in selecting words that are both simple and descriptive. However, the teacher does not exercise the kind of vocabulary control found in many basal readers. The student has a great deal of choice in selecting colorful, sometimes even colloquial, vocabulary.

For beginning readers, the story might be short—possibly only a two-word title for a picture. For example, "The Rattlesnake" might be a perfectly acceptable first "story." You might argue that "Rattlesnake" isn't exactly a high-frequency word; nevertheless it has many advantages. Its configuration (shape) is quite different from "The," and hence you have a good lesson in configuration. The word "The" is the most common word in the English language and one that will come up in almost every sentence, so a very valuable word is learned. Furthermore, the student has written and is reading about something that interests him or her. There might be enough intrigue and enough rebelliousness in writing and reading about a rattlesnake to start getting young persons fascinated with the whole process of writing and reading their own stories.

In a "story" such as "The Rattlesnake," a number of letters are used that are useful handwriting practice. In fact, since it would be unusual for a pupil at this level to know all the letters, this is also a good learning experience.

A child at this stage is also just making the transition to graphic communication. The teacher should not try to make the change too abrupt. for example, during a group presentation of the rattlesnake story, the author might be encouraged to elaborate a little more about the rattlesnake, talking about its size or its awesome virtues. The result provides the basis for the next lesson. "The rattlesnake is big." Now we have repetition plus the introduction of two more high-frequency and highly useful words. You can see how important creative teaching is in the language experience approach.

Students will sometimes work for several days to several weeks on a story. However, it may be difficult to set a time period and announce ahead of time that the students will have exactly two weeks to write their next story. Some of the interesting products that come out of language experience classes are little student-written books, some as long as 15 to 20 pages, with frequent illustrations and a rambling plot. Not only do students enjoy producing them, but sometimes they enjoy reading each

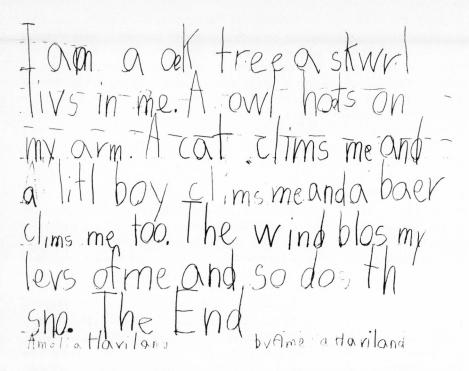

I am a oek tree a skwrl
livs in me. A owl hods on
my arm. A cat clims me and
a litl boy clims me and a baer
clims me too. The wind blos my
levs ofme and so dos th
sno. The End

Amelia Haviland   by Amelia Haviland

Figure 10-1 A language experience story produced by a second-grade girl after hearing a poem about trees.

other's books. Teachers find ways of binding the books with tape, cardboard, and staples that give them a measure of permanence for both the classroom library and trips home to show pleased parents.

One of the strong features of the language experience approach is that it produces an *integration of all the language skills*—speaking, listening, writing, and reading. Hence, the discussion period about stories is important. Many teachers feel that it is necessary to develop speaking and listening skills before developing reading skills. We discussed this in the chapter on reading readiness; however, we might reiterate here that oral and aural (listening) skills are an integral part of the language experience approach.

How much to stress correct penmanship, correct spelling, and correct grammar is a problem. The first goal is communication. If a student can read a story and understand it, this is an important step. However, if the child wants another student to read it, or wants to be able to read another student's story, then it becomes important to have a common code or common system of writing. This is the central argument for so-called "correct spelling," "correct penmanship," and "correct grammar." If writing is very "incorrect," it simply won't communicate, especially to an immature literate who is having trouble learning. To have a common word appear 10 different ways can only confuse learning. Hence, teachers often have students recopy stories in more correct form after they are first put down in a burst of creation.

Experience Charts

A modification of the language experience approach is the use of *experience charts*, which are group rather than individual activities. Experience charts are frequently used in kindergartens and primary grades for both reading readiness and actual reading instruction. Using either the chalkboard or a large sheet of lined chart paper and a crayon or a broad felt-tipped pen, the teacher writes a story that is dictated by the children through group discussion.

A typical experience chart lesson might stem from a common group experience, such as the proverbial trip to the zoo. The teacher tells the student that together they will write a story. A child is asked to suggest a title for the story. Children discuss the title, and it is modified. The story is then written line by line with a kind of group consensus for each line. An actual example follows:

The Rockland Zoo

We all went to the zoo.
The school bus took us.
John fell down getting off the bus.
We liked the tiger cubs the best.
The birds ate our cookies.
We ate lunch at the zoo.
The bus took us back to school.

These aren't the exact words the children used; the teacher modified the sentences a bit as she wrote them down. While there is some freedom of vocabulary in "tiger cubs" and "cookies," there are plenty of basic words in the story. There is even a bit of repetition; "ate" is used twice, "bus" is used twice, "we" is used three times, etc. The story has personal interest, especially for John and the children who fed cookies to the birds.

After the story was written, various children took turns reading each line, and some children were able to read the whole story almost without error. Although some immature pupils could not read even a whole line, they were able to participate in the valuable language experience of seeing talk being written down so that it reinforced the concept that written words do represent speech. This point—and the creative act of writing an original story—are integral parts of the language experience approach.

Language Experience Variations

An interesting variation of the language experience approach can be found in Sylvia Ashton-Warner's novel, "Teacher." She emphasizes the importance of having the children learn emotionally loaded words like "love," "kiss," "afraid," and she encourages children to use them in writing experience stories. She felt that stories that express basic emotions facilitate learning to read. New words are put on a single card for review and copying in later stories.

As Miss Warner was working with a "disadvantaged" population, the Maori people in New Zealand, some educators feel that it might have applications for American disadvantaged children.

In an experience chart lesson, a group of children write a story, then take turns reading it. *(Mike Q./ Coronet Studios)*

The language experience approach has been refined, developed, and published by *Encyclopaedia Britannica* under the title *Language Experiences in Reading* (L.E.I.R.) by Dr. and Mrs. Roach Van Allen. Three large teacher's manuals covering the primary years give numerous teaching suggestions on interesting story stimulation techniques. There are also pupils' books for each level. The pupils' books are not workbooks and not readers; rather, they provide spaces to write stories and illustrate them, stimulating pictures, samples of children's literature for the child to read, and other language-related activities. This program has been used instead of a basal reader series in some school districts.

Fernald Kinesthetic Approach

There is also a famous remedial teaching method that encompasses most of the features of the individualized language experience approach. It is called the "Fernald Kinesthetic Technique," and it derives that name because, in the earliest stage of development, emphasis is placed on the kinesthetic sense. The kinesthetic sense is that body sensory experience you receive from muscle movement. If you put your hand behind your back and wiggle your fingers, you know your fingers are moving because of your kinesthetic sense.

Grace Fernald was a school psychologist in Los Angeles who worked with boys with serious reading problems. She developed a method that they liked and at which they were successful. The clinic school at the University of California at Los Angeles, where she also taught, still uses her technique. The basis of it, like all language experience methods, is to first stimulate the student to write a story. When the student doesn't know how to write a word, the kinesthetic part begins. The student asks the teacher to supply the word. She or he writes it in large cursive writing (the connected-letter type of handwriting most American adults use, as opposed to manuscript or disconnected letters). The student then traces the word with a finger saying the word to himself slowly as his finger passes over it. Thus, the kinesthetic sense is used in the tracing movement, but the process is also tactile (touching) as well as oral and auditory (he hears himself say it). After the student has traced the word several times with his finger, he turns the card over, then tries to write the word without looking at it. If he can successfully write the word (he checks and compares), then he can write the word in his story. If he can't successfully write the word from memory, he must practice tracing and saying the word.

The word cards are saved and placed in alphabetical order in each individual's word box. Thus the student not only builds a personal dictionary, but also gains some alphabetizing skills.

After the student has completed his or her story, usually one per day, the teacher types a clean version of the story which is used as the child's reading lesson the next day. In addition, all the new words are typed in isolation so that special practice is given in reading them.

The Fernald technique and others that involve tracing, speaking, and listening are sometimes called V-A-K-T for the Visual, Aural (or Auditory), Kinesthetic, and Tactual senses used.

Language Experience Limitations and Extensions

A general criticism of the language experience individualized approach is that it is very time-consuming for the teacher; hence, it is often used as only part of the reading program. There is also a tendency for it to be used only when teacher's aides are available.

One of the problems of all the language experience approaches is that children tend to memorize a story and "read" it from memory. While some of this is not objectionable, particularly for some children who never have "read" anything successfully before, one of the objectives of reading instruction is to get children to be able to read anything, not just their own stories. Thus, children are encouraged to read the stories of others.

Teachers can take words from the story and write them in isolation in a mixed order to see if the child can recognize the words by themselves.

Another method is for the teacher to put the child's story away for a few days or a few weeks, then use it for a reading lesson. Nearly all teachers who use a language experience approach also have the children read from other materials, such as trade books and textbooks. In kindergartens, first grades, and remedial situations, the use of other material is often delayed until the child acquires minimal competence in reading the language experience stories.

Some teachers teel that the language experience approach only works well with bright and creative or highly verbal children. It has been used effectively, however, with disadvantaged pupils, in Title I supplementary classes, and with bilingual children. Certainly the experience of Sylvia Ashton-Warner was not with an advantaged population.

Teachers who use language experience might use it as a supplement to some other system, such as a basal reading series, or they might use it along with a major emphasis on trade books or an individualized reading approach. In any event, sooner or later (and usually sooner), the student is exposed to many other types of reading materials in addition to his or her own stories or those of fellow students.

Let us close our discussion of the language experience methods by reviewing some of their strong points:

They provide for individual differences in ability.

The provide for cultural diversity; black culture, Spanish culture, Maori culture, etc.

They integrate and show the relationship of all language arts; speaking, reading, writing, spelling, penmanship, etc.

They provide strong motivation, especially for some children, to learn to read and write.

They are multisensory; vision, hearing, touching, moving, and speaking.

They encourage creativity.

Read some of the references at the end of this chapter by Russell Stauffer, Janette Veach, Roche Van Allen, and others, if you are interested in learning more about the language experience approach.

Children's Writing

The language experience approach, almost by definition, makes heavy use of children's writing. However, many other approaches tie children's writing closely to reading lessons. For example, some of the basal reading series listed in Chapter 7 place relatively more emphasis on integrating all the language arts (including children's writing).

Penmanship is the formation of letters and the physical production of words. It and creative writing, or the production of stories, are both called "writing," though both are different tasks. Children need to do both, of course. In writing lesson plans and in teaching, you must be clear which you are trying to teach. In most American schools, children learn manuscript in grade one and begin the transition to cursive writing in the second or third grade.

Spelling (orthography) is a problem for most children, but it should not be allowed to interfere with story production. A child who is chastised for poor spelling in a story often limits his or her production to short stories with very limited vocabulary usage. It is best to correct stories and teach spelling at another time, unless it can be worked in without interfering in the creative writing process.

Whether they use language experience or not, practically all elementary teachers encourage story writing, and excellent teachers often get excellent stories from children. Many teachers are able to stimulate story writing and story reading by producing a classroom newspaper, a community history, or poetry booklets.

Figure 10-2 *(From Charles Schultz's* You've Had It, Charlie Brown, *Holt, Rinehart and Winston, Inc., New York.)*

Typewriting is a skill that is now being taught in some elementary classrooms. It is usually not taught on a whole-class basis, but is more of a supplementary, remedial, or enrichment activity for certain children. For some children, learning to type is a great motivator for learning the language arts skills of reading and creative writing. It is not difficult to teach regular 10-finger touch typing. All you need is a typewriter (either manual or electric), a set of lessons, and a minimum of adult supervision. I have written a small children's typing booklet that has taught thousands of children ages 8 to 12 to type without a trained typing teacher. They don't become expert typists, but they can type faster than they can handwrite, and it gives them a useful skill in this modern world of typed term papers and computer terminal interaction. Donald Durrell found that teaching typing to fifth-graders slightly improved reading skills besides giving the children a useful skill. Some studies have even found that it improves handwriting, possibly because the children become accustomed to seeing well-formed letters.

A study at Rutgers taught most of the children in the reading clinic to type during reading instruction period. It didn't improve their reading more than the previous semester's group, but—for the same amount of instruction time—they got the same reading improvement *plus* the valuable skill of touch typing. They, incidentally, told their friends not that they were going to remedial reading, but that they were going to typing class. The typing lessons included the Instant Words so that they also were learning a basic vocabulary.

READABILITY

In Chapter 1, we talked about the important principle of *matching*, or getting the child to read a book that is on the correct level. By the correct level, I mean that the book is easy enough. It doesn't hurt children to read a book that is too easy, but to continually give them books in which they can't experience success may kill the desire to read. Of course, children should try a "challenging" book once in a while to see if they are ready to grow up to it. Also, there is another important principle of readability: If the child has especially high interest or very strong motivation, a somewhat more difficult book can be read. But, in general, most children will only read books at an appropriate level of difficulty.

How do you, the teacher, know the readability level of a book? One way is to take the publisher's word for it. In a basal reading series, if the publisher says it is a third-grade book, it probably is a third-grade book. However, if you buy a children's trade book, the publisher either provides no information on level or simply states that the book is "suitable for children ages 6 to 12." This information is not very useful to the teacher, since children in this age span are found in grades one through six, where tremendous differences in reading ability are found, varying from beginning readers to children who can read almost anything. Other school texts are not always graded well; it is not uncommon to find a third-grade science book with fourth-grade readability.

However, there is help for the teacher in judging the difficulty of children's reading material, in the form of *readability formulas*. These are mechanical procedures, sometimes involving use of average sentence length, vocabulary lists, or counts of syllable length, which give you an *estimate of readability* or reading difficulty level.

Figure 10-3 is a nomograph that is used to determine readability by randomly selecting three 100-word passages from a book, then taking the average sentence length and the average number of syllables per hundred words, and entering these two variables to get the approximate grade level of the book. It is one of the simplest and most widely used formulas, and it will grade material from grade one to college.

Two other well-known readability formulas are the Spache Readability Formula and the Dale-Chall Readability Formula. The Spache formula covers grades 1 to 4, and the Dale-Chall formula covers grades 4 through 16. Both of these formulas use a vocabulary instead of syllable count to determine vocabulary difficulty. Each formula gives you a list of common words (4,000 in the case of the Dale-Chall), and you must determine whether or not each word in the 100-word sample is on the list. If a word is not on the list, it is called "unfamiliar." The percentage of unfamiliar words is entered into a mathematical formula along with the average sentence length to calculate the grade level of the book. Syntax difficulty is determined by sentence length.

Hence, the two main factors in determining readability are *syntactic (grammar) difficulty*, which is usually measured by sentence length, and *vocabulary difficulty*, which is measured either as the percent of unfamiliar words or as word length (number of syllables). Other factors which play minor roles in readability include:

Legibility   size of type, white space, shape of letters
Illustrations   which might supplement the story (also graphs and tables)

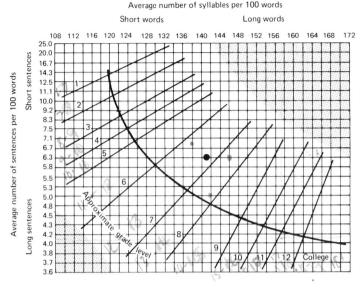

Directions:

Randomly select three 100-word passages from a book or an article. Plot average number of syllables and average number of sentences per 100 words on graph to determine the grade level of the
material. Choose more passages per book if great variability is observed and conclude that the book
has uneven readability. Few books will fall into the gray area, but when they do grade level scores
are invalid.

Example:

	Syllables	Sentences
First hundred words	124	6.6
Second hundred words	141	5.5
Third hundred words	158	6.8
Average	141	6.3

Readability 7th grade (see dot plotted on graph)

Additional Directions for Working Readability Graph

1. Randomly select three sample passages and count exactly 100 words beginning with a beginning of a sentence. Don't count numbers. Do count proper nouns.

2. Count the number of sentences in the hundred words, estimating length of the fraction of
   the last sentence to the nearest 1/10th.

3. Count the total number of syllables in the 100-word passage. If you don't have a hand counter
   available, an easy way is to simply put a mark above every syllable over one in each word, then,
   when you get to the end of the passage, count the number of marks and add 100.

4. Enter graph with average sentence length and number of syllables; plot dot where the two lines
   intersect. Area where dot is plotted will give you the approximate grade level.

5. If a great deal of variability is found, putting more sample counts into the average is desirable.

Figure 10-3 Graph for estimating readability, by Edward Fry, Rutgers University Reading Center,
New Jersey.

Author's style   writing, clarity, and organization
Familiarity   with the subject matter
Density of concepts   number of new ideas

However, these factors are either weak (such as legibility) or difficult to judge objectively (such as style).

Publishers sometimes take advantage, intentionally or unintentionally, of parents or teachers by changing the page format to make a story appear easier to read. For example, they might set a children's story in large type and include frequent childlike illustrations. These create a superficial appearance of ease of reading, but they can't override the essential factors of readability; namely, vocabulary and syntax. Setting a story in large type might improve the legibility, and this can improve readability a little bit, but not much.

There is another simple and direct way of estimating readability, and that is to have a child read a portion of the book aloud. He or she should be able to read about 99 percent of the words fluently without error for the book to be easy reading; that is, for the child to sit down and read it alone. If he or she makes about 95 percent accuracy, then this is a good book for instruction; that is, for use in an oral reading group with supervision. If the child can read only 90 percent or less of the words, then the book is apt to be frustrating, and he or she probably will not continue reading it without extreme motivation or outside pressure. These estimates come from the work of Emmett Betts, and are sometimes called the independent, instructional, and frustrational reading levels. I sometimes teach this as the *1 out of 20 rule*:

If the child misses less than 1 out of 20 words, the book is easy enough; if he misses about 1 out of 20 words, the book is all right for instruction; and if he misses more than 1 out of 20 words, don't use it.

Giving children books or stories to read at their frustration level is bad because it tends to make them dislike reading; it tends to make comprehension poor; it tends to make lessons boring; and, worst of all, it tends to make them stop reading. Betts observed, and you can also, that children reading at the frustration level tend to show signs of nervousness, including:

Excess body movement: fidgeting, foot tapping, hair twisting, finger pointing at words, frowning
    Erratic eye movement: reading same line twice, reversing words, losing place
    Poor comprehension: can't anticipate meaning or remember what was read
    Inattention and short attention span
    Voice problems: high pitch, flat tone, no emphasis, stuttering, whispering
    Rate very slow
    Low eye-voice span
    Vocalizes during silent reading or has lip movement
    Makes oral reading errors: repetitions, omissions, reversals, substitutions, and insertions of extra words

Many of the symptoms of reading at the frustration level are the same as those described for "dyslexic children," or those thought to have some kind of special or inherent reading problem. (Chapter 13 has more to say about dyslexia.) It is possible that many of those children who are labeled "dyslexic" have merely been presented reading material on their frustration level so long that some of the symptoms have become habituated. The "cure" is simply to give the child easier reading material.

Readability formulas or the 1 out of 20 rule is an important part of curing reading problems or, better yet, of preventing many of them in the first place.

Writing Style

Part of the readability problem is poor writing. It is not fair to blame the reader for poor comprehension if the writing is confused, ambiguous, or uncommunicative.

It is very hard to state exactly what poor writing is, and, in most respects, it is a matter of personal judgment. One writer might communicate well to one reader but not to the next reader. Some writers might communicate to a wide variety of readers, but few writers communicate equally well to all readers. There are people who love Hemingway, and those who think he is a bit ordinary.

Teachers themselves sometimes become writers or have to instruct students in the art of clear writing. There are a number of textbooks and courses in English to assist you.

One of the areas of writing style in which I have been interested attempts to explain why two sentences that have exactly the same length and the same vocabulary appear to have different levels of reading ease. This resulted in the Kernel Distance Theory. To explain the theory, it is first necessary for you to know that usually the *kernel of a sentence* is the subject and the verb, or as some linguists might call it, "the noun phrase and the verb phrase." *Distance* is defined as a word or a clause that can be moved around. The theory holds that distance between the parts of the kernel makes the sentence more difficult to read than does distance at either end. For example, "The birds flew north after dark" is easier to read than "The birds, after dark, flew north."

The theory also holds that distance at the end of the sentence is easier to read than is distance at the beginning. For example, "The birds flew north after dark" is easier to read than "After dark, the birds flew north." Thus, if you want to write simply you should not split the kernel, and you should put distance after the kernel rather than before.

Another stylistic consideration for didactic writing (writing intended to teach) is to use some variation of the SER sequence. SER is an acronym for Statement, Example, Restatement. This paragraph and the preceding paragraph attempted to follow the SER sequence. They both made some opening statements, then gave an example followed by a restatement. Sometimes the restatement comes more in the form of a rule or more conclusive statement.

I have obviously just used the SER sequence to apply to a paragraph, but it can also apply to a chapter or an essay. When this is done, the parts are often labeled "Introduction," "Examples," and "Conclusion," or, in the words of the old country preacher, "I tells 'em what I gonna tell 'em," "I tells 'em," and "I tells 'em what I told 'em." This kind of writing can have a beneficial effect on readability and comprehension. The important thing to remember is that examples and restating the idea in different terms both help the student to learn.

Writing to Grade Level

If you are interested in trying to write to grade level, or in taking an article and rewriting it more simply for your lower-level readers, here are seven suggestions.

1 *Watch your vocabulary load* You probably have some natural sense of which words are easy, and this is fine to use, but it also helps to have a basic word list—like the Instant Words or the Dolch Basic Sight Vocabulary—to work from. On higher levels you can use frequency counts, like the Thorndike-Lorge or Carrol list (see references at the end of Chapter 4), to give you some guidance as to which words are easy.

2 *Watch your syntax complexity* This usually means that you should keep your sentence short. But don't be a slave to short sentences. It makes writing boring. Vary the sentence length, but generally keep sentences short for the lowest level of reader. Most, but not all, short sentences are less complex than long sentences.

3 *Style is important* Both the Kernel Distance Theory and the SER sequence will give you hints on how style can influence readability, but there are many others to be found in books on writing style.

4 *Know your audience* There is no substitute for knowing something about the background, previous knowledge of subject, and ability of your intended audience. You really cannot communicate without knowing "where the reader is coming from."

5 *Know your subject* The better you know the topic, the easier it is to write about it and to get the important points in the proper perspective.

6 *Try out and revise* Test out your writing on a sample audience to see how they like it, and to see if the difficulty level is about right. Something that is perfectly clear to you might be difficult for your intended audience. Ask some formal or informal comprehension questions to see if it communicates; if not, rewrite or add explanations, examples, figures, or easier vocabulary.

7 *After you have written, use a readability formula* Don't try to use the formula too early. Write first, then simplify if necessary. But keep in mind the level of your audience so you don't have to change too much. Don't simplify by just chopping sentences in half, but try to use all of these suggestions.

BOOK SELECTION

Readability is one of the factors in selecting a book or story to be read. The other large dimension is interest and motivation.

You won't teach reading for very long before you come across a child who can read but won't. Unfortunately, there is no simple answer, but a lot of partial answers, some of which work some of the time. You might have difficulties with some students in getting them to read anything except short, specific assignments. With others, you might not be able to get them to stop; they would read right through lunch hour if you let them. Both of these groups, as well as all those in between, need some reading guidance by the teacher. Those students who read a lot need suggestions on the variety of books available, and those who don't read need suggestions on getting started.

One problem is that we are not a nation of book readers. Some national surveys have shown that the average adult reads less than one book per year. Children tend to take their parents as models; if the parents read books, the children learn to do so. There have even been correlations established between the number of books in the home and the child's reading ability. While schools can take some of the blame for not turning out "readers," the home and the adult population as a whole share some of the responsibility. Incidentally, there is not much evidence that television is responsible for poor reading habits. There are more books being sold now than before television was available, though this might be due to a number of factors. When books are made into movies or a story is shown on television, it doesn't hurt book sales but tends to increase them. In fact, many teachers take advantage of the fact that a story is being shown on TV to encourage children to read the book, and it often works. Schools regularly show a movie of a classic book, for example, *Tom Sawyer*, before it is suggested for silent reading.

There are numerous professional children's book selection sources. Any school librarian or children's librarian in a public library can get you half a dozen lists of recommended children's books, varying from timeless classics to books recently published, and varying in age level from primary to intermediate to adolescent. Books on children's literature have been written by such well-known authorities as May Hill Arbuthnot, Charlotte Huck, and Nancy Larrick. They give lists of specific titles, such as *Charlotte's Web* and *The Biggest Bear*. If you need more current choices, you can find recommendations from such sources as the University of Chicago Library children's list and the Newbery and Caldecott awards. The Elementary School Library Collection not only suggests children's books that should be in a school library, but gives the readability and interest level for many of them. Since most elementary teachers take a course in children's literature, it is not my purpose to repeat all that information here, but merely to suggest that it is available.

Knowing about children's literature is important because it can frequently catch a spark of interest that a child gives off and turn it into a delightful book-reading experience. It also prepares the teacher to provide for diversity. If a child is sick of animal stories, the teacher can provide "Mike Mulligan and His Steamshovel." It is sometimes easy to pick up signs of interests from children's drawings. If a child continually draws pictures of race cars, it is an indication that certain stories are likely to be of great appeal. Ideas of children's interest can also be obtained from children's writings and conversation.

Reading Interests

Formal *interest inventories* give a lot of suggestions for book selection. They are published in numerous elementary books, or you can use the one in Figure 10-4. Interest inventories have the advantage of being somewhat systematic, and they sometimes plumb areas that the teacher might not have thought about or just didn't get around to trying. They have another advantage in that they are relatively permanent; you can put them in a file folder and use them in parent interviews, or they may be useful when you have to get the child interested at a later time. It is also interesting to compare the

My name is _____

I am _____years old.

Outside of school the thing I like to do best is_____

_____

In school the thing I like best is_____

If I had a million dollars I would_____

When I grow up I will_____

I hate_____

My favorite animal is_____

The best sport is_____

When nobody is around I like to_____

The person I like best is_____

Next summer I hope to_____

My father's work is_____

My mother's work is_____

When I grow up I will be_____

I like to collect_____

The things I like to make are_____

My favorite place to be is_____

The best book I ever read was_____

The best TV show is_____

What's funny?_____

NOTE TO TEACHERS: Filling this out is supposed to be a pleasant experience,
not a chore. Tell the student that every question doesn't have to be
answered. Don't penalize for spelling, but give help if needed. Most of
these answers could use more space so suggest the back of the sheet or almost any of them could be the suggested topic for a theme. Tutors can
orally ask the questions and take notes on the answers.

Figure 10-4 Reading interest inventory.

changes in an interest inventory from the beginning of the year to the end of the year,
or from year to year. I would recommend using the same inventory more than once,
and, if possible, for a few years running. By looking at interest inventories for the
whole class, the teacher can get some good information on selecting books for the
classroom library, or in guiding children around the school or public library.

Teachers are sometimes concerned when children develop *unbalanced reading
interests*; for example, one child may read only books about sports, another child only
books about railroads, etc. There are special charts and wheels that attempt to get the

child to have a balanced reading program—some fiction, some history, some how-to-do-it, etc. If a child loads up in one area, the teacher suggests that he or she try another area. Some studies of eminent men of science have found that they had unbalanced reading programs both as children and as adults, but, all things being equal, the teacher might try to get the child to have wide reading interests. Keep in mind, however, that it is better to read all in one area than not to read at all, and a highly developed special interest just might be more beneficial for the student and for society than a "well-rounded" reading interest.

There have been a number of studies of children's interests by age and by sex. But these studies tend to become outdated. Oceanography and environment were scarcely noticed a decade ago. The role of women has been undergoing both a lot of publicity and a lot of study. Those in the woman's movement charge educators with stereotyping sex roles, but the educators respond that they are merely reflecting the values of society, and that the interest studies are not biased but merely reporting how chidlren respond. In any event, teachers should not assume that girls are not interested in mechanics or that boys don't care about cooking. Publishers of children's reading materials have become much more careful about role stereotyping, and teachers should be just as careful in suggesting books.

One of the best-known sources of information on books for the reluctant reader is George Spache's *Good Books for Poor Readers*, which is published regularly by the Garrard Publishing Company. It combines both readability levels and interest areas, and includes a copy of the Spache Readability Formula.

Good teachers have always had an ear to the ground for good books for all types of readers. They listen to what children tell them; they talk to the librarian and other teachers; they read professional articles on children's books; and they read some children's books themselves. When they find a good one, they bring it to class, read a bit of it to the class, and leave it in a conspicuous spot.

Book Reports

Book reports are a bit of a problem. When overdone or poorly done, they can actually cause a decrease in book-reading behavior. When well done, they can serve to encourage book reading and aid the child to understand what he or she has read, in addition to making it possible for the teacher to check on the child's progress. Oral book reports have the advantage of having the child inform others about a book, and often stimulate interest in it.

The assigning of written book reports should be analyzed carefully. If the purpose is merely to keep a record of books read, perhaps there is a simpler way. If the purpose is to give the child a writing experience, perhaps there are other more interesting ways. Is it to check on reading comprehension? Often the assigning of written book reports is more of a tradition for the teacher and an unpleasant task for the child. Perhaps a well-done or a well-structured, written book report can be a good learning experience, but if the children balk at them, perhaps you should examine your teaching goals for that task.

Teachers usually make up their own book report forms. They vary from a 3 by 5 card with the title and a brief comment, to a somewhat longer form or format which would include a more formal bibliographic reference and specific categories, such as: Main Characters, Setting, and Why I Liked It.

CONCLUSION

In this chapter we have looked at writing, partially from the standpoint of writing that children do in the language experience approach and partially from the standpoint of writing (books) that the children read.

We have discussed two of the most important factors in teaching reading; (1) matching the children's ability levels to the difficulty of the books or readability, and (2) motivating the children to read more books. Readability is basic, because by judging the difficulty level of the material, the teacher is able to make it possible for the child to experience success. Readability is also important in getting the student to read all types of pleasurable and instructional material.

It is one problem to teach a child to read, and another to get him or her to enjoy reading and develop good reading habits. Book selection for the individual child is very important in accomplishing the beginning of lifelong enjoyment from books. For some children, this doesn't need to be taught, but for others, teacher guidance is crucial.

SUGGESTED LEARNING ACTIVITIES

1 Work the readability formula in Figure 10-3 on an elementary subject matter textbook so that you get the practice of doing it. It is one thing to read about readability formulas and another to be able to actually work one. It is a valuable learning experience.

2 Administer the interest inventory to an elementary child, and suggest three books that might interest him or her. Don't forget to pay attention to the readability of the books you suggest, as well as the topic.

3 Try writing your own simple children's story using the suggestions on page 220. If you don't want to write your own, get an elementary science book or social studies book and rewrite a section to a lower grade level.

4 Make a booklist for a classroom showing a balanced selection of a wide variety of interest areas. Use one of the anthologies mentioned in this chapter or one suggested by a children's librarian.

VOCABULARY AND STUDY TERMS

Language experience approach
  Stimulate interest
    Discussions, show pictures
    Provide experiences, trips, displays
    Children draw pictures
  Write
    Teacher writes group story (experience chart)
    Children write individual stories
    Warner likes emotional words

Read
   Your own story
   Other students' stories
   Books
Distinctions
   No vocabulary control
   No skills specified
   Encourage creativity
   Little curriculum structure
   Multisensory
   All language arts included
   Can involve other subjects
   Individual differences provided for
      In interest
      In ability
      In background
Personal satisfactions
Problems
   Children memorize stories
   It takes much teacher time
   Creative teaching needed
LEIR
Fernald kinesthetic technique
   Student writes story
   Teacher supplies unknown words on card
   Student traces with finger
      Says word
      Writes it from memory
   Card filed for reference
   Teacher types story
   Add stories together in book
   Student rereads story
   Drill on unknown words
V-A-K-T
Readability
   Formulas
      Graph, Spache, Dale-Chall
   Range
   Major factors
      Syntax
      Vocabulary
   Minor factors
      Legibility
      Illustrations
      Style

      Familiarity
      Density of concepts
    Oral reading measures readability
      1 out of 20 rule
      Independent, instructional, and frustration levels
    Signs of frustration
      Body movement
      Eye movement
      Poor comprehension
      Inattention
      Voice abnormality (like dyslexia syptoms)
      Slow rate
      Lower voice span
      Vocalization in silent reading
      Errors in oral reading
Writing style
  Kernel distance
  SER sequence
Writing to grade level
  Vocabulary load
  Syntax
  Style
  Audience
  Subject
  Try out and revise
  Formula
Book selection
  Teacher guidance
  Parent model
  TV aids interest
  Book lists
Interest inventories
  Balancing interests
  Interest awareness
Book reports

LIST OF MATERIALS FOR LANGUAGE EXPERIENCE AND TYPING*

Languages Experiences in Reading (LEIR): Roach Van Allen, Richard Venezky, Harry Hahn, and Claryce Allen; Encyclopaedia Britannica; three multimedia kits, cards, filmstrips, records, spirit masters, reading selections, pupil book; **1-3**.
Typing Course for Children: Edward Fry; Dreier; book; **3-6**.

*A list of publishers' addresses can be found at the end of the book.

REFERENCES

Arbuthnot, May Hill, and Z. Sutherland. *Children and Books*. New York: Scott, Foresman, 1972.

Ashton-Warner, Sylvia. *Teacher*. New York: Bantam, 1971.

_____. *Spinster*. New York: Simon & Schuster, 1959.

Betts, Emmett. *Foundations of Reading Instruction*. New York: American Book, 1950.

Bormuth, John R. (Ed.). *Readability in 1968: Committee of the National Conference on Research in English*, a bulletin. Champaign: National Council of Teachers of English, 1968.

Chall, Jeanne S. *Readability: An Appraisal of Research and Application*. Bureau of Educational Research Monographs. Columbus: Ohio State University, 1957.

Dale, Edgar, and Jeanne S. Chall. "A Formula for Predicting Readability." *Educational Research Bulletin*, Ohio State University, 1948, *27*, 11–20; *28*, 37–54.

Durrell, Donald, L. W. Erickson, and W. J. Moore. *The Manual Portable Typewriter as an Instructional Tool in the Elementary Classroom*. Port Chester, New York: Royal McBee, 1960.

Fernald, Grace M. *Remedial Techniques in Basic School Subjects*. New York: McGraw-Hill, 1943.

Fry, Edward B. "A Readability Formula That Saves Time." *Journal of Reading*, 1968, *2*.

_____. "The Readability Graph Validated at Primar. *The Reading Teacher*, March 1969.

_____. "The Readability Principle." *Language Arts*, 1975.

_____. "A Kernel Distance Theory for Readability." George McNinch and Wallace Miller (Eds.), *24th Yearbook*. National Reading Conference, Clemson, South Carolina, 1975.

Guthrie, John T. "Learnability versus Readability of Texts." *Journal of Educational Research*, February 1972, *65*, 273–280.

Hansell, Stevenson T. "Readability, Syntactic Transformations, and Generative Semantics," *Journal of Reading*, April 1976, *19*(7).

Klare, George R. "Assessing Readability." *Reading Research Quarterly*, 1974–1975, *10*(1).

Lorge, Irving. *The Lorge Formula for Estimating Difficulty of Reading Materials*. New York: Teachers College, 1959.

MacGinitie, Walter H., and Richard Tretiak. "Sentence Depth Measures as Predictors of Reading Difficulty." *Reading Research Quarterly*, Spring 1971, *6*, 364–376.

McCuaig, Susannah M., and Barton Hutchings. "Using Fry's Graph to Describe the Variation of Readability." *Journal of Reading*, January 1975, *18*(4).

McDonnell, Gloria M. "Relating Language to Early Reading Experiences." *The Reading Teacher*, February 1975, *28*(5).

Taylor, W. L. "Cloze Procedure: A New Tool for Measuring Readability." *Journalism Quarterly*, 1953, *30*, 415–433.

Van Allen, Roach. *Attitudes and the Art of Teaching Reading*. Department of Elementary-Kindergarten-Nursery Education. Washington, D.C.: National Education Association.

Vaughn, Joseph L. "Interpreting Readability Assessment." *Journal of Reading*, May 1976, *19*(8).

Veatch, Jeannette, et al. *Key Words to Reading: The Language Experience Approach Begins.* Columbus, Ohio: Merrill, 1973.

Vilscek, Elaine C., Donald L. Cleland, and Loisanne Bilka. "Coordinating and Integrating Language Arts Instruction," *The Reading Teacher*, October 1967, *21*, 10.

von Glaserfeld, Ernst. "The Problem of Syntactic Complexity in Reading and Readability." *Journal of Reading Behavior*, Spring 1970–1971, *3*, 1–14.

Part Three

Evaluation, Grouping, and Individual Differences

Chapter 11

Evaluation: Observations, Informal and Formal Tests, Test Management Systems

When you mention evaluation to teachers, probably the first thing that they think about is a standardized test. Tests certainly are an important part of evaluation, but they are one of the least frequently used evaluation devices. By far the most common devices are informal evaluation procedures used by classroom teachers on almost a daily or weekly basis. In this chapter we will discuss both formal and informal evaluation and the related activities of record keeping and reporting procedures.

INFORMAL EVALUATION PROCEDURES

Informal evaluation procedures used by classroom teachers in the reading area vary from incidental individual observations to teacher-made tests for an individual, a group, or the entire class.

Observation of pupil reading behavior is probably the most important part of reading evaluation because it helps the teacher to immediately adjust the curriculum and method to the child's needs. Since it is unstructured, its value depends heavily on the teacher's experience and knowledge. In this text, especially in the chapters on phonics, word attack, vocabulary, and comprehension, there is considerable material which should aid you in observation.

Experience helps the teacher to develop a norm base. Through teaching in a variety of classroom situations, the instructor begins to learn what is typical reading behavior for different types and ages of children. Besides learning about children, experience also gives the teacher familiarity with the content of one or more specific reading programs, plus some supplementary material.

Observations can be general or specific in nature. *A general observation* might be that the child is having some trouble with comprehension. *A specific observation* might be that the student can get the details, but has difficulty relating the main idea of a paragraph. In recent years, a number of school districts have developed long lists of *behavioral objectives* which are very specific kinds of behaviors that a teacher is often asked to observe. In many instances, the teacher is asked to note attainment of the behavioral objective in some kind of record-keeping system.

Incidental observations are those frequent observations that occur during the day inside or outside of lessons, such as noticing that the child has trouble pronouncing the /ou/ sound in a word. Such observations might lead to an immediate correction or brief explanation, or they might lead to a more formal kind of instruction, such as assigning the child a worksheet on the /ou/ sound. One difficulty with incidental observations is that they frequently do not lead to additional instruction. This is one reason for the development of more formal evaluation procedures. Informal observations can often be improved, however, through the use of a *checklist* of skills, objectives, or activities to be observed.

Teacher-made Tests

A more systematic type of observation is the administration of a teacher-made test. This has the advantage that all children in the group are asked to do the same task, enabling the teacher to make direct and immediate comparisons among the individual students. If the students are asked to write down words using the five short vowels, and all but three students succeed, then what is typical or "normal" for the class is fairly obvious. The results also show which students need more instruction in short vowels.

Many good teachers use informal teacher-made tests frequently. It is important for the teacher to avoid placing undue emphasis on the testing process. Tell the students that you merely want to know who needs more work in certain areas of reading instruction. You should also point out that the purpose of these informal tests is not to assign grades, tell parents, or for some other threatening consequence. Elementary school grading should be based on overall performance in many types of activities, not on just one or two big tests. By giving many, brief, informal tests, the children soon learn that they have nothing to fear and that tests are for their own good.

Tests can be motivating. They can cause students to attempt to learn specific things, thereby giving the children a focus for their studying. They can also be used so that a student can check individual progress.

However, like almost anything else, tests for motivation can be misused. Teachers who overuse tests as a motivating device probably not only lack creativity, but probably don't have very good rapport with their children. Not everything in school needs to be tested. Even things that can be tested don't need to be tested all the time. One

Informal teacher-made tests enable teacher and students to check individual progress. *(George Roos/Peter Arnold)*

of the creative parts of teaching is deciding how much or how little testing is to be done. The amount will differ with teacher personality, training, class situation, and many other factors.

Some parts of reading are much more amenable to testing than others. For example, it might ruin motivation and interest to have tests on reading poetry or children's trade books. On the other hand, some reading skills, such as phonics or some specific parts of comprehension or basic word knowledge, are quite easy to test. Not only that, but it doesn't make much sense to test something that is not going to lead to some kind of improvement. A phonics test will suggest to the teacher what kind of lessons are needed. A comprehension test on *The Wind in the Willows* might only be a chore to the child. If the teacher wants to know if the child has adequate reading comprehension, it would probably be better to have specifically designed questions on some selected paragraphs.

Basal Series Tests

Most basal reading series or basal reading systems contain tests that are used either before starting a book or unit, or after the book or unit is completed. The Scott, Foresman system which was discussed in Chapter 7, for example, includes tests to be given upon completion of each of its 12 primary levels. For placing the child into the series at the right level, Scott, Foresman makes available an informal reading inventory which contains selections from each level, thus giving the teacher a chance to check the child's oral reading, silent reading, and comprehension ability.

The Read System, also discussed in Chapter 7, has both screening activities for placement (to be used in starting a child on the proper level) and checkup tests (to be used after a child has completed using a basal reader and accompanying workbook).

It should be pointed out that many of the workbook activities could also be considered as informal tests which give an indication of the child's mastery of the skills and concepts being taught.

The tests which accompany basal readers have good *content validity*; that is, the items are closely related to the subject matter that was just taught. However, they are usually not standardized tests; they do not compare a child with a norm or standardized group. For example, test results might indicate that a student has mastered most of the reading skills taught up through the middle of the third grade of a particular series, but they do not show whether the child reads as well as the typical third-grader in the United States.

Basal series tests are sometimes *diagnostic*; that is, they show particular areas of strength or weakness. In the case of evidenced weaknesses, the test or its accompanying instruction manual will often suggest remedial or supplemental activities that should be engaged in before the child progresses to the next book or level.

It is possible to use a series without using the accompanying tests, but the tests are always recommended by the author and publisher as they are helpful in evaluating the effectiveness of instruction and in discovering individual differences in learning. The only excuses for not using them would be dire poverty on the part of the school district or some excellent alternate system of evaluation.

FORMAL OR NORM REFERENCED TESTS

Basal series tests are printed, have standard directions, and are developed by someone, presumably an authority, outside the classroom. They are much more formal than teacher-made tests. However, really formal tests are those types of reading achievement tests that are made by test companies, and which go through a rather extensive development process including norming or standardization. Formal tests also have evidence of reliability, validity, item analysis, and other factors. These tests are also called *standardized tests*. Austin and Morrison found that formal tests are used by 98 percent of the United States' school districts, so teachers should have some understanding of them. What makes a formal test different from an informal test?

Item Analysis

A formal test has an *item analysis*. This means that there are statistics on each individual item (question) to show that it contributes to the total score. A bad item on an informal test, for example, might actually pull against the total score; all the poor readers get it right, and all the good readers get it wrong. Bad items either are omitted from a formal test or are rewritten so that they become good items. Informal tests might have bad or useless items. Useless items are those items that don't contribute because as many poor readers get them right as do good readers. In testing parlance, the item doesn't "pull" or discriminate.

Weighting

Formal tests also are concerned with *weighting*. In an informal test, a primary teacher might believe that phonics and comprehension are equally important, yet, because phonics items are easier to write, he or she has 20 phonics items and only 10 comprehension items. If the teacher uses total score as a measure of reading competence, phonics will be given twice the importance of comprehension. In a formal test, if phonics, comprehension, and other skills are separate subtests, this can equalize different length (number of items) weighting. However, even when buying published tests, teachers should watch the weighting of the test they are selecting.

It should be remembered that the total score is a sum of the subtest scores; hence, the number and type of subtests are a type of weighting.

Validity

Formal tests also pay much more attention to *validity*. The problem of validity is simply, "Does the test measure what it is supposed to measure?" There are several ways to look at validity. One is to determine *content validity*: Is the test a fair sampling of some specific content? For example, if a phonics test is supposed to cover regular consonants, common vowels, and diphthongs, does it indeed sample from each of these areas? Furthermore, do the items really measure attainment of this knowledge? Some so-called phonics tests might be measuring ability to discriminate between two different sounds when what the teacher really wants to know is whether, given the grapheme, a child can sound out the phoneme. Yet a test measuring each of these skills might contain regular consonants, common vowels, and diphthongs. Lists of objectives or goals can be used to help check on content validity.

The concept of content validity is close to the concept of *face* or *surface validity*. What these latter terms mean is that you just look at the test: If it looks like a reading test, or if it looks like it tests vowel sounds, then it has face validity. A more systematic approach might be used in determining content validity; for example, you might check the kinds of items against a list of objectives or a taxonomy.

Concurrent validity is another kind of information a formal test often provides. Concurrent validity shows how the test compares with another test. For example, if X Test Publishing Company puts out a new reading test, it helps to show the validity of that test if it can pick out the same good and poor readers as another well-known reading test. The test publisher usually tells you this in a rather formal way: "The X Reading Test correlates with the Stanford Reading Achievement Test .80, and with the California Test of Basic Skills .75." To interpret this, you need to know that when correlating reading tests, the 80s (.80 to .89) are high while the 50s would be low.* To further interpret this, you probably need to realize that a very high correlation, such as .90 or better, means that the test is measuring much the same thing as another test, so you might reason, "Why not use the other test?" On the other hand, if a reading test correlated very low with other well-known reading tests, you might wonder if it really measured reading. Hence, there are times when you want concurrent validity to be high, and perhaps times when you want it to be low. Users of informal tests usually don't know the concurrent validity.

Another type of validity is *predictive validity*. It tries to tell you how well the test will predict some future event. For example, reading readiness tests try to predict how well a child will learn to read (is the child ready?). One way of doing this is to correlate the reading readiness test scores given at the beginning of first grade with the reading achievement scores given at the end of the first grade. In other words, we are asking the questions: "Who will succeed in reading?" and "Who did succeed in reading?" If a test had high predictive validity, say in the 70s or 80s, then we could say that the test tended to tell us which students or which class had a good chance of succeeding. Intelligence tests (IQ) also attempt to have predictive validity.

Unfortunately, predictive tests have much more validity for a group than for individuals. They can pretty well tell us that the average reading score for Miss Washington's class will be better than for Miss Lincoln's class, but they are not very good at telling us whether Johnny will do better than Jimmy. Predictive tests are less valid for young children than for older children or adults.

Reliability

One of the major differences between formal tests and informal tests is in the determination of *reliability*. Reliability is really a very simple problem stated something like this: "If I test a child on one day, will he get the same score if I test him on the next day?" Or, another way of putting the reliability problem: "If I test the class on one day, will the same students come out on top if I test them the next day?" (assuming no change of learning in the pupils in between). If the answer to these questions is "no," then the test is no good. If a child can get any score on any day, then how good is the score you get? In other words, one of the first requisites of a test is that it have a measure of constancy—if the scores jump around they are valueless.

Unfortunately, very few things in this world are perfect, and reading tests certainly are not in the perfect category. So what really happens is that if you give a child two identical reading tests on the consecutive days, he or she will get two different scores; hopefully, not too much different, but there is often some difference. In other

---

*It is not the purpose of this text to delve far into statistics, but it is useful to remember that they are not percentages but that a perfect correlation is 1.00. This means that two tests would rank the students in exactly the same order, and hence some would say that they are testing the same thing. A correlation of 0 means that there is no relationship between the rankings.

words, no reading tests are perfectly reliable, so the problem for the teacher is how *unreliable* they are. The test maker tells you this in a statistic called "a coefficient of correlation," and you have to interpret it. The statement about reliability might look something like this: "Reliability was determined by the split half (or Kuder-Richardson or test-retest method) and was found to be .91." A reliability of .95 is very good, a reliability of .85 is just fair; below that, it is inadvisable to use the test.

Another way of stating reliability, and one that is much more useful for the teacher, is the *Standard Error of Measurement* (SEM). In order to understand the SEM, you need a couple of more concepts. One is *true score* and the other is *obtained score*. The obtained score is the only score you can get. It is the score a child gets upon taking the test. We know that that score is unreliable, but if the child theoretically took the test over the over again (and there was no practice effect), we could get a mean or average of those obtained scores, and this would be the true score. Now, the question is: How far away is the obtained score—the one the child actually gets—from the theoretical true score? The answer is: We don't ever know for sure, but we can estimate the distance or the amount it shifts due to unreliability. Using the SEM, we can determine a band of probability which is the obtained score, plus or minus one standard error of measurement. For example, the paragraph comprehension section of the Stanford Achievement Test has an SEM of .2 of a year at the third-grade level. This means that if a child scored 3.1 on the test, his or her band of probability would extend from grade level 2.9 to 3.3. Now, the probability statement is that only two-thirds of the time the true score will lie within the band, and one-third of the time it will be outside the band (one-sixth of the time above and one-sixth of the time below). Looking at it another way, you can say that the test is so inaccurate (unreliable) that only two out of three times do we even know the child's approximate reading level within a band .4 of a year wide (in this instance from 2.9 to 3.3), and in one out of three testings the student is outside that band. In the upper elementary grades, it is not unusual to find major standardized reading tests with an SEM of .5 or, in other words, the band is a full year wide. As a result, we only know reading level within a one-year band, two-thirds of the time. One out of three times, or one out of three children, score outside the band. And that's how unreliable major reading tests are. Why then do we even use them? The answer is very clear: "Because there is nothing better." Not teacher judgment, not informal tests, not anything can judge reading level any better. In fact, most informal and subjective judgments are worse (less reliable) than formal tests.

People who are not professionally informed on the use of tests might think that a child who scores 2.9 is reading worse than a child who scores 3.1. I trust that you know that this isn't true, or more accurately, there is no way of knowing if either child reads better than the other one, at least based on this one test score. Of course, if one child consistently scored lower on a number of tests or on repeated testings, then you might begin to get some confidence in the "direction" of the difference and, after even more testings, in the "amount" of the difference.

Some test makers have tried to get educators to use *band scores* rather than single scores. But educators have resisted the bands; perhaps because they really didn't understand the standard error of measurement concept of tests. Unfortunately, in the past, teachers have not been well-trained in the use of tests, causing them to misuse and misinterpret them. When tests are misused, they are obviously not as valuable, and sometimes even cause harm to students. Harm can be caused: (1) by inaccurately telling the student he is not progressing, or that he is going backward; (2) by too-rigid grouping; (3) by failure to promote based on a single test score; or (4) by failure to give reading instruction because a readiness test with poor predictive validity was used.

Understanding of tests is crucial in evaluating test materials. Test publishers naturally stress the high validity and reliability of their tests rather than stressing their unreliability. In buying tests, like buying anything else, the buyer must be aware of faults.

Standardization

Standardization or *norming* is probably the major factor that differentiates informal from formal tests. Item analysis is important, concurrent validity is important, reliability is important, but the major differentiation is standardization or norming. What standardization means is developing a standard or norm group by administering the test to a large group—say 300,000 children—who are a representative sample of children in all regions of the United States. Then, when one child takes the test, his score is compared to the standardization group. To understand how this works, consider this illustrative example. If we have a brand-new reading test which has been item-analyzed (bad items thrown out) and has at least content validity, we now administer it to 50,000 fourth-graders, 50,000 fifth-graders, and 50,000 sixth-graders. The fourth-graders got 57 items right (mean raw score 57), the fifth-graders got 68 items right, and the sixth-graders got 79 items right. That is, the mean score of all the fourth-graders was 57, etc. Now along comes your student, little Rudy Readall, and he takes the test and gets 68 questions right; we say that he reads like the average fifth grader, or that his reading score is 5.0.

Now please note that the raw score of 68 was a *mean* score of the fifth graders in the norm group. This means that approximately half the fifth graders received a score below 68 and half received a score above 68. Thus, a score of 5.0 is not a standard or a criterion or a minimal satisfactory score; it is a mean score. You must understand this because misunderstanding of this basic little fact causes all sorts of enflamed tempers, hurt feelings, accusations of poor teaching, poor interpretations in the newspapers, inaccurate reports to school boards, misinformation in telling parents about tests, and devastating comments in telling students about test scores. There are many teachers and many principals (and most parents) who don't understand that half the students are supposed to be below the grade level if the school contains a representative sample of children from the United States. *Grade-level scores on standardized tests are not minimum criteria, or mastery, or goals, or anything but averages.*

Tests are one of the many tools that teachers use to try to help children. They need to know how a child is progressing; they need to know a child's strengths and weaknesses; and occasionally they need to compare a child with some kind of norm.

Children are born different. They grow up in different circumstances; they have different experiences in school. All these things cause reading achievement to be different. If children are different, some are better and some are worse. If we put this on a scale and assign numbers to it, we can get an average number. By definition, average is the midpoint and half are above and half are below. By definition, half the fifth-graders in September score below 5.0 and half score above. It is not a fault of the public schools—it is the way the test is constructed.

There are a number of different scores reported on standardized tests. The most often used is the grade level, or as some test makers call it, a *Grade Equivalent (GE) score*. This is the one we have been talking about which compares the student's raw score with the average of the standardization group. Another common score is the *percentile*, which tells you how a student compares with a specific section of the norming group or the whole norming group. For example, a raw score of 68 might give a grade equivalent score of 5.0, and a raw score of 63 might give a grade equivalent score of 4.5; but instead of telling the student that his reading grade equivalent score is 4.5 (which to a fifth-grader might be a little demeaning), you can say that compared to all the fifth-graders who took the test in the standardization sample, he scored at the 41st percentile; that is, he was above 40 and below 58 of a typical hundred fifth-graders. Hence, it is a little easier to see that this student is not far from average or in the middle. Percentiles, of course, can be given in bands (the standard error of measurement for percentile) and hence his band might be from the 33rd to the 49th percentile.

Don't confuse percentile with *percentage*. Percentile tells the student's relationship to the standardization group; hence, you can only get a percentile on a normed test. Percentage is a much simpler statistic and tells the percentage of items the student got right. Informal teacher-made tests often use percentage.

Some test makers report reading scores in *stanines*, which is a system of breaking up the entire range of possible scores into nine areas. The chief advantage of this is that a single digit can be used to tell how the student compares with the standardization group, but it is a little difficult to interpret. See Figure 11-1 for the percentiles covered by the nine different stanines. Basically, stanines four, five, and six are the average or midrange scores, while a stanine of one or nine represents extremely low or extremely high.

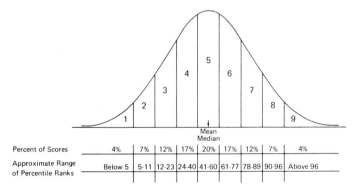

Percent of Scores	4%	7%	12%	17%	20%	17%	12%	7%	4%
Approximate Range of Percentile Ranks	Below 5	5-11	12-23	24-40	41-60	61-77	78-89	90-96	Above 96

Figure 11-1 A normal distribution curve (population) broken up into stanines showing the percent of the population in each stanine and the percentile rank for each stanine. *(Source:* Test Service Notebook No. 13. *Issued by the Test Department, Harcourt Brace Jovanovich, Inc.)*

A *band score*, given by some test makers, is really the score plus and minus a standard error of measurement. For example, a percentile band score might say that this student is the 52d to the 40th percentile; or, in grade equivalent scores, that the score is 3.8 to 4.6. As you recall from our discussion of standard error of measurement, band scores are really just as accurate as single (or point) scores, but many teachers and administrators do not like them. In fact, an argument could be made that they are really more accurate as they point out the unreliability of the test. Look ahead to Figure 11-3 and you will see band scores under "National Percentile."

Range of the Test

Range is another qualification you should look at when selecting a test or interpreting a score. Two different tests which state that their target population is grades 4, 5, and 6 might really have two different ranges. One might yield scores from 3.0 to 7.5. It is is usually possible to score a little higher and a little lower than the target population. The other might score from 3.0 to 8.5; hence, there is a possibility of the latter test yielding a score in a wider range. However, there is a more important factor, and that is the number of items needed or the discrimination of scores between the 3.0 and 5.0 versus the number of items or discrimination ability of the upper part of the test. Stated in tester's slang, one test might have a lot of "bottom" and another a lot of "top." If you have a population of students who are expected to score on the low side, or you want the test to do a good job with low-level students (perhaps so you could find out who should go to remedial reading), then you should select a test with a lot of bottom. If, on the other hand, you have a bright class and you want to know who the good students are (or you want to know just how good your good readers are), then you should select a test with a lot of top.

You can determine meaningful range by looking at the raw scores needed to change grade equivalent scores in the top or bottom ranges. In an intermediate test a raw score of 26 might give a Grade Equivalent Score of 4.6, and a raw score of 27 might give a GE of 4.7. Near the upper limit of the test, however, a raw score of 42 might give a GE of 7.4, and a raw score of 43 might give a GE of 7.9. Hence, the chance missing of one item at midrange of the test would only throw the GE off one-tenth of a year; but at the upper extreme, one raw score point (one more item correct) can change the GE by a whole half a year. Obviously, scores at the extreme upper range of this test are much more subject to chance fluctuations or, to put it in testing terms, "the extreme upper scores are less reliable."

To be on the safe side, you should give students who score near the top and bottom of a test the next upper or lower form, or use another test with more top or bottom.

Chance Score

Another limitation on range on the bottom end is the chance score. I call this the *"orangutan score"* because it is the score that can be made by an orangutan if items are presented one at a time before his cage and he gets a banana whenever he presses button A, B, C, or D. In other words, it is the pure guessing score. You can calculate the pure guessing score easily. If each item has four choices, then on the average, by guessing, you will get one out of four items right or 25 percent. To get the orangutan score, simply take 25 percent of the total items and convert this to a grade equivalent score. This won't work if the test uses a correction for guessing formula, but most reading tests don't. You will be surprised how high a reading score an orangutan could get. Hence, any score at or below the orangutan score should be discarded, and you should administer the next lower level of the test. In any event, please don't use a score at or below the orangutan level; it might be seriously misleading. The opposite applies when a student hits the ceiling or top of a test; the next higher form should be given to get the proper score.

Measuring Growth

Sometimes teachers wish to use standardized tests to measure growth in some skill, such as reading. Since the standard error of measurement is so large, *it is difficult to measure growth of an individual* for a time span of much less than a year, and even that time span is a bit shaky. The reason for this can be seen in the probability bands (plus and minus one SEM). If the SEM is .4 of a year, and if the student scored at the top of the band at the first of the year and at the bottom of the band at the end of the year (even if he really made a year's progress, true score), his obtained scores would show almost no progress. It is even possible for a test to show that a student went backward during a year in which she really went ahead. The way to avoid getting caught in this trap is to have a number of different ways of evaluating the student informally and formally—use more than one formal and informal test, plus observations.

Class means have a much lower standard error than individual scores (the bigger the group, the less the score jumps around), so *it is possible to measure growth of a group* for a year or a bit less with more confidence.

If the test is put away immediately after it is taken, and there is no "teaching to the test," then it is possible to use the exact same test again. However, most tests have alternate forms that can be used. *Alternate forms* have an equivalence or reliability problem. Stated simply, "Is the score obtained on one test exactly the same as the score on an alternate form?" The answer is, of course, "no," as each test has its SEM. The test maker will usually tell you *interform reliabilities* (for example, the reliability between Form A and Form B); hopefully, they are in the high 80s or better; if they are in the low 80s, be cautious; below that, forget the comparison. Incidentally, readministering exactly the same test usually has as high or higher reliability as administering an alternate form. However, this assumes that the teacher has been scrupulously correct about not teaching to the test.

Subtests

Most of the time thus far I have been talking about reading scores as if the normed tests yielded only one reading score. It is true that many reading achievement tests do yield a single score, or a total reading score, which is probably the most reliable score, but many also yield a number of *subtest scores*. These subtest scores attempt to make the test *diagnostic*, or, in other words, they attempt to show specific strengths and weaknesses.

If several subtest scores are given, the most common breakdown is between general comprehension and vocabulary. The most widely used and accepted method of assessing comprehension is to have the child read a paragraph and then answer several comprehension questions about it. This kind of test is also called *paragraph comprehension.*

The *vocabulary test* is an attempt at assessing word meaning, sometimes in the context of a sentence or phrase, and sometimes by having the student select synonyms or antonyms of a chosen word (study Figure 11-2). These two scores are sometimes combined into a total reading score, and sometimes the test maker will only give them separately with no provision (or norms) for combining them into a total score. Other reading test makers include more subskills, such as sentence meaning, study skills, reading for facts, etc.

In Chapter 5 we saw lists of a number of comprehension subtests, and in Chapters 2 and 3 we saw several ways of breaking down word-attack skills.

Subtest scores sometimes have the problem of low reliability, so you should check the test manual before relying on the subtest too much.

Even if only one or two scores are given for reading tests, they are sometimes somewhat diagnostic by virtue of their reporting the raw score item by item and clustering items into content areas. No subtest score for an area is given, but the teacher can glance at the response record and see that Johnny got six of the eight items right in "main idea," but only one of four items right in "paraphrasing." There are so few items in each of these diagnostic categories that the scores are not really reliable, but they do give some indication of the student's strengths or weaknesses. See Figure 11-3: A "+" means the item was answered correctly, and a "−" means that the student got it wrong. Furthermore, if the teacher sees that a large number of students in the class are weak in "main idea," then perhaps some lessons in that area are in order. Curriculum diagnosis is often more accurate on informal tests or on criterion referenced tests, which I will discuss later.

EXPECTANCY OR ABILITY TESTING

Teachers are continually faced with the problem, "Is Sara reading as well as she should be?" The problem obviously hangs on what is meant by the word "should." We all know that some students are brighter and some are duller, some learn more quickly, some learn more of almost anything, some have special abilities in certain areas.

Modern ability testing started with Simon Binet, in France in the early 1900s, when he developed his famous scale for determining intelligence. A little later, in World War I, group intelligence tests came into widespread use; in succeeding decades schools have adopted them to attempt to predict who should be learning easily or more at any given age.

Unfortunately, some educators have misused intelligence tests; but then again, some educators have misused phonics books, audiovisual devices, and nearly anything else they could get their hands on. The misuse of intelligence tests has caused some

TEST 2 · READING Comprehension

This reading test will show how well you understand what you read.

Directions: Read each poem, story, or letter and do the items following it. Choose the **best** answer for each item. Fill in the circle that goes with the answer you choose.

Sample Items: Read the first Sample Item below and see how the right answer is marked.

Choose the word which has **oa** in it.

soup	soap	suit	seat
○	●	○	○

Now do the next Sample Item and fill in the circle that goes with the right answer.

I have a parrot named Perky Pete.

My parrot's name is
- ○ Peter Perk
- ○ Pecky Pete
- ○ Peter Peck
- ○ Perky Pete

► Read the story below and do Items 8 11.

We were playing follow the leader, and Tom was the leader. He started out by walking along the top of a fence. From the fence he climbed a tree. He swung from a branch, hopped up and down, and jumped up on a porch.

8   Mark what Tom did next after he walked a fence.

swung	climbed	hopped	jumped
○	○	○	○

9   Find the third thing Tom did.
- ○ jumped up on a porch
- ○ climbed a tree
- ○ walked along a fence
- ○ swung from a branch

10   Choose the answer that tells **in order** what Tom did after he climbed the tree.
- ○ swung, jumped, hopped
- ○ hopped, swung, jumped
- ○ jumped, hopped, climbed
- ○ swung, hopped, jumped

TEST 1 · READING Vocabulary

The reading test on the next page will show how well you know the meaning of words.

Directions: For each item on the next page, choose the word that means **the same** or **about the same** as the word with the line under it. Fill in the circle that goes with the word you think is right.

Sample Items: Read this Sample Item and see how the right answer is marked.

start to play
- ○ like
- ● begin
- ○ forget
- ○ stop

Now do the next Sample Item and fill in the circle that goes with the right answer.

about the same
- ○ always
- ○ exactly
- ○ almost
- ○ never

10   all <u>but</u> one came
- ○ because
- ○ except
- ○ of
- ○ for

20   <u>mend</u> the tire
- ○ patch
- ○ clean
- ○ change
- ○ fill

30   he was <u>smiling</u>
- ○ grinning
- ○ joking
- ○ laughing
- ○ teasing

40   the earth's <u>path</u>
- ○ orbit
- ○ square
- ○ field
- ○ space

Figure 11-2 Sample items from the *Comprehensive Tests of Basic Skills*, Level 1. *(Source: California Test Bureau, McGraw-Hill Book Company, Monterey, California.)*

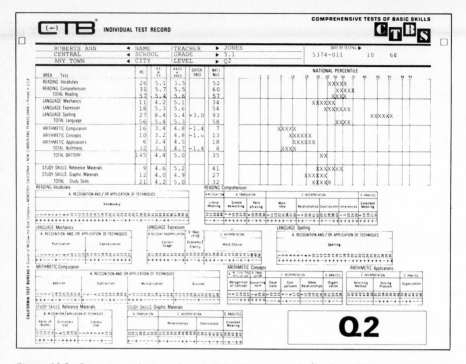

Figure 11-3 Computer printout of an individual test record. *(Source: California Test Bureau, McGraw-Hill Book Company, Monterey, California.)*

groups, particularly minority groups in some areas, to ask schools not to use them at all. An examination of the use of intelligence tests in the schools would reveal that they have had considerable popularity and some recent bad press. However, they are still used widely, and some understanding of them by the teacher is absolutely necessary.

First, let us discuss the good things about intelligence tests and how they should be used, then some of the cautions and indications of when they should not be used.

The best thing about *intelligence tests* is that they help the teacher to pick out *underachievers*; that is, they help the teacher or the supervisor to spot children who should be reading at a better level. They show if a child or the class is reading up to where they might be expected to be.

To do this, intelligence tests attempt to measure a number of mental factors—such as reasoning, spatial relations, vocabulary development, number concepts, and many more—that usually correlate fairly well with school achievement. We shall avoid the argument as to whether intelligence is inherited or environmental (learned)—there are plenty of other texts that provide both sides of this argument. Most experts feel that both are involved, but they disagree as to the relative importance of each. What we are concerned with is not how the child got that way, but where he or she is at some given point in time; say, at the fifth grade. Does the child have the approximate school learning ability of the average fifth-grader, or a bit more, or a bit less? It is also fairly well established that sometimes IQ or ability scores can change either up or down over a period of time.

Intelligence tests, like all other kinds of tests, also have reliability problems. The SEM is frequently about five IQ points. Thus we only know someone's IQ within a band ten points wide two-thirds of the time, at best. IQ determination is not an exact science, as some teachers and parents unfortunately seem to believe, but rather it is an estimation. It is intended to give the teacher some idea of expectancy, to provide additional information about a child. If an IQ score doesn't correlate with a child's demonstrated ability to learn, then obviously the IQ test is wrong. On the other hand, some pupils who the teacher might have thought of as "dumb" might receive another look when their scores on an IQ test come out surprisingly high.

Since "intelligence" test has a rather harsh sound, some test makers use other words to describe the same thing, like *mental ability, educational ability, mental maturity,* or *anticipated achievement.*

The IQ score itself is sometimes used in schools as a general indication of brightness, but it is probably more useful when it is converted into *grade expectancy* for comparison with Grade Equivalent scores on reading tests and other achievement tests.

Let us briefly review what an IQ score is based on, and how it relates to grade levels. If we test a large number of seven-year-olds, we might find that their mean raw score on a test number of items they got right would be 30, and a large number of eight-year-olds would get 40 items right. An individual child getting 30 items correct would have the mental ability of the average child who is seven years old; or, in other words, his *Mental Age (MA)* would be 7.0. If this child is also seven years old (*Chronological Age* or *CA* 7), then we say that he is normal and that he has an IQ of 100. If, on the other hand, this seven-year-old scored 40 items correct, he would score like the eight-year-olds and have an MA of 8.0. To calculate his IQ, we divide his CA of 7 into his MA of 8 and, moving the decimal point over two places, say that he has an IQ of 114. Hence, IQ is theoretically a ratio of CA to MA.

Since most children in the United States enter first grade at about the same age, about 6.3 or 6.4 years old, we can also easily convert MA into grade placement or grade expectancy. Hence, a seven-year-old would have spent about six months in first grade, so we can say that his or her grade expectancy or placement would be 1.6. If you want a simple formula for converting either Mental Age (MA) or Chronological Age (CA) into Grade Equivalent (GP for grade placement), simply subtract 5.4. Stated in algebraic form:

$$CAGP = CA - 5.4 \quad (7.0 - 5.4 = 1.6)$$
$$MAGP = MA - 5.4$$

For example, if a child is 8.5 years old and you wonder what grade he should be in according to age (birthdays) or CA, just deduct 5.4 from 8.5 and you can see that she should be in the beginning of third grade (3.1). If you have a test that gives you a mental age, and if the child's Mental Age (MA) is 9.7, then we deduct 5.4 and see that the child should be achieving at 4.2; in other words, her reading score should be at least fourth grade if she is working up to expectancy.

Incidentally, if the child's cumulative folder only gives you IQ and chronological age, there is also an easy way to get mental age: simply multiply chronological age times IQ and move the decimal two places

$$MA = \frac{CA \times IQ}{100}$$

For example, if a child is seven years old and has an IQ of 110, then multiplying these two together we find that the MA is 7.7; by deducting 5.4, the grade expectancy is 2.3. Note that by CA this child would probably be in first grade, yet should be reading on second-grade level. That's one of the things an IQ test shows us; it gives the teacher different expectations than those derived from just knowing that the child is seven years old. It also helps to show why some other children are behind grade level in reading.

Limitations of IQ Testing

Some of the major limitations of IQ testing are based on the kind of norming or standardization group used. Most major ability tests are based on the "whole" United States population. If a child comes from a different background, or speaks a different language in the home, then the tests tend to lose validity. I say lose validity, not totally destroy validity, as even with children who have a foreign language background, the tests retain some validity as the instruction is in English, the same language as the test. For example, a child who speaks mostly Spanish and only a little English will do poorly on an IQ in English, but he or she will also do poorly in learning to read; as the child's English improves, so will the IQ score and the reading ability. The same argument applies to other cultural differences.

IQ tests tend to predict school achievement, not outside-of-school activities. For example, an IQ test tends to show who will do well in learning mathematics, but not who will do well in baseball, salesmanship, or interpersonal relations.

A serious limitation of many IQ tests in evaluating students who are below average in reading is that they require reading ability. It is illogical to test a child on an IQ test that requires reading ability, then (when he or she scores low on the IQ test and low on the reading test) say that the child shouldn't be reading any better because of the IQ expectancy. This is one of the misuses of IQ testing that has caused it to be removed from some schools. One way around this problem is to give an IQ test that does not require reading, or to look at only that section of the test that does not require reading. For example, some IQ tests have a section that often requires no reading at all, and issues a separate IQ subtest score. Incidentally, individually administered IQ tests, like the WISC or Stanford-Binet that are usually given by a school psychologist, do not require reading, and are more accurate than group tests.

Another problem with IQ tests, in fact all tests, is that they are accurate only if the child tries. If the student balks or won't answer the questions, the test is invalid. A normal amount of motivation is assumed in all test norms.

As we showed earlier, IQ or mental maturity (or whatever you want to call it) can be compared to reading achievement by using grade scores. The British tend to use age scores to do the same thing. For example, they talk about Reading Age to compare it to Mental Age. However, in America we tend to use reading achievement grade equivalent (GE) scores in comparison with mental age (MA) grade equivalent scores.

Understanding the Computer Printout

Since much of the standardized test scoring is done by computers these days, it is beneficial for a teacher to have some knowledge of the kind of information the computer provides.

Study Figure 11-3 while you are reading this section. This is the printout or report for a single child who took an achievement test called the California Test of Basic Skills (CTBS), and an IQ test called the California Short Form Test of Anticipated Achievement. The full report of the IQ test is not shown, but it was used to estimate the *Anticipated Achievement Grade Expectancy* or AAGE. In reading across the top line, we see that Ann received a Raw Score (RS) of 26 which gave her a reading vocabulary Grade Equivalent (GE) of 5.1. By glancing up at the heading material, we can see that she took the test at the beginning of fifth grade (5.1), so that her reading vocabulary and her grade placement are exactly the same. Now, when we look at her expectancy or AAGE, we find that the test shows that she is doing a little bit worse than expected; but the computer did not note this in the "Difference" column because it was not significantly worse (they use the 20 percent level of confidence). Another way of saying this is that the difference is not reliable.

In case you are wondering why there are different AAGE figures for each achievement test, here is a brief explanation. The method that I suggested you use—of calculating expectancy based on MA—is fundamentally correct; however, it is based on gross or total scores. Computers make more complex determinations possible. Instead of just using a table of norms, the computer actually takes a number of factors into account in determining the AAGE for each subtest of the achievement battery. The computer searches its memory banks for members of the standardization population that are alike in age, grade, and scores on a number of subtest scores on the IQ test (more than just verbal and nonverbal). It can frequently find between 500 and 1,000 students to give you an AAGE score. However, more meaningful than the AAGE score is the "+" or "−" in the *significant difference* column. The actual numbers in the difference column are not as important; it is the "+" or "−" that counts.

The raw score of 26 gives Ann a percentile of 52 based on national norms, and that percentile is also reported in a band of X's that range from about 40 to 65. This, of course, means that chances are two out of three that her true score lies within the band. Hence, don't take the single figure of 52d percentile too seriously. The band of X's is really the obtained score (52d percentile) plus and minus one standard error of measurement.

There are two subtest scores for reading, vocabulary and comprehension, each with a separate score, which can be combined to get a total score. Other scores are given in the language, arithmetic, and study skills areas.

Down below the scores is information on how Ann did on every single item in the test. A "+" means the item was correct, and a "–" means the item was wrong. The items are clustered according to skill to make the test somewhat more diagnostic. For example, under reading comprehension she got wrong four out of five items related to literal meaning. Hence, one reason Ann might not be reading better is that she is having trouble with literal meaning. In case you wonder what exactly is meant by "literal meaning," you can get a copy of the test and look at items 12, 17, 33, 40, and 44—the item numbers printed in the literal comprehension box.

The computer can also print out two different kinds of class summaries of item information: a right response record, which shows how each child scored on each item, and a summary of the right response record which tells the percentage of students in the class who successfully answered each item. The items are grouped and summarized so the teacher has available the average percent of items passed in each diagnostic skill area, such as main idea, paraphrasing, etc. Another class record sheet gives the numerical scores for each member of the class on each part of the achievement and the IQ test. Other summaries can be printed for the school and the district. Figure 11-4 shows a class report for the SRA testing program. Note that different test companies use slightly different terms for achievement and ability. It is necessary for the teacher to learn the terms for the test used in his or her school.

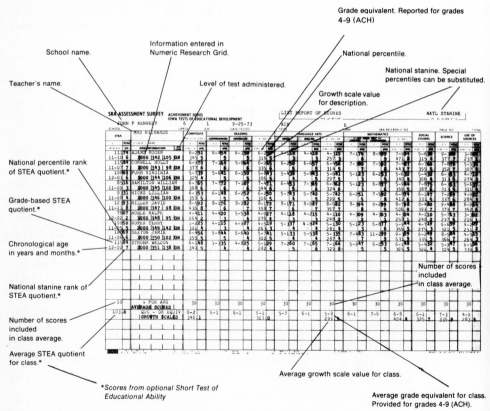

Figure 11-4a Class report for the SRA assessment survey.

The Assessment Survey growth scale values measure incre-
ments of educational growth as students progress from
grade 1 to grade 12. All growth scale values are the same
size, just as all inches on a yardstick are the same length.

When growth scale values from several years of testing are
plotted on Growth Scale Charts, they form patterns of educational growth. These patterns show how a student's present
performance compares with his past performance and are
much more meaningful than scores from a single year. By
comparing the student's growth patterns to the national performance curves on the charts, you can also predict his
future growth.

Plotted growth scale charts emphasize educational growth
as students pass through the grades. Thus they are particularly valuable when working with faculties, parents,
and students.

Average growth scale values for groups are also reported.
They can be plotted on a growth scale chart to provide a
graphic picture of what is happening educationally in a school
or district. Because growth scale values are small units,
even slight changes in performance are discernible. This is
particularly important with very high- or very low achieving
students.

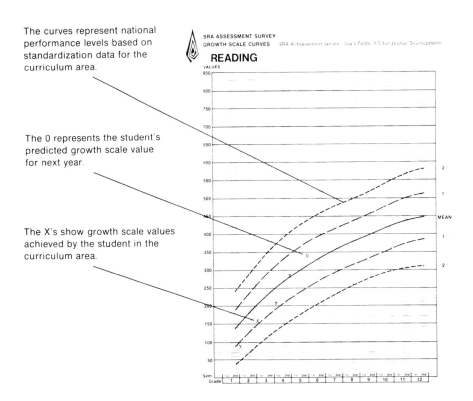

The curves represent national
performance levels based on
standardization data for the
curriculum area.

The 0 represents the student's
predicted growth scale value
for next year.

The X's show growth scale values
achieved by the student in the
curriculum area.

Figure 11-4b Longitudinal growth chart.

An additional valuable service of some test companies is to have the computer develop *local norms*, usually on a district-wide basis. Once local norms are developed, percentiles can be found for each child. As a result, the teacher can make useful statements, such as, "Ann is at the 40th percentile for students in this district in total reading." National norms compare Ann with a cross section of all the students in her grade in the United States, while local norms compare her only with the other fifth-graders in her district. Tests taken in past years can be plotted on a *longitudinal growth chart* (see Figure 11-4b).

Record keeping is also facilitated by computer printout. There are district-wide summaries for the superintendent and supervisors, school summaries for the principal, class summaries for the teacher, and individual test records for the student or parent. Of course, teachers, principals, and supervisors are interested in larger and smaller units than those specific concerns. A principal might not study each individual child's score, and a superintendent of a large district can't look at each individual class score. Besides printing out the individual student's report, like the one in Figure 11-3, the computer will print out test scores on self-sticking label strips so that a relatively permanent report can be kept in the child's folder.

Even though the computer is facile at printing out all kinds of information about scores, it is useless in using the information. That is the teacher's job. Don't be dismayed if you don't instantly comprehend the first bundle of results you receive. It takes a little time and effort. Every company uses a slightly different format, a different set of abbreviations, and different subtest names, so take a little time to learn to read the printout. Study the manual that accompanies the printout or the test administration manual. These will help you interpret the scores. Particularly question very low and very high scores. Look at the children reading and see how you think the test scores compare with actual performance. If there is discrepancy, try to confirm it by informal testing. You may have some surprises when you see some students scoring high, and you find that you have them in the medium or poor reading group. Perhaps you should change them. You might have other students who show poor silent reading comprehension, but who might be reading orally relatively well. They perhaps need more work on comprehension, and perhaps should not progress "through" a set of basal readers so fast; in other words, the child shouldn't be rushed into the next more difficult book. Both individual and class right-response sheets give further suggestions for more specific lessons.

CRITERION REFERENCED TESTS

Now that we have looked at completely informal teacher-made tests and completely formal norm referenced tests, we are better able to discuss criterion referenced tests, which might be conceived of as being somewhere between the two. Some criterion referenced tests are close to formal norm referenced tests, and some are quite close to classroom teacher-made tests.

A criterion referenced test places its main effort on curricular validity. It derives its strength from the closeness to the curriculum. It attempts to answer the question,

"How much does the child know?" This question is answered by setting up a criterion, and seeing how close the child comes to meeting the criterion. For example, a typical reading criterion might be to know all the most-used beginning consonant blends (note the relatively narrow objective or criterion). Since there are only about 25 such blends, a criterion test might have one item for each blend, thus sampling 100 percent of the curriculum matter. At other times, a criterion referenced test might sample only 50 percent or 25 percent of the subject matter; but, generally speaking, a criterion referenced test would have many more items per diagnostic area than the standardized test we saw in Figure 11-3. In short, a criterion referenced test is more "diagnostic." It also has more direct implications for what to teach next.

A formal normed-standardized test, on the other hand, is more useful in comparing individuals with another group or other individuals. The big question that it can answer is, "How well can Johnny read, compared with the average fifth-grader?" or "Is my class as a whole (on the average) reading as well as should be expected?"

Advocates of criterion referenced tests are not very interested in expectancy. They tend not to use IQ or anticipated achievement tests. They downplay the use of expectancy formulas, and are interested in specific criteria. "Can Johnny read the 600 Instant Words?—Who cares what his IQ or age are?" See Figure 11-5 for an example of a criterion referenced test that measures sight recognition of the Instant Words.

There is nothing to prevent makers of criterion referenced tests from using many of the formal test construction techniques. For example, there is nothing to prevent

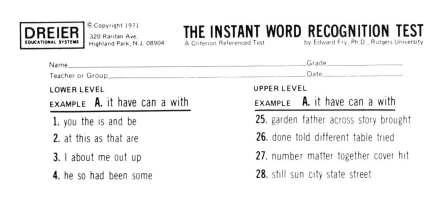

Figure 11-5 A sample of items from a criterion referenced test. *(Source: Dreier Educational Systems, Highland Park, New Jersey.)*

them from doing an item analysis, getting concurrent validities, or calculating relia- bility and standard error of measurement, and some do, but most do not. Of course, whether they calculate the SEM or not, it still exists.

Another way of talking about a reading criterion is *mastery*. This is sometimes called *mastery learning*. "Has the student mastered such-and-such segment of the cur- riculum?" Mastery might be defined as scoring 90 percent on a test covering the area. This information is often useful to the teacher because once a student has demon- strated mastery, or has shown that he or she has reached a criterion, then the next unit can be attempted. Both criterion and mastery people frequently assume that there is a specific order in which units of curriculum should be introduced, and that mastery on lower units is necessary to master upper units. This idea works well for mathematics, fairly well for some parts of reading (such as word-attack skills or some specific parts of comprehension), but rather poorly for other areas of the curriculum, such as appre- ciating literature, writing creative stories, or using such critical reading skills as, "Does this poem engender a feeling of tenderness?" The 90 percent or any other criterion in percentage is an arbitrary figure; the real difficulty of the test is of course determined by the difficulty of the items.

Most formal tests rely heavily on multiple-choice items. While criterion referenced tests also use multiple-choice items, they are more apt to use other types of testing procedures, such as those which ask the student to fill in the blank, read the word or nonsense syllable aloud, listen to the difference in various sounds, circle the main idea, draw a line between, etc. Formal tests also tend to focus more on global objectives like "reading comprehension," while criterion tests measure much more specific objectives like "following directions."

Some standardized norm referenced tests tend to be relatively more diagnostic than others; that is, they mention many more specific objectives, and even have many subtests listed and scored separately. Conversely, some criterion referenced tests might even have some norming; that is, they will suggest that some specific objectives are usually mastered by the end of third grade, etc. Therefore, the line between criterion referenced tests and norm referenced tests is not always clear.

Since it is usually much more time-consuming to construct a formal test, the user of published tests can often be a little more assured of quality, but not always. Some criterion referenced tests are little more than teacher-made tests that have been sent to a printer and appear in a neater format.

EVALUATING THE TEST

Evaluating the quality of tests is a difficult procedure. Fortunately, Buros *Mental Measurements Yearbooks* (MMYs) are of real help in evaluating most normed tests and some criterion tests, and can be found in virtually all college libraries and many school districts. Every published test in the English language is critically evaluated by test experts in the yearbooks.

In case you have to evaluate a test on your own, here are some basic questions to ask about the test. Most of them should be answered by looking at a copy of the test, the administration or examiner's manual, and a technical manual (which may be separate from the examiner's manual). Read over these questions carefully; if you don't understand them, reread relevant parts of this chapter.

Checklist for Evaluating Tests

Content validity:

  Do the test items test items you think are important? (Use goals or list of objectives.)

  Are the subtest titles and content useful?

Concurrent validity:

  What does the test correlate with?

Predictive validity:

  Usually used only for readiness and IQ or expectancy tests; however, occasionally a reading achievement test will be used to predict school achievement in another area.

  How does the test correlate with future achievement?

  Buros Yearbooks give references to other correlational studies.

Reliability:

  Does the test have good reliability, usually near .90 or better?

  Is the standard error of measurement reported? How large is it?

  Are band scores given?

Standardization:

  Are the students in the norm group like your pupils?

  Is the norm group large?

  How old are the norms?

  Can local norms be provided?

Scoring:

  Is computer or self-scoring convenient and rapid? Is self-scoring easy?

  Are useful scores—such as percentiles, grade scores, stanines, band scores, and others—given?

Range:

  Does the test cover the range of abilities of your students?

  Does it have more top or more bottom?

  What is the orangutan (chance) score?

  If the form you would use is inadequate in range for some pupils, are there other levels available with the same standardization and scoring?

Alternate forms:

  Are alternate forms for retesting available?

  What is the interform reliability of the alternate forms? (It should be a correlation in the mid- to upper 80s.)

Subtests:

  Are there subtests? Are they useful?

  Does each of them seem valid?

  Are the subtest scores reliable?

Weighting:

  How are the subtests weighted to make up the total score?

  What kind of items make up the bulk of the items for the total or subtest score?

  Are these the kinds of items you want? (This is really making you take another look at validity, which is extremely important.)

Costs:
> How much does it cost per pupil to buy or rent a booklet?
> Are booklets consumed, or are answer sheets available?
> How much does scoring cost?
> Are there extra charges for local norms, class summaries, district summaries, individual child score sheets, self-stick labels with scores for folders, etc.?

General administrative factors:
> Is the test easy for teachers to administer?
> Is the format pleasing and convenient for children?
> Are the explanations of scores clear and understandable?
> How much time is taken up by the testing?
> How long does it take to get the scores back?

Ultimate purpose of the test:
> Will the test show growth?
> Will the test help you compare your pupil or district with national norms?
> Will the test help you find curriculum strengths or weaknesses?
> Will it help teachers and administrators?
> Will it help in reporting progress to parents and the public?
> Is it worth the time and cost, considering what else could be done with the time and money?
> Is there any other way you could get the same information?

TEST MANAGEMENT SYSTEMS

We have discussed basic reading systems which are primarily based on a series of textbooks, accompanying workbooks, and instructions in the teachers' manuals. These systems have some evaluative procedures built in, such as tests at the end of units and some assessment procedures in the workbooks and manuals, but the primary source of control is the instructions in the teacher's manual. Now we will discuss reading systems that are based on tests which control the use of materials.

The test management systems start with a list of objectives or specific goals which covers all or some major areas of the learning-to-read process. They then develop a large number of criterion referenced tests which match the skill areas at differing levels of development.

After the criterion referenced tests are given, specific teaching suggestions are given, and reference is made to a large number of different publishers' materials that teach the specific skill tested. Test management systems like the Wisconsin Design or the Fountain Valley system list dozens of different sources, ranging from basal reader systems to supplementary audiovisual materials, for each of the skill areas they test. As a rule, test management systems do not sell their own materials for the child to use. They do, however, have lists of materials for the teacher to use, some teaching suggestions, and, of course, tests and scoring services. In addition to telling the teacher about a large amount of commercially published material, the teacher is encouraged to develop his or her own skills lessons.

Though I am calling these *test management systems*, other authors might call these or similar systems the *diagnostic-prescriptive* approach, *continuous progress*, or

Table 11-1 A Boxful of Information

Test edition	Abbreviated test titles	Publisher	Form	Level used at grade 4	5	6
Calif. Achievement Tests (1970 ed.)	CAT	CTB/ McGraw-Hill	A	3	3	4
Comprehensive Tests of Basic Skills (1968 ed.)	CTBS	CTB/ McGraw-Hill	Q	2	2	2
Gates-MacGinitie Reading Tests (1964 ed.)	GMT	Teachers College, Columbia University	1M	Survey D	Survey D	Survey D
Iowa Tests of Basic Skills (1971 ed.)	ITBS	Houghton-Mifflin	5	10	11	12
Metropolitan Achievement Tests (1970 ed.)	MAT	Harcourt Brace Jovanovich, Inc.	F	Elemen- tary	Inter- mediate	Inter- mediate
Sequential Tests of Educational Pro- gress, STEP Series II (1969 ed.)	STEP II	Educational Testing Service	A	4	4	4
SRA Achievement Series (1971 ed.)	SRA	Science Research Associates	E	Blue edition	Blue edition	Green edition
Stanford Achievement Tests (1964 ed.)	SAT	Harcourt Brace Jovanovich, Inc.	W	Inter- mediate I	Inter- mediate II	Inter- mediate II

If you are using any one of the above eight major reading tests and a new student comes to your school who has had one of the other tests, and you want to know how the new student compares with your students, you can get comparable scores by simply looking them up in the *Anchor Test Study*. It is in many major libraries, or you can get your own copy by writing to the Superintendent of Documents, U.S. Government Printing Office, Washington, D.C. 20402 (Stock Number 1780-01312, $1.90), or it is available from ERIC on microfiche.

mastery learning. Commercial publishers tend to have test management systems, in varying degrees of completeness, under such names as "Prescriptive Reading Inventory" or SRA's "Diagnosis," or the "Skills Monitoring System." A variety of systems is listed at the end of this chapter.

Perhaps you will understand these systems a bit better if we look at one in more detail. I will choose the Wisconsin Design because it is widely used and has gone through extensive development by Wayne Otto and a number of his colleagues at the University of Wisconsin. Much of the development was funded by the U.S. Office of Education through a Regional Development Laboratory. Test management systems developed by commercial organizations do not always have such extensive tryouts and revisions.

The Wisconsin Design began in the Madison public schools in 1964, when Otto and his team took the existing curriculum guide and developed assessment exercises to check on specific skill development. At the same time, they began to work on record-keeping systems. The design evolved and grew over the next 10 years to include more formal criterion referenced group tests, much more carefully developed skill assessment procedures, more sophisticated record keeping, and extensive lists of commercially published lessons from dozens of sources. The outline of reading skills has also developed, but it still represents more or less a consensus of the lists of skills found both in many public school curriculum guides and in the skills outlines of the publishers of basal series. The skills also have been divided into developmental levels which roughly correspond to grade levels, but the authors resist equating levels with grade for the simple reason that one of the main purposes of the design is to allow children to progress as they master the levels, and not wait for September to get to the next level. Hence, bright children go through the levels relatively quickly, and slow children take relatively longer. Also, provision is made for children to progress rapidly in some areas and slowly in others. In other words, management systems tend to provide for individual differences.

Perhaps it will help you to grasp the idea of the design if we show you the plan in three levels of detail. First is the "big picture." In Figure 11-6, we see that there are six skill areas and seven developmental levels roughly corresponding to grade levels kindergarten through sixth grade. The first three skill areas (word attack, comprehension, and study skills) are relatively more developed, with more detail in the outline, assessment procedures, and teaching suggestions, than the latter three areas.

In Figure 11-7, there is a section from the outline of reading skills in the word attack level C. This is an expansion of the circled part of Figure 11-6. It illustrates the amount of detail that can be expected in the outline.

Next, we have an expansion of word attack level C, skill 2a, consonants and their variant sounds. Figure 11-8 contains a *behavioral objective* giving exactly what is meant by the outline, and it gives a skill-assessment procedure that can be followed by the classroom teacher. The teacher can use this exact procedure, and is encouraged to develop his or her own procedures to measure the same objective. While the behavioral objective specifies the skill in detail, it is helpful to have an example of an assessment

Skill Area	Grade						
	K	1	2	3	4	5	6
Word Attack	A	B	Ⓒ	D	—	—	—
Comprehension	A	B	C	D	E	F	G
Study Skills	A	B	C	D	E	F	G
Self-directed Reading	A	B	C	D	← E →		
Intrepretive Reading	A	B	C	D	← E →		
Creative Reading	A	B	C	D	← E →		

Figure 11-6 Wisconsin Design general plan showing skill areas by traditional grade level. *(Source: The Wisconsin Design for Reading Skill Development, The Board of Regents of the University of Wisconsin System, copyright 1972.)*

Level C

1. Has a sight word vocabulary

2. Has phonic analysis skills
   a. Consonants and their variant sounds
   b. Consonant blends   ➙e. Consonant digraphs
   c. Vowel sounds
      1) Long vowel sounds

      2) Vowel plus *r*
      3) *a* plus *l*
      4) *a* plus *w*
      5) Diphthongs *oi, oy, ou, ow, ew*
      6) Long and short *oo*

   d. Vowel generalizations
      1) Short vowel generalization
      2) Silent *e* generalization
      3) Two vowels together generalization
      4) Final vowel generalization

3. Has structural analysis skills
   a. Base words with prefixes and suffixes
   b. More difficult plural forms

4. Distinguishes among homonyms, synonyms, and antonyms
   a. Homonyms
   b. Synonyms and antonyms

5. Has independent and varied word attack skills

6. Chooses appropriate meaning of multiple meaning words

Figure 11-7 Wisconsin Design sample segment from the statement of skills and objectives. *(Source: The Wisconsin Design for Reading Skill Development, The Board of Regents of the University of Wisconsin System, copyright 1972.)*

procedure to further specify the meaning of the outline. Take your time, read the objective carefully, and you will get a good idea how behavioral objectives are written.

The skill-assessment procedure, in this skill and many others, is individually administered. While this is excellent instruction, it is very time-consuming for a teacher with 30 children, so group assessment procedures, in the form of criterion referenced tests called the "Wisconsin Tests of Reading Skills Development," were developed as

Skill 2
Phonic Analysis Skills: Consonants and Their Variant Sounds

Objective

Given words containing variant sounds of *c, s,* and *g* (e.g., cake – city, sit – trees, go – giant), the child indicates whether the underlined letters in given pairs of words have the same or different sounds.

Note: Although the consonants *c, g, s, q, d, x, t,* and *z* have more than one sound, variant sounds of *c, s,* and *g* are most common at this level.

Procedure

Give the child the word list. Say, "Read to me the two words by each item number and tell me whether the underlined letters in the words have the same sound or different sounds."

	Child Reads		*Answers*
1.	picnic	– circus	same
2.	giant	– good	different
3.	trees	– please	same
4.	drag	– strange	different
5.	cage	– colt	same
6.	ask	– seven	same
7.	police	– city	same
8.	house	– busy	different
9.	begin	– gift	same
10.	come	– cent	different

Figure 11-8 Wisconsin Design sample behavioral objective and guide to individual skills assessment.

part of the Wisconsin Design. These tests are helpful when starting up the system in a school that has not previously used it, and they provide a systematic way of looking at the skills development of all children after the system has been in operation for a year or more. They can be computer-scored with the results printed out in various forms, such as self-stick labels for the child's folder and skills summaries for the teacher.

Another important part of the Wisconsin Design and other test management systems is the *record-keeping procedure.* Folders with the skills printed inside are one standard method; as the child demonstrates mastery on either the skill-assessment procedure or on the test, a notation is made. Mastery can be determined by the local school. Generally, 80 percent is acceptable, but local districts might vary the percentage from 70 percent to 90 percent, depending on the specific skill and their experience with their students. Teachers are also instructed to make classroom skill charts which list each child by name and by skills he or she has mastered. Another interesting type of record keeping is a McBee-type card which has holes around the periphery (see Figure 11-9). As each skill is mastered, the hole next to the skill name is notched.

WISCONSIN DESIGN FOR READING SKILL DEVELOPMENT

LEVEL A:
1 Rhyming phrases
2 Rhyming words
3 Shapes
4 Letters, numbers
5 Words, phrases
6 i—Colors
7 All A skills

WORD ATTACK

© 1972-The Board of Regents of the University of Wisconsin System   V36037X

LEVEL C:

1 i — Sight vocabulary
2 Consonant variants
3 Consonant blends
4 Long vowels
5 Vowel + r, a+l, a+w
6 Diphthongs
7 Long & short oo
8 Middle vowel
9 Two vowels separated
10 Two vowels together
11 Final vowel
12 Consonant digraphs
13 Base words
14 Plurals
15 Homonyms
16 Synonyms, antonyms
17 i — Independent application
18 Multiple meanings
  All C skills

NOTE: Skills marked i are assessed by a performance test or teacher observation.

WISCONSIN DESIGN FOR READING SKILL DEVELOPMENT

PUPIL NAME   DATE

UNIT	GRADE	SPECIAL CODE	LEVEL

SKILL	RS	M	%C

LEVEL B:

  All B skills
13 Possessives
12 Plurals
11 Base words
10 Contractions
9 Compound words
8 Consonant digraphs
7 Short vowels
6 Rhyming elements
5 Consonant blends
4 Ending consonants
3 Beginning consonants
2 i — Left-right sequence
1 i — Sight vocabulary

DATE	NO. OF SKILLS	GROWTH

LEVEL D:
1 i—Sight vocabulary
2 Consonant blends
3 Silent letters
4 Syllabication
5 Accent
6 Unaccented schwa
7 Possessives
  All D skills

Figure 11-9 Wisconsin Design sample of record keeping for skills mastery on a McBee card. *(Source:* The Wisconsin Design for Reading Skill Development. *The Board of Regents of the University of Wisconsin System, copyright 1972.)*

When the teacher wishes to know who needs instruction in a specific skill, she takes the pack of McBee cards (one for each student in her class) and a skewer is inserted into the hole next to the skill. When the skewer is lifted up, only those cards which have not been notched will remain on the skewer, and this is the group of students who need instruction in that skill. For example, if the teacher wants to know who needs instruction in diphthongs, she inserts the skewer in hole 6. If the example card in Figure 11-9 is notched at hole 6 indicating mastery, it would not stay on the skewer.

In the future, test management systems like the Wisconsin Design will lend themselves to *computer managed instruction*. Instead of having McBee cards, the teacher will be able to use the computer terminal to determine which children need which skill instruction. The computer will keep a permanent record of the child's skill progress in all areas. This information could be utilized in having it print out part of the report card for parents, and it could be used by the principal or supervisor to see which materials should be ordered. It is even possible for the same computer to score the tests, so that with a single input of information there is automatic record keeping and a variety of useful outputs. Please note that this is an example of computer "managed" instruction, and this is not the same as *computer assisted instruction*, which utilizes the computer as a teaching device.

The final component of test management systems is the *instructional unit*. The Wisconsin Design has teacher resource files for most of the skill areas. These contain sheets of skill development activities similar to those found in teachers' manuals but not particularly dependent on specific commercial materials. See Figure 11-10 for several activities. The teacher resource file also contains long lists of both printed and audiovisual materials that are referenced in detail so that the teacher can find exactly where to find material for the skill. Figure 11-11 gives an example of some of the commercial materials. In addition, local school districts are encouraged to add to their

Computer printouts, recording students' skill progress, are useful to the school principal or supervisor in assessing learning outcomes and ordering materials. *(Mike Q./Coronet Studios)*

C.2.a

Skill 2
Consonants and Their Variant Sounds

Word Attack
Level C

SKILL DEVELOPMENT ACTIVITIES

Rationale: The child learns to pronounce the appropriate variant sound of c *in words.* (*Note:* Before e, i, and usually y, c *has an* s *sound, otherwise* c *is sounded like* k.)

1 **Materials:** Word list, basic reader, picture dictionaries, spelling books, chalk, chalkboard.

Procedure: The teacher reads a list of words beginning with the *s* sound. Some of the words begin with *s,* some with *c.* The children are asked to give the beginning sound for the entire group of words. Then the teacher writes the words on the board and asks the children to group the words according to their first letter, noting that *c* sometimes has an *s* sound. Finally he writes *e* and *i* on the board and asks the children to use various books and dictionaries to find more words that begin with *ce* and *ci.* The children note that words in which *c* appears before *e* and *i* frequently have an *s* sound.

Samples:

city	circle	certain
sink	sit	center
cent	cell	simple

2 **Materials:** Mimeographed copies of soft *c* pictures (worksheet 1).

Procedure: As the teacher re-emphasizes the *s* sound in *ce* and *ci* words, the children are given the pictures illustrating these spellings.

Figure 11-10 Wisconsin Design sample of instructional material from the teacher's resource file. *(Source:* The Wisconsin Design for Reading Skill Development, *The Board of Regents of the University of Wisconsin System, copyright 1972.)*

files from commercial materials that may not be listed and from lessons or materials developed by creative teachers in the district.

In summary, then, these are essentially the elements of a test management system:

1 *Skills outlines* and specific objectives

2 *Assessment procedures* to measure the objectives by informal teacher assessment and more formal criterion referenced tests

3 *Record keeping* by individual child's folder, special data (hole) cards, class record charts, or computer printout, to show specific skill mastery

4 *Instructional procedures* and information on where to find specific skill lessons

Test management systems may be supplemental to a basal reading system or might control the use of the basal reading system. Stated another way: Reading instruction in the classroom might be *book-controlled* or *test-controlled.*

Figure 11-12 shows a list of objectives from another test management system so you can compare it with Wisconsin Design objectives in Figures 11-6, 11-7, and 11-8.

Printed Material

Allyn and Bacon, *Arrivals and Departures,* Teacher's Ed. (1968), pp. 60–61, 174, 192, 330.

American Book, *Ideas and Images,* Teacher's Ed. (1968), pp. 172, 268.

Continental Press, *Phonics and Word-Analysis Skills,* Grade 3: Part 1 (1968), p. 14.

Economy, *Phonetic Keys to Reading,* Grade 1 Teacher's Manual (1967), pp. 50–51, 70, 109.

Audiovisual Materials

Colonial Films, *Consonants With Two Sounds* (1967).

Ideal, *Phonic Analysis,* Tape No. 8, 9 (1969).

(This is only a sample; there were approximately 110 printed material references and 15 audiovisual references.)

Figure 11-11 Wisconsin Design sample of information on where skill 2, level C, word-attack commercial material can be found. *(Source:* The Wisconsin Design for Reading Skill Development, *The Board of Regents of the University of Wisconsin System, copyright 1972.)*

ORAL READING TESTS

The tests that we have been discussing thus far in this chapter are chiefly silent reading tests. When one thinks about silent reading tests, comprehension is usually the major factor considered, though there are often a number of other subtests, such as sight-word recognition, word meaning, word analysis, and study skills. However, oral reading tests have a long and honorable history, particularly at the elementary level. In fact, the first published test in the reading field was William Gary's "Standardized Oral Reading Paragraphs" in 1916. This test, which has been revised by Helen Robinson, is still in print and used by many teachers. Since it is typical of many other oral reading tests, a brief description of it is in order. There is a set of 10 paragraphs ranging in difficulty from approximately first to tenth grade. The child is asked to read the paragraph aloud. On a separate copy of the test the teacher marks the kind of errors made, such as mispronunciations, repetitions, omissions, and "needing aid" (examiner tells the student the word he or she doesn't know). Following the reading of the paragraph, several comprehension questions are asked. A grade-level score is obtained based on the number of errors made during oral reading and on the time it took to do the oral reading. The comprehension questions are scored separately or not at all.

There are a number of other standardized oral reading tests on the market by such authorities as George Spache and Donald Durrell (see list of tests at end of

Behavioral Objectives for the PRI

Recognition of Sound and Symbol
1. Vowel Sounds: Matching Like or Variant
2. Consonant Sounds: Letters
3. Vowel Sounds: Unlike
Phonic Analysis
4. Consonant Substitution: Blends
5. Consonant Substitution: Initial and Final
6. Consonant Substitution: Final
7. Syllables: Number
8. Rhyming Word Parts
9. Silent Letters
10. Silent Vowels
11. Variant Vowel Sounds: y
12. Variant Vowel Sounds: r-controlled
13. Variant Vowel Sounds: Digraph, Diphthong
14. Phonetic Parts: Variant Sounds
15. Phonetic Parts: Blending
Structural Analysis
16. Inflected Words: Singular/Plural
17. Inflected Words (Endings) and Affixes
18. Possessives
19. Adjectives: Positive, Comparative, Superlative
20. Prepositions and Prepositional Phrases
21. Pronouns
22. Pronouns: Referent
23. Contractions: Word Pairs or Verb Phrases
24. Compounds: Recognition
25. Compounds: Forming
26. Word Structure: Endings, Spelling Changes
27. Verb Tense
28. Subject-Verb Agreement: Irregular Verb
29. Sentence Building: Subject-Predicate
30. Sentence Building: Phrase Selection
31. Phrase Information
32. Affixes: Identifying Prefixes, Suffixes
33. Affixes: Building Words
34. Defining Affixed Words
35. Defining Affixes
36. Punctuation: Commas
37. Punctuation: Exclamation Point
Translation
38. Like and Unlike Entities: Word Definition
39. Like and Unlike Entities: Synonyms
40. Like and Unlike Entities: Antonyms
41. Like and Unlike Entities: Positive and Negative Sentences
42. Use of Context: Sentence Completion

Translation (Continued)
43. Homonyms in Context
44. Sentence Sense
45. Meaning of Related Words in Context
46. Most Precise Word in Context
47. Phrase Definition in Context
48. Word Definition in Context
49. Word Definition in Isolation
50. Multi-meaning Words and Definitions
51. Multi-meaning Words and Synonyms
52. Synonyms: Selection
53. Antonyms: Selection
54. Homonym Pairs: Selection
55. Homographs: Selection
56. Heteronyms: Selection
Literal Comprehension
57. Event Sequence
58. Story Setting
59. Story Detail: Recall or Descriptive Words
60. Story Detail: Recall by Parts
61. Story Detail: Identify True Statement
Interpretive Comprehension
62. Cause or Effect
63. Inference
64. Conclusion: Formation
65. Conclusion: Factor Identification
66. Predicting Future Action
67. Main Idea: Summary, Title, or Theme
68. Character Analysis: Feelings
69. Character Analysis: Motive or Cause
70. Character Analysis: Descriptive Words, Traits, or Attitudes
71. Descriptive Words and Phrases
72. Sensory Imagery
73. Idioms or Figures of Speech
74. Figurative Expression: Definition
75. Simile
76. Metaphor
77. Mood
78. Time Span and Period
Critical Comprehension
79. Problem Solution
80. Literary Forms: Fable
81. Literary Forms: Satire
82. Literary Forms: Myth
83. Reality and Fantasy
84. Reality and Fantasy: Possibility
85. Fact and Opinion
86. Author Technique: Persuasion
87. Author Technique: Irony, Fanciful Language
88. Author Technique: Altered Syntax
89. Author Purpose
90. Symbolism

OBJECTIVE

32. The student will demonstrate recognition of affixes and endings by identifying prefixes and suffixes in an affixed or suffixed word. (Affixes: Identifying Prefixes, Suffixes)

33. The student will use affixes to build words by adding the correct affix to a word so that it will complete a sentence or phrase. (Affixes: Building Words)

Figure 11-12 A list of behavioral objectives used in the prescriptive reading inventory in outline form, with two items written out completely. *(Copyright CTB/McGraw-Hill, Del Monte Research Park, Monterey, California.)*

chapter). Oral reading tests are frequently included as part of a diagnostic battery that also contains some individual testing of phonics or word-analysis skills, reading words in isolation, silent-reading comprehension, and other tests. These oral reading tests and individually administered batteries are most frequently used by remedial reading teachers dealing with students at the elementary level of reading skills; however, many classroom teachers now use oral tests also. Since the comprehension section of both the oral reading and silent reading sections of these batteries is usually very short, most test specialists feel that comprehension is best measured on standardized silent reading tests.

Oral reading tests have a great value in their obvious face validity. When you hand one child a paragraph and she can read it aloud with few mistakes, and you hand the same paragraph to another child and he makes many errors or can't read it at all, the difference is most striking. It is far more "real" than looking at some numbers printed out by a computer.

Informal Reading Inventories

One technique initiated by Emmett Betts is the use of *Informal Reading Inventories* (IRI). To make one of these, a teacher is told to select passages from books at various levels, such as beginning first grade, upper first grade, beginning second grade, upper second grade, etc. The child is then asked to read the passage, frequently 50 to 150 words long, aloud while the teacher counts the number of errors. Following this, the child is asked some comprehension questions, typically five or six. Betts then gives a rule of thumb as follows:

95% pronunciation with 90% comprehension → Independent Level
 (5% errors)
90% pronunciation with 75% comprehension → Instructional Level
75% pronunciation with 50% comprehension → Frustration Level
 (or worse)

Betts states that the independent level is for reading independently for pleasure or study; the instructional level is where reading instruction might most profitably occur (this level of book might be used in a reading group or in a study situation where help is readily available); and the frustration level should not be used at all. In fact, a number of strain symptoms occur when the child is forced to read on the frustration level, such as losing place, nervous body movements, high-pitched voice, and word calling. "Word calling" is reading a sentence aloud without expression and often as if each word was an independent word from a word list.

The benefit of the IRIs is that they have great surface validity. The passages are often chosen from the exact reading series that is being used in the classroom.

The problems of IRIs are that they lack reliability and their validity is sometimes open to question. For example, if you work a readability formula on a number of 100-word passages from a third-grade basal reader, you will quickly discover that not every hundred-word passage is at third-grade level; some are second-grade, some are fourth-grade, some might even be at fifth- or sixth-grade level. Now, if you must select at random one 100-word passage, which level did you get out of the grab bag? Many a teacher has found in constructing an IRI that the fourth-grade passage was easier for the children to read than the third-grade passage. The comprehension part of the IRI, which includes oral questions after oral and sometimes silent reading of a passage, is also of questionable reliability and validity; one teacher thinks up difficult questions on the passages and another thinks up easy questions. Why then have IRIs survived and why are they being used? First of all, they are considerably better than nothing, and nothing is what is often available to many teachers. Secondly, they are cheap and easy to make. Next, they often have some validity; and after they have been used for a while, the teacher gets to know how they work—where they are too easy and where they are too difficult. It gains a measure of predictive validity when the teacher immediately places the child in a book and sees how well he or she does in that book. Last but not least, the Betts levels make a lot of common sense.

There are also some published criterion referenced oral reading tests which choose a middle course between the formal standardized oral tests and some of the problems of the informal teacher-constructed oral tests.

Miscue Inventory

A relatively new way of talking about oral reading errors is to call them *miscues*. Kenneth and Yetta Goodman and some of their colleagues have developed the reading miscue inventory, which is far more concerned with the type of error a student makes while reading than with just determining level. The old Gray's Oral did instruct the teacher to record different types of errors, probably with the idea that these errors could be corrected with specific types of drills—"Slow down if you are making too many ommissions," etc. However, Goodman is more interested in classifying errors, or "miscues," as he prefers to call them, according to various linguistic categories:

Semantic

Some miscues demonstrate that the child is getting the meaning of the passage; hence, the mere substitution of one word for another is not important (Gray would count this as an error).

Syntactic

Some miscues show that the child misses the meaning but that [he or she] is at least putting in a word that makes grammatical sense.

Sound-Symbol

Some miscues tell you something about the child's knowledge of phoneme-grapheme correspondences.

When giving a miscue inventory, a relatively hard and long passage is chosen so that there will be plenty of miscues to analyze. It is usually tape-recorded so that analysis can be done later. The analysis is too complex to be done as the child is reading. Goodman feels that the miscue inventory tells the teacher more about the "process" of the child's reading, and is potentially more helpful, than a simple grade-level score or the older type of error counting. Others find the miscue inventory fine for research but cumbersome for the classroom teacher.

Teachers have long observed children during oral reading as an informal check on their use of phonics. One of Goodman's great insights is that some oral errors demonstrate that the child is reading with meaning. These errors are not serious if one accepts that the goal of reading is understanding. Aware classroom teachers can make use of the three types of errors—semantic, syntactic, and sound-symbol—in informal observation of any oral reading.

The Cloze Technique

The cloze technique is simply the process of deleting words from a passage, every fifth word, for example, and asking the reader to fill in the blanks. The construction of a cloze passage is very simple—just type a blank for every fifth word. The instructions are simple—fill in the blanks. The scoring is simple—are the author's words filled in?

Cloze scores have been found to correlate fairly well with comprehension tests, so the teacher can use cloze as a test of comprehension for a passage. Both Rankin and Culhane, and Bormuth, found that 35 percent on a cloze passage was equal to 70 percent on a multiple-choice comprehension test.

Some research by John Bormuth, aimed at discovering if a book is readable, found that cloze scores of 55 percent or better (using every fifth word deleted) were necessary for the pupil to gain much information from the text. This is similar to Betts' 90 percent comprehension score on multiple-choice comprehension tests which yields the independent level.

Cloze can be used to find out if the text you are using in any subject is suitable. It can be used to test reading comprehension of a passage. It can be used to help you determine who are your better readers and who are your poorer readers. To make your own reading comprehension test is often very time-consuming; making a cloze test is not.

There is nothing to prevent a teacher from using other deletion patterns. For example, you might like to use every tenth word; it makes the test a little easier and the students a little less frustrated. (If you do that, however, you can't use Bormuth's 55 percent.) If you are particularly interested in *testing comprehension of the subject matter*, you might just delete a content word (noun, verb, adverb, or adjective). If you are interested in *syntax* or *a student's language ability*, you might delete just structure words. Cloze can be used in a lot of ways. I talked about its use as a teaching method in Chapter 9.

PARENT REPORTING

Evaluation can be used in many ways. Its major purpose is to provide feedback to the teacher so that the aim of the instructional process can be corrected. Feedback to the school administration is another important outcome. Now, however, I will discuss feedback to the parent.

Parent reporting used to consist chiefly of a report card to the parent which showed a single grade given in each subject for some set period of time, such as a month, a quarter, or a semester. Formal reports to the parent are now usually issued on a quarterly basis in elementary schools.

The single grade for reading has often been replaced or supplemented by parent-teacher conferences, written evaluations, and skills mastery checklists. Some report cards look like a checklist of behavioral objectives; others look like a blank space for the teacher to write comments.

It is doubtful if parents want too many skills details; knowing that Joan has mastered diphthongs might only cause you to have to explain what a diphthong is. However, parents are interested in their child's progress, both in terms of how well he or she is doing in comparison to past progress or individual expectancy, and how well he or she is doing in comparison with the rest of the class. Parents are also usually interested in attitude and work habits. Any way that the teacher can convey this information is good. Usually there is little choice in the reporting method or the card form as this is determined by the district. It is a little difficult to have to tell a parent that a child is at the bottom of the class and that that is all you really expect of the student, but most teachers can learn to do it gracefully. It helps to know something about a child's good points in another area: "He isn't strong in reading, but he does better in arithmetic and he is one of the best in kickball."

There is sometimes a problem when parents ask for the results of formal standardized tests. School districts have different policies (and state laws vary) about giving exact scores; you will probably have to follow the policy in your district. One problem in giving exact scores is that you really need to know the standard error of measurement to interpret the scores. Rather than explaining the concept, you are probably better off in giving scores as "about fifth grade." But, even to understand what "fifth grade" means, you have to know that it is a mean score, not a criterion. There is nothing wrong with giving parents exact scores if you give them enough background information in testing to use the score properly. If not, you had better word your report in more general terms. The same applies in giving scores to children.

Since court cases in some areas have held that the parent has a right to see anything in the child's folder, you may not be able to avoid giving exact scores if the parent demands to see them; however, then you must give a further explanation of what they mean.

SUMMARY AND CONCLUSIONS

This chapter on evaluation has been a long and somewhat detailed chapter, but it covers an increasingly important part of what a teacher of reading must know. Tests are now mandated in many districts and states. Their proper interpretation, criticism, and use are a teacher's professional responsibility.

Informal teacher observations and teacher-made tests are the most common type of evaluation done in the schools. They can be strengthened by the use of lists of objectives or goals, but by and large they stress content validity; that is, they are closely related to what the teacher is teaching.

Formal or standardized tests have many more technical terms and concepts related to them, but they also give more accurate assessments of the pupil's progress and his or her strengths and weaknesses. They also give the school administration and the public outside comparisons. Familiarity with the terms and concepts takes both practice and study. Perhaps we can help by reviewing some of them briefly:

Item analysis tells how well an individual item correlates with the total score.

Content validity tells how well the content of the test correlates with the criterion, goals, or subject matter.

Concurrent validity tells how well the test correlates with another, similar test given about the same time.

Predictive validity tells how well the test correlates with some other test given at a later time.

Reliability tells how well the test correlates with itself. (Would a retest rank the students the same?)

Standard error of measurement and band scores tell how well the obtained score relates to the true score.

Percentile and grade equivalent and stanine tell how well a student compares to the norming group.

Range tells you the top and bottom possible scores, but some tests have better scores at the top or at the bottom.

Orangutan scores are guessing scores and are one way of determining the bottom of the range.

Weighting tells how much of what contributes to the score, and is another way of looking at validity.

Formal tests often have computer printouts for reporting scores back to the teacher. It takes a little time to learn how to read these as each company uses a slightly different format and terminology, but with the basic concepts in this chapter, you should be able to understand them fairly readily. Remember the difference between a norm and a criterion—a grade equivalent score is a norm—half the children are below the norm by definition.

Criterion referenced tests have curricular validity. They don't give norms; they tend to tell how much of the curriculum the student has learned.

A major use for criterion tests is now in test management systems that not only tell how much a student knows but which curriculum materials teach missing skills. Test management systems are also strong in providing lists of goals or objectives and in providing record-keeping systems.

This chapter contains a checklist for evaluating tests. If you really want to see the differences between informal tests (for example, your own classroom-made test), formal tests (norm referenced), and criterion referenced tests (for example, those in a test management system), try applying the checklist to all three.

SUGGESTED LEARNING ACTIVITIES

1 Using the checklist in this chapter, evaluate a formal reading test. Compare your report to the evaluation in *Buros Mental Measurements Yearbook*.

2 Administer either a formal or a criterion referenced reading test to yourself, a friend, or a child, and score it.

3 Get a computer printout for a reading test from a school district, or a sample one from a publisher, and write an explanation of what it says. Try to get both an individual and group (class) printout.

4 Make an Informal Reading Inventory.

5 Examine the components of a test management system. See how each of the four elements—objectives, evaluation, records, and prescription—are handled.

VOCABULARY AND STUDY TERMS

Informal evaluations
  Observation: general or specific
  Behavioral objectives
  Incidental observation
  Checklists
Teacher-made tests
Basal series tests
  Content validity, diagnostic
Formal, norm referenced, or standardized tests
Item analysis
Weighting
Validity
  Content validity (face or surface)
  Concurrent validity
  Predictive validity

Reliability
Standard error of measurement
  Obtained score
  True score
Standardization or norm
  Mean score not a criterion
Grade Equivalent score (GE)
Percentile (not percentage)
Stanine
Band scores
Range
  Top-bottom concept
Orangutan score
Measuring growth
  Alternate form reliability
Subtests
  Skills breakdown
  Reliability problem
Expectancy or ability
  Underachievers
  Intelligence test factors
  Grade expectancy
Limitations of IQ or expectancy
Computer printout
  AAGE
  Significant differences
  Subtest scores, band scores, single item, class summaries
  Local norms
  Record keeping
Criterion referenced tests
  Curricular validity
  Mastery
Evaluating tests
  Buros—MMY
  See checklist
Test management systems
  (Diagnostic: prescriptive or continuous progress)
  Skills outline
  Assessment (criterion tests)
  Record keeping
  Instructional procedures
Oral tests
Informal reading inventories
Betts levels
Miscue inventory
  Semantic

Syntactic
Sound symbol
Errors
Cloze technique
Test comprehension
Test language ability
Parent reporting
CAGP

LIST OF MATERIALS

The list of materials at the end of this chapter is in a little different format and is a little more complicated than the lists of materials at the end of most other chapters.

The tests are listed in a shortened form of just title, range, and publisher. To save space and repetition, publishers' addresses are listed on pages 323–326.

This list of materials has the following subdivisions:

List of Normed Reading Tests
    Group tests
    Individual tests
    Readiness tests (group)
List of Criterion Referenced Reading Tests
Test management systems that refer students to other teaching materials
Diagnostic systems that rely heavily on teacher training
Miscellaneous

It is true that the distinction between a test management system and a diagnostic system is somewhat arbitrary. The distinction used here is that a true test management system is diagnostic-prescriptive, does not contain teaching material, but does refer the student to other teaching material. The diagnostic system tends to contain its own teaching materials, though it may also do some referring. A test management system may contain some teaching lesson suggestions, but these are more on the order of a teacher's manual rather than a workbook page.

Tests which are published as part of a basal series or which are closely related to a basal series are not included in the criterion referenced list; these tests are usually noted as part of the basal series listed at the end of Chapter 6.

List of Normed Reading Tests

Group Tests
American School Achievement Tests, Grades 1–9 (Bobbs-Merrill)
California Achievement Tests: Reading, Grades 1–14 (CTB)
Comprehensive Tests of Basic Skills, Grades 2.5–10.0 (CTB)
Cooperative Primary Tests, Grades 1–3 (Addison)
Diagnostic Reading Tests, Grades K–13 (Comm. on Diagnostic Reading)
Durrell-Sullivan Reading Capacity and Achievement Tests, Grades 2.5–6.9 (Psych. Corp.)

Gates-MacGinitie Reading Tests, Grades 1-12 (Teachers College)
Iowa Tests of Basic Skills, Grades 1-9 (Houghton)
Iowa Silent Reading Tests, Grades 4-8 (Psych. Corp.)
Lee Clark Reading Test, Grades 1-2 (CTB)
Metropolitan Achievement Tests: Reading Tests, Grades 2-9 (Houghton)
SRA Assessment Survey, Reading, Grades 1-12 (SRA)
Stanford Achievement Test: Reading Tests, Grades 1.5-9.0 (Psych. Corp.)
Stanford Diagnostic Reading Test, Grades 2.5-8.5 (Psych. Corp.)
STS Educational Development Series: Scholastic Tests, Grades 2-12 (Scholastic)

Individual Tests

Diagnostic Reading Scales (Spache), Grades 1-8 (CTB)
Durrell Analysis of Reading Difficulty, Grades 1-6 (Psych. Corp.)
Gates-McKillop Reading Diagnostic Tests, Grades 2-6 (Teachers College)
Gilmore Oral Reading Test, Grades 1-8 (Psych. Corp.)
Gray Oral Reading Test, Grades 1-16 (Bobbs-Merrill)
Peabody Individual Achievement Test, Grades K-Adult (AGS)
Wide Range Achievement Test, Grades 1-Adult (Psych. Corp.)
Woodcock Reading Mastery Tests, Grades K-12 (AGS)

Readiness Tests

American School Readiness Test (Bobbs-Merrill)
Analysis of Readiness Skills (Houghton)
Gates-MacGinitie Reading Tests: Readiness Skills (Teachers College)
Harrison-Stroud Reading Readiness Profiles (Houghton)
Lee-Clark Reading Readiness Test (CTB)
Metropolitan Readiness Tests (Psych. Corp.)
Murphy-Durrell Reading Readiness Analysis (Psych. Corp.)

List of Criterion Referenced Reading Tests

Basic Reading Rate Scale, Grades 3-12 (Revrac)
Botel Reading Inventory, Grades 1-12 (Follett)
Classroom Reading Inventory, 2nd Edition, Grades 2-10 (Wm. C. Brown)
Cooper-McGruire Diagnostic Word-Analysis Test, Grades 1-5 (Croft)
Diagnostic Reading Test: Pupil Progress Series, Grades 1-8 (Scholastic)
Dolch Basic Sight Word Test, Grades 1-4 (Garrard)
Doren Diagnostic Reading Test, 1973 Edition, Grades 2-8 (AGS)
Durkin-Meshover Phonics Knowledge Survey, Grades 1-12 (Teachers College)
EDL Reading Versatility Tests, Revised, Grades 5-8 (EDL)
Gillingham-Childs Phonics Proficiency Scales, Grades 1-12 (Educators)
Group Phonics Analysis, Grades 1-4 (Dreier)
Individual Phonics Analysis 1-6 (Dreier)
Instant Word Recognition Test, Grades 1-4 (Dreier)
Oral Reading Criterion Test, Grades 1-7 (Dreier)
Phonics Knowledge Survey, Grades 1-6 (Teachers College)
SPIRE Individual Reading Evaluation, Grades 1-6 (NDE)

Test Management Systems That Refer Students to Other Teaching Materials

The Wisconsin Design for Reading Skill Development: Wayne Otto, Eunice Askov, Karlyn Kamm, Pamela J. Miles, Deborah M. Stewart, Virginia L. Van Blaricom, and Margaret L. Harris; National Computer Systems; criterion tests, computer, record keeping, prescriptions; **K-6**.

Prescriptive Reading Inventory: California Test Bureau; criterion test, computer, prescription; **1-6**.

Fountain Valley Teacher's Support System in Reading: Richard L. Zweig; tests, cassettes, reference guides; **1-6**.

High Intensity Learning Systems—Reading (HILS): S. Allen Cohen and Anne Marie Mueser; Random House; tests, prescriptions, record books; **1-12**.

Diagnosis: And Instructional Aid Program: SRA; two kits, tests, cassettes, prescription; **1-6**.

Ransom Program: G. A. Ransom; Addison-Wesley; tests on spirit masters, skills correlation booklets; **K-6**.

Individualized Criterion Reference Testing: Educational Progress; testing kits, computer, objectives cross-indexed to selected materials; **1-6**.

Skills Monitoring System—Reading: Lenore Ringler; Psychological Corporation; tests, individual records, prescriptions; **3-5**.

Mastery: An Evaluation Tool—Sobar Reading: Center for the Study of Evaluation at the University of California; test booklets, or custom-made test booklets, computer; **K-9**.

Individual Pupil Monitoring Systems: Houghton Mifflin; tests, progress records, prescriptions.

Diagnostic Systems That Rely Heavily on Teacher Training

Croft Teacher Training System for Diagnostic and Prescriptive Reading Instruction: Marion E. McGuire, Marguerite J. Bumpus, and J. Lewis Cooper; inservice teacher training materials, skill packs, tests; **1-6**.

Reading Diagnosis: Kenneth M. Ahrendt, Gary Anderson, Lou E. Burmeister, Donald Carline, Jane Catterson, John George, Michael Graves, David Hill, Jack Humphrey, James Layton, Leona Mackler, Doris Nayson, Florence Nelson, Joan Nelson, Eunice Newton, Effner Reid, Joanna Sullivan, Dorothy Watson, A. Pollard Williamson, and William Woolbright; Scholastic Reading Center; cassettes, workbook; **1-6**.

Miscellaneous

Reading Miscue Inventory: Yetta Goodman and Carolyn Burke; Macmillan; coding sheets, profile sheets, tapes; **1-6**.

Read On: Sandra M. Brown, Patricia A. Ruckle, and Marie N. La Rosa; Random House; tests, cassettes; **1-4**.   .

IOX Criterion-Referenced Tests: Instructional Objectives Exchange; spirit masters, tests; **K-6**.

Customized Reading Systems—Mainstreaming: Price and Summit; Economy; tests, tapes; **K-6**.

REFERENCES

Berg, Paul C. "Evaluating Reading Abilities." In Walter M. MacGinitie (Ed.), *Assessment Problems in Reading*. Newark, Del.: International Reading Association, 1973.

Bliesmer, Emery P. "Informal Teacher Testing in Reading." *The Reading Teacher*, December 1972, *26*, 268–272.

Bloom, Benjamin S., et al. *Taxonomy of Educational Objectives, Handbook I, Cognitive Domain*. New York: David McKay, 1956.

Bormuth, John. "Cloze Test Readability: Criterion Reference Scores." *Journal of Educational Measurement*, 1968, *5*.

Buros, Oscar K. (Ed.). *Reading: Tests and Reviews*. New Brunswick, N.J.: Gryphon Press, 1968.

_____. *The Seventh Mental Measurements Yearbook,* Vols. 1, 2. New Brunswick, N.J.: Gryphon Press, 1972.

Chomsky, Norman M. "Age, IQ, and Improvement in Reading." *Journal of Educational Research*, 1963, *56*, 439.

Dore-Boyce, Kathleen, Marilyn S. Misner, and Lorraine D. McGuire. "Comparing Reading Expectancy Formulas." *The Reading Teacher*, November 1975, *29*(1).

Ekwall, Elden E. "Informal Reading Inventories: The Instructional Level." *The Reading Teacher*, April 1976, *29*(7).

Farr, Roger. *Reading: What Can Be Measured?* Newark, Del.: International Reading Association, 1969.

Farr, Roger, and Nicholas Anastasiow. *Tests of Reading Readiness and Achievement: A Review and Evaluation*. Newark, Del.: International Reading Association, 1969.

Flanagan, John C. "The PLAN System for Individualizing Education." *NCME Measurement in Education*, January 1971, *2*, 1–8.

Goodman, Kenneth S. "Miscue Analyses: Theory and Reality." In John E. Merritt (Ed.), *New Horizons in Reading*. Newark, Del.: International Reading Association, 1976.

Gronland, Norman E. *Preparing Criterion-Referenced Tests for Classroom Instruction*. New York: Macmillan, 1973.

Jaeger, Richard M. "The National Test-Equating Study in Reading (The Anchor Test Study)." *NCME Measurement in Education*, Fall 1973, *4*(4).

Johnson, Dale D., and P. David Pearson. "Skills Management Systems: A Critique." *The Reading Teacher*, May 1975, *29*(8).

MacGinitie, Walter H. "An Introduction to Some Measurement Problems in Reading." In W. H. MacGinitie (Ed.), *Assessment Problems in Reading*. Newark, Del.: International Reading Association, 1973.

Mager, Robert F. *Preparing Instructional Objectives*. Belmont, Calif.: Fearon Publishers, 1962.

Maginnis, George H. "Measuring Underachievement in Reading." *The Reading Teacher,* May 1972, *25*, 750–753.

Niles, Olive (Reviewer). "System for Objective-Based Assessment Reading (SOBAR)." *The Reading Teacher,* November 1973, *27*, 203–204.

Norris, Eleanor L., and John E. Bowes (Eds.). *National Assessment of Educational Progress: Reading Objectives*. Ann Arbor, Michigan: National Assessment Office, 1970.

Otto, Wayne, and E. Askov. *Rationale and Guidelines: The Wisconsin Design for Reading Skill Development.* Minneapolis: National Computer Systems, 1972.

Pikulski, John J. "Assessing Information About Intelligence and Reading." *The Reading Teacher*, November 1975, *29*(2).

Rankin, Earl F., and Joseph W. Culhane. "Comparable Cloze and Multiple-Choice Comprehension Test Scores." *Journal of Reading*, December 1969.

Scanlon, Robert G. "Individually Prescribed Instruction: A System of Individualized Instruction." *Educational Technology*, December 1970, *10*, 44-46.

Simmons, G. A. and B. J. Shapiro. "Reading Expectancy Formulas: A Warning Note." *Journal of Reading*, May 1968, *11*, 626-629.

Sipay, Edward R. "A Comparison of Standardized Reading Scores and Functional Reading Levels." *The Reading Teacher*, January 1964, *17*, 265-268.

Thompson, Richard A., and Charles D. Dziuben. "Criterion-Referenced Reading Tests in Perspective." *The Reading Teacher*, December 1973, *27*, 292-294.

Thorndike, Robert L., *The Concepts of Over- and Underachievement*. New York: Teachers College Press, 1963.

Chapter 12

Grouping:
Organizing the Class,
Management, Control

It might be well and good to know about teaching phonics, increasing vocabulary, or using basal readers, but every classroom teacher is faced with another very real problem: "How do I organize my class?" Do you try to teach all 30 children at once, or do you try to teach one child at a time? How did the children get into the class in the first place? Are they children of like age, or like ability, or like achievement?

In this chapter you will read about various methods of sorting children into groups. Research is not very conclusive about which type of grouping is "best," but this does not mean that schools aren't continually trying out new grouping arrangements. One grouping might be favored over another because of the teacher's personality or "style," because of the characteristics of the pupils, or because of a variety of other factors such as school or community values, school board wishes, or even popular trends. Changing from one grouping to another sometimes adds stimulation or new interest in the education process in general and reading lessons in particular. Since many of the elementary grouping plans so specifically revolve around reading abilities or reading instruction methods, it is quite appropriate that they be discussed here.

Reading programs must fit into overall school organizational patterns, though, in some instances, reading organization helps to determine school organization. The first graded elementary school in America is believed to have been started in 1848. Before that time, all schools were ungraded, and long after 1848 "one-room schools" continue to exist.

CLASS AND INDIVIDUAL GROUPING

Self-contained Classrooms

In this century, most schools have a system of *self-contained graded classrooms* containing a teacher and 25 to 35 children. The children progress one year or grade at a time. Acceleration (skipping) or retention (failure) is rare; hence, the teacher tends to get children that are similar in one respect—age. This is sometimes called *heterogeneous grouping* because the students are dissimilar on most educational variables, such as I.Q. or reading ability. Placement of students in classes on the basis of age has been called the *birthday method of promotion*. A more technical term is *chronological age grade placement* or CAGP. See Figure 12-1 if you wish to see how CAGP is calculated. Schools sometimes call this *random* grouping because there is no plan or policy behind it other than age. Often, however, it is not truly random since some subconscious or accidental selection factors are involved.

Schools which have more than one class per grade level might use *tracking or homogeneous grouping based on ability*. Bright students or high achievers (who usually, but not always, tend to be the same students) are placed together in one room, with separate placement of other students. Larger schools might have three or four tracks or ability level groupings. One of the benefits of this type of grouping is that it tends to minimize the spread of abilities within groups. A large third grade might be separated into a fast group—which might have children with reading abilities

---

Most schools require a similar specific age for entrance and they promote children every year; hence, it is fairly easy to estimate if a child is near the average age of his grade. Since schools often admit only once a year, there is always a 12-month spread and sometimes a bit more in every grade.

The following formula is for median or average placement. It tells you if a child is older or younger than his class average.

$$CAGP = C.A. - 5.4$$

For example: If a child is 8 yr and 7 mo old
subtract 5 yr and 4 mo
his CAGP is 3 yr and 3 mo or 3.3

In other words, he should be in the third month of third grade, and if he just happened to have a completely normal IQ (IQ 100) and everything else was normal, we might expect him to be reading at third-grade level or, more specifically, his reading test score would be 3.3. This formula is based on the fact that the average child enters kindergarten at age 5.4 in the United States. It, of course, can't be applied too rigidly, but it does give you one useful way of looking at a child and suggests one type of placement.

Figure 12-1 Determining CAGP (Chronological Age Grade Placement)

spanning fourth to sixth grade and a slower group, with students having reading abilities ranging from second through fourth grade. However, the grouping is never too exact as tests are inaccurate and children progress at different rates. It would not be unusual for a teacher of a fast group to discover that some students were reading on third-grade level, while others had eighth-grade reading ability. The same inexactitude and increased spread will show up in a slow group.

While there are advantages for both the pupils and the teacher to have a class that is more alike and can move at a similar pace, one of the drawbacks is that children don't like to be identified as belonging to the slow group. (No matter what you call it, they find out.) Parents sometimes object when their children are placed in a slow group, and have been known to make vociferous complaints. Another problem in using tracking with self-contained classrooms is that when students are selected on the basis of reading ability, there may be a wide divergence of ability in mathematics or other skills. Because of this, some schools that have self-contained patterns avoid the problems of tracking and settle for the problems of random selection. Some schools use heterogeneous grouping in primary grades and homogeneous grouping in intermediate grades. Research is inconclusive as to which method of grouping gives better reading results.

Cluster grouping is a modification of homogeneous grouping for assigning children to classrooms (or, at times, even reading groups). Its aim is to cut down the range of differences without having some of the disadvantages of complete homogeneous grouping. You might say that it is halfway between heterogeneous and homogeneous grouping. In a large school, students in a given grade might be divided into six different ability groups with group six being the best readers. The first teacher might get students in ability groups one through four; the second teacher might get children in groups two through five; and the third teacher might get children in groups three through six. Thus, each classroom includes some pupils of greater ability and some of lesser ability, but none includes the full range.

Within a classroom, the traditional method of grouping is to have *three reading groups*: sometimes two and occasionally four, but usually three. Two groups don't seem to provide for the spread of abilities, and might be a little large to work with. With four groups, there are sometimes organizational problems as well as more difficulty for most teachers in preparation. If you are using a basal reader series, the teacher's manual will often give you instructions on how to group your children, and often provides progress tests on which you can make your *provisional grouping*. I say "provisional" because any grouping should be sufficiently flexible to allow for the shifting of individual students from one group to another depending on their rate of progress and need for review.

Standardized *achievement tests* can also be used for grouping within the classroom as can *recommendations* from the teacher who taught the students in the previous year. However, many teachers prefer not to take anyone else's word. They give *informal tests* of their own, rather than relying on prior assessments, before provisionally assigning students to groups. Informal tests might be only part of an informal evaluation procedure that includes observations like listening to the child read aloud. Note that here I have mentioned three major criteria for grouping: standardized achieve-

Problem

If you have 29 pupils and 3 reading groups, how do you decide which pupil is assigned to which group? (or which class next year?)

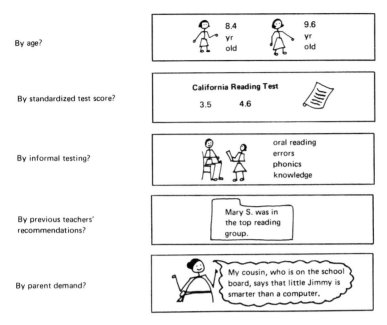

By age?

8.4 yr old

9.6 yr old

By standardized test score?

California Reading Test

3.5   4.6

By informal testing?

oral reading errors
phonics knowledge

By previous teachers' recommendations?

Mary S. was in the top reading group.

By parent demand?

My cousin, who is on the school board, says that little Jimmy is smarter than a computer.

Figure 12-2 Criteria for assigning pupils to groups.

ment tests, previous teacher's recommendations, and informal evaluation made by the teacher doing the grouping just before assignment.

In the traditional class, most direct reading instruction takes place within the group. The children read both aloud and silently out of their books with guidance by the teacher and are assigned workbook exercises which are usually discussed, or stem out of, a teacher presentation of some new or retaught skill.

Some teachers regularly form *special-purpose groups* or *special-skills groups*, for one lesson or a series of lessons, which cut across the regular reading groups. Perhaps a teacher will identify a group of students who need more help in short vowels, for whom special lessons may be designed using charts, audiovisual equipment, supplementary workbook pages, or teacher-made seatwork exercises or games.

Another type of grouping that has been tried successfully in some schools is the *staggered attendance* plan in which half the class, for example, the better readers, comes to school 45 minutes early and leaves school 45 minutes early, while the other half of the class comes to school 45 minutes later in the morning but stays 45 minutes later. This gives the teacher a smaller group to work with during reading lessons, with more time for individual attention.

I have already mentioned *individualization* which is *no group* instruction. Individualization can, however, be used in some group lessons. Individualization might

Individualization can be applied in group lessons, when comprehension is checked after silent reading. *(Mike Q./Coronet Studios)*

occur during part of "reading" lessons. For example, the teacher might use individualized reading, which is essentially silent reading plus some type of comprehension check. Group lessons would involve the teaching of many reading skills (affixes, vocabulary improvement, homonyms, etc.), or as part of language arts, spelling, or grammar instruction. There are many test-based management systems which have as one of their strong points the diagnosis and individualization of skills teaching. The language arts are all interrelated, and many so-called "reading" skills can be taught just as easily as part of writing or other language arts lessons.

Materials Influence Grouping

Whether or not individualization or group instruction is used depends to a great extent on the materials available as well as the kind of lesson the teacher wishes to provide. For example, if the teacher is going to use the SRA reading laboratory, individualization is built into the system; there is almost no way to use such a system in group instruction as each of dozens of reading selections is entirely different. On the other hand, if the teacher wishes to use (or is given by the school district) a set of basal readers, then group instruction is fairly inherent, at least if the teacher follows the teacher's manual and uses the materials as intended. Even if the teacher uses some combination of individualization and group practices, there are certain lessons which are inherently grouped—such as *choral reading*, where groups read aloud together to get a choruslike effect—and certain lessons which are necessarily individual, like silent reading in trade books. Some audiovisual materials encourage or mandate individualization and others do not.

Cross-Class Grouping

Ways of grouping within and between classes are almost infinite and there is a tendency for each school to have its own method. There are several varieties of *cross-class grouping* in which two or more teachers combine their good or poor readers. For example, at 10 A.M. every morning all the good readers in the third grade from two different teachers' classes meet together with one of the teachers, while the poor readers go to the other teacher's room. Occasionally, cross-class grouping becomes *cross-grade grouping* so that the best readers of grades 3, 4, and 5 all go to one room, etc. The aim in this regrouping for reading is to get more homogeneous grouping; this means grouping where the pupils tend to be alike.

This type of grouping is often called by different names in different areas. Cross-grade grouping is sometimes called the *Joplin plan*, sometimes called *redeployment*, and sometimes called the *platoon system*. There might be fine differences in these various plans or systems, but they are some type of cross-class or cross-grade homogeneous grouping.

Departmentalization

Departmentalization is similar to a grouping arrangement, but it really applies more to teacher assignment than to pupil assignment. Departmentalization is the type of organization in the typical high school where one teacher teaches mathematics all day, another teaches English all day, etc. This organizational method has been used in the intermediate grades of many elementary schools and occasionally in the primary grades. Departmentalization can be complete—that is, it may be used for every subject, as in the high school—or it may apply only to certain subjects, such as art or music. When departmentalization occurs in the reading area, several teachers (usually regular elementary teachers) are responsible for most of the reading instruction, while others teach only math or science. This system may be combined with a homeroom, where pupils first come in the morning and where some of their instruction may be done by the homeroom teacher, say in some subject like social studies. Sometimes the teachers move from room to room, and sometimes the pupils go to the teachers' rooms. Departmentalization might be combined with homogeneous grouping or clustered grouping (limited homogenization).

Grouping Problems

Some of the problems with cross-class homogeneous grouping and departmentalization are:

1 They tend to reduce individualization; in some instances, the teacher assumes that the children are all at the same level, and hence gives them all the same lesson. The fact is that in no grouping system are all the children the same. Even in groups which originally contain students on the same level, the students soon evidence various levels.

2 Reading tends to become isolated from other subjects. In self-contained class-rooms the teacher doesn't hesitate to try to get the child to apply phonics skills to an unknown word in a science lesson, but there is sometimes a tendency in departmental situations for the science teacher to teach only science. There is also the tendency to develop a lack of communication between teachers of various disciplines.

3 The clock dominates the extent of the lesson. When three other teachers and three-fourths of the other students will be seriously inconvenienced if you run 10 minutes overtime in a lesson, you tend not to do it. In a self-contained classroom, if the lesson is interesting or not quite complete, you tend to adjust the schedule to the pupils' needs.

On the other hand, there are problems involved in self-contained classrooms:

1 The students are likely to vary considerably in their abilities, which can complicate teacher's lessons. Just having reading materials ranging from first- to sixth-grade levels (which might be a usual spread of abilities in a third or fourth grade) is difficult and almost impossible in some schools. To provide interesting and challenging lessons for this range of pupils can be exceedingly demanding for the teacher.

2 Not all teachers are equally competent in all areas of the curriculum. Some elementary teachers enjoy teaching math while other prefer reading. It is not just a matter of preference; some teachers know more about math and others are more competent in reading instruction. The argument for departmentalization is that the teacher should teach in the area of his or her competence.

3 Last but not least, whatever kind of grouping you have in your school or select for your classroom, it is certain to displease someone.

Team Teaching

Team teaching is another type of organizational method or way of utilizing teachers that is similar to some of the plans we have already discussed. In this approach, several classes or grades are combined and two or more teachers plan a joint curriculum, perhaps dividing up subjects in a kind of departmentalization, and perhaps dividing up

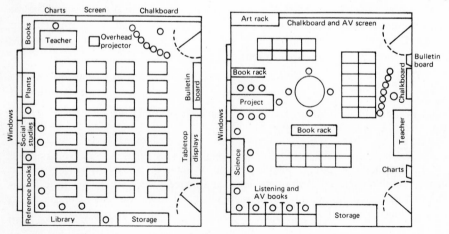

Figure 12-3 Room arrangement for traditional and progressive classrooms.

lesson presentations. They might even divide up parts of lessons so that each teacher makes only part of the presentation or prepares only part of the seatwork for individual activity. Open classrooms, where two or more classes are joined together, provide many opportunities for team teaching. Open classroom arrangements will be discussed later in this chapter.

While team teaching might be cross-class or cross-grade, it is seldom cross-team; in other words, children once assigned to a team seldom get instruction from another team.

Teacher's Aides

Team teaching might utilize *teacher's aides*, noncertified personnel working under the direction of a teacher. However, teacher's aides can also be used in a self-contained classroom. The amount of teaching-type activities that the aide engages in vary from school to school and sometimes from classroom to classroom. Some schools use aides only for discipline in the cafeteria and others use them as reading teaching assistants who do tutoring of individual students or supervise lessons of small groups.

When aides are used to assist the teacher, it might be part of a more general plan called *differentiated staffing*. Differentiated staffing is comparable to the medical field, in which different services are provided by different personnel (*e.g.*, doctor, nurse, medical secretary, lab technician). In education, differentiated staffing enables the extension of a trained professional, the teacher, by relieving him or her of many clerical and lower-level tasks.

Sometimes a teacher's aide has had some community college training on how to be an aide, and sometimes school districts which employ aides provide formal training sessions. However, most aides really learn on the job by working with a regular teacher. Aides are usually paid by the district or by some special funding project, but sometimes they are *volunteers* or *parents* working without pay. Use of teaching aides can be beneficial in that they can extend teaching services with much more attention to individual children.

At the end of this chapter is a list of reading teaching materials specifically designed for use by aides or tutors.

Nongraded Classes

Organization of students in nongraded classes is usually an attempt at more or less homogeneous ability grouping while ignoring, or at least paying less attention to, (1) age or (2) years in school. In a nongraded primary classroom, for example, there might be children of different ages who have spent the same time in school as children who are in the first, second, and sometimes third grade. However, these children would be more or less alike in reading ability and other academic achievements. Nongrading is often an attempt at minimizing the range of abilities. It can engender a few social problems. For example, some older children object to being in a room with younger children, or some younger children might be at a continuous disadvantage in physical education games. It also poses some curriculum and materials problems for children who have used the same books for two or three years; but these problems can be solved by an alert teacher and a well-supplied school. The same problems come up in nongraded rooms as do in other homogeneous rooms, such as those involved in teaching children whose reading development is similar but who may differ in their abilities in math and other subjects.

Remedial Reading

The overall organizational pattern for reading instruction includes a provision for remedial reading in many school districts. Remedial reading is usually taught outside the regular classroom by a specially trained teacher. It is usually reserved for children of normal intelligence who are very poor in reading, that is, children who are underachievers or not working up to their capacity. Unfortunately, in some schools remedial reading classes are provided for any pupil who is below his or her class in reading achievement, even though the child may have low intelligence; hence, the functions of remedial reading and special education get confused.

Remedial reading instruction is supplementary to the regular classroom instruction in reading; hence, the remedial reading student is called out of class at some time other than reading period.

Children join remedial reading classes in several ways. One is by referral from the classroom teacher. If a child is very poor in reading, and doesn't seem to be making any progress, the teacher can refer the student to the remedial reading teacher, who evaluates the child. Depending on such factors as availability of space in the remedial program and the child's ability (IQ) and achievement (reading test scores), a decision is made on accepting the child. Sometimes the child is rejected because he or she can read better than indicated by classroom performance; such a case may not involve a reading problem and might be motivational. In other cases, children are rejected because they are mentally retarded or have some other handicap, such as a visual or hearing defect, that has gone undetected.

In good schools, children also get remedial reading instruction when the reading specialist analyzes standardized reading test scores in comparison with ability scores, thus spotting underachievers; in other words, there is no wait for teacher referral. In the best schools, children reading on grade level receive remedial reading instruction when their ability (IQ) scores indicate that they should be reading way above grade level. This is one of the major ways IQ scores can be used to help children.

Parent complaints about reading progress are seldom a good basis for referral to remedial reading. If a parent complains, however, the teacher might take extra care in reviewing tests and performance to be certain that possible candidates for remedial reading are not being overlooked.

Remedial reading teachers do not do anything the classroom teacher couldn't. However, remedial teachers usually have a better understanding of evaluation and teaching. That is, they have more and better tests, and they are better equipped to read the scores because they usually have had more graduate training. They usually also have had more experience teaching reading and have a better knowledge of materials and methods. If a child is failing in a class that uses primarily the whole word approach, a remedial reading teacher might use a heavy phonics approach.

Because the teacher works with smaller groups, it is possible to provide more individual attention and to get the children on an easy reading level, so that success is more likely and more attention can be paid to the diagnosis of special skill weaknesses.

If the remedial reading program is full, the remedial teacher can give some suggestions and materials to the classroom teacher that will aid the child who needs remedial instruction. Often the remedial reading teacher can be of great assistance to new teachers in planning reading lessons for the whole class as well as the few remedial pupils. In some good schools the remedial reading teacher will even come into the classroom and give demonstration lessons.

At the end of Chapter 8 is a list of series books often used in remedial and supplemental instruction.

Supplemental Instruction

Supplemental instruction is additional instruction in reading for weak pupils. It is done either within the classroom or outside the classroom by some person other than the regular teacher. It differs from remedial instruction in the selection of pupils and in the training of the teacher. Remedial reading is usually taught by a specially trained teacher who holds a reading specialist certificate or at least has had special training in remediation. Supplemental instruction might be done by a regularly trained teacher, a teacher's aide, or even a volunteer tutor.

Pupil selection for supplemental instruction is usually on the basis of low achievement. In other words, supplemental instruction is provided for poor readers; no measure of potential or IQ is involved.

Supplemental instruction has been popular in urban areas where additional federal funding, such as that provided for in Title I of the ESEA (Elementary and Secondary Education Act), is available for intensified instruction, and where minority groups, including bilingual children, have a tendency to score inaccurately on traditional measures of intelligence. Supplemental instruction can also be used in districts that have a policy of not removing retarded or dull children from the regular classroom.

Supplemental reading instruction methods are similar to both remedial and regular classroom methods and materials. The supplemental teacher might use exactly the same basal reader used by the regular classroom teacher; the remedial reading teacher would seldom do this. Supplemental instruction is less limited to reading, and often includes supplemental help in mathematics, language arts, and other subjects. The supplemental instructor may use only materials and methods suggested by the classroom teacher while the remedial instructor not only designs his or her own curriculum, but may suggest materials to the classroom teacher.

Supplemental instruction is usually individual or small-group instruction. Sometimes it takes on a definite ethnic slant; for example, a school in a predominantly black neighborhood might be careful to select black teachers' aides from the community to conduct the supplemental instruction on the theory that they are better able to communicate with the children.

MANAGEMENT AND METHODOLOGY

Time Management

How to allocate your time during the school day is part of an overall curriculum and values problem. It is related to what you think is important and to the teaching methods you are using. In many schools today, teachers are required to prepare *lesson plans* or a time planning book showing the approximate time allotted to various subjects and approximately when they will be taught, so that a principal or supervisor coming into the class will know the overall plan the teacher is following. Time planning on a daily or weekly basis also helps the teacher to keep time in perspective so that trivial problems or difficulties in a minor subject area will not use up the one irreplaceable resource—time. Special projects, such as school plays, newspapers, trips, displays, experiments, art exhibits, holiday celebrations, public appearances of various types, and even interclass sports or music activities have a way of stealing large amounts of time from fundamental subjects, such as reading. Without a firm hand on the planning chart, such activities can steal hours and hours of valuable reading teaching time.

In a recent survey of the elementary schools in New Jersey, James Swalm and Barbara Hunt found that about nine hours per week were devoted to reading in the primary grades and about six hours per week in the intermediate grades.

Curriculum Outlines or Guides

Lesson plans, in addition to time planning, also contain a curriculum outline or plan for teaching content.

In many schools, the curriculum outline for reading is essentially the outline of the basal reading series. This can be a good curriculum to follow, especially if the teacher adapts it to the class's special needs or specific interests.

Evaluation in the form of either formal tests or informal evaluation techniques, which we discussed in Chapter 11, can be a valuable source for suggesting modifications in the curriculum outline supplied by the publisher of the basal readers.

Many schools have independently prepared their own curriculum outline. Committees of teachers and supervisors have worked out an overall curriculum for a given grade or group of grades; for example, the primary grades, all of the elementary school, or (in a few rare instances) all the grades from kindergarten through high school. These *district curriculum guides* are usually in outline form and may vary in length and detail. Curriculum guides for reading in elementary schools can range in length from a few pages to several hundred pages. The school will usually select a basal reading series or system that is in harmony with a major portion of its curriculum guide. Not infrequently, however, the guide suggests a different emphasis or something additional to the materials found in any one commercially published reading series. If you are teaching in a district that has a curriculum guide for reading, it makes good sense to read it over and compare it with the basal series or system that you are using. Frequently, your lesson plans will have to contain something in addition to what is provided by the teacher's manual of a reading series.

If you find your basal series does not cover all the curriculum in the district guide, you can frequently get help from a supervisor or more experienced teacher on where to find supplementary materials or how to conduct lessons which include that part of the curriculum not covered adequately by the basal series.

Teachers who do not follow a basal reader, or perhaps use a mixture of several basal readers, must be especially careful in planning. They may need at least two types of lesson plans or curriculum outlines. One would be more general, covering the whole year or semester, and the other would be a more detailed daily or weekly plan.

The problem with not having any kind of plan is that important areas are overlooked. Daily teaching tends to fall into a rut of convenient and familiar activities. Creative teachers, of course, continually try to make lessons different and stimulating; lesson plans should encourage this, but variety in content can best be seen if an overall curriculum guide is followed.

While individual teachers can emphasize the things they deem important, curriculum guides are useful in that they reflect some kind of collective thinking aimed at broadening the experience of children and systematically covering a given subject area, such as reading. Curriculum guides are made to aid teachers, not control them. In a few rare districts, the supervision may be so close, and the insistence on following the district guide so strong, that much of the fun and creativity is taken out of teaching. In most cases, however, the many valuable hours put into developing the guide can be wasted if teachers pay little attention to it.

Behavioral Objectives

Curriculum guides are a relatively traditional method of outlining the curriculum, and they are by no means outdated. They still form the basis of instruction in most large school districts (small districts tend to just use the textbooks). However, a relatively new phenomenon in curriculum writing has emerged: *behavioral objectives*. These are quite specific statements about what the teacher should expect the child to be able to do. For example, the traditional curriculum guide might state:

Paragraph Comprehension
   [or, if a bit more wordy]
The pupil should be able to understand the meaning of a paragraph taken from a third-grade science book.

However, behavioral objectives might look like this:

Given a paragraph from a third-grade science book, the pupil will be able to answer questions of a factual nature.

Given a paragraph from a third-grade science book, the pupil will be able to answer questions about the implications for daily life.

Given . . . . etc., the student will be able to restate the paragraph in his or her own words.

Words like "comprehend" or "understand" are anathema to the behavioral objective writer. Behavioral objectives should (1) state the specific observable behavior that can be expected and (2) specify certain given conditions. They would maintain that old-style curriculum goals or objectives (which might be called cognitive objectives) are too fuzzy, that the teacher doesn't know exactly what the child is supposed to do, and that consequently teaching is inefficient.

Opponents of behavioral objectives find them overly detailed, boring to read and follow, and stiflers of creativity.

Behavioral objectives are an outgrowth or an application of *behavioral psychology* in the reading classroom. They are more or less related to the theories of behaviorists like Watson, Skinner, and Pavlov, whose concerns are primarily observable, measurable phenomena, and who are opposed to such cognitive terms as "thinking," "understanding," and "feeling."

Some school curriculum guides have been heavily influenced by behavioral objectives and are written in straight behavioral objective fashion. However, these school districts are in the minority. A somewhat larger number of curriculum materials has at least been influenced by behavioral objective thinking. You were introduced to this influence partially when we discussed some of the test management systems, like the Wisconsin Design and the Fountain Valley System, in Chapter 11. Other basal and supplementary reading materials will discuss their content or goals in pure or modified behavioral objective terminology. Likewise, reading tests have felt the influence of the behavioral objective movement.

A few districts even require their teachers to state their lesson plan goals in more or less formal behavioral objective form. Needless to say, there are some teachers who rebel at this, but others find it quite helpful in reminding them in a more specific fashion just what it is they are trying to teach.

Methodology in Lesson Plans

We have just been discussing two important ingredients of lesson plans—time and content. However, there is a third important factor—methodology to be used.

While the curriculum guide may specify that certain times should be allocated to reading instruction (which, in most elementary schools, is an hour-and-a-half to two hours in the morning), and that a certain content should be covered, the problem then becomes one of methodology: How do you teach that content during that time? For example, you have an hour-and-a-half tomorrow morning and the curriculum guide tells you that comprehension skills and phonics skills are important and even goes into some detail to tell you what is included in those more general topics; what specifically do you do? If you are following a basal reader series, your problems are solved because the teacher's manual will tell you to get your reading group together, discuss the story to be read, perhaps have the students read the story silently, then have them read it orally, then discuss the meaning of the story and see if the pupils understand it. The students are then given instruction on how to do the workbook exercise.

If you are not using a basal reader, you will probably be using some kind of instructional material, perhaps an SRA lab, some phonics ditto sheets, some filmstrips, some free reading in trade books, or a lesson that combines reading and language arts in word usage. Or perhaps the children will play a teacher-made game that teaches a specific skill.

While not all methodology planning is provided for in instructional material selected by the teacher, materials and methodology are strongly interrelated. Teacher's manuals for both basal series and supplementary materials frequently suggest teaching methods, such as games, chalkboard explanations, and pupil activities, that go beyond use of the specific material.

Throughout this text, we shall discuss and point out various methods that can be used in different teaching situations. Experience, of course, is the best teacher, and you will find some methods more suited to your teaching than others. There are, for example, many different ways in which short vowels can be taught. In any case, your lesson plan should include some planning as to the methods you will use. Note that "methods" is in the plural because frequently one method is not enough; you must teach and reteach to get many concepts and points across. Some children can learn best from one method and others from another method. Most children can benefit from the reinforcement which comes from teaching content by use of several different methods. Teachers should build some type of *review* or *reinforcement* into their lesson plans.

Room Arrangement

It might not surprise you to learn that the way the furniture within the classroom is arranged is influenced by the methodology used.

Traditional classrooms tended to have the students' desks all in a row facing the front of the room with the teacher's desk at the front. There was usually some area where a subgroup of the class—one reading group, for example—could sit apart from the students' regular desks. Better traditional classrooms tend to have various areas around the room designated for special interests, such as a science table, a classroom library, bulletin boards, and art materials.

More modern or progressive classrooms tend to have a less formal arrangement of student desks (see Table 12-1). The students' desks might be grouped in reading groups or they might be grouped in social clusters—students who can get along well together or who work well together. Frequently they are in several clusters with more developed interest centers (also called learning centers) around the room. In some progressive classrooms pupils do not have specific desks: They have a locker or shelf space in which to keep their own papers and books, but they sit at various places depending on the learning activity.

The *learning centers* or *interest centers*, which might include a "reading center," a "science center," an "art center," etc., are areas of the room which may include a large table with seating for groups of five to ten children each, groups of small desks, or several easels, depending on the nature of the activities. A center often has a bulletin board with interesting material such as posters, photographs, realia (objects such as coins, bird nests, etc.), and samples of the children's work.

A *reading center* might contain stories that the children have written in a language

Table 12-1 Traditional and Alternative Answers to Some Grouping and Assignment Problems

Question Area in which decision must be made	Answer Traditional	Answer Alternate
Arrival time?	all arrive at same time	staggered attendance: one half of class comes one hour earlier for reading
Intraclass grouping?	three reading groups	individualized reading individualized skills special-purpose groups
Interclass grouping?	self-contained class	cross-class grouping cross-grade grouping
Instructor assignments?	one teacher does everything	departmentalization team teaching aides or volunteers
Pupil assignment to class criteria?	age (CAGP) (heterogeneous)	homogenous grouping; by reading ability by IQ or general abilities (tracking) cluster grouping (limited homogeneous)
Housing?	one class per room	open classroom two or more classes per room
Materials?	basal readers some supplementary skills workbooks and trade books	multibasal individualized reading diagnostic skills (tests) language experience
Goals?	general (cognitive)	specific behavioral objectives

experience approach, a chart of books read by pupils, a variety of supplemental reading books, games that teach word-attack skills, phonics charts, a phonograph for listening to stories while the pupil follows the words in a book, and a tape recorder for taping children while they read their own stories or produce a radio play. In short, the reading center contains a wide variety of materials and equipment that are used in formal lessons and in stimulating voluntary activities related to reading use and improvement.

The *open classroom* is a room arrangement, used most often in primary rather than intermediate grades, that combines several "rooms." Two or more teachers, with 25 children each, occupy a large space (double room). Each teacher has a separate area which the children come to the first thing in the morning. As the day progresses, there is intermingling with the other pupils in the room for teacher-conducted small-group lessons and for student-directed and independent activities. During reading time, for example, one teacher might take the beginning readers from both teacher groups, the other teacher might be instructing a more advanced group in word-attack skills, a teacher's aide might be supervising a third group in completing a workbook exercise, a number of other children might be reading out of trade books, and several children might be listening to a story with earphones plugged into a tape recorder.

Like other room arrangements, the open classroom implies something about the curriculum and time management organization. Open classrooms became popular in America as an adaptation of a British plan. However, some teachers have misinterpreted the plan in thinking that it could be reduced to breaking down walls between classrooms (which in some instances has actually been done), thus dispensing with formal reading instruction, and thereby providing less direction and discipline. In short, they confused the open classroom with recess or the school playground. Learning in an open classroom can be very carefully directed, skills can be diagnosed, group instruction can occur, and definite assignments can be made. There are, however, both curriculum areas and time periods when children are encouraged to develop their own interests and skills. In the reading and language arts area, these periods are often used for self-selection of reading materials varying in topic from animal training to fairy tales. They also provide freedom to develop projects that include reading activities with social studies or science. These reading activities can include looking up reference articles, writing reports, developing specialized vocabularies, and making charts.

CONTROL AND DISCIPLINE

Beginning teachers are often worried about "behavior problems" or the class "getting out of control." While these problems do occur, they are frequently not as difficult as imagination can make them. Nonetheless, they are a legitimate concern of the teacher and may be more prominent in schools where children come from lower socioeconomic families, although they exist to some extent in every type of community.

In the open classroom, seating arrangements allow for small-group lessons and individual student projects. *(Mike Q./Coronet Studios)*

A first principle of teaching is to somehow or other get the children to go along with you rather than fight you. As the teacher, you have several advantages. Someone else has already gotten the children to come to your room, you are older, usually stronger, more experienced in life and schools, hopefully know more about the subject being taught, have a role already defined by the culture—in short, you have a lot of things going for you to begin with. However, you still need to continue to create respect for yourself, the classroom, other pupils, and the subject matter. The first prerequisite, of course, is that you like children and enjoy teaching.

Essential to classroom control are interesting and meaningful learning activities. Classrooms in semichaos are frequently classrooms where there has been little curriculum planning. Teachers are continually looking for *interesting lessons* and learning activities because they know this. *Attention span* is another important factor. Some lessons work well for 10 minutes but are a boring, fidgeting horror if they run a half-hour. As a beginning teacher, have too many activities planned; if one doesn't work, you can go on to another.

Some kinds of reading lessons require more *student involvement* than others. Having children sit around in a circle and wait for their turns to read might not be the most stimulating kind of activity. Maybe it is necessary or useful, but don't overdo it. A bingo game might teach phonics better than a lecture, particularly if the teacher conducting it slips in a few content comments or explanations during the game and its directions. Furthermore, the bingo game might better "control" the class. Good control provides for an environment that is not disruptive to learning activity; absolute silence is not necessary.

You should remember that you are not completely alone. There is a lot of help around you—the teacher next door, the principal down the hall, and visits by a supervisor. All of these people are aware of control and discipline problems because they have had to face them themselves, and frequently they have some good suggestions. Don't be afraid to consult your principal; that's what he or she gets paid for.

From a reading standpoint, you need to be aware of difficulty level. Reading material and lessons need to be easy enough so that the child can be successful, but difficult enough to be challenging. In Chapter 10 we discussed readability formulas which will help you to judge the difficulty of reading passages or books. You might not think that a readability formula is related to discipline and control, but it is. And so are a lot of other things in this book.

One type of control procedure that is used by a good number of teachers is *behavior modification*. The basic idea is simple—you identify a type of behavior you desire and reward it when it occurs. For example, if you want a child to sit and read quietly, you praise the child when he or she does so.

On a more formal level, behavior modifiers set up token economies in which tokens (plastic chips, gold stars, marks on a chart, etc.) are awarded when a specified behavior occurs. Perhaps completion of a workbook page or successful passing of a criterion referenced test on consonant blends would award the child one token. Tokens could then be exchanged for something deemed of value—being at the head of the line to go to recess, a set of crayons, getting a good job such as office messenger, etc.

Some teachers complain that token economies are too rigid or materialistic; however, they are effective in some instances. They can be abused, but so can a laissez-faire creative atmosphere.

CONCLUSION

Teachers are traditionally allowed a great deal of freedom in grouping the children within their own classroom. Hence, it is well to consider alternate criteria and plans for grouping. Teachers are frequently allowed quite a bit of freedom in room arrangement and the development of learning centers. Some learning centers involve expenses like the purchase of listening equipment which requires administrative approval, but most involve ideas and a little special effort.

Larger grouping patterns, including such problems as cross-class grouping or which children will be assigned to which class, involve not only other teachers but the school administration. However, the teaching staff frequently has considerable input into such decisions. Figure 12-1 summarizes alternative grouping and teaching plans.

It should be stated again that the comments on classroom discipline are only a partial view of the subject, and that many discipline problems are really curriculum problems; they are a failure of the teacher to adjust the curriculum and methodology to the students. Hence much of this book will help you have a better class, and that means a class with relatively few "discipline problems" and a class where interesting and varied lessons occur.

SUGGESTED LEARNING ACTIVITIES

1 Visit two different elementary schools and see what organizational patterns they are following. Try to visit one that is more or less traditional and one that uses some type of modern plan, such as cross-grade grouping, open classroom, etc. If you can, visit both a primary grade or area and an intermediate grade in each school. Write a brief report using as many of the descriptive terms in this chapter as possible.

2 Draw a floor plan for a classroom. Assume that you have 30 student desks, a teacher's desk, and room for other activity areas. Remember that you usually have windows along one wall and a hall with two doors along the opposite wall. You may be either progressive or traditional, and for this glorious exercise you are not particularly limited by budget (but try not to be unreasonable). You might remember that one of your most important subjects is the teaching of reading.

3 Assume that a fellow teacher is complaining about a disruptive traditional class. Make several suggestions regarding materials, methods, room arrangement, and grouping that might help during reading lessons.

4 A large elementary school wants to consider several different grouping procedures that might improve reading instruction. Write a brief description of two interesting grouping arrangements, including pupil assignment practices, with the pros and cons of each.

VOCABULARY

Age-graded school
Acceleration—retention
Heterogeneous grouping
Birthday method of promotion (CAGP)
Tracking
Homogeneous grouping
  Benefits and problems
Cluster grouping
Three reading groups
Provisional grouping
Grouping criteria
  Standardized tests
  Teacher recommendations
  Informal evaluation
Special-purpose groups
Staggered attendance
Individualization of reading or skills
Materials influence on grouping
Cross-class grouping
Cross-grade grouping
Joplin plan—redeployment—platoon system
Departmentalization
Grouping problems
Team teaching
Teacher's aides
Differentiated staffing
Nongraded class
Remedial reading
  Criteria for admission
  Referral source of methods
Supplemental instruction
  Contrasted with remedial
Time management
Curriculum guides
Behavioral objectives
  Observable behavior
  Given conditions
  Behavioral psychology
  Contrast with cognitive goals
Lesson
  Time
  Content
  Methodology
  Review

Room arrangements
  Traditional
  Progressive
Learning (interest) centers
  Reading center
Open classroom
Class control (discipline)
  Socioeconomic-related
  Get children on your side
  Plan interesting lessons
  Watch attention span
  Use student involvement
  Consult other teachers or principal
  Check reading difficulty level
Behavior modification

LIST OF CURRICULUM MATERIALS DESIGNED TO BE USED WITH A TUTOR*

Grolier Reading Improvement Program: I: Grolier; kit; **1-2R**.
Letters and Words: Joanne Beebe; Harcourt; kit; **1-3**.
The Macmillan Tutorial System: Douglas Ellison, Larry Berber, Phillip Harris, Renie Adams, and Beatrice Moran; three kits; **1-3**.
The Reading Series: H. Grush and A. Seronde; Addison-Wesley; 5 books; **1-3**.
Tutor Student System: John E. George; National Tutoring Institute; kit, books, cards, materials; **1-3**.
The Emergency Reading Teachers Manual: Edward Fry; Dreier Educational Systems; manual for tutors.

REFERENCES

Austin, Kent C. "The Ungraded Primary School." *Childhood Education*, February 1957, 260–263.
Braun, Frederick G. "Individualization: Making It Happen." *The Reading Teacher*, January 1972, *25*, 316–318.
Brekke, Gerald. "Actual and Recommended Allotments of Time for Reading." *The Reading Teacher*, 1963, *16*, 234–237.
Earle, Richard A., and Richard Morley. "The Half-Open Classroom: Controlled Options and Reading." *Journal of Reading*, November 1974, *18*(2).
Frager, Stanley, and Carolyn Stern. "Learning by Teaching." *The Reading Teacher*, February 1970, *23*, 403–405, 417.
Goldberg, Miriam. "The Effects of Ability Grouping." New York: Teachers College Press, 1966.
Goodlad, John I. "Ungrading the Elementary Grades." *NEA Journal*, March 1955, 1970–1971.
Lee, Dorris M., and R. Van Allen. *Learning to Read through Experience.* (2d Ed.) New York: Appleton-Century-Crofts, 1963.

*A list of publishers' addresses can be found at the end of the book.

Miller, Wilma H. "The Joplin Plan—Is It Effective for Intermediate-grade Reading Instruction?" *Elementary English*, November 1971, *46*, 951–954.

Newport, John F. "The Joplin Plan: The Score." *The Reading Teacher*, November 1967, *21*, 158–162.

Rogers, Janette Stanton. "Reading Practices in Open Education." *The Reading Teacher*, March 1975, *29*(6).

Snapp, Matthew, Thomas Oakland, and Fern C. Williams. "A Study of Individualizing Instruction by Using Elementary School Children as Tutors." *Journal of School Psychology*, March 1972, *10*, 1–8.

Swalm, James E., and Barbara C. Hunt. *The Three R's—Reading, Reading, Reading*. A Survey of Procedures and Practices Used to Teach Reading in New Jersey Schools. Trenton, N.J.: Department of Education, 1974.

Tanner, Daniel, and Laurel Tanner. *Curriculum Development Theory into Practice*. New York: Macmillan, 1975.

Wilson, Richard C. "Criteria for Effective Grouping." In J. Allen Figurel (Ed.), *Forging Ahead in Reading*. Proceedings: International Reading Association, 257–277.

Chapter 13

Individual Differences: Socioeconomic Status, Dialect, Intelligence, and Emotional Maturity

The fact that children differ in many aspects is both a joy and an educational problem. The joy is that it certainly makes life more interesting to have a variety of abilities, ethnic backgrounds, and personality types. The problem begins when the teacher tries to provide for different levels of reading ability, different strengths of motivation, and different cultural values. Many of the reading techniques that we have discussed previously, such as the test management systems in Chapter 11 or the individualized reading techniques in Chapter 7, provide for individual differences.

In this chapter we shall look at some of the causes or correlates of reading success or failure. Causes are very hard to determine. In medicine we know that the flu is caused by a particular virus. So far not much can be done about it, but at least knowing the cause is a step along the way to finding a cure. In reading success or failure we seldom know the cause; however, we do know some of the correlates. Correlation is not necessarily causality; just because something is often found with reading failure does not necessarily mean it was the cause.

Teachers need to know about the range (amount) of individual differences in reading ability so that they can do a better job of ordering materials and improving lessons for their classes. The last chapter provided some information on how individual differences are determined. This chapter will give you some of the reasons why they exist, or more accurately, what correlates. By looking at some of these factors, it might help you to plan lessons and select materials that will more adequately provide for the individual differences that are certain to exist in your classroom. By thinking about these different factors, you also might develop more understanding about the reading problems that exist in your school or you state.

SOCIOECONOMIC STATUS

Reading educators have sometimes accepted a lot of blame for reading failure which may not belong to them.

We do not know a lot about reading failure or superior reading, but we do know that, in general, reading achievement is related to socioeconomic level. More specifically, reading scores correlate well with family dollar income. They correlate well with number of years of education that the parents have completed. They correlate well with the type of community in which a child is raised.

The National Assessment of Educational Progress confirmed these findings unequivocally. The assessment tested thousands of children during the school year 1970–1971 in all areas of the United States. The tests were conducted with four age groups: 9-year-olds, 13-year-olds, 17-year-olds, and young adults aged 26 to 36. About three-fourths of the 9-year-olds were in fourth grade, and most of the remainder were in third grade. Likewise, about three-fourths of the 13-year-olds were in eighth grade, with most of the remainder in seventh grade. Statistics were kept on sex, race, region (northeast, southeast, central, west), and community type (rural, suburban, etc.). Reading was assessed in five comprehension areas. The assessment used a modified norming; no total scores are given, but percentages of pupils passing specific items are reported. Note that this is not the typical percent score used in reporting comprehension (percentages of items correct) but a *tally* comprehension score (number of students reaching a criterion).

A composite of socioeconomic factors is reflected in *community type*. Poor and less-well-educated people tend to live in the inner city; conversely, richer and better-educated people tend to live in the suburbs. Table 13-1 shows the percent of students who could successfully pass a typical item.

If we wish to look at just the influence of *parent education*, we see a similar correlation between the amount of maximum education by either parent and the per-

Table 13-1   Socioeconomic Level Effect on Reading Achievement: Percent of Students Passing a Typical Reading Study Skills Item in Different Neighborhoods

Lowest	Extreme inner city	60 percent
	Extreme rural	80 percent
	Small city	82 percent
	Medium city	80 percent
	Rest of big city	83 percent
	Suburban fringe	86 percent
Highest	Extreme affluent suburb	90 percent

Source: National Assessment of Educational Progress.

Table 13-2 Percent of Nine-year-old Students Passing a Study
Skills Item, Grouped by Parent Education Level

No high school	64 percent
Some high school	75 percent
Graduated high school	84 percent
Post-high school	86 percent

Source: National Assessment of Educational Progress.

centage of nine-year-olds passing a study skills item. Table 13-2 shows that only 64 percent of the children with parents who have no high school education passed the item, while 84 percent of the children who have at least one parent with some post-high-school education passed the item. Of course, a higher percentage of 13- and 17-year-olds passed the item than 9-year-olds, but the exact same trend followed in respect to parent education level.

Federally funded programs, such as Title I of the Elementary and Secondary Education Act (ESEA), have attempted to give special help to children from impoverished homes, but these programs have had only limited success on reading achievement scores. Given the impact of total family income, living conditions, and parent educational background, it is not surprising that the addition of several hundred dollars a year for a child's schooling should result in disappointing responses on objective tests. It is extremely difficult to offset the influence of socioeconomic status on educational achievement, especially for large numbers of students.

Teachers should be cautioned that the kinds of data shown in Tables 13-1 and 13-2 are large-group data (mean scores). Within any group, even the very lowest possible socioeconomic group, the normal distribution curve still applies. This means that there are some individuals who will learn to read brilliantly, and there are many more children who will be good readers. It is not sound educational practice to prejudge any individual child on the basis of his or her background. Group statistics help you to understand groups—individuals vary widely.

Race and Family

It is not clear whether race is a factor in poor reading achievement. In the National Assessment, blacks' mean scores were lower than whites' in almost all general categories, but it is also evident that there are many more blacks in the lower socioeconomic levels. For example, at the nine-year-old level in their sample, it was found that 44 percent of the blacks were in the inner city, but only 4 percent of the whites lived there. Education of parents showed a similar trend: 34 percent of the white parents had some post-high-school education, but only 19 percent of the black children had a parent with post-secondary education.

Another problem associated with race, but not itself a part of race, is the family constellation. As Robert Zajonc at the University of Michigan has pointed out, the higher the ratio of adults to children, the higher the ability of the children. Thus, large families with relatively more children than adults tend to have, on the average, children with less ability. If, however, the children are spaced farther apart, then there is some benefit to the family average as the older children approach adulthood.

Firstborn children (the eldest) tend to do better than later siblings, perhaps partly because they have a higher ratio of adults around, at least when they are young. An exception to this is that only children do not do quite as well as firstborns, perhaps because they don't have the benefit of teaching things to their younger brothers or sisters.

The 1970 census shows that there are over three times as many single-parent families among blacks (38 percent) as among whites (10 percent), and children from single-parent homes tend to have lower school achievement. The number of children in the family and the spacing between children also affect school achievement. Black families were larger (3.05 children, as opposed to white families which had 2.27 children). The black children were also spaced closer together; the average intervals between first and second child, second and third child, and third and fourth child, was 23.1 months, 23.0 months, and 22.3 months. White families spaced their children further apart: 26.7 months, 31.8 months, and 30.6 months. The ultimate in close spacing, twins, on the average, have lower ability than singletons.

However, there were some bright spots for the blacks. On the National Assessment at the 17-year-old level, they did as well as the whites in items requiring map reading and answering details on a story (incidentally, about a city setting). At the 13-year-old level, they could use a telephone directory as well. And, though the sample was small, at the extremely fast reading speeds (over 750 words per minute), there were more blacks than whites.

These are just a few examples, and there are more. Since the normal distribution curve operates for blacks as well as for whites, there were many blacks that could read better than some whites in all categories. Also, socioeconomic levels apply to blacks as well as whites. As one wag has said "the easy way to get blacks to read better is simply to make all their parents rich." However, this is a bit outside the capacity of the elementary school teacher.

The term "race" refers to inherited or genetic factors. It is not clear that race influences reading scores. What is abundantly clear is that socioeconomic levels do influence reading achievement. Family composition also seems to be a factor in reading achievement.

DIALECT

A dialect is a version of a language. By definition, persons speaking the same language can, with perhaps a little difficulty, understand each other and communicate. In general, persons speaking a different language cannot communicate.

For example, an American cowboy and a cockney chimney sweep could talk to each other, perhaps with a bit of difficulty, but the cowboy would have to resort to pointing and gesturing if he were in France.

Dialects differ on several factors. The following three examples from so-called "black dialect" show three kinds of differences:

Syntax   "He be home" (verb use)
Phonology   "I didn do nu-tin" (speech sounds)
Semantics   "Hey, man, gimme some skin" (word meaning)

The first thing that teachers should know is that everyone speaks a dialect. When I asked a class of undergraduates if I spoke a dialect, only about half the hands in the class went up. It is impossible to speak any language without some dialect. Most well-educated people in the United States speak a dialect called something like "Standard English," or, as some linguists might call it, "Great American." However, there are variations in this, and there is disagreement among linguists. There are many regional differences in speech among people in the South, New England, the Midwest, etc. Whether or not these regional differences are enough to constitute a dialect is a matter of degree and dispute. But certainly very few Americans speak the same kind of English that Queen Elizabeth does, and neither Americans nor Englishmen speak the same dialect of English spoken by an East Indian.

There are also social class differences in language. It is particularly evident in England, where the difference between "Oxford English" (also called "Received Pronunciation" or "BBC") is noticeably different from the speech of some people in the working classes, but even in America there are noticeable differences. Bernard Shaw wrote a delightful play called "Pygmalion" about such differences—its musical version, "My Fair Lady," has charmed audiences around the world.

A number of people in the reading field have been concerned with "black dialect," and there have even been beginning reading books written in black dialect on the theory that they would help black children to learn to read better. Such books have not been particularly effective, but some experimentation is still going on. One problem is that even among blacks there is wide disagreement as to what constitutes black dialect, and further disagreement as to whether it should be used in the teaching of reading. Many upper-class or college-educated blacks do not speak black dialect, or if they do, they have equal facility with Standard English. Many of them do not want their children growing up speaking like the culturally deprived families in the inner city. Some other blacks, with equally good college education and community standing, purposely speak black dialect because they believe that it will help the black cause.

Looking at the problem from a different perspective, there is ample evidence that black children do not have much trouble understanding Standard English, even if they don't speak it or write it. When school is out, black children as well as white go home and quite voluntarily turn on the television set and are entertained for hours listening to programs in which Standard English is spoken.

There is another insight that might help the future classroom teacher, and that is that most written English is different from spoken English. In a sense, written English is a dialect. If you doubt this, just turn on a tape recorder sometime when you are giving a lesson to your class, or record one of your phone conversations. Then write down your spoken language word-by-word (if you can distinguish them) and sentence-by-sentence (if you can locate them). Paragraphs are not a part of the pattern of spoken speech. If you have never done this, you will be amazed how different your spoken syntax is, how different your phonology is from anything written, and even how different your word usage is. You might argue that written English is more formal. I would argue that it is a dialect.

Linguists who have studied the complexities of syntax find that all dialects are of about equal complexity and equally capable of expressing ideas. From a scientific point of view, one dialect is not inferior or easier to learn than another. There are certainly social class value systems which influence the desirability of some dialects in some places, but linguists don't take the position that one dialect is better than another.

What relevance does this discussion of dialect have for the classroom teacher? First of all, from the standpoint of teaching reading, there isn't much evidence that writing books in a dialect greatly facilitates the acquisition of reading skills; on the other hand, there isn't much evidence that it harms reading skills. The same might be said for your own speaking. Very few people would advocate teaching children to write in anything other than standard written English, even though this is different from everybody's spoken English. However, in acquiring writing and reading skills, the teacher might sometimes allow children to write more like they talk without undue harm.

Since most black children learn to understand Standard English, it can be used by teachers in teaching reading. It is advisable, however, for a teacher to learn to understand the dialect of the children that he or she is teaching, whether it be black dialect, white mountain dialect, or whatever is prevalent locally.

The teacher might help children to express themselves in standard dialect, but certainly should not denigrate the child's own dialect. All of us had to learn some dialect, and we had no choice in the first one we learned.

Bilingual Children

A dialect may or may not be a problem depending on how you look at it, but a child who speaks a language different from English definitely has a problem. The problem is intensified if the child lives in a community in which the foreign language is prevalent.

In the good old "melting pot" days, when European children were arriving at East Coast public schools, the problem of bilingualism was not as serious because there usually was not a major dominant language. Many of the immigrants were Irish or English and may have had a dialect problem, but not a language problem. Children who spoke German or Hungarian or Ukranian could not communicate with each other except through the medium of English. Hence, though Hungarian words, for example, were used on the playground, children were amply exposed to the English language.

The major second language in the United States is Spanish, with such large groups as the Puerto Rican–Americans in New York, Cuban-Americans in Miami, and Mexican-Americans from Texas to California. Spanish-speaking children often live in a Spanish-speaking community, so that school and television are their main contacts with an English-speaking world. Both school and television are often largely *receptive language* situations where the child listens but does not speak, or reads but does not write. Teachers should try to insure that bilingual children get plenty of practice in the *productive language* skills of speaking and writing.

There is another serious problem with Spanish-speaking children, and that is that many of them come from lower socioeconomic homes. Hence, they not only have the language handicap, they also have the socioeconomic handicap.

There is currently much discussion and even debate about whether reading should first be taught in Spanish with the children later learning to read in English, or whether reading instruction should be only or chiefly in English.

Teachers in schools in Texas and California regularly teach the reading of Spanish using books very similar to supplementary readers in English. Although the books look much like a regular basal series translated into Spanish, they do not have as elaborate teacher's manuals, workbooks, or other supplementary aids. If you will recall my description of basal series in Chapter 7, major basal series have well-developed teacher's manuals, workbooks, and a host of supplementary materials. The most effective use of these Spanish reading books requires a teacher who can speak Spanish and who has been trained in methods of teaching reading.

A good bit of the problem of teaching children who speak different languages revolves around understanding the different cultures from which these children come. Each culture is unique, with different values, different jokes, and different approaches to work and the school setting. If you find yourself in a school with bilingual students, one of the first things you should do is to learn something about the children's culture. American Indians are certainly different from Puerto Ricans even though they may both speak Spanish. A school district can show that it values the other culture of the children by holding formal classes part of the day to teach the children about their cultural background, and sometimes to read and write both languages.

In bilingual teaching programs, texts in the children's native language are often used in reading instruction. *(Mimi Forsyth/Monkmeyer)*

Speaking in English is often a problem for children raised to speak a foreign language. Each language uses slightly different phonemes. Spanish, for example, does not use the /j/ sound. It is not uncommon for a Spanish-speaking child to say "heneral" for "general." Spanish children need special help in learning to make the /j/ sound. Children from other language backgrounds might omit, substitute, or alter English phonemes. The same is true for syntax. English words in Spanish syntax, while often intelligible, are not usually Standard English.

If you have children in your class that come from a foreign-language background, talk to a speech correction therapist about characteristic errors and what you can do about them. Some educators would argue that a child should learn to speak English before being given any reading instruction in English. Other educators proceed to give both reading and speaking instruction in English at the same time.

Some specialists in bilingual education maintain that the child should be given reading instruction in his or her major language first. In other words, a child from a Spanish-speaking home, who lives in a predominantly Spanish-speaking environment, should be taught to read and write Spanish when he or she first comes to school. The child should simultaneously be given large doses of oral-aural (speaking-listening) instruction in English. After mastering, to at least some extent, spoken English, then, and only then, should the child be given reading and writing instruction in English.

It is probably economically feasible to give Spanish reading instruction before English reading instruction in districts which have large numbers of Spanish-speaking children. As a classroom teacher, you will have to follow the policies of the district which employs you regarding reading instruction for bilingual children, but it is well to be aware of the trends and controversies in this field.

In many districts, reading methods do not differ for bilingual or bicultural students, but reading content often does. Like any child, bilingual or bicultural children need to start with simplified reading material, often including a gradual introduction of vocabulary and a systematic teaching of phonics and word-attack skills. Reading comprehension skills likewise need to be taught. However, teachers have often found motivation to be higher, particularly in the upper grades, if the content of the passages is more relevant to the child's life setting. Thus, some publishers have readers and comprehension drills aimed at black inner-city children and at Spanish-speaking children.

ADULT ILLITERACY

While this book is concerned with teaching at the elementary level, it is important to know about adult illiterates because they are a special population and their very existence is related to earlier education efforts.

America has a relatively high literacy rate compared to the rest of the world, but it is doubtful if we have the highest. Higher literacy rates are reported for Japan and some Scandinavian countries. However, estimates of illiteracy vary from 40 percent to 60 percent of the world population, depending on who did the study and what criterion for literacy is used.

In the United States, the illiteracy level is probably between 5 percent and 10 percent, again depending on who did the study and what criteria for "literacy" were used. For example, when Louis Harris and Associates did their Survival Literacy Study in 1970, they found that 13 percent of the American population made an error rate of at least 10 percent on filling out common forms, such as those used for drivers' licenses and those obtained at social security offices. An estimated 3 percent of the population (4.3 million) had an error rate of more than 30 percent. The National Assessment found that 9 percent of the 26- to 35-year-olds could not glean significant facts from a passage. The Census Bureau uses even more lenient criteria (self-report on ability to read and write a simple statement—this is similar to UNESCO criteria), and the 1969 census found only 1 percent of the U.S. population over 14 to be illiterate.

A certain percentage of illiterates are mentally retarded or have other types of handicaps that could seriously interfere with literacy skills. However, many illiterates have mental abilities in the normal range.

Not infrequently, teachers of Adult Basic Education (ABE) courses are persons with training or experience in teaching elementary reading. Some of you reading this book and planning to teach reading to children will, at some point in your lives, teach adults to learn to read on either a full-time or part-time basis. As in bilingual or bicultural education, the basic methods of teaching are not different; however, the content is usually aimed at adult interests. Readers don't include illustrations of little children and puppy dogs, but vocabulary and syntax are simplified and comprehension drills work away at the same old skills of facts, main idea, and sequence.

The level of reading required for an adult is again somewhat variable. Thomas Sticht, in a study done for the Army, found that a mechanic needed eighth-grade reading ability, and that the lowest trade (cooks) needed seventh-grade reading ability. The goal of most GED (General Educational Development) or high school equivalency training programs for adults is ninth-grade reading ability.

Unfortunately, people who write for the public do not often take reading ability into consideration. Various studies of newspaper front pages show that they are written at the tenth- or eleventh-grade level, which is probably a year or more above the "average" adult's reading ability. Ballot propositions are even worse. Studies of ballot referendums and constitution changes show that they are written at the college level or higher; as a result, ballot authors are disenfranchising a majority of the population by poor writing.

It is, of course, easier to train the relatively few newspaper reporters and ballot authors to write on a simpler level than it is to raise the reading ability level of the United States. Reading teachers have an obligation to inform the general public and writers, in particular, the facts about using reading as a communication tool.

BIOLOGICAL FACTORS IN READING SUCCESS OR FAILURE

In this and a few of the following sections of this chapter I will discuss a number of factors that influence reading success or failure. A common question asked of all teachers is "Why do so many children fail to learn to read?" There isn't any simple answer. There are many reasons. We have already discussed some, such as socioeconomic and family factors, but there are many more.

Sex is a factor in reading. There are many more boys than girls in remedial reading classes. On a national basis, studies have found that there are about four boys to every girl in remedial reading. This trend is found in city after city and clinic after clinic. It is no accidental finding, but there is no ready explanation.

There is some evidence, that of the National Assessment for example, that girls generally read better than boys, but the difference is slight and in a few studies it is so slight that it is not significant. At the top end of the scale, it is not clear that the very best readers are predominantly of any one sex. A difference is not found for adults.

In searching for reasons, some reading authorities have pointed out that most first-grade teachers are women, and thus present a better role model for girls or somehow are more empathetic toward girls. Another speculation is that girls tend to develop fine motor skills, including talking, slightly earlier than boys, and reading and writing require fine motor activities.

You might not like the answer, but one response to "Why can't Johnny read?" is that "He is a boy." However, people seem to prefer some other answer, such as "Because he wasn't taught enough phonics." Other answers popular in the barroom or at the coffee klatch have to do with "old-fashioned discipline" or the presence of TV. Research studies have not validated these "common sense" explanations.

Vision is an obvious part of the reading process, yet, curiously, it isn't a major factor in influencing statistics on reading failure. One interesting finding is that children with a slight degree of myopia (nearsightedness) tend to do better at near-point tasks (such as reading) than do normal children, and this may cancel out the below-average readers who tend to have hyperopia (farsightedness). However, any vision problem should be corrected if, in the judgment of a specialist, correction is needed. Classroom teachers should be scrupulously careful in seeing that their children have a vision screening by the school nurse, or through other sources, on a regular basis. Furthermore, they should refer children with suspected vision problems whenever they become apparent. Serious vision problems can cause serious reading problems.

Incidentally, there are a few unusual factors related to vision that are not problems. For example, a child who is blind in one eye has no special problem learning to read, provided the other eye is normal. Occasionally, teachers of young children think that if a child writes words in reverse or says words in an inverse order ("saw" for "was") some kind of visual perception problem is involved. This is usually not the case. You can walk into any first grade in the country and find children who sometimes reverse words. It seems to be a thing that many beginning readers do. Even at upper grades, reversals most often occur in children who have immature reading habits.

Hearing problems, as discussed in Chapter 6, can cause reading problems. This is why auditory acuity screening tests should be regularly given to elementary children.

Speech problems are often related to hearing problems. In the extreme instance of deafness, the child has complete inability to talk, and this, of course, makes reading instruction a very difficult process. It can be done, but only by specially trained experts. However, even a partial hearing loss causes partial speech problems; these in turn often cause some difficulty in children learning to read. When there is no hearing problem, speech problems can still exist. In the elementary school, immature speech patterns ("baby talk," lisping, phoneme omissions, etc.) are the most common problem and are easily cured by a speech correctionist. Stuttering or stammering—speech flow problems—are more difficult. Some speech problems are caused by physical impairment, such as malformation of the mouth area; some are the result of brain damage; some are emotional problems; some are environmental; and some have no apparent cause. But for whatever reason, speech problems exist. There is some tendency for them to be associated with reading failure. Many teachers find that correcting the speech problem definitely aids learning to read. (There is also a section on speech in Chapter 6.)

General health can affect learning problems. There are more children with general health and development problems (undersize, for example) in remedial reading classes than in the overall normal population. The classroom teacher can't often do a lot about the child's general health, but I mention it here to remind you that it can be a cause of reading failure or underachievement.

A small percentage of children have *minimal brain damage* (MBD) which also can affect learning. Minimal or mild brain damage can be caused by a lack of oxygen during the birth process or anytime subsequent, or by damage to the brain cells from such causes as high fever, a blow, a destructive virus, or poison. When brain damage is greater and affects motor functions, it is often called cerebral palsy (CP), of either the athetoid (shaking) or spastic (rigid) type. When brain damage seriously affects intellectual functioning, the child is usually called mentally retarded (MR). Brain damage can also affect personality and general behavior. For example, some brain-damaged children are described as "motor-driven"; they can't sit still, and have short attention spans. Others are just the opposite, and sit in lethargy. Brain damage can be very specific or more generalized. For example, many cerebral-palsied children have high IQs and are excellent readers; others might be mentally retarded. The point the teacher should remember is that brain damage in the motor area does not necessarily mean damage in areas which affect reading.

Brain damage affecting language areas, such as speaking, listening, or writing, is called *aphasia*. When it affects the reading area, it is called *alexia*. This term is usually applied to adults who have lost the ability to read through a stroke or localized damage from a trauma, though it could be applied to children who have a pathological inability to learn to read. Alexia is probably very rare (that is, less than 1 percent of the population), but it can exist.

Inability to learn to read, or difficulty in all areas of learning, can also be caused by *endocrine* problems. The endocrine system of the body includes the glands and the chemicals they secrete into the blood which keep the body working normally. For example, adrenaline is secreted into the blood when you are excited to make your heart beat faster and give you some immunity to pain. Insulin is secreted into the blood when you eat food (particularly starch and sugars) so that the body will store the glucose (food) for later use. If, for example, there is too much insulin—a condition called *hyperinsulinism* (or hypoglycemia)—then too much glucose is stored, and there is a depressed energy level and sometimes a depressed learning ability. The field of endocrinology is beginning to have more and more relevance to learning problems.

People in the field of special education sometimes use the term *dyslexia* to describe a child who has difficulty learning to read. Dyslexia is a medical word to describe a symptom—the symptom is inability to read. It does not really describe a disease or even a cause. It could be that some children described as dyslexic have minimal brain damage; others might have endocrine problems; for others, there is no apparent explanation for their inability to read. In some schools, the term "dyslexic" simply refers to a child who is an underachiever; that is, any child who is not working up to his or her presupposed ability level in reading. Expensive tests done by neurologists usually do not show evidence of brain damage in cases that are termed "dyslexic" by special educators.

The rare case of alexia (aphasia) is difficult to teach, but children labeled "dyslexic" by special educators can usually be taught to read by ordinary developmental or remedial reading methods.

In some states, labeling children "dyslexic" really has more political or economic importance than educational significance. In these states, special funding is available if a child is called "dyslexic"; if the child is only a "poor reader," no special funds are available. A truly scientific definition of dyslexia is lacking, and there is dispute in the field as to whether there really is a special condition called "dyslexia" or whether children labeled "dyslexic" really have minimal brain damage, some other problem, or essentially no problem at all other than the obvious fact that they need to have reading instruction.

MOTIVATION

Teachers have known since time immemorial that it is easier to teach a child who is *motivated* to learn, and nearly impossible to teach a child with no motivation, or worse, negative motivation or aversion. A good deal of the "art" of teaching is how to motivate children who have little or no motivation. Teachers use reward systems, now dignified by the term "behavior modification," and all sorts of devices to attempt to induce higher motivation. Behavior modification was discussed in Chapter 12; however, it might equally be a part of this section on motivation.

Motivation springs from a variety of sources. One very prominent source for children is the home. If there is a positive attitude and encouragement of learning in the home, this usually carries over to the child's motivation to learn in school.

Lack of motivation might be cultural—"My Pa don't care nothin' about readin', he likes huntin' "—or it might be a protest by the child against parents—"I (subconsciously) hate my home situation; they want me to read; I won't, and that will show them."

Psychologists, even after thousands of experiments, still know relatively little about motivation. What makes Sammy run is still largely unknown. Theorists from the field of psychotherapy, such as Freud and Jung, have attempted to provide some answers. Experimental psychologists working with rats, prisoners, and college freshmen have attempted to give other answers. Still, motivation is only very partially understood.

A good deal of the "art" of teaching is motivating children. *(Mike Q./Coronet Studios)*

The classroom teacher will hear parents say over and over again, "How can I get my child to read better?" or even "How can I get my child to read anything?" There aren't any easy answers or any single answer that works for all children, but some partial answers may be found below.

Provide easy-to-read books.

Provide books or articles on high-interest topics, such as snakes or adventure.

Use a reward system: "You have read three books, so we will go to the circus."

Use encouragement: "You are doing great—you read two pages!"

Use facilitation: get the child a library card, a book club membership, a birthday gift of books.

Use environment: a decent chair with a good light and a respite from radio and TV.

Use examples: read some books yourselves; discuss them at dinner.

Keep trying: attitudes don't change in a day.

INTELLIGENCE

Classroom teachers should think of intelligence in several ways. The first concept to consider is that of mental age (MA). We know all children do not have the same ability, and mental age is a concept used in deriving IQ. Students who are brighter and learn faster tend to learn like children who are older. A bright child, one with a high IQ, has a higher mental age than his or her chronological age, and tends to have the academic abilities of an older child. Conversely, a slower child, one with a lower IQ, tends to have the abilities of a younger child. Figure 13-1 shows the normal distribution curve of mental ages (abilities) that can be found in a typical fourth grade. Note that it is perfectly normal to have one child with first-grade ability and three children with sixth-grade ability.

True, some grouping situations will cut down this range, but if a teacher had a completely normal sampling of the United States population of fourth-graders in the

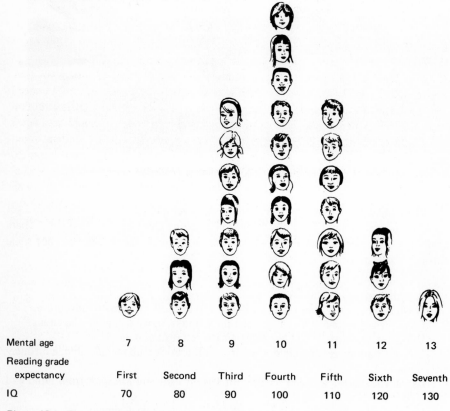

Mental age	7	8	9	10	11	12	13
Reading grade expectancy	First	Second	Third	Fourth	Fifth	Sixth	Seventh
IQ	70	80	90	100	110	120	130

Figure 13-1 The normal distribution of mental ability and expected reading ability for an average fourth-grade class of 32 10-year-olds.

classroom, it would look exactly like Figure 13-1. Study it slowly and carefully so that you will not be surprised when you enter your own classroom and find such a range of abilities.

The second concept about intelligence is that it is an index of brightness of learning ability. A 10-year-old girl with an IQ of 120 has a mental age of a 12-year-old, but more than that, she has a capacity to handle abstract thinking and symbolic thinking better than a normal or below-average child. In fact, the 10-year-old with an IQ of 120 and a mental age of 12 has more "brightness" than a 15-year-old with an IQ of 80 and a mental age of 12. Theoretically, both children would have sixth-grade expected reading achievement, though one would be in a fourth grade and the other would be in the ninth grade.

Time to learn is another way of interpreting IQ or MA. A way of looking at the typical fourth-grade class is to consider that it will take the average child two years to get sixth-grade reading ability, but it will take those three children with an IQ of 80 (those in the figure with MA 8) four years to get to sixth-grade reading ability.* If more teachers realized this, they could relax and give more equal treatment to all children, and all areas of the curriculum, rather than "fret" about some of the children in their class that are "not reading up to grade level."

This is not to say that teachers should give up on any child, or that standards should be lowered; however, teachers should have realistic expectancy standards. I have seen too many classes where the teachers somehow perceived of themselves as failing—or decided that their reading methods were not any good—because a few slow children were not "keeping up" with the class. Worse, such teachers might spend hours of special preparation and tutoring on slower children, with too little attention to the bright and even normal children in their classes. All children should have equal opportunities to learn, and should receive equal effort from the teacher. Perhaps problem children, by their very nature, take a little more time and effort; but if the drain becomes too heavy, the teacher should get assistance for the problem from special service personnel. Many schools all but ignore their bright pupils, while giving all sorts of special help to slow or retarded pupils. This is not only undemocratic to the children involved, but in the long run is harmful to the nation. Special education is desirable for very slow children, like the child with an MA of 7 in Figure 13-1, either within or outside the classroom.

There are many ways to err in the teaching profession. Teachers who spend a majority of their time with just a few bright children are committing just as grave an error as are those teachers who devote large portions of class time to the slow learners.

We have already discussed intelligence tests in Chapter 11. Let me just remind you that they are sometimes inaccurate and that the alert teacher will notice many ways in

---

*By definition, the average child (IQ 100) develops mentally two years in two years' time, but a dull child develops slowly:

$$IQ\ 80 \times CA\ 12 = MA\ 9.6;\ MA\ 9.6 - 5.4 = MAGP\ 4.2$$

Chapter 11 explains the formula. Thus, a child with IQ 80 would have to be 12 years old and in sixth grade before his or her expected reading score would be about fourth grade.

which children show intelligence. But whether or not intelligence tests are used in your school, children will come with the same range of abilities.

We have been talking about intelligence as though it were a general factor. Psychologists have studied IQ, and there is some disagreement whether intelligence is a general factor or whether it is several special abilities. Most psychologists feel that intelligence is composed of both a general factor and special abilities. For example, special ability in art or music might not correlate too highly with verbal abilities. Some children seem to have greater mechanical ability and others greater social abilities. Though it is not often discussed, there are probably special talents involved in reading; some children just take to reading like Bach took to the organ. And if there are unknown reasons why some children have special facility with reading, there probably are unknown reasons why some children lack facility with reading skills. We have pretty good measures for some differences, but for other differences, like special facility in reading, we have almost none.

Children with an IQ of around 70 and below are often called *mentally retarded*, and they can usually learn to read up to approximately their mental age, provided that their IQ is above 50. The lower their IQ, however, the more difficult it is to teach them. It requires a great deal of effort, repetition, and individual attention. Most children with low IQs will never be great readers, but they can achieve some functional reading skills. Some people in the field of special education advocate special methods to teach such students reading—tracing letters on sandpaper, for example. Others assert that these children need essentially the same kind of reading lessons used in a regular classroom or in regular remedial instruction, but that more total time must be expended and shorter lessons with more repetition should be used. Even when they reach adulthood, persons with an IQ of 70 seldom read above the fifth-grade level, and persons with an IQ of 60 seldom read above the third-grade level.

EMOTIONAL MATURITY

Perhaps a majority of the emotional problems encountered in elementary school might be considered as emotional immaturity. What do we mean by "emotional immaturity"? A child characterized by this problem, when faced with an emotional situation, reacts like a younger child. Children who cry easily when frustrated, or who throw temper tantrums in the classroom when they can't get their own way, are essentially acting like preschool children. It is part of the classroom teacher's job to attempt to guide these children into more mature behavior. Of course, if the teacher finds that he or she can't help, or that the problem is getting worse, it is advisable to call for a consultation with the school psychologist.

Emotional maturity can definitely affect learning to read. Some children are so "nervous" that they literally can't pay attention to the reading lesson for any extended period of time. A short attention span is often a sign of emotional immaturity. Unfortunately, it is also a sign of some types of brain damage and is frequently present in low-IQ children. In fact, almost any symptoms of immaturity can also be caused by brain damage. There is no simple way of dealing with or identifying the cause of emotional problems. It is often difficult to tell if the nature of immature behavior is physical, cultural (the treatment of a child at home), or psychological. Although it would be helpful, it is not the classroom teacher's responsibility to determine the cause. However, one thing that the classroom teacher can do is to try to educate the whole child, that is, to help the child grow to greater maturity whatever the cause. This growth is often an interaction between teacher and child. Sometimes firmness or discipline is beneficial, and sometimes a more relaxed and accepting attitude is better. Discussing a child's problems with school psychologist or social workers can be beneficial. In some cases, a transfer of the child by the principal to another teacher helps. However, if you ask the principal to transfer a child with whom you are having problems, then you must be willing to take on some other teacher's problem child.

Inability to read or underachievement in reading can often be a symptom of an emotional problem. Children who are too insecure to attempt any new task also apply this insecurity to the new task of reading. Success is a great remedy for some insecurity. Try to place the child in as many situations where he or she can be successful as possible, both during reading lessons and at other times during the school day.

Occasionally, teachers have a problem with a child who reads too much. Withdrawn bright children, who cannot relate to other children or who disdain any physical exercise, should probably be encouraged to engage in a variety of activities. Allowing for individual differences, it is normal that some children will enjoy reading more than others and some will spend more time reading than others, but great excesses of anything are often a warning sign of some kind of trouble.

Proper content of reading material can often contribute toward increased emotional maturity. This process is often called *bibliotherapy*, and the general idea is to have children read books about other children with similar problems or books that describe emotional growth. For example, there are books for children and about children whose parents are getting divorced, children with all sorts of physical handicaps, children who have to move, children who have deaths of family or friends, children who have difficulty getting along with brothers and sisters, and yes, even children with school problems. School librarians can help you locate lists of books suitable for almost any problem.

School is a place for growing. Emotional immaturity is like ignorance; it's something good teachers help children grow out of. If for no other reason than because emotional immaturity hinders learning to read, this is important.

There are several other interesting considerations about emotional immaturity. First, the definition of emotional maturity, or what is called a "psychological problem," is partially culturally determined. Behavior that might be called abnormal in one district may go unnoticed in another. Second, the new teacher should be aware that some children will test the limits of permissiveness. Some psychologists believe that children need to have some structure, and that the structure needs to be defined. Individuals, frequently those individuals who have emotional problems, will probe and "try things" to find out what kinds of behavior are allowed. Once other children see what is permitted, they will act accordingly. The teacher need not feel hostile or malevolent toward the child who is testing the limits. It is to be expected that usually someone will test them. Thus, the teacher should set the limits of behavior, expect them to be tested, and go on about the business of teaching reading. If you are spending more time paying attention to discipline or setting limits than in teaching or performing creative acts, then something is wrong. If you expect never to have to set a limit, however, then your expectations need adjusting.

There is a movement in education called *mainstreaming*, which means that all types of special-education children, including emotionally maladjusted, are being placed in the regular classroom. Many children who formerly would have been placed in special classes are now being put into regular classrooms for at least part of the day. When this is done, hopefully there is extra help for the classroom teacher in one or more forms: a teaching aide, frequent consultation with special service personnel, supplementary classes for the child with the problem for part of the day, additional counseling for the child, additional counseling for the parent and teacher, special curriculum materials available, inservice training for the classroom teacher, or an extra materials budget. Sometimes mainstreaming results in slightly smaller regular classroom size.

Last but not least, emotional problems often do not come in a pure form; that is, they are mixed with other handicaps. For example, there are emotional problems mixed with mental retardation, emotional problems mixed with reading problems, brain damage mixed with a variety of problems, etc. Children with problems frequently have more than one. Interestingly enough, when you can cure or definitely improve any one problem, such as poor reading, there frequently is a beneficial effect on the child's other problems. Many a teacher who has successfully taught an older child to read has seen relations with other students improve, bed-wetting stopped, hostility toward the school lessened, and any manner of other improvements. While reading improvement is not the key to everything, it is surprising how many other areas, from grades in other subjects to general attitude, can be beneficially affected by it.

SUMMARY AND CONCLUSIONS

In this chapter we have been discussing individual differences or, more specifically, causes or correlates of reading failure. However, these causes or correlates can be looked at from the obverse side and seen as factors in reading success. There isn't any easy answer to why some children fail and some children succeed in learning to read, but we have tried to discuss some of the known and suspected factors which are related.

Socioeconomic status is seen as a strong and rather definite influencing factor, but race is considered doubtful. Family factors, such as parent education, single-parent homes, and spacing of children, seem to have some effect on children's reading abilities.

Dialect, which is composed of differing syntax, phonology, or semantics, certainly exists, but its relationship to reading ability or type of reading instruction is somewhat controversial. Similarly, some of the educational factors with bilingual children (such as teaching them to read in a foreign language first) are still under debate.

A number of other factors, such as sex of child, vision, hearing, speech, general health, minimal brain damage, and endocrine problems, probably affect reading achievement. However, the special educators' classification of dyslexia seems to have some confusion surrounding it as to whether it is (1) a unique entity, (2) some combination of the above factors, or (3) no entity itself, but rather just a way of describing children who haven't learned to read. In any event, most children who are poor readers, whether or not they are called "dyslexic," can learn to read by using the materials and methods discussed in this book.

Motivation is seen as an important but evasive factor. Some practical suggestions were given for trying to enhance it.

General ability, often defined as IQ, is seen as following a normal distribution curve, and this means that the classroom teacher can expect a fairly wide range of abilities in any one classroom. Besides viewing intelligence (MA) as expectancy—what level of reading ability a child should have—it is seen as a time-to-learn factor, which means that lower-IQ children simply take longer to learn things and that mentally retarded persons have limits even as adults.

Another important but evasive factor in learning to read is emotional maturity or the lack of it. Emotionally immature children tend to act like younger children and have such characteristics as a short attention span. The teacher can help them to grow by a number of ways including bibliotherapy. However, just what constitutes an emotional problem is partially a cultural or local definition.

One trend in American education is mainstreaming or taking special education children, such as those with lower IQ or so-called emotional problems, and placing them in regular classrooms for at least some of the school day. If this happens, these children and the regular teacher need some outside help. Unfortunately, children with one problem often have another problem; in other words, problems are often multiple. Fortunately, helping them with one problem will often help them with another problem.

The classroom teachers' main job is not to diagnose the causes for failure, but rather to accept the children as they are and to move them ahead in reading ability. It is interesting to know some of the causes and correlates of individual differences, but good teaching is the important thing.

SUGGESTED LEARNING ACTIVITIES

1   Try to find a school district nearby that makes reading test scores (average scores by school) available to the public. For example, they might say something like Meadowbrook School sixth-graders scored 6.8 in reading comprehension on the Stanford Achievement Test and Martin Luther King School scored 7.1, etc. Then go to the library and get the census report of family incomes for the area surrounding each school. See if the family income and the reading comprehension scores rank the schools the same.

2   Tape-record two students who have different dialects under two conditions: (1) reading a set passage and (2) telling a story about a picture. Write down differences in phonology (pronunciation) which will show up under condition (1) and differences in syntax which might show up under condition (2).

3   Observe a class that has a number of bilingual students, a class that has a number of culturally different students (such as inner-city blacks), a special education

class, or an adult basic education class. What are some of the differences you see between a regular elementary class and one of these classes in the materials or methods that the teacher uses?

4 Try a small experiment using behavior modification in a classroom, or with a child in your neighborhood. Specify the desired behavior, such as reading a number of pages in a book or learning phonics rules or sight vocabulary. Use some type of reward to try to improve performance. Keep a chart of improvement or total amount of learning.

5 Develop a small bibliography for children with a specific problem (bibliotherapy), such as physical handicap, divorce in the home, or other problems.

VOCABULARY AND STUDY TERMS

Socioeconomic status
  National assessment
  Community type
  Parent education
  ESEA
Race and family
  Single parent
  Sibling spacing
  Black bright spots
Dialect
  Syntax, phonology, semantics
  Region and class differences
  Black dialect?
  Books in dialect?
Bilingual children
  Receptive-productive language
  Reading in a foreign language
  Different cultural values
  Phoneme problems
  Same skills—different content
Adult illiteracy
  U.S. amount
  ABE
  Occupational requirements
  Readability of written materials
Biological factors
  Sex: girls better readers?
  Vision problems
  Hearing problems
  Speech problems
  General health
  MBD—aphasia

Endocrine problems
  Dyslexia
Motivation
  Behavior modification
  Home influence
  Suggestions for improving
Intelligence
  Normal distribution
  MA—expectancy
  Learning ability
  Time to learn
  General versus specific IQ
  Retarded limits
Emotional immaturity
  Like younger children
  Short attention span
  Help child grow
  Bibliotherapy
  Cultural definition of problem
  Testing limits
  Mainstreaming
  Multiple problems

LIST OF CURRICULUM MATERIALS OFTEN USED WITH CULTURALLY DIFFERENT OR SPECIAL EDUCATION CHILDREN*

Supermarket Recall: William Orr; kit, label cards, question sheets; **3-12**.
Special Language Series: Learning Resources; audio cards, worksheet pads, cards; **K-1**.
Peabody–Rebus Reading Program (REBUS): Richard Woodcock, Charlotte Clark, and Cornelia Oakes Davies; American Guidance; workbooks, readers, cards; **K-1**.
Hip Pocket Stories: Leonore Itzkowitz; Random House; kit, pamphlets, tape, workbooks; **2.8-3.3**.
Action Reading: George Cureton; Allyn and Bacon; cards, charts, spirit masters; **K-1**.
The Electric Company Sentence Comprehension Kit: Shirley C. Feldmann, Elisha J. Bartlett, Linda Lerner, and Linda Roberts; Addison-Wesley; kit, activity books, cassettes, filmstrips, minibooks, games; **1-3**.
Breakthrough to Literacy: Brian Mckay, Brian Thompson, and Pamela Schaub; Bowmar; kit, cards, pocket charts, booklets; **K-1**.
Distar Reading: Siegfried Engelmann and Elaine C. Bruner; SRA; kit, books, cassette; **1-3**.
Breakthrough: William D. Sheldon, George E. Mason, Nicholas J. Silvaroli, Warren H. Whellock, and Nina C. Wossner; Allyn and Bacon; paperback books, spirit masters; **1-6**.

*A list of publishers' addresses can be found at the end of the book.

Plus 4 Reading Booster: William D. Kottmer; Webster/McGraw-Hill; cassettes, book, workbook, cards, word wheels; **4.**

Play That Game: Robert McAdam; Bomar; books, cassette; **2.5–4.0.**

Corrective Reading Program: Siegfried Engelmann, Julie Becker, Wesley Becker, Linda Carnine, Gary Johnson, and Linda Meyers; SRA; book, tests; **4–12.**

Reading Success Series: Xerox; skills practice books; **2–4.**

REFERENCES

Archer, Marguerite P. "Minorities in Easy Reading through Third Grade." *Elementary English*, May 1972, *49*, 746–749.

Asbury, Charles A. "Selected Factors Influencing Over and Under Achievement in Young School Age Children." *Review of Educational Research*, Fall 1974, *44*(4).

Baratz, Joan C. "Beginning Readers for Speakers of Divergent Dialects." In J. Allen Figurel (Ed.), *Reading Goals for the Disadvantaged*. Newark, Del.: International Reading Association, 1970.

Baratz, Joan C., and Roger W. Shuy. *Teaching Black Children to Read*. Washington, D.C.: Center for Applied Linguistics, 1969.

Cianciolo, Patricia Jean. "A Recommended Reading Diet for Children and Youth of Different Cultures." *Elementary English*, November 1971, *48*, 779–787.

Figurel, J. Allen (Ed.). *Reading Goals for the Disadvantaged*. Newark, Del.: International Reading Association, 1970.

Goldberg, Miriam L., and Marion S. Taylor. "Working with the Urban Disadvantaged: Beginning Reading Project." In J. Allen Figurel (Ed.), *Reading Goals for the Disadvantaged*. Newark, Del.: International Reading Association, 1970.

Goodman, Kenneth S. "Dialect Barriers to Reading Comprehension." *Elementary English*, December 1965.

Hall, Maryanne. *The Language Experience Approach for the Culturally Disadvantaged*. Newark, Del.: International Reading Association, 1972.

Johns, Jerry L. "What Do Inner City Children Prefer to Read?" *The Reading Teacher*, February 1973, *26*, 462–467.

Johnson, Kenneth R. "Black Dialect Shift in Oral Reading." *Journal of Reading*, April 1975, *18*(7).

Johnson, Laura S. "Bilingual Bicultural Education: A Two-Way Street." *The Reading Teacher*, December 1975, *29*(3).

Kaplan, Robert B. "On Conditions of Bilingualism." In Robert P. Fox (Ed.), *Essays on Teaching English as a Second Language and as a Second Dialect*. Urbana, Ill.: National Council of Teachers of English, 1973.

Knapp, Margaret O. "Black Dialect in Reading: What Teachers Need to Know." *Journal of Reading*, December 1975, *19*(3).

Lahaderne, Henrietta M. "Feminized Schools—Unpromising Myth to Explain Boys' Reading Problems." *The Reading Teacher*, May 1976, *29*(8).

Lang, Janell Baker. "Self-Concept and Reading Achievement—An Annotated Bibliography." *The Reading Teacher*, May 1976, *29*(8).

Lawrence, Dolores. "Sparta Revisited (Youths of Six Grade Tutors)." *The Reading Teacher*, February 1975, *28*(5).

Loban, Walter W. "Teaching Children to Speak Social Class Dialects." *Elementary English*, May 1968, *45*.

McNinch, George. "Determining the Reading Preferences of Third, Fourth and Fifth Grade Disadvantaged Pupils." *Journal of Reading Behavior*, Spring 1970–1971, *3*, 32–38.

Naiden, Norma. "The Ratio of Boys to Girls among Disabled Readers." *The Reading Teacher*, February 1976, *29*(5).

National Assessment of Educational Progress. *Reading Rate and Comprehension*. Denver, Colo.: Education Commission of the States, 1972.

Smith, Nila Banton. "Cultural Dialects: Cultural Problems and Solutions." *The Reading Teacher*, November 1975, *29*(2).

Somerville, Marian. "Dialect and Reading: A Review of Alternative Solutions." *Review of Educational Research*, Spring 1975, *45*(2).

Spache, George D. *Good Reading for the Disadvantaged Reader: Multi-Ethnic Resources*. Champaign, Ill.: Garrard, 1971.

Stanley, Julian C. (Ed.). *Preschool Programs for the Disadvantaged: Five Experienced Approaches to Early Childhood Education*. Baltimore: Johns Hopkins, 1972.

Stewart, William A. "Negro Dialect in the Teaching of Reading." *Teaching Black Children to Read*. In Joan C. Baratz and Roger W. Shuy (Eds.), Washington, D.C.: Center for Applied Linguistics, 1969.

Strickland, Dorothy. "The Black Experience in Paperback (Kindergarten through Grade 6)." In M. Jerry Weiss, Joseph Brunner, and Warren Heiss (Eds.), *New Perspectives in Paperbacks*. York, Pa.: Strine, 1973.

Vacca, Joanne L. "Bidialectism—Choose Your Side." *The Reading Teacher*, April 1975, *28*(7).

Zajonc, Robert B. "Family Configuration and Intelligence." *Science*, April 16, 1976.

Postscript: Continued Professional Growth

Learning to teach reading is a lifelong task. Don't be disappointed if you are not an expert after one course. Most teachers grow in professional competence by combiing practice with further study. For example, if you haven't taught before, you will now engage in student teaching, then, in due course, become an elementary teacher. Similarly, experienced teachers who may be reading this book will get insights that they might not have gotten or have forgotten from their first course in reading. There is almost too much to absorb at one sitting. Furthermore, after mastering some of the basics, new priorities in knowledge needs emerge. Beginning teachers might need to master use of a basal series and the teaching of supplementary phonics; more experienced teachers might need more help with testing and the study skills part of comprehension. All teachers need fresh ideas on how to teach skills and generate interest.

College courses and advanced degree programs are the major method of self-improvement. Many teachers find a course in remedial reading to be very helpful, and this course is included in most advanced degree programs. Remedial reading helps the teacher with those few children in every class who do not seem to profit from regular reading instruction. There are not any real secrets to remedial instruction, but often it emphasizes refinements to principles found in this text, better diagnostic testing, more attention to individual type instruction, high interest methods, and at least a partial search for physical and psychological underlying causes for failure.

Professional organizations offer much part-time in-service instruction for teachers.

Nearly every state and locality has a chapter of the International Reading Association (IRA) which conducts day-long conferences and after-school meetings that are truly educational in nature. At these meetings, the classroom teacher can frequently meet the author of the curriculum materials, the textbook, or the journal articles, and ask questions. The stimulation of exchanging ideas about reading with colleagues is also very beneficial. The National Council of Teachers of English (NCTE) also has a similar organization pattern and educational function. Their somewhat broader language arts approach includes many reading topics. Other organizations, such as state teachers' associations and some college and universities, also regularly include special programs on reading instruction.

Many professional meetings include exhibits prepared by textbook and media publishers. At these exhibits, the teacher can see the latest instructional materials and usually ask questions of a company representative. Teachers can also get good ideas on conducting lessons by simply looking at commercially prepared materials. Materials exhibits also help to keep you informed of current trends and what is going on in other areas of the country. In selecting materials for the school, you should use all the evaluation tools available. For example, you might use the readability graph in Chapter 8 on texts, and compare phonics skills taught against the list of phonics skills in Chapter 2.

Journals are also an important source for continuing your professional education. Probably the main journal devoted to reading for the classroom teacher is *The Reading Teacher* published by the International Reading Association (Newark, Delaware). However, interesting articles on reading can be found in a variety of sources. *Language Arts*, published by NCET (Urbana, Illinois), regularly carries quality articles on reading of interest to elementary teachers. On a less regular basis, reading articles are found in the *Elementary School Journal*, the *Instructor*, and the *Grade Teacher*.

Should you wish to read research reports, papers given at conventions, or projects carried out in schools with grants from the Department of Health, Education, and Welfare, you should become acquainted with the ERIC system which produces both abstracts and microfische of thousands of reading titles. You can obtain bibliographies on many topics, such as successful reading programs for Spanish-speaking children, or sex differences, by writing to ERIC/NCTE at Urbana, Illinois. ERIC titles categorized by subject matter can be found in their publication, *Research in Education* (RIE). In another publication of theirs, *Current Index to Journals in Education* (CIJE), they also list reading articles that have appeared in most education magazines. Most major university libraries and state departments of education libraries contain all the ERIC materials on microfiche. Since the ERIC system covers all of education, you should start by finding reading categories in the *Thesaurus of ERIC Descriptors*.

Listings of reading articles can also be found in standard reference works. The more popular articles are listed in *Reader's Guide to Periodical Literature*, and the more recent research articles are listed in *Psychological Abstracts*. Both IRA and NCTE also regularly publish bibliographies on reading topics.

All university and many public libraries have good holdings of textbooks on reading which you can use for reference of either general or specific information. If you would like to see a rather complete list of reading texts take a look at *Textbooks in Print*, which can be found in the reference section of most libraries. The bibliography at the end of this section lists some of the major textbooks in reading for your further information.

This should be enough sources of further information for you. Probably what you need now is some practice in teaching and applying some of these ideas. But remember, becoming a good reading teacher is a lifelong process. Don't get in a rut. Try different approaches and continually try to learn more by taking courses, by attending meetings, and by keeping up on your professional reading.

This book limits itself in the topics of children's literature or what to read. I have given a few important references, but most teachers take a separate course to enrich their knowledge in this area. I have also suggested where further information about the teaching of reading can easily be located in the current journals.

POSTSCRIPT BIBLIOGRAPHY

Betts, Emmett Albert. *Foundations of Reading Instruction*. New York: American Book, 1954.

Bond, Guy L., and Eva Bond Wagner. *Teaching the Child to Read*. Macmillan, 1966.

Carroll, John B., and Jeanne S. Chall (Eds.). *Toward a Literate Society*. A Report from the National Academy of Education. New York: McGraw-Hill, 1975.

Chall, Jeanne. *Learning to Read, The Great Debate*. New York: McGraw-Hill, 1967.

DeBore, John J., and Martha Dallmann. *Teaching of Reading*. New York: Holt, 1970.

Durkin, Dolores. *Teaching Them to Read*. Boston: Allyn and Bacon, 1970.

Durrell, Donald D. *Improving Reading Instruction*. New York: Harcourt, Brace, and World, 1956. p. 367–392.

Effective Reading Programs, *Summaries of 222 Selected Programs*. National Right to Read Effort, U.S. Office of Education (ERIC) 1975.

Freedle, Roy O., and John B. Carroll (Eds.). *Language Comprehension and the Acquisition of Knowledge*. New York: Wiley, 1972.

Fry, Edward. *Reading Instruction for Classroom and Clinic*. New York: McGraw-Hill, 1972.

Harris, Albert J., and Edward R. Sipay. *How to Increase Reading Ability*. (6th ed.) New York: David McKay Co., 1975.

Heilman, Arthur W. *Principles and Practices of Teaching Reading*. (3rd ed.) Columbus, Ohio: Merrill, 1972.

Karlin, Robert. *Teaching Elementary Reading*. Second Edition. New York: Harcourt, Brace, Jovanovich, 1975.

Olson, Joann P., and Martha H. Dillner. *Learning to Teach Reading in the Elementary School*. New York: Macmillan, 1976.

Ruddell, Robert B. *Reading-Language Instruction: Innovative Practices*. Englewood Cliffs, N.J.: Prentice-Hall, 1974.

Spache, George D., and Evelyn B. Spache. *Reading in the Elementary School*. (3rd ed.) Boston, Mass: Allyn and Bacon, 1973.

Smith, Frank. *Understanding Reading: A Psycholinguistic Analysis of Reading and Learning to Read*. New York: Holt, 1971.

Smith, Henry P., and Emerald D. Dechant. *Psychology in Teaching Reading*. Englewood Cliffs, N.J.: Prentice-Hall, 1961.

Zintz, Miles V. *The Reading Process*. Dubuque, Iowa: William C. Brown, 1970.

Addresses of Publishers
of Curriculum Material
and Tests

Acropolis Books; 2400 17th St., N.W.; Washington, DC 20009
Addison-Wesley Publishing Co.; 2725 Sand Hill Rd.; Menlo Park, CA 94025
Allyn and Bacon, Inc.; Pond Rd.; Rockleigh, NJ 07647
American Book Co.; 450 West 33d St.; New York, NY 10001
American Guidance Service, Inc. (AGS); Publishers' Building; Circle Pines, MN 55014
Paul S. Amidon & Associates, Inc.; 1966 Benson Ave.; St. Paul, MN 55116
Audiotronics Corp./Acoustifone Corp.; P. O. Box 3997; N. Hollywood, CA 91609
Bantam Books, Inc.; 666 Fifth Ave.; New York, NY 10019
Barnell Loft & Dexter Westbrook Publications; 958 Church St.; Baldwin, NY 11510
Clarence L. Barnhart, Inc.; P. O. Box 50; Bronxville, NY 10708
Behavioral Research Laboratories; P. O. Box 577; Palo Alto, CA 94302
Bell & Howell Co.; 2201 West Howard St.; Evanston, IL 60202
Benefic Press; 10300 West Roosevelt Rd.; Westchester, IL 60153
Bobbs-Merrill Company; 4300 West 62nd St.; Indianapolis, IN 46368
Bowmar Publishing Corp.; 622 Rodier Dr.; Glendale, CA 91201
Califone International; 5922 Bowcroft St.; Los Angeles, CA 90016
CTB/McGraw-Hill (California Test Bureau); Del Monte Research Park, Monterey, CA 93940
Cambridge Book Co.; 488 Madison Ave.; New York, NY 10022
Center for Study of Evaluation, Univ. of Calif.; Los Angeles, CA 90016
Childrens Press; 1224 West Van Buren St.; Chicago, IL 60607

Committee on Diagnostic Reading Tests; Mountain Home, NC 28758
Communacad; P. O. Box 541; Wilson, CT 06897
The Continental Press, Inc.; 520 E. Bainbridge St.; Elizabethtown, PA 17022
Coronet Instructional Media; 65 E. South Water St.; Chicago, IL 60601
Craig Corp.; 921 W. Artesia Blvd.; Compton, CA 90220
Creative Teaching Associates; P. O. Box 7714; Fresno, CA 93727
Croft Educational Services; 100 Garfield Avenue; New London, CT 06320
Croft, Inc.; 283 Greenwich Ave.; Greenwich, CT 06830
Developmental Reading Distributors; 1944 Sheridan Ave.; Laramie, WY 82070
Dexter and Westbrook (same address as Barnell Loft)
Walt Disney Educational Media Co.; 800 Sonora Ave.; Glendale, CA 91201
Dreier Educational Systems, Inc.; 300 Raritan Ave.; Highland Park, NJ 08904
The Economy Co.; P. O. Box 25308; Oklahoma City, OK 73125
Edits Publishers; P. O. Box 7234, San Diego, CA 92107
Educational Development Laboratories (EDL/McGraw-Hill); 1221 Avenue of the
    Americas, NY 10020
Educational Development Corporation (EDC) (Learning Research & Educational Pro-
    gress); P. O. Box 25308; Tulsa, OK 74145
Educational Insights; 20435 S. Tillman Ave.; Carson, CA 90746
Educational Progress (see Educational Development Corp.)
Educators Publishing Service (EPS); 75 Moulton St.; Cambridge, MA 02138
Encyclopaedia Britannica Educational Corp.; 425 N. Michigan Ave.; Chicago, IL 60611
ERIC/RCS, NCTE; 1111 Kenyon Rd.; Urbana, IL 61801
Essay Press; P. O. Box 5, Planetarium Station; New York, NY 10024
Fearon Publishers, Inc. (Pitman Publishing Corp.); 6 Davis Dr.; Belmont, CA 94002
Follett Publishing Co.; 1010 W. Washington Blvd.; Chicago, IL 60607
Garrard Publishing Co.; 1607 N. Market St.; Champaign, IL 61820
Ginn and Co. (see Xerox Education Publications)
Globe Book Co., Inc.; 175 Fifth Ave.; New York, NY 10010
Grolier Educational Corp.; Instructional Systems Div., 845 Third Ave.; New York, NY
    10022
Harcourt Brace Jovanovich, Inc.; School Dept., 757 Third Ave., New York, NY 10017
Harper & Row School Division; 10 E. 53rd St., New York, NY 10022
D. C. Heath and Co.; 125 Spring St.; Lexington, MA 02173
Hertzberg New Method, Inc.; Vandalia Rd.; Jacksonville, IL 62650
Highlights for Children, Inc.; 2300 W. Fifth Ave., P. O. Box 269; Columbus, OH 43216
Hoffman Educational Systems; 4423 Arden Dr.; El Monte, CA 91731
Holt, Rinehart and Winston, Inc.; 383 Madison Ave.; New York, NY 10017
Houghton Mifflin Co.; One Beacon St.; Boston, MA 02107
Ideal School Supply Co.; 11000 S. Lavergne Ave.; Oak Lawn, IL 60453
Imperial International Learning Corp.; P. O. Box 548; Kankakee, IL 60901
Instructional Fair, Inc.; 4158 Lake Michigan Dr.; Grand Rapids, MI 49504
Instructional Objectives Exchange; P. O. Box 24095; Los Angeles, CA 90024
Instructo/McGraw-Hill; Cedar Hollow Rd.; Paoli, PA 19301
The Instructor Publications, Inc.; 7 Bank St.; Dansville, NY 14437
International Reading Assoc.; 800 Barksdale Rd.; Newark, DE 19711
Jamestown Publishers; P. O. Box 6743; Providence, RI 02940
Jones-Kenilworth; 8301 Ambassador Row; Dallas, TX 75247
King Features; 235 E. 45th St., New York, NY 10017

Laidlaw Brothers; Thatcher & Madison; River Forest, IL 60305

Learn, Inc.; Mount Laurel Plaza, 113 Gaither Dr.; Mt. Laurel, NJ 08057

Learning Systems, Inc.; 4150 Chippewa St.; St. Louis, MO 63116

Learning Through Seeing, Inc.; P. O. Box 368; Sunland, CA 91040

Learning Resources Co. (Educational Development Corp.); 202 Lake Miriam Dr.; Lakeland, FL 33303

Learning Ventures (see Bantam Books)

J. B. Lippincott Co.; E. Washington Square; Philadelphia, PA 19105

Lyons and Carnahan (see Rand McNally)

Macmillan Publishing Co., Inc.; 866 Third Ave.; New York, NY 10022

McCormick-Mathers Publishing Co. (Litton-American Book); 450 W. 33rd St.; New York, NY 10001

McGraw-Hill Book Co.; 1221 Avenue of the Americas; New York, NY 10020

Media Materials, Inc.; 2936 Remington Ave.; Baltimore, MD 21211

Charles E. Merrill Publishing Co.; 1300 Alum Creek Dr.; Columbus, OH 43216

Milliken Publishing Co.; 1100 Research Blvd.; St. Louis, MO 63132

Milton Bradley Co.; Springfield, MA 01101

Mind, Inc.; 1133 Avenue of the Americas; New York, NY 10036

Modern Curriculum Press, Inc.; 13900 Prospect Rd.; Cleveland, OH 44136

"My Weekly Reader" (Xerox Educational Publications); Education Center; Columbus, OH 43216

National Council of Teachers of English; 1111 Kenyon Rd.; Urbana, IL 61801

National Computer Systems; 4401 W. 76th St.; Minneapolis, MN 55435

National Tutoring Institute, Inc.; 5911 W. 94th Terrace; Overland Park, KS 66207

New Dimensions in Education, Inc.; 160 Dupont St.; Plainview, NY 11803

New York Times (see Cambridge Books)

Noble and Noble; 245 E. 47th St., New York, NY 10017

Open Court Publishing Co.; P. O. Box 599; LaSalle, IL 61301

William Orr; 111 Row Blvd.; E. Patchogue, NY 11772

Oxford Book Co.; 11 Park Place; New York, NY 10262

Personnel Press; 191 Spring St.; Lexington, MA 02173

Phonovisual Products, Inc.; 12216 Parklawn Dr.; Rockville, MD 20852

Prentice-Hall, Inc.; Englewood Cliffs, NJ 07632

The Psychological Corp.; 757 Third Ave.; New York, NY 10017

Psychotechnics, Inc.; 1900 Pickwick Ave.; Glenview, IL 60025

Rand McNally & Co.; P. O. Box 7600; Chicago, IL 60680

Random House, Inc.; 201 East 50th St.; New York, NY 10022

Reader's Digest Services, Inc.; Educational Division; Pleasantville, NY 10570

Revrac Publications; 1535 Red Oak Drive; Silver Spring, MD 20910

Right to Read Effort; 400 Maryland Ave., S.W.; Washington, DC 20202

Frank Schaffer Publications; 1926 Pacific Coast Highway; Redondo Beach, CA 90277

Scholastic Magazines & Book Services; 50 W. 44th St.; New York, NY 10036

Scholastic Testing Service; Bensenville, IL 60106

Science Research Associates, Inc. (SRA); 259 E. Erie St.; Chicago, IL 60611

Scott Education; Lower Westfield Rd.; Holyoke, MA 01040

Scott, Foresman and Co.; 1900 East Lake Ave.; Glenview, IL 60025

Singer Education Systems; 3750 Monroe Ave.; Rochester, NY 14603

Slosson Educational Publications; 140 Pine St.; E. Aurora, NY 14052

Society for Visual Education (SVE), Inc.; 1345 Diversey Parkway; Chicago, IL 60614

Steck-Vaughn Co.; P. O. Box 2028; Austin, TX 78767

Teachers College Press; 1234 Amsterdam Ave.; New York, NY 10027

Webster/McGraw-Hill (see McGraw-Hill)

Westinghouse Learning Corp.; 100 Park Ave.; New York, NY 10017

Winston Press; 2211 Michigan Ave.; Santa Monica, CA 90406

Xerox Education Publications; 191 Spring St.; Lexington, MA 02173

Richard L. Zweig Associates, Inc.; 20800 Beach Blvd., P. O. Box 73; Huntington
    Beach, CA 92648

Name Index

Aaron, Ira, 46, 143, 151
Adams, Ann H., 189
Adams, Renie, 295
Adell, Marion Young, 150
Ahrendt, Kenneth M., 274
Allen, Claryce, 226
Allen, Harold B., 151
Allen, R. V., 153
Allington, Richard L., 206
Allyn and Bacon, Inc., 46
Almy, Millie, 132
Amble, Bruce R., 107
American Book Company, 36
Amidon, Paul S., 188
Ammon, Richard, 152
Anderson, Gary, 274
Andres, Michaela C., 133
Arbuthnot, May Hill, 203, 206, 221, 227
Archer, Marguerite P., 318
Armstrong, Mary K., 152
Artley, Sterl, 143, 151
Asbury, Charles A., 318
Ashton-Warner, Sylvia, 211, 227

Askland, Linda C., 152
Askov, Eunice, 273, 275
Atkins, Ruth E., 46
Atkinson, Richard C., 189
Auckerman, Robert C., 107
Austin, Kent C., 295
Austin, Mary C., 19, 102, 103, 107, 124
Axelrod, Jerome, 152

Backer, Julie, 318
Bagget, May E., 66
Bailey, Mildred H., 47
Bamman, H. A., 166, 185, 187
Baratz, Joan C., 318
Barbe, Walter B., 151
Barnes, Donald L., 46, 107, 205, 206
Barnhart, Clarence L., 18, 151
Barrett, Thomas, 87, 107
Bartlett, Elisha J., 131, 317
Batty, Dorothy, 188
Becker, George J., 189

Subject Index

Ideographs, 20
Illiteracy, adult, 304-305
Individual differences, 297, 299-321
Individualized instruction, 172
Individualized reading, 145
Informal Reading Inventories (IRI), 160, 264-265
Instant words, 73-74, 83
Intelligence, 310-312
Interest centers, 289
Interest inventories, 221
  (*See also* Betts levels)
International Phonetic Alphabet, 55
IQ, 244-247, 310-312
IRA (International Reading Association), 323
ITA (Initial Teaching Alphabet), 30-31, 53, 173-174

Joplin plan, 281
Junior high, 141

Kernel Distance Theory, 219
Key words, 85

Language activities, 121
Language experience approach, 208-214
Latency or response time, 13
Learning centers, 289-290
Learning systems, 46
Lesson plans, 286, 288-289
Librarian, 221
Listening comprehension, 121-122
  instruction, 180
Literature selection, 202-203
Long vowel digraphs, 27
Long vowels, 27

McGuffey Readers, 35-36, 50, 54, 72, 135, 164, 167
MAGP, 245
Mainstreaming, 314
Mastery learning, 255, 312
Matching, 5
  (*See also* Readability)
Mental age, 115, 245-246, 310-312
Mental Measurements Yearbooks, 252
Metropolitan Readiness Tests, 113
Miscue inventory, 13, 265-266
Models, 8-16
Morpheme, 63, 68

Motivation, 7, 308-309
Murphy-Durrell Reading Readiness Analysis, 113

National Assessment of Educational Progress, 298-299
NCTE (National Council of Teachers of English), 231
New England Primer, 50-52, 59, 72, 135, 167

Objectives, 168
  (*See also* Behavioral objectives)
Open classroom, 290-291
Open syllable rule, 28
Oral reading, 13, 90-91, 98-100, 156, 159, 262-264
Orangutan score, 240
Orthography, 24

Parent education, 298
  help, 125-127
  reporting, 266-267
Patterns of frequency, 80
Penmanship, 214
Percentile, 239
Phoneme, 23
Phoneme-grapheme correspondence, 22-24
Phonics, 6, 20-48
Phonograms, 57-59
Phrase, 91, 99
Physical health, 129
Plays, 161
Practice, 7
Prefix, 63-64, 77
Preprimer, 136
Primer, 137
Professional growth, 320-322
Programmed instruction, 167-173
Propaganda analysis, 193-195

Race, 299-300
Rate of reading, 91, 200-202
Readability, 216
Readability formulas, 216
Readiness (*see* Reading readiness)
Reading:
  content areas, 191
  definition of, 4, 10, 90
Reading center, 289
Reading interests, 221-223
Reading Miscue Analysis, 13

Books are to be returned on or b
below.

B 20109